D0149610

BUILDINGS OF EMPIRE

BUILDINGS OF EMPIRE

ASHLEY JACKSON

OXFORD
UNIVERSITY PRESS

OXFORD
UNIVERSITY PRESS

Great Clarendon Street, Oxford, OX2 6DP,
United Kingdom

Oxford University Press is a department of the University of Oxford.
It furthers the University's objective of excellence in research, scholarship,
and education by publishing worldwide. Oxford is a registered trade mark of
Oxford University Press in the UK and in certain other countries

First Edition published in 2013

Impression: 1

Published in the United States of America by Oxford University Press
198 Madison Avenue, New York, NY 10016, United States of America

British Library Cataloguing in Publication Data

Data available

Library of Congress Control Number: 2013940860

ISBN 978–0–19–958938–8

As printed and bound by
CPI Group (UK) Ltd, Croydon CRO 4YY

On the occasion of our 'tin' anniversary, this book is dedicated to my global companion, Andrea Karel Bidgood Jackson, with all my love.

Preface

Wood, stone, and metal structures and transformational urban and rural land-scapes were leitmotifs of the British imperial experience, forming puissant legacies that shape the world to this day. Wherever they went, the British profoundly affected the environment. They were the greatest creators of municipalities, establishing cities and towns that are part of the furniture of the world in which we live, so definitive that they have become unremark-able. Away from the urban centres that they created or commandeered, the British transformed the natural environment with pasturelands, plantations, forest clearances, and green belts and through the global transplantation and cross-pollination of all manner of flora and fauna. On what Palmerston described as a barren island 'with hardly a house upon it' sprouted the great city-state of Hong Kong; racially zoned conurbations multiplied, town squares and open spaces (often known as maidans or padangs) were planted at the heart of scores of cities, and cosmopolitan ports studded the sea routes of a thriving British world. The things the British built and the landscapes they damaged or improved became a part of the history of new nations when the Empire ended.

The choice of buildings and building sites selected for this book has been entirely subjective. Some readers might wonder why this building or that has not been chosen, why the Pacific is not represented, why Lutyens and Baker do not feature, why there are no viaducts or granaries and why, for heaven's sake, no bungalows or planters' mansions. The answer is that the author has chosen buildings that appealed to him, that were public rather than private, and that have—in as much as one can achieve any breadth when selecting so small a sample—a degree of representativeness across time and geographical regions and that allow for the consideration of a wide range of themes in the history of the British Empire. In choosing them, an effort has been made to avoid the obvious; endlessly fascinating though they are, New Delhi and the Union Buildings in Pretoria were never in the running for inclusion. To be perfectly honest, some choices were better than others, but of course this was not known when the project was embarked upon, and it has proven impossible to deselect a building just because access to reliable sources has left something to be desired. It is hoped that what has emerged is an informative introduction to some of the key themes in the Empire's history through a detailed examination of some of its buildings and sites of interest.

This is *not* an architectural history of the British Empire, it should be emphasized though it is possible even at this distance to anticipate reviews that will judge it as such, and find it wanting. Definitive, indeed essential, histories of colonial architecture and colonial cities have been written by, among others, Mark Crinson, Philip Davies, Robert Home, Antony King, and Thomas Metcalf. Robert Fermor-Hesketh produced a memorable illustrated work in the mid-1980s, *Architecture of the British Empire*, and Jan Morris and Simon Winchester wrote an architectural elegy for the Raj. *The Oxford History of the British Empire* is currently preparing a companion volume on architecture. The architectural history of the Empire is a highly developed field, one not to be trespassed upon lightly. What this book *is* is an exploration of British colonization and imperial rule, from Europe and the Caribbean to Asia and the Far East, viewed through a series of significant buildings and building sites. Its spans a period from the Norman Conquest of Ireland in the thirteenth century to the hand-over of Hong Kong in the late twentieth century and the construction of the new Wembley Stadium in the early twenty-first. It embraces a diverse range of buildings that the British constructed or appropriated as they established themselves amidst alien cultures and propagated their own forms of social and political organization, communications and leisure facilities, and religious, educational, and commercial institutions.

The buildings selected represent various intriguing aspects of Britain's imperial story. These include migration and overseas settlement, urbanization, the transplantation of flora and fauna, and the functioning of the colonial state, including legislatures and governors-general. Other themes include the role of the Royal Navy and the expansion of empire through warfare, the role of hotels and clubs in catering for a worldwide colonial elite, and the role of education and display in recruiting indigenous collaborators and reaffirming imperial pride and confidence. Still standing and functioning to this day, these buildings of empire became buildings of post-colonial states as decolonization proceeded apace, and their continued existence and utilization is a crucial facet of their story.

Acknowledgements

Thanks are due, in no particular order, to Dr Donal Lowry; Barry Webb; David Barber of the Football Association; Dr Andrew Gordon; Christopher Boutcher; Luciana O'Flaherty; Matthew Cotton; David Tomkins; Tom Cosgrove; Kate Alderson-Smith; Jeremy Langworthy; His Excellency Fra John Cretien, Knight Resident, Fort St Angelo, Malta; Reno Capuana, Joseph Amodio, and Marlene Gouder at Malta National Archives; Tonio Hili of the Cottonera Waterfront Consortium; Matthew Balzaon, Heritage Malta; Leslie Danker, Resident Historian at the Raffles Hotel, Singapore; Jane Hogan, Archivist of the Sudan Archive, University of Durham Special Collections; Francis Gotto, Mike Harkness, Richard Higgins, and Danielle McAloon of the Durham University Archives and Special Collections; Dr John Clemens, Curator, Christchurch Botanic Gardens; Professor Dominic Fenech, Dean of Arts, University of Malta; Dr Charlotte Smith, Senior Curator, History and Technology Department, Museum Victoria, Melbourne; Steve Le Feuvre, webmaster, Old Cambrian Society; Professor Peter Ronald de Souza, Director, Indian Institute of Advanced Studies, Shimla; Rear Admiral Sir Oswald Nigel Cecil, former Commander-in-Chief Malta; Annie Choy, Director, Marketing Communications, Raffles Hotel Singapore; Mark Khng, Retail Coordinator, Raffles Hotel Singapore; Simon Edwards, Royal Institute of British Architects Library and Information Centre; Louis Vincent, author of *Walk along the Tracks*, a memoir of the Malaysian Railways; Hambali Parjan, Curator, KTMB Museum, Malaysia; Carl Lounsbury, Senior Architectural Historian, Colonial Williamsburg Foundation; Noel Rands, Secretary, The British Egyptian Society; Nick Millea, Map Room, Bodleian Library, Oxford; John Harris, Cairo resident and Gezira Sporting Club member; Sayad Hessn, Gezira Sporting Club administrator; Denis McCarthy, Marketing Manager, Dublin Castle; Angela Cassidy, Dublin Castle; Aisling Gaffne, Dublin Castle; Commander Cate Pope, RN; Colin Ord; Jack Ord; Eng. Ibrahim Zaher, President, Gezira Sporting Club; Jean-Marc Oppenheim, Teachers College, Columbia University; Professor John MacKenzie;

Debbie Usher, Archivist, Middle East Centre Archives, University of Oxford; Professor Arthur Goldschmidt, Penn State University; Professor Robert Tignor, Princeton University; Neil Hewison, Associate Director for Editorial Programs, American University in Cairo Press; Samir Raafat; Max Rodenbeck, Middle East correspondent, *The Economist*; Nicola Duffett, Professor Khaled Fahmy, Chair of History Department, American University in Cairo; and Marianne Martin, Visual Resources Librarian, Colonial Williamsburg Foundation.

The Defence Studies Department of King's College London generously sponsored this research, particularly visits to Cairo, Dublin, Kuala Lumpur, and Valletta. Sponsorship from the King's College–Hong Kong University Partnership Award scheme permitted a visit to Hong Kong on college business that gave me the opportunity to visit the HSBC Headquarters building, and a grant under the King's College–National University of Singapore Partnership Award scheme allowed me to spend a month in Singapore, which gave me the opportunity to visit the Raffles Hotel. Oxford University Department for Continuing Education kindly hosted a lecture series based on the research for this book, and the attendees provided many illuminating insights.

Contents

List of Colour Plates

1. Michelangelo Hayes (1820–77), *Military Parade in Dublin Castle*, 1844.
2. Aerial view of Fort St Angelo with Kalkara creek on one side, Dockyard creek on the other.
3. Plan of the Botanic Gardens, Christchurch, New Zealand, 1958.
4. Detail from a map of Cairo produced by The Survey of Egypt in 1936.
5. Contemporary view of the Old Railway Station in Kuala Lumpur, with the Railway Headquarters building.
6. Painting of Viceregal Lodge by Viceroy Lord Lansdowne's Private Secretary.
7. Contemporary view of the Viceregal Lodge, now the home of the Indian Institute of Advanced Study.
8. Opening of the First Parliament of the Commonwealth of Australia by HRH the Duke of Cornwall and York (later King George V), 9th May 1901.
9. Historical postcard advertising the Raffles Hotel in Singapore.
10. Exterior of HSBC Building, Hong Kong.
11. London Underground Museum poster advertising the 1924 Empire Exhibition.
12. *Metro-Land* guide-book, showing one of Wembley Stadium's famous twin towers.

List of Illustrations

Figure 1. Map of the British Empire *c*.1920.

Introduction

Buildings are badges of sovereignty, and usually outlast monarchs and empires and survive into new ages. No matter where we are in the world we encounter the constructions and urban designs of those who have imposed their building styles and purposes upon us. A disproportionate number of these buildings and cityscapes are remnants of British endeavour, dating from as far back as King John's fortification of Dublin until as recently as the construction of an airport on East Falkland in the 1980s. The physical and material marks left by the British Empire were profound, and in many parts of the world still inform people's quotidian experience. The colonial structures of New England, elegant Georgian squares in the Caribbean, Gothic piles in India, and the fine stone country houses of Tasmania are testament to British imperial expansion. So, too, are road, rail, irrigation, and sanitation networks, derelict whaling stations in the wastes of the Southern Ocean, and infrastructural hardware such as dry docks, bridges, barracks, and runways.

As the British Empire expanded to cover over a fifth of the habitable globe, its representatives on the ground built things, bridged things, and dug things up.* Some of their buildings were completed in a hurry, in order perhaps to repel imminent attack from local people opposed to their desire to settle, trade, or conquer. A surprising number of buildings were prefabricated elsewhere before being shipped to their destinations, from early settler bungalows in New South Wales and hotels in India to the headquarters of the Hongkong and Shanghai Bank designed by Sir Norman Foster in the early 1980s. Many of these buildings were intended to symbolize ruling narratives such as majesty, knowledge, divinity, justice, and might. From the nineteenth century, architects and those who

---

* For military purposes, they also tunnelled; underground caverns near Cairo were used to repair salvaged fighter aircraft; there were the tunnels of Malaya Command's headquarters in Fort Canning Park Singapore; extensive facilities created inside the Rock of Gibraltar; and emergency tunnelling in Grand Harbour Malta as the Axis bombing campaign gripped the island.

commissioned them sought to convey through buildings a sense of the imperial unity that they ardently desired but that was never in fact real. Some buildings conveyed messages of economic stability and individual prosperity, while others, more prosaically, were constructed simply to store grain or gunpowder or to treat sewerage.

Many buildings were created in the image of home, which the British missed, and which they propagated all over the world. Settler cities such as Sydney and Toronto adopted familiar forms of architecture, such as classical and Gothic, reassuring people that, though they were far from 'home', they remained British. 'Braeside' might look different in the Southern Hemisphere—a bungalow rather than a house, a veranda and bougainvillea in place of the porch and roses—but it was unmistakably British. So, too, were the Surrey stockbroker-style houses of Maymyo in Burma, along with the generic town hall and cathedral square, the masonic lodge and baronial mansion, even if they happened to have been set down amidst the Himalayan foothills or the African bush.

But what was more impressive than the individual buildings of the colonial period was the sum of their parts—the *settlements* that they comprised. The Empire created complex city centres, ports, and suburbs, and fundamentally altered landscapes and ecosystems. These urban and rural transformations are arguably the Empire's most powerful legacies. So powerful, in fact, that they are easy to miss, because they are all around us—in the street lay-outs of Bombay, Boston, or Khartoum; in roads and railway terminals; universities and churches; and in farms, ranches, tea plantations, green belts, and game reserves. Herds of Hereford cattle, flocks of Romney sheep, and the rabbits that afflict Australia's pasturelands are as much a part of this legacy as Lutyen and Baker's New Delhi and Ottawa's famous High Gothic Parliament Building.

On whatever shores the British washed up, they brought with them their own conceptions of how to organize the built environment, and how to organize life. Whether constructing towns and cities from scratch, laid out with military precision by the Bombay Engineers and designed by obscure British-trained architects, or adopting to their purposes settlements founded long before their arrival, they created facilities for governance and administration, the dispensation of military power, for worship, accommodation, and leisure, for communication and education, and for commercial and civic functions. Imperial buildings both contained and projected British power— offices, courts, barracks, governors' and district commissioners' residences, prisons, and police stations—and proclaimed the superiority of British ways, along with the subjugation or co-option of indigenous people and their culture.* Surveyors, engineers, sanitation and public health experts, town planners, and those who theorized about 'model' forms of settlement and colonization were as important to the imperial project as explorers, soldiers, and missionaries.

Of course, not all of these colonial buildings—in fact, the outright minority—were particularly grand or designed to impress, though they sometimes did this despite themselves, as witness the haunting ruins of the Port Arthur penitentiary in Tasmania. They were above all else practical structures: 'Royal Engineers Gothic' and 'Public Works Department Gothic' flourished all over the Empire long before noted metropolitan architects or proud-hearted civic bigwigs got in on the act and sought posterity in stone. 'From corrugated iron to colonnades' is how Henry Gunston captures the essence of the Empire's architectural journey: corrugated iron fastened over basic wooden or steel frameworks provided a whole range of adequate structures, from small bungalows and railway stations to large industrial complexes.[1]

But adornment was soon to follow: Gothic became the generally established High Victorian idiom and was eagerly adopted as an imperial medium too. Like an invading army, Fermor-Hesketh writes, Gothic architecture swept across the British Empire, rearing its pinnacles, turrets, and finials wherever the flag flew.[2] Other architectural trends followed, in particular the style widely known as Indo-Saracenic, which become almost universally accepted as the appropriate style for substantial public buildings in India and the greater Asian region. The British gamely experimented with minarets and domes as they ceased so ardently to proclaim their civilizational superiority and sought instead to insinuate themselves into the culture and history of the societies they had come to rule.

But all told, there were many other imported styles, hybrid designs, European influences, and one-off creations as the Empire's built environment emerged. There was High Gothic, classical, Georgian, mock Tudor, Scottish baronial, Palladian, even Garden City. Italian Renaissance influences were widespread, Cape Dutch established itself in South Africa, Louis XVI in

---

* In *Burmese Days* George Orwell wrote of the British 'Creeping round the world and building prisons. They build a prison and call it progress.'

Canada, and American style was influential in Australia. European architects were inspired by local influences too, often fancifully, leading to structures such as the Anglican Memorial Church in Mombasa, built in an Oriental style to blend with the region's Arab culture, and Bombay's Gateway of India, designed by George Wittet with sixteenth-century Gujerati architecture in mind. Local forms were often adopted by early settlers and one of them, the bungalow, became a global export.

In the early days of empire, military engineers turned their hand to almost any type of structure; convict architecture was common in certain colonies, and improvisation was the order of the day. What was striking was the amateur nature of the architects, many of them young military officers or men from the colonial public works departments. On beholding Simla, the renowned architect Edwin Lutyens exclaimed: 'If one was told the monkeys had built it all, one would have said what wonderful monkeys! They should be shot in case they do it again.'[3] The amateur builders often relied on architectural handbooks such as Colin Campbell's *Vitruvius Britannicus* (1725) or James Gibbs's *Book of Architecture* (1728). The 1840s and 1850s saw increasing uniformity as buildings began to spread throughout the colonies. In 1890 Swinton Jacob, Jaipur State's Engineer, published his six-volume *The Jeypor Portfolio of Architectural Details*. The work contained 600 large-scale drawings of detail from an array of north Indian buildings. With this publication, a distinct style of Indian architecture—commonly known as Indo-Saracenic—came of age.

The range of buildings varied enormously, including slave forts on the West African coast, the urban villas and country mansions of the gentry and gentry manqué, prefabricated bungalows, classic 'English' town squares and promenades, and business districts such as Shanghai's Whangpoo waterfront with its banks and clubs. There were grandstands and racetracks in Colombo, Hong Kong, and Port Louis, and the emporiums of famous department stores, such as the Army and Navy Stores in Bombay, Haddon and Sly in Bulawayo, and Cargill's in Colombo. Bombay University was planned by Sir Gilbert Scott from his London office. In Jerusalem the British built Wingate Square as well as St Andrew's Church, the General Post Office, and Government House, erected on the Hill of Evil Counsel. Old North Church (or Christ Church) in the City of Boston was inspired by Sir Christopher Wren and bore a peal of bells inscribed with the words: 'We are the first ring of bells cast for the British Empire in North America, A. R. 1744. Made in Gloucester.'

The British were proud of their towns and cities. The guidebooks published by Baedeker and John Murray evinced a fascination with their growth and celebrated the development of Western architecture, modern modes of transportation, civic memorials dedicated to Victoria and imperial notables, and public gardens and leisure areas.[4] The Empire's major urban centres were generally to be found around ports. British creations included Auckland, Baltimore, Bombay, Calcutta, Karachi, Melbourne, Philadelphia, Sydney, and Vancouver. Half the cities of the American east were established by British settlers as well as most Canadian cities, many African, and all the cities of Australasia. There were then the phenomenal city-states of Hong Kong and Singapore. In India, even though cities such as Agra, Delhi, Lahore, and Lucknow were important and civilized centres long before the British set foot on the subcontinent, the biggest cities of them all—Bombay, Calcutta, and Madras—were all in effect British creations. So too were a host of smaller towns including railway towns, garrison towns, government enclaves, and the incredible range of hill-stations, including Darjeeling and Simla in India and Nuwara Eliya in Ceylon.[5] The Empire's cities were engines of monumental change, radiating 'European power and culture into their hinterlands, redirecting the economies and cultures of the tropics outward, toward the sea and the distant West'.[6]

The colonial city had distinct characteristics, as the seminal work of Anthony King explains. It was characterized by the physical segregation of its ethnic, social, and cultural component groups resulting from the process of colonialism: 'native quarters' were made separate from a city's civic and business districts, and from the European residential areas. Calcutta was boldly divided into 'White Town' and 'Black Town', while in Singapore Raffles marked out separate Arab, Chinese, and India quarters that influence the city to this day. Often there was also a separate military district or 'cantonment'.[7] This city-building, a phenomenon of the mass movement of Britons and other migrants, utterly changed the world.

★ ★ ★

Imperialism is a global process which occurs across regions—but even in its most marauding forms it takes hold through *the local*, through the places where people live and through which they pass in their daily lives.[8] Processes of colonization were very much about place, whether it was the kind of colonization which imposed an alien culture upon an existing, indigenous one, forming a synthesis with it, or the kind that took over the land and recreated it as a new place—as happened to a great extent in the major zones of white settlement, especially the Americas and Australasia.[9] The purpose of this book is to look closely at a selection of these places—ones in which the British grafted themselves onto indigenous places, as well as those that they created from scratch. Buildings, and the institutions that they served (government, church, the military, schools, the post office) were central to the nation-building that was one of the main by-products of the colonial era. Studying the manner in which buildings developed and how they were used presents a portrait of British perceptions of themselves, the messages they sought to convey to their subjects, and the manner in which the Empire functioned.

The British built new buildings and adapted pre-existing ones. Architects were inspired by buildings with which they were familiar, such as St Martin-in-the-Fields, Ypres Cloth Hall, and Osborne. Government House, Ootacamund, built in 1877 while the Duke of Buckingham was Governor of Madras, had a pillared portico copied from His Grace's seat at Stowe. In Calcutta, a city built by the British on classical lines, a prototype of Kedleston Hall (the Curzon family's Palladian pile in Derbyshire) was chosen as the design for Government House. It was approached through arched gates modelled on those at Sion House in Middlesex, surmounted by lions and sphinxes. It contained six state apartments, a throne room, an Ionically columned ballroom, a Marble Hall with Doric columns, and a drawing room, breakfast room, and supper room, each over 100 feet in length.

Sometimes the British adopted buildings that pre-dated their arrival. Fort St Angelo in Malta, famed for its role in the defence of the island when attacked by Suleiman the Magnificent in 1565, became the nerve centre of the Royal Navy's Mediterranean Fleet and was commissioned as one of His Majesty's Ships. Government House Lahore was built around the tomb of Mohammed Kasim Khan (died 1635). Its centre was a domed dining room, formed from the upper part of the tomb itself; below it was a kitchen, in which the sarcophagus served as a chopping-board. When Delhi was conquered in 1803, the British commandeered a Mughal style palace to serve as their residency. Soon they affixed to its façade a grand colonnade of Ionic columns. In Kandy, Sri Lanka, red post boxes and the colonial façade of the Queen's Hotel frame Sri Wickrama Rajasinghe's beautiful lake beside the Temple of the Tooth, while in Cairo the British created their own enclaves in Garden City and on Gezira Island.

There were always salient non-British influences in the buildings of the colonial era, too, often involving non-British designers, financiers, and craftsmen. Some were utterly incongruous, such as the Sasson Institute in Bombay, commissioned by a Baghdadi Jew in Venetian Gothic. Indian princes funded building projects and erected their own incredibly lavish and eclectic palaces; and non-British entrepreneurs developed merchant houses, hotel chains, and banks throughout the Empire. The iconic Taj Mahal Hotel in Bombay was built by the Indian industrialist Jamshetji Tata. The equally famous Raffles Hotel in Singapore was founded by four Armenian brothers born in Isfahan. Aligarh Muslim University, meanwhile, was founded by Sir Sayed Ahmed Kahn to prepare Muslims for the Indian Civil Service.

George Town, Penang and Richmond, Tasmania

Most imperial settlements were (of course) inhabited overwhelmingly by non-Europeans, both indigenous *and* alien. George Town, founded by Francis Light in 1786 and named for King George III, is a case in point. Situated on a swampy part of Penang Island off the Malayan coast, it was an important base for the spice trade. As a trading post, Penang provided the East India Company with a strategic base from which to challenge Dutch supremacy and to expand trade with China.[10] George Town was founded with the blessing of the Sultan of Kedah, as it provided a bulwark against the predations of local rivals. It attracted settlers and traders because of Britain's free trade policy, at odds with the practice in Dutch ports where irksome restrictions and taxes were imposed. George Town was also attractive because it offered better security than native ports afflicted by piracy and the random impositions of rival chieftains. Soon George Town's population began to grow, fuelled by the migration of disparate groups. Its ranks were swelled by Malays escaping Siamese attacks in Kedah, Eurasians fleeing religious persecution in Siam, Chinese moving away from the oppressive Manchu regime, and South Indians seeking a better life.

As the population grew, buildings proliferated. The hybrid town that developed from Light's classic gridiron street design entered a brief golden age fuelled by tin, rubber, and shipping, before the foundation of Singapore signalled its eclipse. An extraordinary range of Anglo-Indian buildings emerged, along with South Indian Muslim architecture and Chinese shop-houses and temples. Diverse building traditions were adapted to the wet tropical climate, incorporating Malay building forms and materials. Used as a penal settlement for India from 1789, convict labour built the government buildings and the roads. Light imported Chinese and Indian bricklayers, who worked with bricks fired in East India Company kilns. Malay *nibong* palm gave way to Chinese- and Indian-built masonry; early nineteenth-century terra cotta tiles began to replace attap roofing.

George Town developed along lines that were to become familiar all over the colonial world. In a town named for a British king, the seat of government was on Downing Street and a grand administrative complex stretched to King Edward Street. Zones for worship, leisure, civic events, and military activity were laid out. Drury Lane was George Town's West End; there was a splendid town hall, St George's Church, and Fort Corn-wallis. There were the State Assembly Buildings, Government House, a Supreme Court, the elite Penang Sports Club, and a Protestant cemetery. Hill bungalows were built along the ascending line of the funicular Penang Hill Railway.[11]

Opulent mansions, with names such as Homestead and Hardwicke, appeared, along with the usual array of memorials, such as the Light Memorial of 1886 commemorating the town's centenary, and the Logan Memorial, commemorating the Edinburgh lawyer James Logan, a champion of the rights of the town's non-European population. There was hybridity beneath the colonial, as non-British people contributed to the town's development: the Victoria Memorial Clock Tower, built for the queen's 1897 jubilee and measuring sixty feet in height to represent each year of her reign, was donated by Cheah Chen Eok. In similar fashion, in 1930 the Governor unveiled the Queen Victoria Memorial, featuring lions bearing Union flags, which had been erected by 'the Queen's Chinese'. The Chinese community experienced a period of affluence in the late nineteenth and early twentieth centuries which caused bungalows and gardens to mushroom on the town's fringe, while earlier wooden shophouses were rebuilt in brick.

In other parts of the world, too, the British Empire caused swamp and bush to give way to modern towns and cities. Tasmania's architectural heritage featured both the convict architecture of Francis Greenway and the restrained Georgian buildings of John Lee Archer. Fine stone mansions were built by convict workmen to the design of convict architects—country houses of curiously solidified English allusion, in Joan Woodberry's words, attended by their own English-style inns and parish churches, encircled by oaks, elms, beeches, poplars, and hawthorns brought especially from home. The proximity of the small town of Richmond to good building stone, and its growth during the period when Georgian architecture was the style, gave it an English appearance in harmony with, yet alien, to the surrounding eucalyptus landscape.[12]

Even today, Richmond looks like a Jane Austen film set. Located in the Coal River Valley, once known for its abundant deposits of fossil fuel (now for its vineyards), handsome buildings were erected to serve the requirements of an expanding settler community. It was a police district, convict station, military outpost, agricultural market town, electoral district, and municipality. Buildings included a post office, gaol, court house, dispensary, village store, race ground, school house, taverns, and hotels such as the Richmond Arms, decorated with iron laced verandas upstairs and down. There were two churches: St Luke's Anglican church designed by John Lee Archer, and St John's, Australia's oldest Catholic church, erected after a visit from Bishop Polding in 1835 following which tenders were put out for a 'typical English style' parish church.*

A mill house and windmill supplied the town's flour; convict labour built Richmond Bridge in the early 1820s, the oldest bridge still in use in Australia. The names of the houses betray Richmond's English heritage: Belmont, the Old Rectory, Fernville, Emerald Cottage, Churchill, Mayfield, Carrington, Daisy Bank, Craigow, Strath Ayr, Laburnum Park, Sadlers Court, and Oak Lodge. The house named Prospect was owned by Colonel Crawford, ex-Indian Army and a dedicated imperialist, who installed a canon for the celebration of royal and military occasions. Its first performance shattered all the windows in the neighbourhood, and it was promptly decommissioned. The houses of Richmond are known for their established gardens: Oak Lodge, for example, on the corner of Bridge Street and Blair Street and built between 1831 and 1842, has a garden of raised beds on a cobbled courtyard, medicinal plants, a peppercorn tree, a common walnut, and two English oaks.

The buildings of empire were more than just monuments to British pretensions and surprisingly few became gravestones of a defunct imperium. Not all symbolized arrogance and oppression, and some betrayed cultural empathy. What is more, many significant buildings existed long before the arrival of the

---

* Churches were the type of building most unchanged from British prototypes as they spread around the Empire, many churches derived from the designs of James Gibbs, designer of St Martin-in-the-Fields.

British and were adopted by them as imperial power came to overlay that of defeated empires or usurped civilizations, or to lodge, uncomfortably, in robustly nationalist and anti-British locations such as Cairo. Perhaps most importantly, the buildings constructed or borrowed by the British continued to have relevance long after their departure, in the affairs of state, the everyday lives of ordinary people, and the functioning of society.

The arrival of the British could have significant consequences for many landmarks of indigenous culture and civilization, or those built by previous colonizers: violence was a perennial theme in the history of British expansion and rule. Peking's Summer Palace was burnt to the ground in an act of retributive vandalism; the Catholic Chapel of the Red Cross and many other Spanish buildings in Jamaica were razed to the ground by Oliver Cromwell's troops; the Sultan of Zanzibar's Palace was reduced to ruins after a short naval bombardment in which 500 people died; the Mahdi's Tomb was destroyed by Kitchener in revenge for the death of Gordon; Bulawayo and Delhi were built on sites of great cultural importance to the indigenous people; and the Taj Mahal, it is widely rumoured though still unproven, was nearly stripped of its marble by Governor-General Lord Bentinck. The British arrogated to themselves the right to pronounce upon the merits and provenance of indigenous buildings, and to be their guardians. In Central Africa, generations of settlers believed that the ruins of Great Zimbabwe belonged to some lost white tribe or vanished Sudo-Nilotic civilization, too sophisticated, they insisted, to have been crafted by African hands. Further north, meanwhile, British administrators and archaeologists became the rulers of Pharaonic Egypt; soldiers and other itinerant Britons scrambled to the top of the Great Pyramid or clambered onto the Sphinx to pose for photographs, and many of its treasures were removed to the British Museum.

But while these destructive and arrogant tendencies cannot be overlooked, they were not universal and nor were they unalloyed. The British were conservators of indigenous buildings and monuments too, and often displayed cultural sympathy and respect, even reverence and emulation. Furthermore, they built all manner of physical infrastructure still in use today, connecting subregions through railways, ports, and roads and developing modern cities from the sewers up. They constructed bridges, dams, dry docks, and urban spaces for which many people were grateful. In 1809 for example, as the tides of war swept British troops into distant islands such as Madeira and Rodrigues, it also brought them to the Ionian islands of Ithaca, Kefalonia, and

Zanthi. On Kefalonia a major public works project was immediately undertaken which saw the construction of a lighthouse, roads, and the Bridge of
Trapano which united the two parts of the capital, Argostoli. In the middle
of the stretch of water to this day stands an elegant stone obelisk, inscribed
'To the Glory of the British Nation 1813', erected by the inhabitants of the
province of Levatho in honour of the road network.

In the chapter that follows we travel to Ireland, and an English building
erected in the thirteenth century. The journey then continues across the
world and across the centuries, as we alight in Cairo, Christchurch, Hong
Kong, Khartoum, Kuala Lumpur, London, Malta, Melbourne, Shimla, Singapore, Spanish Town, and Williamsburg.

I

Dublin Castle

Britain's nearest and longest-contested imperial domain lay across the Irish Sea. Here, the streets of Dublin trace successive waves of invasion, as well as shifts in architectural requirement and style. Curtain walls and dungeons contrast with elegant drawing-rooms and striking Georgian squares. The history of Ireland's tempestuous relationship with its overbearing neighbour can be read through the city's buildings, and Dublin Castle captures it all in terms of architecture, archaeology, and historical resonance. Spanning a millennium, from the Viking period through centuries of English occupation to the achievement of independence in the twentieth century, the Castle has remained at the heart of Irish affairs. During seven centuries of British rule it served variously as viceregal residence, court of justice, parliament, bureaucratic and police headquarters, army barracks, prison, treasury, mint, and archive. The building was a daily reminder to Dubliners of their colonial status, viewed by many as a stark symbol of oppression and of the chasm that divided the rich from the poor, the Protestant from the Catholic. To the British, it was the chief symbol of their power.

During its thousand-year history the Castle complex evolved as the requirements of imperial power altered, as fashions changed, and as new architectural styles were embraced and buildings fell into ruin or were destroyed by fire or the accidental detonation of gunpowder. Finally, and in some ways incredibly, the Castle became a central part of independent Ireland's national heritage, and stands today as eloquent testament to the extent to which a building can be transformed across the ages, both physically and in terms of its symbolic utility.

From the reign of King John (1199–1216), Dublin Castle developed as a four-square fort standing behind a moat crossed by a drawbridge, a classic castle design aimed primarily at defence, indicating the hostility with which the invading English were viewed. It was a dominant high-walled building

Thefe trunckles heddes do playnly fhowe, eache rebeles fatall end,
And what a haynous crime it is, the Queene for to offend.

Although the theeues are plagued thus, by Princes trufty frendes,
And brought for their iniquuyties, to fondry wretched endes:
Yet may not that a warning be, to thofe they leaue behinde,
But needes their treafons mult appeare, long kept in feftred mynde.
wherebby the matter groweth at length, vnto a bloudy fiefbe,
Euen to the rebells ouerthrow, except the traytours yelde.

6

For he that gouernes Irifhe foyle, prefenting there her grace,
whofe fame made rebeles often flye, the prefence of his face:
He be I far, he goeth forth, with Marsis noble trayne,
To intl ifie his Princes caufe, but their bemernures bayne:
Thus Queene he will haue honored, in middeft of all her foes,
And knowne to be a royall Prince, euen in defpight of thofe.

Figure 2. Sir Henry Sidney, Lord Deputy, riding in state in Dublin, with rebel heads suspended over the gate of Dublin Castle, from *The Image of Irelande*, 1581, by John Derricke.

in a town that was itself enclosed by defensive walls. But from the seventeenth century, the Castle's physical appearance began to alter, as it became a partially fortified centre of government and administration, its fortress-like features gradually giving way to more genteel architecture and the atmosphere of a stately home. From early days as a grim fortress, sporting enemy heads on spikes, the Castle became a centre of bureaucratic control and of elite society gatherings and the dispensation of royal patronage. Yet the gradual demilitarization of the site did nothing to alter the perception of the Castle among the bulk of the native population, or its centrality to the affairs of the colonial state.

The Castle buildings

Sir Henry Sidney, Lord Deputy of Ireland on three occasions in the 1560s and 1570s, moved his family into the Castle. The first viceroy to live there, Sidney converted it from a 'ruinous, foule, filthie and greatly decayed place' into a 'verie faire house for the lord deputie or the chiefe governor to reside and dwell in'.[1] By 1570 he had completed the Deputies House with Clock Tower and Chapel and a new Council Chamber. He extended and planted The Castle Gardens and erected a drawbridge across the south ditch. There were new buildings for officials, including the Master of the Rolls and Offices of the Auditor at the north wall. The Courts of Justice, Exchequer, Pleas, King's Bench, and Chancery were situated in the Great (or King's) Hall at the west wall. This was an 80-feet by 120-feet building which also served as the Parliament House, situated on the first floor above the munitions store ('a source of much complaint').

The most dramatic alterations were caused by conflagration. The great fire of 1684 effectively ended Dublin Castle's function as a medieval fortress, and when the building housing the State Apartments was destroyed it was replaced by more sophisticated accommodation designed by the Surveyor-General, Sir William Robinson. Absolving the then Justiciar* of responsibility for the fire, the king issued a royal warrant declaring that it had been an accident and ordering reconstruction for a governor's residence 'the same to be still and forever called by the name of the Castle of Dublin'.

Although much of the present architecture dates from the eighteenth century, sections of the original moat, curtain wall and town wall, as well as the Record Tower and the bases of the other massive corner towers, remain. What is known today as Upper Castle Yard corresponds closely with the rectangular enclosure of the original thirteenth-century Norman castle. The main hall of today's Conference Centre is partially supported by the remains of the Corke Tower, visible from its roof garden. This three-storey tower had 10-feet-thick walls and contained a dungeon. Loopholes allowed archers and gunners to direct flanking fire along the curtain wall towards the next tower. Built on boulder clay, it became structurally unsound: an explosion in 1596 undermined it, and in 1624 it collapsed with the weight of the ordnance mounted upon it. Opposite this, in the southern curtain wall, a D-shaped middle tower stood approximately where the Octagonal Tower stands today. It was three storeys high with loopholes for defenders to repulse attack from the south and to provide effective fire along the adjoining curtain walls. It collapsed in 1689.

The main buildings around today's Upper Castle Yard are the Bedford Tower and Corke Hill main gate on the northern side, faced opposite by the

---

* Justiciar: a term for the monarch's main representative in Ireland, later altered to lord lieutenant and later still to viceroy.

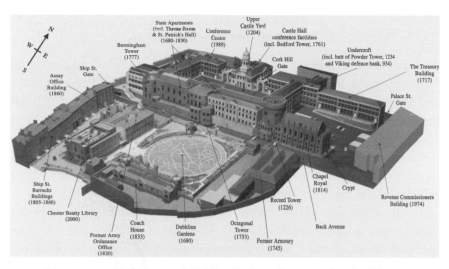

State Apartments
(incl. Throne Room
& St. Patrick's Hall)
(1680-1830)

Conference
Centre
(1989)

Upper
Castle Yard
(1204)

Castle Hall
conference facilities
(incl. Bedford Tower, 1761)

Bermingham
Tower
(1777)

Cork Hill
Gate

Undercroft
(incl. butt of Powder Tower, 1234
and Viking defence bank, 934)

Ship St.
Gate

Assay
Office
Building
(1860)

The Treasury
Building
(1717)

Palace St.
Gate

Ship St.
Barracks
Buildings
(1805-1860)

Chester Beatty Library
(2000)

Chapel
Royal
(1814)

Crypt

Record Tower
(1226)

Revenue Commissioners
Building (1974)

Coach
House
(1833)

Former Army
Ordanance
Office
(1820)

Dublinn
Gardens
(1680)

Octagonal
Tower
(1753)

Former Armoury
(1745)

Back Avenue

Figure 3. 3-D diagram of Dublin Castle and surrounding buildings.

extensive State Apartments, finished off at the western end by the Bermingham Tower (1777) and the Conference Centre, an extensive 1980s development behind the façade of earlier buildings. The Bedford Tower was built on top of the thirteenth-century entrance towers and causeway. Completed in 1761, it was the centre-piece of the new-look Upper Castle Yard. The new tower was nothing like the medieval stone structures of the other towers, built with the grim practicalities of defence and security in mind. Instead an elegant Georgian structure emerged, rusticated arches supporting Ionic columns and pediment from which rose a circular Corinthian lantern and cupola. Its balcony was used by state musicians and it was first occupied by the Dean of the Chapel Royal. The Bedford Tower was (and still is) flanked by two large internal arches, their heavy broken pediments supporting the lead sculptures of Fortitude and Justice by Van Nost the Younger. For most Irish people, these prominent statues stood for nothing other than the vanity and perversity of their oppressors. The statue of Justice was a particular source of jest; not only did she face away from the city and not wear a blindfold but, until holes were drilled to solve the problem (the popular story goes), her scales tipped off balance when it rained. A rhyme well-known in areas such as the Liberties ran:

> Lady of Justice
> Mark well her station

With her face to the Castle
And her arse to the nation.*

This part of the Castle once housed the Genealogical Office and the Guard
House. Today it is used mainly as part of the Castle's conference facilities
and acts as the office of the European Union president when Ireland holds
the presidency. To the immediate right of the Bedford Tower (known also as
Castle Hall) stands the main castle gate, the town entrance known as the
Cork Hill Gate (on the top of which stands the figure of Justice). In former
days it was a D-shaped guard house and prison block with portcullis, above
which Justiciar Edmund Butler spiked up to seventy severed heads in 1315.

On the other side of the Upper Castle Yard 'quad' are the range of buildings known as the State Apartments. These were, and remain, the main
buildings in which the Castle's ceremonial and social functions took place.
In an earlier period, a stately Long Gallery (1624) stood upon pillars in the
nature of a piazza, with a grand entrance and staircase (where the present
one stands) leading up to the State Rooms, Chapel, and Presence Chamber,
or Battleaxe Hall. In 1737 George II issued a warrant for the demolition of
the Great Staircase, Battleaxe Hall, the Chaplain's Apartments and the castle
entrance—'being in most ruinous condition'. Lord-Lieutenant Chesterfield
initiated the construction of the new State Apartments, the main rooms of
which were completed by 1761 including the present grand entrance, the
Battleaxe staircase, a new suite of bedrooms, the State Corridor, the Throne
Room, the Picture Gallery, and the ballroom (now St Patrick's Hall). In 1787
Vicenzo Waldré was commissioned to execute ceiling paintings in St
Patrick's Hall to commemorate the founding of the Order of St Patrick.
They include make-believe depictions of Henry II receiving the submission
of the Irish chiefs and George III supported by Justice and Liberty. The
Castle complex was taking on a character more akin to the court of a Ren-
aissance viceroy than the quarters of the commander of a military outpost.
As well as a viceregal home, the Castle served as the seat of parliament from
the early seventeenth century until it moved to a new purpose-built parliament building on College Green in 1731.

The Bermingham Tower, standing nearby at the south-west corner of the
castle wall, was an advanced military design adjoining a dungeon block used
for the detention of state prisoners in the sixteenth century. From 1537 until

* Thanks to Aisling Gaffney for this reference.

1810 the State Records were also stored here. These included important documents such as the Patent, Plea, and Pipe Rolls on which exchequer accounts were recorded. The records were removed following structural damage caused by an explosion in the nearby Armoury, and the tower was taken down to its sloping base and rebuilt in a more slender style in 1777, creating the tower that we see today. Now with thinner walls, on one of its three levels it connected to the Wedgewood Room, a dainty room of blue walls, candelabra, and plaques and a striking carpet, dating from the 1920s, which shows a phoenix rising from the ashes, symbolizing the birth of the Irish Free State. Nearby the Wedgewood Room is George's Hall, built in 1911 as a supper room to accommodate the vast demands of the visit of George V, and to avoid a repetition of the embarrassing spectacle of temporary marquees erected in the castle grounds to cater for a previous royal visit in 1903. There was also a kitchen on the lower ground floor of this tower until the twentieth century. The Square Tower abutted the Bermingham Tower where the southern wall crossed the castle ditch. It was eventually reduced in height to form a gunnery platform and the remains are still visible.

Over the centuries, therefore, Upper Castle Yard was gradually transformed. The total effect, with its red brick and cream stone trimmings, segment-headed windows, and arcades, is charming in an intimate, almost collegial fashion. It can almost persuade one, Maurice Craig suggests, to forget the evil role of the Castle in Irish affairs. The original quadrangle arrangement of castle buildings (Upper Castle Yard) was joined by a second quadrangle, as Lower Castle Yard took shape. This second quad is formed by a walkway joining the two, the Undercroft, adjoining Treasury Building (1717), the Chapel Royal (1814) and Record Tower (1226), and the Revenue Commission Building (1974). Beneath the Undercroft the butt of the Powder Tower (1234) remains visible, and beneath *that*, extensive Viking stonework is exposed to view. The Record Tower, the most impressive thirteenth-century structure still standing, was the mightiest of all the Castle's keeps, featuring 15-feet-thick walls suited to its function as a top-security jail.[*]

The moat was U-shaped and averaged a depth of 28 feet and a width of 69. It looped around the eastern end of the castle site—from the Undercroft,

---

[*] Previously known as Gunners' Tower and Wardrobe Tower, its present name was adopted in 1814 when it was converted to house the Public Records of Ireland. The upper section and battlements were added later to match the style of the adjoining Chapel Royal.

around the Record Tower, and towards a deep pool of water known as the Dubhlinn or the Pool of Dublin, created by the confluence of the Liffey and Poddle rivers. The Poddle lapped the walls of the other two sides of the Castle. The moat was used extensively as a dump and also served as the Castle's sewerage pit. An archway and steps cut through the curtain wall allowed small boats to land provisions across the moat, transferred from larger boats on the Liffey.

The pool is now underground, beneath the Castle Gardens, an intricate mural design tattooed into the grass. The Castle Gardens came to house important facilities as part of the Castle complex. There was an Artillery Ground and an Armoury, erected in 1745. On the opposite side of the garden were an Ordnance Office and an army barracks on Ship Street.* Ammunition previously stored in the towers and the ground floor of the old Parliament House had been moved into the powder house in the garden, which exploded in 1689, leading eventually to the construction of a large magazine in Phoenix Park (1732). A new castle munitions store, workshop, and laboratory was built in the garden area near the Ship Street Gate. This too blew up in 1764, damaging the roof of the ballroom and the remaining superstructure of the old Bermingham Tower which, as we have seen, was then rebuilt. The Castle's Coach House (1833) forms the backdrop of the garden, fronted by a castellated façade erected, allegedly, to screen the slums beyond. The grounds also contained police facilities, home, for instance, to the notorious 'G men', the political agents of the Dublin Metropolitan Police, who were approached clandestinely by people telling tales on their neighbours.**

The changing role of the Castle: from Vikings and Anglo-Normans to the Ascendancy

Founding new settlements in disparate parts of the world made specific demands upon those involved; safety was a pressing need, especially if their

---

* The Armoury is today a Garda station and the Ordnance Office part of the Chester Beatty Oriental Library.
** One of the most famous 'G men' was the double-agent David Neligan, Michael Collins's main mole inside Dublin Castle, who was able to gain vital intelligence from the heart of the British security state at the Castle. See his book *The Spy in the Castle* (London: MacGibbon and Kee, 1968).

arrival initiated conflict with indigenous inhabitants. So, too, was the requirement to worship God. Another primary requirement was the need to trade,
which is what had often led settlers to their fragile coastal bridgeheads in
the first place. Dublin's strategic significance rested on the fact that it provided an ideal port, offering shelter from, yet easy access to, the Irish Sea.
Also favouring settlement here, the Liffey gave access to the Irish interior;
many of the Empire's most significant settlements developed at the mouth
of navigable waterways. Lying on a bay fed by a navigable river, it commanded the shortest sea crossing to Britain carrying shipping to north Wales
and to the estuaries of the Mersey and the Dee.[2]

In its earliest incarnation, a Gaelic ring fort probably existed on the site
of today's Upper Castle Yard, which traces the square castle structure that
was built by King John in 1204. The site was at the eastern end of the Hazel
Wood Ridge, overlooking the Liffey and Poddle rivers above the flood
plains. Vikings remained in control of Dublin until at least 1042, though
they were increasingly assimilated. In the twelfth century the English Crown
acquired a stake in Ireland when Henry II helped Diarmait Mac Murchada,
king of Leinster, to regain his kingdom. Proposals for the conquest of Ireland were explored at the Royal Council at Winchester in 1155, and a papal
bull issued by the English pope Adrian IV permitted Henry to invade and
enforce religious conformity to Canterbury after Dublin had been 'illegally'
transferred to Armagh by the Synod of Kells in 1152.* This began an English
attempt to take Ireland by force and make Dublin their stronghold, and an
Anglo-Norman invasion fleet appeared off Wexford in 1169, led by Richard
fitzGilbert, known as Strongbow. The Vikings tried to retake the town in the
following year under Asculf MacThorkil, the recently deposed king of Dublin, but his forces were routed. Asculf was taken captive to the Castle and
beheaded.

Strongbow, Earl of Pembroke, invoked Henry II's concern, as there was a
chance that he might establish a base in Ireland from which to contest the
throne. Henry therefore became the first English monarch to visit the
embryonic colony, landing in 1171 to establish his authority. He received
the submissions of the Irish chiefs and bishops (romantically depicted on
the ceiling of St Patrick's Hall). He gave Dublin to the freemen of Bristol,
and it developed as a colonial city state facing more towards the sea than the

---

* The nascent Christian community had refused to submit to the authority of the see of Armagh,
  insisting instead on remaining under the protection of Canterbury.

Gaelic hinterland. King John issued a mandate to his cousin, Justiciar Meiler
FitzHenry (1199–1208), to build a proper castle:

> You have given us to understand that you have no safe place for the custody
> of our treasure, and because of this reason and for many others, we are in need
> of a strong fortress in Dublin. We command you to erect a castle there, in such
> a competent place as you may consider to be suitable if need be for the
> defence of the city as well as to curb it, if occasion shall so require, making it
> as strong as you can with good fosses and strong walls. But you are first to
> build one tower, to which a castle and palace and other requirements may
> conveniently be added; for all of these you have our authority.[3]

Covering about one and a quarter acres, for its day Dublin Castle was an
enormous structure. Despite its might, however, the fledgling colony was
vulnerable, and English power weak or non-existent in the rest of Ireland.
It was a colonial state characterized by incompetence and brutality, which
bore the usual fruits of colonial excess: the neglect and near bankruptcy of
the colonial administration prompted an Irish cultural and military resur-
gence. Attacks against the English and their castle were commonplace
throughout the thirteenth and fourteenth centuries. The colonial state also
faced threats from abroad, a trend that continued into the Napoleonic era
and even beyond. On 25 May 1315, for example, Edward Bruce landed at
Larne with 6,000 soldiers following his victory over the English at Ban-
nockburn. Dublin Castle prepared for a siege, military specialists arriving to
prepare the defences. The mayor and bailiffs were ordered to supply the
Castle with 1,000 crossbow arrows, coal, wheat, salt, grease, lead for the towers and internal buildings, and a ship for the transportation of stones.[4] The
Castle's armoury, meanwhile, produced crossbows and other weapons. Those
people crucial to the functioning of the royal treasury and the Castle's
defences were ordered to live within the Castle walls. The bell tower of St
Marie del Dam was demolished because it overlooked the Castle, the stone
debris used to strengthen the Castle walls. People took refuge in the Castle,
including the Bishop of Down, and Irish leaders wishing to demonstrate
their loyalty to the regime sent hostages to reside there.

 In the fighting that ensued, Irish garrisons were massacred, and after one
particularly brutal episode, 'four score of their heads' were set upon the
ramparts. Remnants of Bruce's Isle of Man garrison were imprisoned in the
Castle, along with survivors of a battle against privateers fought in the Irish
Sea. Bruce's army twice came close to the town, the sight of its campfires
terrifying the inhabitants. Panic spread, the bridge over the Liffey was

torched as were the western walled suburbs and farms, denying the enemy food at a time of widespread famine. Dublin was saved from Bruce, but only at the cost of burning much of the new development beyond the walls.

As if famine and invasion were not enough to contend with, by Christmas 1348 the Black Death had killed around 14,000 people in the city and fire was a constant hazard (in 1283 much of Dublin had been lost in flames). The Castle administration was weakened by the high death toll among civil servants and administrators and fearing that the colony might fail, Edward appointed his son, Lionel of Clarence, as Justiciar (1361–6). The Castle was refurbished in anticipation of his arrival, and during his stay he developed its facilities, establishing a jousting ground complete with wooden castle. He also had a barge built, possibly to ferry members of the court from the postern gate adjoining the Powder Tower to the Castle Gardens and arbour.

The Castle contained kitchens, laundries, dungeons, quarters for the garrison, administrative offices, court rooms, and a chapel. It was the most visible symbol of English rule—which was becoming more oppressive—and the religious feuds that it fuelled. Clarence introduced the Statutes of Kilkenny (1366) which sought to exclude the 'inferior, degenerate' Irish from the colony and to eradicate the 'contamination' brought by Irish language, customs, and dress (and even hair-cuts). In 1394 Richard II landed with 10,000 men in order to halt the colony's decline. On his departure from the Castle he left a stockpile of weapons including 2 chests of bows, 31 pipes of arrows, 141 coats of mail, 335 large shields and lances, and 16 cannons from the Tower of London.[5] The power of the Dublin government was effective in a territory only 30 by 50 miles. As in many other parts of the colonized world, the process of subjugation, or 'pacification' as it euphemistically became known, was a long and drawn-out one, and for the time being, England remained an enclave power in Ireland.

Henry VIII sought to assert English power across the island as he strove to centralize his kingdoms and secure the Protestant Reformation. Reaction against the Crown's assertion of absolute power and its break with Rome came to a head in the revolt of Silken Thomas, which was comprehensively defeated by English arms. In preparation for Thomas's assault on Dublin, the Castle Constable, John White, had the following supplies delivered: 'Twentie tun of wine, four and twentie tun of beer, two thousand dried ling, sixteen hogsheads of salted beef and twentie chambers [guns] with an iron chain for the draw bridge of the castell'.[6] Thomas cut off the town's water supply and, following a short siege, Dublin surrendered. Thomas could then enter the walled town and lay siege the Castle. When word that reinforcements were on their way reached the Castle garrison, a flag was raised proclaiming the end of the truce. The citizens turned on the besiegers, many of whom were killed or imprisoned in the Castle. Thomas's attack switched to Ship Street Gate, but cannon fire from the Castle dislodged his men, at the same time destroying adjacent thatched houses. An attempt to storm New Gate failed, the defenders charging out from the Castle and scattering Thomas's men.

Silken Thomas surrendered on 24 August 1535. He was taken to the Tower of London and hanged, drawn, and quartered at Tyburn Tree, his head set on a spike on London Bridge together with those of his uncles. Hatred of the English grew, and the Castle was its focal point. The 'New English' of Queen Elizabeth's colonial administration saw Ireland as a territory to be conquered and civilized—much as the Spanish Conquistadors of the same century viewed South America. As the Attorney and Solicitor General, Sir John Davies, put it, 'A barbarous country must first be broken by war before it will be capable of good government.'[7] The tenure of Lord Deputy Arthur Grey de Wilton (1580–2) was marked by severity and massacres. A conspiracy to capture the Castle was foiled, and Fíach McHugh O'Beirne's severed head was spiked above the Castle gate. By the end of Elizabeth's reign in 1603, Ireland had been totally conquered and the Castle had become the centre of English government throughout the island.

Yet still the colonial state was insecure. In 1689 King James II arrived in Ireland intending to use it as a base from which to regain his crown. Accompanied by 6,000 French soldiers, Dublin welcomed him enthusiastically. Entering through St James's Gate with Lord Deputy Tyrconnell displaying the sword of state, forty dancing women ran alongside the parade through streets freshly covered with gravel and lined with soldiers of the garrison. Upon reaching the Castle, James dismounted and was accompanied into the chapel to witness a sung 'Te Deum' in his honour before retiring to the State Apartments.[8] On 7 May he processed from the Castle to the King's Inn and convened parliament, and presided over the reversal of the Act of Settlement and the resolution that the Parliament of England could not legislate for Ireland. For a brief time, Ireland possessed a complete and independent government. In response, William of Orange landed at Carrickfergus with 36,000 soldiers and defeated James at the Battle of the Boyne on 12 July 1690. James returned to exile in France after spending a last night in the Castle. Soon after, two battalions of William's Dutch troops secured Dublin, and William himself moved into the Castle.

The Ascendancy and Castle society

The Ascendancy was an exclusive social class comprising Protestant families of Norman, Old English, Cromwellian, and occasionally Gaelic origin. It was founded upon the penalization of the majority Catholic population, which was assigned a subservient role and denied the right to vote or serve in parliament. As late as the 1790s, armed rebellion and invasion forces deployed by Britain's European rivals threatened English rule. Revolutionary groups inspired by events in France emerged, and French troops arrived to aid them. The Castle authorities promulgated harsh new laws and the Lord-Lieutenant ordered rebels to be disarmed, sparking a reign of terror which fuelled a rebellion in 1798. A generous secret service fund incubated a network of spies and informers linked to the Castle; there were street battles in Dublin; and people were hanged from bridges and bodies were brought into Upper Castle Yard following a cavalry charge.

During these upheavals, the Castle site was constantly being adapted to changing circumstances. The Robert Emmet insurrection of 1803, for instance, highlighted its vulnerability. In response, the internal route from Palace Street to Ship Street was closed, and the stone bridge linking the State Apartments and the garden removed. The houses off Cole Alley, adjoining the western perimeter where the old curtain wall once stood, were compulsorily purchased and demolished. The present Ship Street Gate, Guard House, and high perimeter wall with return along Castle Street were constructed as a reaction to the Emett rebellion, to allow the more rapid movement of troops around the Castle site. The tower of St Werburg's Church was removed as its occupation by enemy sharpshooters would threaten Upper Castle Yard. Houses and shops on the east side of Great Ship Street were also purchased and demolished, and new buildings that became Ship Street Infantry Barracks were erected. There were other additions in this period too, notably the rebuilt Chapel Royal, designed by Francis Johnson, an architect of the Board of Works and Civil Buildings, one of Ireland's finest examples of Gothic Revival architecture.

After the upheavals at the turn of the century, the British government determined to get rid of the Irish parliament and remove legislative powers

to London. Lord-Lieutenant the Earl Cornwallis steered the necessary act
through the Irish parliament, which met for the last time in August 1800.
Peerages and other forms of patronage were distributed to ease the vote,
and the United Kingdom of Great Britain and Ireland came into existence
on 1 January 1801. The Union flag incorporating that of St Patrick flew
from the Castle's Bedford Tower for the first time. In the Throne Room, the
magnificent gilt chandeliers with interwoven shamrocks, roses, and thistles
were cast to mark the event. The giant gilded throne was installed for the
visit of George IV in 1821 (its attendant footstool subsequently adjusted for
the diminutive figure of Queen Victoria upon her visit to Ireland in
1849).

By the beginning of the eighteenth century the life of the Castle had
taken on many of the characteristics of the London Court of St James. The
Throne Room was modelled on that in Buckingham Palace and there
developed an extravagant formal court similar to that in England, centred
on the viceroy as the monarch's official representative. Charles II had dispatched the Duke of Ormond as viceroy, and he supervised the creation of
an English ruling class, rooted in lands taken from Catholic owners. The
development of a powerful Ascendancy reduced the burden on the viceroy,

Figure 4. Throne Room, State Apartments, Dublin Castle.

whose main task was to see that the will of the monarch was obeyed. The viceroy needed to keep the leading Ascendancy lights in good humour. Appointed in 1757, John Russell, 4th Duke of Bedford, stiffened the ceremonial side of things, insisting on proper court dress. Meanwhile, the development of affluent new accommodation in the city made the Castle more accessible to privileged families.

Because of all this, the Castle 'Season' became a central feature of court life at Dublin Castle. The Season was a six-week period culminating in the Grand Ball on St Patrick's night, 17 March. Proceedings were opened by the Viceroy's Levee, an evening on which Dame Street was packed from end to end with a stream of carriages, looked upon with envy, wonder, and disdain by the poor people lining the streets. The windows of the Castle, a contemporary reminiscence recorded, 'blaze with light, scarlet cloth covers the staircase and corridors, which are filled with lovely debutantes and handsome matrons. There is a frou frou of silken dresses and the chatter of many voices.'[9]

The Ascendancy developed a hedonistic lifestyle and built large, richly furnished mansions in the country and town-houses in Dublin for their visits during the Season. Here they would host the viceroy when he toured the country, and the Castle and its manifold social and ceremonial activities provided access to the centre of patronage and power. Lady Essex, whose husband was viceroy between 1672 and 1677, was the first vicerine to entertain lavishly as a great hostess. From May 1682 to September 1683, 6,000 gallons of French, Canary, and Rhenish wines and large quantities of other alcohol were consumed by the viceroy's household and his guests. Discrimination against Catholics was staunchly upheld: a proclamation of 1678 forbade Catholics from entering the Castle without a special order from the viceroy himself. As the oppression of Catholics and the depression of the Irish poor continued, the court became more extravagant. Dame Street was crammed with fashionable shops including a 'button maker to the Lord Lieutenant', purveyors of wine and spirits, tobacco and snuff, gun manufacturers, and the premises of John Michaels, 'Furrier to Viceroy and Vicereine Clarendon'. Castle Street meanwhile was home to confectioners, tailors, drapers, lace makers, glovers, bonnet and hat shops, chemists, solicitors, and numerous taverns.

Balls, banquets, drawing-rooms, levees, and elaborate festivities were held to celebrate royal birthdays and other anniversaries. The importance of these courtly frivolities was that an invitation to the Castle was a special token of good standing and prestige. Castle social events allowed the Lord-Lieutenant and his staff to gauge opinion and woo influential members of the Ascendancy. Those invited manoeuvred for advancement, for the monarch's representative in Ireland dispensed significant patronage in the form of pensions, jobs, sinecures, and promotions within the army, church, judiciary, and government. The ennoblement of loyal Anglo-Irish notables ensured willing collaborators. In a single day in 1777 Viceroy Buckinghamshire advanced five viscounts to earldom, seven barons to viscounts, and created eighteen new barons.

Ralph Nevill, a sharp-tongued observer of the Castle court and its pretensions—himself epitomizing its variegated snobberies—wrote a recollection of Dublin Castle and Dublin 'Society'. He noted how English (as opposed to Anglo-Irish) people would play up being 'pure English' because of the status attached to such 'pure bloods':

> The chief 'make-believe', however, was the Viceregal Court, or 'Coort', that strange, theatrical installation, whose tawdry influence affected everything in the place right down to the commonest little tradesman, or to the 'Castle Waiter', whose services it was a great comfort to secure, even at a higher fee... This theatrical make-believe of a Court leavened everything. Everybody played at this sham Royalty, and, I am convinced, firmly believed in it, or fancied they did. The 'Kestle' was no cynosure. To be asked to the 'Kestle', to know people at the 'Kestle', or even to know people who knew people at the 'Kestle', was Elysium itself![10]

Nevill describes the pomp and extravagance of the Castle and the court:

> The Castle, where this Card King [the Viceroy] lived, was a great centre of the city. In my childhood, boyhood, youth, manhood, I suppose no word rang out more loudly or more frequently in one's ears, or inspired such an awesome feeling. Often I passed it, often I was in it. There were held the 'levys', 'draw'n rooms', 'Pathrick's balls', dinners, concerts, and dances *galore*... It was rather an imposing place, with a great gateway and a guardhouse adjoining... Within, there is a large and stately courtyard, and on the left an archway, opening on a second, viz., 'The Lower Kestle yard'; though it seems undignified to call these august enclosures 'yards'. Round the first court were the residences of the high and mighty officers—the Chamberlain... Comptroller, all squeezed, sorely cribbed and cabined into a little set of rooms... And the household!—that awe-inspiring word! There was the 'Private Secretary', the 'Additional Private Secretary', and, odd to say, 'Assistant Private Secretary', State Steward, Comptroller, Gentleman Usher, Chamberlain, and actually a 'Master of Horse'.[11]

There were many posts to fill, and members of the Ascendancy coveted them. In addition to the positions listed by Nevill, there were also aides, gentlemen-at-large, and gentlemen-in-waiting. There was the Physician-in-Ordinary, the Surgeon-in-Ordinary, the Surgeon to the Household, the Surgeon Oculist, and the Surgeon Dentist. There were gentlemen of the bedchamber and gentlemen ushers who presented ladies to the viceroy and vicerine, and began balls by dancing with the first 'lady of quality'. There were grooms of chambers, footmen, coachmen, postilions, and pages, all with their own colourful and distinctive uniforms.

The increase in the extension of invitations to Irish people as well as members of the Anglo-Irish Ascendancy led to the blurring of social distinctions. Arrivistes arrived, along with members of the 'professions' and those from the broader Anglo-Irish community—even the occasional Catholic as attitudes softened. The 'Castle Catholics'—a pejorative term applied by nationalists to those Catholics admitted to viceregal circles, particularly under the Aberdeens—were a largely petit-bourgeois element, according to historian Joseph Robins, who opted for status as supporters of British rule in Ireland and of British culture rather than be identified with the largely peasant and increasingly nationalistic population from which many of them had sprung.[12] To many traditionally Protestant members of the Ascendancy, this marked the indigenization of the viceregal court—in essence, a measure of the success that British imperialism was having in broadening its collaborative base within Irish society. Quite apart from the tension this caused as Catholics entered the Protestant citadel of Dublin Castle, it upset deep-seated social values. P. L. Dickinson, a member of the Castle circle in the late nineteenth century, wrote with indignation about the impact of Viceroy Aberdeen's opening up of Castle society. 'Without being a snob, it was no pleasure, and rather embarrassing, to meet the lady at dinner who had measured you for your shirts the week before.'[13] The rapid extension of the peerage debased the currency, and strengthened the English perception that their Irish counterparts were a lesser breed, the Irish court a pretentious imitation.

The facilities at the Castle required constant modification to make them fit for a viceregal court. Prestige was important, and the Castle was not very well equipped, due to its age, to compete with the stunning new municipal buildings that were being erected around it, such as James Gandon's Four Courts for the legislature, the Irish parliament on College Green, and the mansions of the Ascendancy. The apparatus of the Irish court expanded,

Irish Ascendancy society grew in wealth and sophistication, and Georgian Dublin developed physically and socially into a more attractive city. Changes in the Castle's functions also reflected the construction in Phoenix Park of the new Vice-Regal Lodge as a residence for the viceroy (now the residence of the Irish president). The viceroy's life was ensconced in formality and ceremony from the moment he set foot in Ireland, met at his point of disembarkation by the Lords Justice and conveyed in a procession of carriages and mounted militia through decorated streets lined with foot soldiers and onlookers. At the Castle an elaborate ritual was performed, including the administration of an oath by the Archbishop of Dublin. The same levels of attention attended a viceroy's departure: when Lord Carlisle left in 1782 he was accompanied to the port by over 150 coaches bearing the nobility and gentry.

The life of the court at Dublin Castle involved feasting and drinking on a grand scale—to the point that many diaries and letters complained of the effects of over indulgence. Carlisle wrote that:

> almost before I have lost sight of the knives and forks of one, the soup of the other makes its appearance...My levee on Sunday is a consumptive business; the insulting myself and every gentleman in Dublin with some nonsensical questions for two hours makes me feel very thin and bilious indeed.[14]

The Duke of Shrewsbury, viceroy from 1713, was central to this process. Under Shrewsbury, dinner at 'His Grace's Table', even on normal, non-public occasions, consisted of a course of sixteen dishes, four removes, and a dessert on Sundays, Wednesdays, and Fridays. On one occasion a course of thirty-four dishes and six removes was accompanied by fourteen dishes of sweetmeats. One viceregal incumbent sent an emissary to France to procure the best food and wines and most attractive *objets d'art*. His principal cook was dispatched to France to gain skills at the royal court of Fontainebleu as well as the kitchens of the Duke of Orleans and the Archbishop of Narbonne, both notable gourmets. In December 1786 his man in France dispatched 500 bottles of Sillery champagne of the very best quality and 300 of Hautevilliers champagne. He also procured snuff boxes, paintings, sporting guns, and shoe buckles. Dinner was usually served in the Old State Room, which towards the end of the century was improved and redesigned to become St Patrick's Hall. About a hundred people were employed in cooking, serving, and maintaining the personal apartments of the viceroy. Sometimes there were largesse days, on which the poor were admitted and allowed to take away the remains; unfortunately, it was often considered fun, by the invited attendees, to watch the common people fighting over the food.

But some had no complaints whatsoever. Viceroys such as Thomas, Earl of Wharton, were notorious for their profligacy. Under Wharton (1708–10) the Castle became a centre for debauchery, where prostitutes and card-sharps gathered. Jonathan Swift, a chaplain to the court, wrote that Wharton was 'the most universal Vilain I ever knew'.[15] Mrs Scion, a friend of Swift, noted the unrelenting pursuit of pleasure among the ladies of Castle society: 'nothing about them Irish but their souls and bodies: I think they may be compared to a city on fire which shines by that which destroys them'.[16] During parliamentary sittings, members were allowed into the viceroy's cellars to drink from hogsheads. At the departure of Lord Townshend as viceroy in 1772, the *Freeman's Journal* published the couplet 'Drunkards, pimps and whores go mourn/Townshend shall never return'.[17]

The abuses of the viceroys could be astonishingly egregious. Walpole wrote that Viceroy Harcourt was proficient only at hunting and drinking. Viceroy Rutland, meanwhile, bestowed on Margaret Leeson the accolade of running the best brothel in Dublin, being so taken by her 'art of pleasing' that he had her included on the pension list for £300 a year under an assumed name. On one visit to her establishment in Pitt Street, Rutland was accompanied by two aides-de-camp and an escort of cavalry, who remained on duty at the brothel from one in the morning until five in the afternoon.[18] In 1787 Rutland set out on a punishing three-month tour of the country, during which he was entertained lavishly. He died shortly after, aged thirty-three, a post-mortem revealing a decayed liver.

Throughout the eighteenth century the social pace sped up under a succession of viceroys inclined to regal living on a grand scale. All of this, of course, was in contrast to the poverty of the Irish masses. Viceroy Chesterfield added new rooms, including the ballroom, to ensure that the Castle's social programme continued to dazzle, though he also attempted to discourage jobbery and 'the pernicious and beastly fashion of drinking'.[19] By the latter half of the eighteenth century all the trappings of a self-contained monarchy were in place in Dublin Castle and the Irish court reached its pinnacle of brilliance and extravagance.

Viceroy the Earl Temple's (1787–9) major contribution to court grandiosity was the establishment of the Order of the Knights of St Patrick, its extravagant ceremonies necessitating the refurbishment of the main hall of the viceregal apartments. The St Patrick's Day Ball of 1784 started with the knighting and investiture of Lord Carysfort, using the Sword of State following the delivery of proofs of blood. Later there was a fancy-dress ball, at which the ladies were dressed as Circassian slaves, Turks, and also 'Paddies', as the gentry and nobility found increasing amusement in the images of deprived and unsophisticated Irish peasantry.[20] Temple attempted to curb peculations and launched a campaign to root out fraud and corruption by directing that every office and store of the ordnance service be sealed and locked while all accounts were checked. Indicating the corruption endemic in the Castle administration, the comptroller of the ordnance laboratory cut his throat in the Castle Gardens, a senior official of the bullion ended his life in similar manner, and one of the commissioners for the impress office shot himself.[21]

The Castle underwent a further period of significant refurbishment in the first few years of the nineteenth century. The reception areas and the long suite of rooms of the State Apartments were improved and linked with wide connecting arches, newly furnished and with crimson silk covering the wall panels. Lavish entertainment was still the order of the day. A dinner in honour of the lord mayor in 1815 featured no fewer than twenty-six toasts, and the state visit of George IV in 1821 excited a great deal of attention. The first monarch to cross the Irish Sea on a non-martial mission, he arrived drunk after passing the voyage eating goose pie and drinking whisky.

When the Marquess Wellesley arrived as viceroy in 1833 his entourage was bedecked with shamrocks and the ceremonial carriage was drawn by shamrock-festooned horses. The former Governor-General of India, Wellesley found the viceregal apartments poorly appointed. He had designed his own residence in Calcutta, at the cost of £180,000 to the East India Company, and he soon set about improving Dublin Castle. The viceroy's role was increasingly associated with pomp, as political power was invested in the office of the Chief Secretary. Hugh Percy, 3rd Duke of Northumberland (appointed 1829), thought that the best way to rule Ireland was to ensure that his attire, modes of transport, and other elements of consumption were particularly conspicuous, and to subscribe to all manner of public charities and institutions. During Queen Victoria's visit in 1849, 4,000 people attended the Castle levee and 900 ladies were presented at the Drawing Room, where she wore a dress of emerald green poplin embroidered with golden shamrocks. During the 1891 Season, 16,310 persons were entertained at viceregal

functions in the Castle. Balls featured formal dances, often borrowed from
the French court, such as the minuet and gavotte. Practice and tuition were
required to master dances of increasing polish and precision. Ladies were
seated in tiered rows around the ballroom to address matters of ventilation
and heat. It was a world in which crinoline and manners mattered dispro-
portionately; people would worry about the style in which they bowed, or
judge a person's gentility according to the manner in which he lifted his hat.
There was lavish fabric and fashion, indicating breeding, wealth, and taste.
Luxury shops thrived in the streets around the Castle, providing the silk,
satin, brocade, lace, and whalebone creations that were considered *de rigeur*.
Men were expected to wear court dress while women appeared in the latest
London and Paris fashions. Among other things, Castle balls and drawing-
rooms acted as an important marriage mart.

By the 1890s, the flag-waving and cheering that had accompanied viceregal arrivals and tours of the country was a thing of the past. The predomi-
nant attitude was one of indifference among the people, tinged with violent
hostility. Viceroy for a brief spell in 1886, Lord Aberdeen espoused nationalist

Figure 5. Dublin Castle: 1893 engraving of the centre of administration in
Victorian Ireland. With the Chapel Royal on the extreme right next to the
Record Tower and the rear of the State Apartments, the view from the Castle
Garden remains much the same today.

ideas and was committed to Irish Home Rule—then one of the most controversial issues facing Westminster politicians—and a mark of how much things had changed. As a keen advocate of Home Rule, Aberdeen was unpopular with the Unionists—those who had traditionally flocked to Castle events—including the majority of the Castle administration. Many refused to attend the viceregal court, and their places were taken by army officers and civil servants and professionals. The days of the Castle court were coming to an end. Britain was attempting to manage increasingly intractable, not to say violent, nationalism in its nearest and oldest colonial territory.

During the First World War, Lord and Lady Aberdeen (returned for a much longer stint as viceroy and vicerine) turned the area of the State Apartments into a Red Cross hospital. In addition to wounded British troops and recusant aristocratic families (as described in Daisy Countess of Kenmare's autobiography), during the Easter Rising of 1916 the Castle accommodated Irish nationalist fighters too, including James Connolly, shot in the leg at the GPO. He remained at the Castle until he was executed, and now a room in the State Apartments is named in his honour, an example of how the Castle, long associated with British oppression, was invested with symbols of Irish nationalism. The bodies of deceased British and Irish fighters were buried in the Castle Gardens. During the Rising, the Castle reprised its role as a military redoubt, acting as a stronghold, a mustering point for troops, and a military hospital. When the insurgents attacked the Castle, they were not aware, however, of just how unguarded it was, despite war and the building's menacing symbolism. After the war, as unrest deepened and a war of insurrection unfolded, the Castle reverted to its historic role as a fortress in the midst of a hostile territory. The gates of Upper Castle Yard remained closed, and as the threat of terrorism took hold English civil servants working in other departments moved into Castle living quarters for safety.

The last ceremonial event of the viceregal court took place on 16 January 1922 when members of the provisional Irish government, led by Michael Collins, arrived by taxi and met the viceroy, Viscount FitzAlan, in order to receive the handover of the Irish state. It was Collins and his companions for whom the red carpet was laid down on this, the last occasion on which Dublin Castle would be British. Over seven centuries of continuous occupation was at an end. As the *Irish Times* wrote the following day: 'Having withstood the attacks of successive generations of rebels, it was quietly handed over yesterday to eight gentlemen in three taxicabs.' Collins himself summed up the magnitude of the change that he had affected: 'How could I have expected to see Dublin Castle itself—that dread Bastille of Ireland—formally surrendered into my hands by the Lord Lieutenant, in the brocade hung Council Chamber?'[22] As a measure of the Castle's role in Irish history, and the hostility of Irish people towards it, once independence had been achieved senior Irish politicians considered razing it to the ground, as other postcolonial states removed monuments considered too painfully or embarrassingly reminiscent of the colonial era.

Dublin Castle remains the centre stage on which Irish political and cultural affairs are played out. It is where the investiture of new presidents takes place; it acts as headquarters when Ireland holds the presidency of the European Union, and hosts major events such as the 2011 Global Economic Forum. It provides the backdrop for visits from foreign monarchs and leaders, such as the state visit of Elizabeth II in 2010. It is a major tourist attraction and home to a remarkable collection of state-owned art, and it is the site of the internationally renowned Chester Beatty Collection of Asian and Middle Eastern art. It also remains an important bureaucratic site, the Lower Castle Yard housing the offices of the state revenue.

2

A Tale of Two Towns: Spanish Town, Jamaica and Williamsburg, Virginia

The heart of the early British Empire lay in America and the West Indies, not in the African and Asian domains added to the imperial estate later on. Indicating the region's importance, in the eighteenth century the Caribbean was home to three of the ten largest cities in the Empire—Charleston, Kingston, and Spanish Town—as European powers went about the extraordinary business of opening up (a euphemism for breaking into) a 'new world'. This chapter explores the foundation of two of the region's most distinctive towns, colonial settlements that shared many similarities including their attainment, and then loss, of capital status. The history of both Spanish Town in Jamaica and Williamsburg in Virginia featured the displacement of indigenous peoples by European invaders and their African slaves. Thereafter, the evolution of both towns was intertwined with the slave-based plantation economy that was a key feature of early British expansion, and both developed after the original settlements—St Ann's Bay in the case of Jamaica and Jamestown in the case of Virginia—had been deemed unsatisfactory for reasons of swamp-bred disease and vulnerability to attack.[1] The history of both towns illustrates the vacillating fortunes of colonial settlements across the centuries, as well as the capricious role played by natural disasters, particularly hurricanes, earthquakes, and fires, in the ordering of human affairs.

Around an elegant square in Jamaica exists a facsimile of Georgian England. It is an imperial piazza once known as King's Square, framed by a court house, a House of Assembly, an ornate classical memorial to Admiral Lord Rodney, and the King's House, built in 1762 as a residence for the island's governors. Thus were gathered together three buildings representing the

major functions of the colonial state and a cupola'd memorial, with colonnades extending either side, that celebrated the sea power that secured it.
These buildings looked at each other across a central square planted with
palm trees. Located in the centre of Spanish Town, they are considered by
many to form the finest group of British buildings in the West Indies.

Having been a Taino Indian settlement from AD *c.*500, Spanish Town
became the seat of Spanish and then British colonial government, a status it
retained for 333 years, making it the oldest continuously occupied city in the
Western Hemisphere. But throughout most of its history Spanish Town
struggled to remain Jamaica's political and cultural hub in the face of robust
competition from other towns—Port Royal and its successor, Kingston.
Eventually, Spanish Town lost out to Kingston in 1872 and went into steep
decline, leading to the state of dilapidation that now pervades King's Square.

Created half a century earlier, in the American state of Virginia is a unique
town made up of scores of pristine early colonial buildings. Apparently preserved in aspic, Williamsburg is a monument to early British settlement in
America, and to the inclination towards self-government that led to the
foundation of the independent United States. Virginia was one of the showcase colonies of the first British Empire and its old capital Williamsburg—
plain 'Middle Plantation' before it was renamed to mark the accession of
William of Orange to the British throne—is the second town explored in
this chapter. America's first Capitol building was constructed here, its early
members including George Washington and Thomas Jefferson. Nearby
stood the Governor's Palace and the mansions of the well-to-do, as well as
the facilities required to service a new town including taverns, courthouse,
gaol, and magazine. All of these brick buildings were completed by 1722,
establishing a capital for the Virginia settlement capable of both governing
itself and repelling attack from Indians or Spaniards.

The Capitol stood at one end of Williamsburg's main thoroughfare, Duke
of Gloucester Street (named after Queen Anne's son). It was an impressive
mile-long, 90-feet-wide road, with the College of William and Mary's Wren
Building at the other end. Throughout the eighteenth century the Capitol,
along with the Governor's Palace, was at the social and political heart of
Virginian society, and was the scene of epoch-making decisions. The 1776
Resolution for Independence was adopted here, and Thomas Jefferson's bill
for religious freedom was proposed in its chamber. The General Court, the
colony's highest court, also convened in the Capitol building. Fire destroyed
it in 1747, though within six years it had been rebuilt. But in 1780 Richmond

Old Capitol Building and Colonial Coach,
Williamsburg, Va.

Figure 6. The Capitol Building, Williamsburg

replaced Williamsburg as the colony's capital. With the seat of government gone, the Capitol building, like most of the other public buildings, lost its *raison d'être* and subsequently experienced considerable change of use as the town entered a long period of eclipse. Williamsburg, therefore, underwent a rise and fall that paralleled Spanish Town's, though unlike the Jamaican city, in the twentieth century Williamsburg experienced a spectacular revival.

Dispossession of the locals and the establishment of new settlements

A major theme in the foundation of the European empires was the dispossession of indigenous inhabitants, their resistance to European impositions and, in some tragic cases, their abject destruction. So, too, was the forced movement of millions of non-Europeans for the purposes of European economic prosperity as slave-worked plantations fed the developing world economy. In Jamaica, the gentility epitomized by the King's House and its neighbouring civic buildings and mansions was firmly based on the inhumanity of slavery, as was the evolution of Williamsburg. In the one colony sugar and slaves was the foundation of prosperity, while in the other it was the eponymous Virginian tobacco and the slaves that produced it.

In this beautiful island, trills the Jamaica travel guide, 'Mother Nature has concentrated all the splendours she elsewhere sows parsimoniously throughout the tropics—cascading waterfalls, lush green mountains, ribbons of talcum-fine sand, the rustle of trade winds teasing the palms, flowers that spill their petals everywhere.'[2] But Jamaica's history has been a particularly violent one, belying the beauty of its landscapes. In 1494 Christopher Columbus, legendary discoverer of the New World, attempted to land at St Ann's Bay during his second voyage. From the carvel *Niña* he surveyed the shoreline, declaring it 'the fairest island that eyes have beheld'. But in a scene reminiscent of events elsewhere, as white strangers in frightening vessels attempted to land on islands from the Caribbean to the Pacific, he was driven off by canoes laden with angry warriors. Moving round the coast Columbus landed at Discovery Bay, in need of wood and water, and quelled resistance with crossbows and a large dog, which terrified the Taino. Columbus named the island St Jago, or Santiago, after St James, and took possession of it in the name of the king of Spain. In 1510 the Spanish established a permanent colony, though interest in the island faded as it became clear that it was not laden with the gold that they had expected to find in abundance. The Taino Indians were brutalized and enslaved, their population decimated. By the time the British arrived they had been virtually wiped out through overwork, murder, smallpox, infanticide, and thousands of suicides. In one of the saddest ironies of the colonial encounter, as an indigenous population suffered genocide, a new immigrant population began to grow when, in 1517, the first African slaves were imported.

For thirty years Spanish colonists settled around St Ann's Bay, until it became clear that the area was unhealthy because of its swamps. Instead, they looked south to a town on a wide fertile plain, a town they named Villa de la Vega (Town of the Plain), also known as San Jago de la Vega—what the British later named Spanish Town. Jamaica was ruled as a personal fief by Columbus and his sons until the Spanish Crown took control of the island in 1640. Located 7 miles inland, the site of the new town was protected from seaborne attack and stood in the midst of fertile agricultural land, and its proximity to the Rio Cobre afforded it a reliable supply of fresh water. But Jamaica was not valued strategically by Madrid, and its governors feathered their own nests at the expense of the colony's well-being and security. Nonetheless, Spanish Town thrived, and was described by a Carmelite missionary in 1628 as 'marvellously attractive...very well built and laid out'.[3] When the English pirate William Jackson invaded Jamaica with 500 buccaneers in the 1640s, he recorded that it was a fair town 'consisting of four or five hundred houses, five or six stately churches and chapels, and one monastery of Franciscan friars [all] situated on descent of a Delectable and spacious plaine'.[4] Jackson and his men held Spanish Town to ransom, threatening to raze it to the ground. For not doing so they were rewarded with 200 head of cattle, 10,000 pounds of cassava bread, and 7,000 pieces of eight.[5] While his pirate fleet was repaired in the harbour of Passage Fort, Jackson's men roamed the streets of the deserted capital, feasting on hogs and hens and searching for gold.

The Virginia Company had been formed in London in April 1606 in order to establish a colony to challenge the Spanish, find a western route to the Indies, and preach to the American natives. To attract settlers, the company promoted Virginia as a refuge and a land of fortune for England's rapidly expanding population. The enclosure movement had forced thousands of peasants off the land, swelling the urban population. The prospect of land ownership and concomitant status drew many Englishmen and women to Virginia. As an added incentive, settlers were offered English liberties once they arrived in the New World.

Captain Christopher Newport commanded an expedition which took four months to reach Chesapeake Bay, making landfall on 26 April 1607. Earlier settlements had failed, overcome by the predations of other European powers as well as the native peoples. A chronic shortage of funds and the challenge of attracting more settlers to risk their lives on the Atlantic crossing hampered their chance of becoming self-sufficient. The first permanent settlement in what later became the United States, Jamestown, and the river on which it developed, were named in honour of the British monarch. It offered a good defensive position against both the indigenous people and the Spanish, though it lacked fresh water and languished amid mosquito-breeding swamps.

As was the case for the first Europeans to settle Jamaica, this marvellous new land inspired both fear and wonder; it was viewed as wilderness and forbidding forest inhabited by 'savage' indigenes on the one hand, and as a new promised land, unspoiled and abundant, on the other. The fledgling settlement's survival depended on its ability to trade with the Powhatan Indians, who viewed it with understandable anxiety: though willing to trade corn for copper and beads, mistrust and misunderstanding leading to violence was inevitable. By 1616, only 351 of 1,500 settlers remained. Rein-forcements arrived, 3,750 between 1618 and 1621 alone. Another significant arrival was '20 and odd Negroes', the first slaves landed in a Dutch frigate, probably from Ndongo in Angola. The settlement lived precariously, rela-tions with the Powhatans veering from friendliness to violence. Settler numbers were greatly reduced by disease, starvation, lack of clean water, and war. The Great Assault of 1622 killed at least 347 settlers. The English responded with a declaration of 'perpetual warre without peace or truce'.[6] The second Great Assault of 1644 killed 500, about 8 per cent of the settlers, sparked by rampant land acquisition and a concerted effort to drive out the invaders. One of the colonists, John Rolfe, married Pocahontas, daughter of the Powhatan chief.

Despite being buffeted by numerous threats, the settlement soon devel-oped landmark political institutions. The creation of a legislative assembly was authorized in the company's royal charter and on 30 July 1619 twenty-two elected delegates, or burgesses, convened with the new governor, Sir George Yeardley, and his advisory Council of State. They met in the wooden Jamestown church to discuss company rules and enact laws of governance and public order. This was the first elected representative body in the New World, and it established the principle of self-government that would become a leitmotif of American and Caribbean settlement. In 1625 Virginia was declared a crown colony by King Charles I, the company having been deemed a failure and dissolved. In 1643 the burgesses won the right to sit independently of the council, which now became an upper house.

Jamestown fell out of favour as a settlement and Governor John Harvey signed 'An Act for the Seatinge of the Middle Plantation'. It encouraged colonists to settle on a new site protected by a wooden palisade designed as a defence against Indian encroachment. In 1699 Nathaniel Bacon torched the Statehouse in Jamestown, so a new political chamber was required, as well as a healthier and safer environment. Thus Williamsburg was established on high ground on the peninsula between the James and York rivers, the move partly motivated by the desire to escape the malarial swamps that bedevilled Jamestown. Williamsburg grew from these modest roots to become one of colonial America's most important commercial and political centres and in 1699 was named capital of Virginia, after which Jamestown simply ceased to exist. So began an experiment in the construction of a model society replicating the best elements of the Old World on the fringes of the New.

The invasion of Jamaica

Jamaica was constantly threatened by the predations of pirates and the consequences of raiding and smuggling. Sir Anthony Shirley landed in 1597 and plundered and burnt Spanish Town. Six years later the Spanish governor, Fernando Melgarejo, defeated an invasion attempt led by Christopher Newport. Spain used Jamaica as a supply depot for the conquest of Cuba and much of the American mainland. The island's immense agricultural resources and strategic position were undervalued, however, and it was left virtually defenceless. Oliver Cromwell, Lord Protector of England following the execution of Charles I, was aware of this and appreciated the strategic and political value of the Caribbean islands: Jamaica had the potential to be a dagger pointed at Spain's Caribbean underbelly. On 10 May 1655 two Spanish fishermen beheld a fleet of thirty-eight warships which were soon crammed into the harbour of Passage Fort. Messengers spread out to warn of the impending arrival of the British, and people left Spanish Town and made for the hills. But this was not just another raid; it was a full scale invasion force sent from England under Admiral William Penn, his fleet bearing an army commanded by General Robert Venables.

The British conquered Jamaica as part of Cromwell's Western Design, a scheme intended to expand Britain's holdings in the Caribbean at the expense of Spain's. The expedition had begun badly with an ill-judged attack on Hispaniola, which ended in a rout. In response to this failure, and spurred by fear of Cromwell's reaction, it was decided to attack some other Spanish possession instead. Thus Jamaica's fate was sealed. Around 7,000 men disembarked from the ships, and were faced by 1,500 ill-prepared Spanish settlers. Rather than march directly on the capital, General Venables allowed the Spanish governor time to consider his terms, time used by the settlers to turn loose their cattle and flee. (Cromwell had both Penn and Venables imprisoned in the Tower of London on their return to England, unhappy with their campaigns in Hispaniola and Jamaica.) The remaining slaves fled to the mountains and hills and formed the Maroons, autonomous communities of escaped slaves and the tiny handful of remaining Taino Indians.

The military action was swiftly concluded and Jamaica's capital fell within days. When the British realized that many Spaniards had fled taking their valuables with them, Spanish Town was burned in anger. Much of the town was razed to the ground, its churches torched and the bells melted down for shot; the Chapel of the Red Cross, a little to the east of King's Square on Red Church Street and the first cathedral in the New World, was destroyed by Cromwell's soldiers.* This wanton vandalism inconvenienced the British themselves, because their destruction of buildings and slaughter of livestock necessitated expensive reconstruction and threatened their food supply.

Jamaica was one of the Empire's earliest colonies of conquest, denoting the manner in which many possessions were to be gained in the future. The precarious situation in Jamaica led to the strategic use of settlers to make good Britain's new claim: Cromwell encouraged settlement in the new colony, providing grants of land and guaranteeing settlers freedom from customs duties, and laid down that all persons born in the island should enjoy the same rights as the people of England. Hundreds of colonists soon arrived from Barbados and Bermuda, and 1,600 came from Nevis. A Spanish attempt to retake Jamaica was defeated at the Battle of Rio Nuevo in 1658, in which over 300 Spaniards were killed. So grave was the threat that, for the first six years of British rule, Jamaica was administered by a military court martial, meeting once a month in Spanish Town.

The Spanish had good reason to try and wrest the island from the British, for it had been speedily turned against them, used as a base for disrupting Spain's extensive interests in the region. Illustrating how intertwined piracy and official policy could become, shortly after the capture of Jamaica its governor, Thomas Modyford, gave buccaneers royal protection to harass Spanish colonies and ships from their base at Port Royal. Having been appointed governor in 1664 with express orders to suppress buccaneers, the onset of the Second Dutch War, and London's inability to spare a fleet for the West Indies, meant that they now had to be enlisted as the island's main defence. The year 1664 also witnessed the first general representative assembly, which convened in Spanish Town, allowing the island's growing population of white colonists to make their own laws providing that they were not repugnant to the laws of England.

---

* The Anglican Cathedral of St Jago de la Vega was erected on the site, a second building appearing in 1714 after a hurricane had destroyed the first. One of the prettiest churches in Jamaica, the red-bricked cathedral is topped by an octagonal steeple with Corinthian columns. The original black and white chequered floor is studded with graves dating from 1662. The beautiful interior features wooden fluted pillars, carved pews and choir stalls, a beamed ceiling, stained glass and a large organ from 1849. In 1843 it was named the Cathedral of the Jamaican Diocese of the Anglican Church. A mixture of different architectural styles, including medieval, the Cathedral is shaped like a cross and includes a number of monuments by John Bacon.

Though the island was formally ceded to Britain at the Treaty of Madrid (1670), its new rulers had plenty of challenges to contend with, both internal and external. Disease and a dearth of imports took their toll on early British settlers—the 7,000 members of the invading army, for instance, shrank to around 2,500 within a year. In 1670 a Spanish man-of-war appeared off the coast, prompting the Jamaica Council in Spanish Town to take defensive measures. They commissioned Henry Morgan as 'Admiral and Commander-in-Chief of all the ships of war belonging to this harbour', and instructed him to attack the Spaniards and Spanish possessions. This led, among other things, to Morgan's famous attack on Panama City. In 1690 a slave rebellion occurred, in which Clarendon slaves allied with the Maroons and launched the First Maroon War, which was brutally supressed.

In 1694 a French fleet under Admiral du Casse attacked Jamaica and destroyed sugar plantations and factories, kidnapping slaves and killing white colonists. Natural disasters also played a significant role in shaping the colony's history. In 1692 an earthquake destroyed Port Royal, killing 2,000 people. What was a disaster for Port Royal served to confirm Spanish Town's prominence—though its destruction led to the growth of Kingston on the opposite side of the harbour, which was eventually to eclipse Spanish Town. Hurricanes were also a threat, the one of 1722 sinking forty-four of the fifty ships in Kingston Harbour and causing the water to rise 15 feet above the usual mark.[7]

Williamsburg's Capitol and other buildings

In 1699 the assembly passed an act for the building of the Capitol and the 'City of Williamsburgh'. It specified that the new Statehouse built to replace that destroyed by Nathaniel Bacon in Jamestown be known as 'the Capitoll', the first use of the term in America. It called for a two-storey brick building with two 75-feet wings, each terminating at one end with a semi-circular apse. These two wings were joined by a cross gallery 30 feet in length and 15 feet wide, raised upon piazzas. Its 'H' shape meant that the Capitol was actually two buildings joined by a third (the piazza) with a conference room above. Steeply pitched roofs were topped by a tall, glazed wooden tower, with a gallery and a flagpole. Classical architecture and design ideals were employed, inspired largely by Christopher Wren's rebuilding of London

Figure 7. House of Burgesses, Capitol building, Williamsburg, Virginia.

after the Great Fire of 1666. Governor Francis Nicholson, who had previously served as governor of Maryland and laid out the plans for Annapolis, developed the scheme for Williamsburg. Although the design source is unknown, the plan for the Capitol building was produced at the request of the council and may have been procured from England by Governor Nicholson.

Kiln after kiln of bricks was burned and bricklayers and carpenters crossed the Atlantic from England. Materials unavailable locally, such as stone, glass, and ironware were also imported.[8] The Capitol's double form physically expressed the two-house legislature of Council and House of Burgesses, one on each side of the building, a bicameral legislature under one roof. *Oeil-de-boeuf* windows lit the chambers on the ground floor.[9] The use of the projecting apsidal ends on the south façade was one of the earliest examples of this feature in American architecture and may, as with the conscious choice of the building's name, have been a commemoration of antiquity since Roman basilicas, or halls of justice, often contained apses in which judges sat. The original building had no chimneys due to the fear of fire, although they were added in 1723.

The Capitol was decked with symbolic features and specialist fixtures and fittings. A cut brick cartouche symbolized the light of God shining on Virginia and her courts and legislature. The coat of arms of Queen Anne

was emblazoned on the cupola by order of the General Assembly, later supplanted by the arms of Governor Nicholson. The Speaker's Chair, taken to
Richmond when the capital moved, was later returned to its original home.
Governor Botetourt presented an iron warming machine to the House of
Burgesses in 1770, built in London and decorated with the arms of the
colony of Virginia and figures of Justice and Mercy. The entrance hall ceiling, walls, and stairway were decorated with weaponry.

The east wing contained the House of Burgesses on the first floor and
committee rooms on the second. This, the lower house, consisted of two
members elected by the landowners of each county and one member each
from Jamestown, Williamsburg, Norfolk, and the College of William and
Mary. The west wing housed the General Courtroom on the first floor and
the Council Chamber on the second. The Council, made up of twelve leading colonists appointed for life by the king, constituted the legislature's
upper house. The councillors assisted the governor by acting as a council of
state. Each wing had its own staircase, and if the two houses reached dead-
lock in trying to pass a bill already accepted by one or the other, representatives from the Council and the House of Burgesses met jointly in the second
floor chamber over the piazza.

Spring and fall sessions of the General Court, summer and winter sessions of the criminal court, and sessions of the General Assembly were the
formal occasions that brought the town to life. There were other more
informal bureaucratic functions and events all year round. By 1700 a small
number of settler families had established themselves as local and provincial power brokers, their status based upon the tobacco and slave economy. Those who ran for election in Virginia's counties, where the franchise
was an all-male affair, tended to be from the wealthy gentry class, men
such as George Washington and Thomas Jefferson (who came to oppose
the colony's social hierarchy). Although small by today's standards, Williamsburg was a unique centre of power and activity. During the eighteenth century the members of the assembly increasingly came into conflict
with the governors and their councils as the House of Burgesses evolved
into an assertive legislative assembly with greater authority than the king's
appointed governors.[10] By the 1720s governors had come to realize that
they could not dominate or bully the assembly or the council, and chose
instead to work with them to solve the colony's problems, a cordial relationship that remained until the final decade of the colonial period. By mid-
century, therefore Virginia's 'squirearchy' or 'self-perpetuating oligarchy of

plantation owners' were more powerful than the governor. It controlled the colony's tobacco wealth and land sales, and dominated social, intellectual, cultural, and political life. The squierarchy controlled the county court and formed the governor's council, and was a close-knit, small (maybe 5 percent of Virginia's population), self-conscious elite.[11]

Fire destroyed the Capitol in 1747, but within six years it had been rebuilt. The new Capitol took a different architectural form, incorporating the surviving walls of the original but differing in the placement of second-floor windows, without apsidal ends, and including a two-storey entrance porch. Reoriented, the new Capitol now faced west down Duke of Gloucester Street.

The King's Square

Like Williamsburg, Spanish Town in its heyday was a centre of power with a legislative assembly prepared to take issue with the governor sitting in the King's House across the square, alive with political goings on and social gaiety. It had been laid out according to the regular Hispanic template, with a grid of streets and squares containing churches and principal administrative buildings such as the Hall of Audience, centred upon a central plaza (King's Square, also called The Parade). When Cromwell's troops took the town this plan was left in place, and over the remainder of the seventeenth century it was haltingly anglicized with new churches and houses. Thus the Cathedral of St James was erected on the site of the demolished Spanish Chapel of the Red Cross (1525), bricks from the old church used in the construction of the new as the Protestant church supplanted Rome. A new barracks complex appeared in 1791 and an iron bridge was shipped from England to cross the Rio Cobre at the entrance to the town, the oldest surviving cast-iron bridge in the Americas. Constructed from 87 tons of cast iron sent from Britain in forty-one pieces, it spanned the river in an 80-feet rainbow, enabling it to withstand the floods that had destroyed previous bridges.[12]

Dissatisfaction with the 'old' King's House (erected in 1711) was one of the main causes of the extensive redevelopment of King's Square that took place in the middle of the eighteenth century, as was earthquake damage. Making do with the old King's House, the Duke of Portland, governor from 1721 until his death in Spanish Town five years later, complained about the expense of its upkeep. The £4,000 voted for the purpose by the assembly had to be supplemented by a further £2,000 from his own purse in order to recondition the place. The duke had accepted the relatively lowly post of governor of Jamaica after losing a fortune in the South Sea Bubble. The old King's House was considered too dilapidated to dwell in by some of the noblemen representing the king, and they borrowed the mansion of the Royal Africa Company's local agent instead. To make way for the new King's House (1762) on the western side of the square, the old wooden Spanish Hall of Audience, the Island Secretary's Office, and the earlier King's House were demolished, and protruding stubs from the gateway of the Spanish White Church removed. Unfortunately, with the demolition of the Hall of Audience, the last of the buildings from the Spanish period was lost.

The new King's House was built by Thomas Craskell, the island's military engineer.* Upon its completion, the governors of Jamaica were able to represent their monarch while residing in a replica of an English Palladian pile. Its main exterior feature was a giant portico, home to dozens of nesting swallows, which shaded the long, plain façade.[13] The King's House was a mansion of considerable pretensions in the New World. Walter Roberts remarked, 'It would be an error of historical emphasis to see in it merely a sign of routine progress. The King's House expressed Jamaica's current mood and owed something to the dramatic nature of these times. The surge of sugar from a gamble to a bonanza was fully underway.'[14] In the opinion of the architect Hubert Corlette, King's Square was 'a fine architectural conception of what a dignified civic centre could or should be. The King's Square in Spanish Town has seldom been equalled as a heart or local zone, a nucleus, of corporate life.'[15]

All of the new buildings that were erected around King's Square were official commissions proclaiming the town's importance as Jamaica's capital—and Jamaica's status as the jewel in the imperial crown. In the second half of the eighteenth century Jamaica provided a third of Britain's imports, and the duty on sugar entering Britain provided a whopping third of the total customs revenue (up to a twelfth of total government revenue). The Palladian style employed made deliberate statements about prosperity and self-confidence, a measure of the plantocracy responsible for commissioning the buildings.[16] Jamaica's planters were ambitious, rich,

---

* Many of the Empire's early buildings were built by military engineers. In India in particular, the frequency with which one encounters the names of British Army or Indian Army engineers as architects of churches, houses, and administrative buildings, is astonishing.

Figure 8. Archive photograph of the King's House, Spanish Town, Jamaica.

optimistic, and powerful, and were often able to block the policies of the monarch's representative and pass their own self-serving legislation. The growth of Spanish Town and its elegant central square was firmly based on profits derived from slave-grown sugar. When, for example, the Revolutionary and Napoleonic Wars ended and peacetime sugar exports resumed, the assembly commissioned a new range of public buildings on the south side to house the law courts, thus completing the square.

The centre of the square was enclosed by a brick wall as an ornament, though it proved unpopular because it looked like a cemetery wall and was replaced by a post and chain fence. The massive new King's House on the west side of the square balanced the House of Assembly opposite. The house was first occupied by William Henry Lyttelton, who came to Jamaica from the governorship of South Carolina. It cost a fortune—over £30,000—to construct and furnish. But observers were dazzled by the results. Edward Long's account of 1773 remarks that:

It is now thought to be the noblest and best edifice of the kind, either in North America or any of the British Colonies in the West Indies...The

> cornices, key stones, pediments, copings and quoins, are of a beautiful free-
> stone, dug out of the Hope River course...The entrance is by a lofty por-
> tico...supported by twelve columns of Portland stone, of the Ionic order.The
> pediment which rises above the Attic story [sic] is superb, and very properly
> ornamented with the imperial arms of Great Britain carved in work well
> executed...The portico gives an air of grandeur to the whole building.[17]

Stone pillars and a huge lintel were shipped from England to provide the
King's House with its imposing portico. Constructing this feature alone cost
a small fortune as the assembly had to pay for the work of the local stone-
mason who erected it, as well as the cost of the materials shipped out from
England, freight, insurance, the 'Boatage, Haulage, and Wainage' required to
move the materials to Spanish Town, the dog-tooth carving around the
edge of the portico, scaffolding, and the cost of erecting the King's Arms on
the structure.[18] The house featured plain sash windows protected by external shutters. In an unusual architectural arrangement, the portico framed
not one but two front doors, one on the right opening onto a small hall and
a staircase leading to the governor's private apartments. There were three
large rooms on the ground floor on this side of the house and a long gallery
above, designed for dinners during official balls or other public events. The
left-hand front door led into what was variously described as the 'great
saloon' or the 'hall of audience', about 73 feet by 30 in dimension, a lofty
two-storeyed hall panelled in mahogany, and a row of pillars dividing it into
a ballroom and a side aisle.

A contemporary account describes the interior:

> From the ceiling, which is coved, hang two brass gilt lustres. A screen of seven
> Doric pillars divides the saloon from an upper and lower gallery of commu-
> nication which ranges the whole length of the west wide; and the upper one
> is secured with an elegant entrelas of figured iron work. The east or opposite
> side of the saloon is finished with Doric pilasters, upon each of which are
> brass girandoles double gilt, and between each pilaster, under the windows of
> the Attic story [sic] are placed, on gilt brackets, the busts of several ancient and
> modern philosophers and poets.[19]

At the north end over the door was a small movable orchestra, a forest of
mahogany chairs and settees below. The superlative social facilities incorporated into the King's House reflected the priorities that the assembly's building committee assigned to the house and its public role. But in addition to
its social function, the King's House was also integral to the formal processes
of the colony's governance: leading off from the ballroom, three folding

doors opened into a spacious apartment. This room, the Council Chamber, contained paintings of George III and Queen Charlotte by Sir Joshua Reynolds. Here the governor's official council, a body similar to the Privy Council in England and the third component of Jamaican governance, would meet to discuss the colony's affairs.

Running away from the building at right angles was a loggia leading to library stacks, with a picture gallery on the ground floor beneath. The King's House compound stretched across the whole western side of the square, whereas its previous incarnations had been crammed onto the site of the former Spanish city hall wedged alongside the Hall of Audience. The King's House complex accommodated the governor's household, including offices for his three private secretaries. To the west there were the kitchen, pantries, and servants' quarters and a servants' hall, all linked by covered walkways; to the south, the coach house, stables, and a granary. There was also a manicured tropical garden of flowering shrubs and fruit trees. As well as its gubernatorial, administrative, and legal functions, Spanish Town was a garrison town and accommodated a large proportion of Jamaica's military establishment, and for many years a company of the West Indies Regiment guarded the King's House. A new dormitory for the governor's bachelor guests was erected, linked to the main King's House complex by a bridge across the road, and a two-storey residence was built for Governor the Duke of Manchester (1808–27), at the corner of today's Manchester Street. Now the King's House was a working space and a comfortable home. Earlier governors had left the King's House to stay in rural houses or mountain retreats; this new building provided a suitable domestic refuge.

Insecurity: the American rebellion and the Battle of the Saintes

Insecurity from within and without plagued both Jamaica and Virginia in the latter half of the eighteenth century, as Britain struggled to contain rebels and to resist the challenge of imperial rivals. In Spanish Town, the new King's House was erected at the height of the Seven Years' War, and soon the American colonies were in rebellion, a situation which prompted France to join forces with the rebels and profit from the old enemy's incapacitation.

During the 1760s and 1770s the Virginia Assembly spent more and more time in Williamsburg's Capitol debating remonstrations to be submitted to the British king and Parliament. As tension between London and the American colonists mounted in 1768, George III sought to mollify Virginians by sending out Norborne Berkeley, Baron de Botetourt, as his governor. The burgesses passed a series of resolutions strongly protesting additional British taxes the year after, which caused Botetourt to adjourn the Virginia house. Banished from the Capitol building, the burgesses reconvened at the nearby Raleigh Tavern on Duke of Gloucester Street, and it was here, in the Apollo Room, that they drew up non-importation resolves, in association with other colonies, aimed at thwarting the duties. Virginia broke its allegiance to the Crown and many of Williamsburg's prominent figures became directly involved in signing the Declaration of Independence.

When news reached Williamsburg in 1774 that the British Parliament had closed Boston in retaliation for the Tea Party, the burgesses, already in session in the Capitol building, declared 1 June a day of fasting, humiliation, and prayer. The resolution was spearheaded by members including Thomas Jefferson, Richard Henry Lee, his brother Francis Lighthood Lee, and Patrick Henry. The day was also observed by George Washington. Governor John Murray, 4th Earl of Dunmore, objected to the resolution and prorogued the assembly. Most of the burgesses remained in Williamsburg and met at the Raleigh Tavern where eighty-nine of them formed an association to lobby against British imports and proposed a general congress of representatives from all the colonies to meet and discuss items of mutual interest, and voted for an association to interdict trade with Britain. The Raleigh Tavern meeting resolved to boycott East India tea and called on the other colonies to meet in general congress. Special delegates were elected to attend the first continental convention, and they voted for a complete non-importation of British goods and threatened moves towards non-exportation too. American history was in the making. Peyton Randolph, Richard Henry Lee, George Washington, Richard Bland, Patrick Henry, Benjamin Harrison, and Edmund Randolph were picked to represent the colony in the Continental Congress that duly convened in Philadelphia. Peyton Randolph was elected as its first president because of his experience as Speaker of the Virginia House of Burgesses during long sessions in Williamsburg's Capitol.[20]

In 1775 HMS *Fowey* anchored in the York River. Feeling threatened, the Virginia Convention moved to St John's Church in Richmond. Dunmore soon called the burgesses to assembly to consider a resolution from the

British Parliament offering to let the colonies raise their own revenue to support military and administrative needs. But men such as Jefferson wanted nothing to do with this compromise offer from London. When news reached Williamsburg of the battles of Lexington and Concord, the opening engagements of the War of American Independence, the *Virginia Gazette* wrote that 'The *Sword is now drawn*, and *God* knows when it will be sheathed.'[21] Governor Dunmore ordered sailors to remove barrels of gunpowder from the Williamsburg magazine, which brought the town's population onto the streets for a march on the Governor's Palace. There was stalemate in Williamsburg and Governor Murray refused to hand over the keys to the magazine. Soon militia from across Virginia's counties prepared to march on Williamsburg. Patrick Henry marched from Hanover County to Williamsburg with 150 men, demanding that Murray return the gunpowder or pay for it. On 8 June, Dunmore and his family removed themselves to the safety of HMS *Fowey*, effectively ending British rule in Virginia. Authority passed to the assembly, and then the Virginia Convention of Delegates.

In May 1776 the fifth Virginia Convention of Delegates, meeting in the Capitol at Williamsburg, drafted a resolution calling on the Continental Congress to declare the colonies free and independent states, ultimately leading to the Declaration of Independence in July. Patrick Henry was elected as the first governor of independent Virginia. Lord Dunmore's remaining possessions were auctioned off, and Henry moved into the Governor's Palace. While the British government decided that a show of force would put the colonists back in their place, the colonists stockpiled weapons and Williamsburg became an armed camp. Royal government had collapsed.

In 1779 Henry was succeeded as governor by Thomas Jefferson and the question of moving the capital to a safer and more central location was raised. After this had been achieved and the seat of government moved to Richmond, the Capitol building, like many public buildings in Williamsburg, experienced considerable change of use, as the town entered a long period of decline. When the British invaded Virginia in 1781, Williamsburg became the headquarters of the combined American and French forces. The Governor's Palace was used as a hospital for American soldiers, the College of William and Mary performing the same role for the French. By the second half of 1781 Cornwallis was camped near Williamsburg with an army of 7,000 men. When he moved to Yorktown, his opponent Lafayette moved to

Williamsburg with his army. Washington came through Williamsburg after he had defeated Cornwallis at Yorktown in 1781.

While these events were taking place on land, the French were busy hampering British activities by attacking shipping and taking colonies in the wider Caribbean region. Only Antigua, Barbados, and Jamaica remained in British hands, and Admiral de Grasse joined forces with the Spanish with the intention of taking Jamaica. Admiral George Rodney's fleet was the only thing capable of preventing him from doing so, and colonists in Jamaica prepared to defend their island should the enemy land. When the two fleets met in 1782, Rodney broke the enemy's line and scored a decisive victory off a group of islets between Dominica and Guadeloupe known as the Saintes. This victory saved Jamaica from capture and helped restore British prestige, which had been badly knocked by the success of the American rebellion. It was also vital to retain Jamaica for the sake of Britain's financial credit, crucial to its capacity to wage war. It also enabled Britain to secure more favourable terms under the Treaty of Versailles which ended the American Revolutionary War.

King's Square was the scene of unbridled celebration when news of the battle reached Jamaica. Soon Rodney himself arrived, his warships leading the captured French vessels into port, including the 100-gun flagship *Ville de Paris*. Rodney was accompanied by Admiral de Grasse, now his prisoner. The celebrations went on for weeks, and soon the Jamaica assembly decided that a lasting memorial was called for. It voted £1,000 for a marble statue of Rodney—though the final costs of the temple to contain it, and of the land for the public offices either side, was almost £31,000. Indicating the growing challenge posed by the rise of Kingston, Spanish Town nearly lost out on the statue: when news that it was on its way from England reached Jamaica, the people of Kingston and Port Royal petitioned the assembly so that it might be placed in Kingston Parade. The assembly divided equally at the vote, Spanish Town winning the decision only by virtue of the Speaker's casting vote.

To make way for the new monument a range of buildings on the north side of King's Square was demolished. Dating from the 1680s and 1770s, they included a chapel, guardhouse, tavern, and printing office. The Rodney Memorial, standing at right angles to the King's House, took the form of an octagonal dome and cupola over a highly romanticized statue of the hero by the sculptor John Bacon. This shrine to British naval prowess is linked to the adjacent buildings by an Ionic colonnade and a parapet at first-floor level. Dressed as a Roman emperor, the statue of Rodney illustrates the way in which the classically educated British thought of themselves as rulers. Heraldic symbols on the pediment told the story of the battle, and two finely decorated, hand-finished cannon, stripped from the French flagship, were positioned either side of the statue. (The flagship *Ville de Paris* and *Le Glorieux* were sunk in an Atlantic storm when Rodney was returning to England, with the loss of 1,200 lives.)[22] Soon the new Court House rose opposite the Rodney Memorial and its colonnaded approaches, completing the King's Square. As Walter Roberts wrote in 1959, when the Jamaica assembly first voted funds for a King's House and Assembly Building in Spanish Town, 'it cannot be said that anyone foresaw the beautiful harmony that would finally emerge. The Rodney Memorial to the north was not erected until thirty years later, and the Court House not until the nineteenth century.'[23]

Spanish Town and its central square were hubs of activity associated with some famous and infamous events and characters. For so long at the heart of British affairs in the Caribbean, all of Jamaica's distinguished visitors, including famous sailors such as Bligh, Nelson, and Rodney, were entertained at the King's House. Simón Bolívar, hero of Venezuelan independence, was a guest of the Duke of Manchester there in 1815. New governors were feted in style upon their arrival, and then required to repay the colonial gentry by holding 'open house' during the sitting of the assembly, a practice that pirate-turned-governor Henry Morgan claimed cost him $1,000. In 1720 the pirate 'Calico' Jack Rackham was tried and convicted by the Court of Vice-Admiralty in Spanish Town after being apprehended at a rum punch party while at anchor in Negril Bay. In 1739, the treaty that recognized the Maroons as the first autonomous people of African heritage in the New World was passed. In 1773 Lewis Hutchinson, the 'Mad Master of Edinburgh Castle', who tortured and killed visitors and disposed of their bodies down a sinkhole, was hanged in the square after killing up to fifty people. In 1780, a group of armed Maroons marched to Spanish Town holding aloft the mutilated head of the bandit 'Three-Fingered Jack' Mansong, which had been preserved in a bucket of rum, to claim a £300 reward. (His legendary story even made it to the London stage.)[24] In 1791 the body of the Countess of Effingham lay in state in the Great Hall of the King's House prior to her interment in the cathedral, to be followed to the grave by her husband three weeks later. In the nineteenth century, Paul Bogle marched through the bush to meet Governor Eyre in order to explain the plight of the peasants who would go on to riot in the Morant Bay rebellion of 1865. Bogle and his fellow petitioners waited on the King's House steps, but Governor Eyre refused to meet them.

King's Square and the King's House are strongly associated with the end of slavery in Jamaica and, to mark this fact, King's Square was recently renamed Emancipation Square. The full emancipation of Jamaica's slaves came in 1838 at the end of a long period of disturbance to the colony's social fabric, first brought on by an influx of American Loyalist evangelical preachers, keen to empower slaves and free blacks through conversion to the Baptist and Methodist faiths.[25] By December 1831 the situation had become tense, many slaves believing that William IV had already granted emancipation. Slaves rose against their masters, leading to an extensive military campaign, and there was widespread mob violence as pro-slavery elements took on pro-abolitionists. King's Square buzzed with activity as civilians and military officers haunted the House of Assembly and the King's House, and look-outs were posted on the roof.

During the Slave Revolt of 1831–2 arson attacks were directed at both plantations and slave villages, and pilfering and murder were common. Mobs of whites attacked missionary chapels across the island. But mob violence had the reverse effect to that intended by the pro-slavery colonists: it hardened opposition to them and to the institution of slavery in Britain, where reports of the emergency in Jamaica were closely monitored, and the brutality of the plantocracy widely condemned. Parliament passed the Abolition of Slavery Act in 1833, authorizing Treasury payments to slave owners in compensation. It was a convoluted process, especially for the slaves who wanted nothing other than their freedom. On 1 August 1834 the governor read William IV's proclamation ending slavery. Thousands of Jamaicans attended divine service, and many walked up hills or climbed trees in order to witness the literal dawning of their freedom. It was only a partial manumission, however, immediately freeing those under six years of age but leaving older slaves as 'apprentices', obliged to work for their former owners for a specified number of years. It was to be another four years, and following much abuse of the new apprentice system, before proper freedom was granted.

On the day of Queen Victoria's coronation in 1838, the Jamaica assembly voted to release the slaves. Soon afterwards, Governor Sir Lionel Smith read Victoria's proclamation from the steps of the King's House opposite the House of Assembly, declaring the emancipation of all slaves. The royal standard flew as the governor, accompanied by the Anglican bishop and the

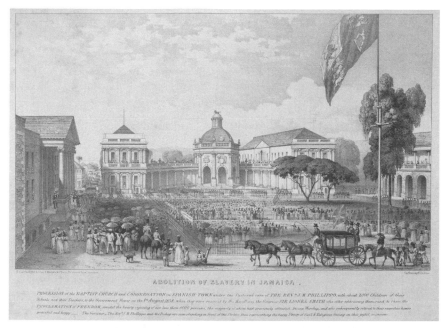

Figure 9. Lithograph depicting the Abolition of Slavery in Jamaica, published by R. Cartwright, London, 1838, by Thomas Picken (fl.1838–70). In this view of King's Square, King's House appears on the left, opposite the Assembly Building, with the Rodney Memorial and its attendant buildings in the centre.

Reverend James Phillippo, addressed the throng. Over 7,000 Spanish Town residents and 2,000 schoolchildren had assembled at the Baptist church and then walked in procession to King's Square, carrying flags and banners bearing mottos such as 'Freedom's bright light hath dawned at last'; 'Victoria'; 'The slave is free'; and 'England, land of liberty, of light, of life'. The official ceremony closed with three cheers for Victoria and three for the governor.[26] The day has been celebrated in Jamaica ever since. It is a national holiday, and the reading of the proclamation is enacted across Jamaica through parish vigils, particularly in the square in King's Square.

The two towns decline: the loss of capital status

Proposals to move Jamaica's capital from Spanish Town to Kingston were voiced from as early as the 1750s, while Williamsburg's strategic vulnerability saw it lose out to Richmond in 1780. The removal of Virginia's capital to

Richmond transformed Williamsburg's historical trajectory. The town became a backwater, buildings decayed, and commerce followed the seat of power to Richmond. Williamsburg's population declined, and fire destroyed important buildings such as the Wren Building at the College of William and Mary as well as the Capitol. The eastern half was demolished in 1794 and its materials sold to meet the maintenance expenses of what remained; the western portion burned down in 1832, followed by demolition. In 1816 George Tucker in his *Letters from Virginia* described the streets as 'paved with grass... This poor town has very little to recommend it to a stranger except the memory of its ancient importance, and this is but a sad sort of interest at best.'[27] Touring Williamsburg in 1835, Sir Augustus Murray, grandson of the last royal governor, Lord Dunmore, wrote that:

> The centre of the palace where the governor resided has long since fallen down, and even the traces of its ruins are no more to be seen. Two small wings, which formed part of the range of offices, are still standing... It may be imagined with what mingled and undefinable feeling I viewed this spot, as a stranger and a foreigner, where my grandfather had lived, surrounded by the pomp and pageantry of vice-royalty—then all was bustle, and gaiety, and life within those halls... the ancient capital, on the site of which I was now standing, has dwindled in half a century, into a paltry village, without even a venerable ruin to rescue its decay from insignificance![28]

In 1861 the *Southern Literary Messenger* wrote that:

> This old town, now a quiet and sleepy village, with only the life and animation imparted by a college and its inmates, was once the scene of Virginia's greatest social refinement, hospitality, statesmanship, and literature. Its history is so full of great incidents, that one is surprised to contrast the bright narrative with the dull and dozing appearance of the present town.[29]

Spanish Town also endured a decline, though it was a lengthier one. Mid-Victorian visitors were unimpressed by the town: it was increasingly dilapidated and compared less and less favourably with the buildings of modern Britain. Measured against the burgeoning centres of trade and industry in the mother country, Spanish Town's one- and two-storey wooden buildings, with their yellow plaster and green-painted woodwork, appeared unprepossessing. Reflecting a sense of inadequacy amongst the town's elite, Spanish Town may well have been unique in being the only colonial capital not to have a street named after Queen Victoria, because it was thought that it had no thoroughfare of sufficient scale to warrant the honour. In addition to this, as the Spanish Town historian James Robertson points out, when the

Victorians began to sneer at their forebears neo-classical Georgian buildings, they devalued the architectural legacy of the late eighteenth-century sugar boom.

Governor Knowles had attempted to transfer the capital from Spanish Town to Kingston in 1755, which was a very unpopular move. The town's Achilles heel as a capital was its poor communications links. Moving the capital was favoured by the Kingston merchants and people of the eastern parishes, but strongly resisted by the residents of Spanish Town and the western parishes. Nevertheless, Knowles succeeded in passing an act for the removal. Various public offices and the Jamaica archives were moved to Kingston and it was three years before petitions to England caused the act's disallowance. The archives were duly returned, loaded onto thirty wagons, and carried back to Spanish Town under a strong armed guard. The return of the archives caused great rejoicing. Illuminations, firework displays, and other entertainments marked the event, including the burning of an effigy of Governor Knowles.[30]

Despite competition from Kingston, easy access for planter-assemblymen from other parts of the island and a less deadly disease environment kept the administrative capital in Spanish Town. Its status was bolstered by the flurry of public buildings in the second half of the eighteenth century, as the English colonists stamped their classical style on a place that had, up to that point, still looked remarkably Spanish. But the 1838 down-turn in the world sugar market and the gradual removal of administrative functions to Kingston signalled Spanish Town's demise. Despite a new railroad and a brief flourish as a centre of banana production and tourism, the town's fortunes never looked like recovering. With fading sugar profits, the planters who had supported Spanish Town's economy through their political activities and leisure pursuits fell from power, taking the town with them.[31]

Spanish Town had its critics. Matthew Gregory Lews wrote that the King's House was 'a large clumsy looking brick building with a portico, the stucco of which has suffered by the weather, and it can advance no pretensions to architectural beauty'.[32] Anthony Trollope, meanwhile, wrote that the town was 'stricken with an eternal death. All the walls are of a dismal dirty yellow... In this Square there are no sounds; men and women never frequent it: nothing enters it but sunbeams.' Predictably, the whinging Trollope didn't much like the sunbeams either.[33] Visiting the King's House to meet the governor, Trollope—at the time a Post Office official—left the King's House and marched around the town rather than wait for a cab back to the railway station. He got lost, could not find a place to have a drink, paid a large tip to be shown round the corner to the Wellington Arms, and quite literally became hot and bothered. This flying visit in 1859, which stimulated a dreary short story, led him to write that 'on the whole face of the inhabited globe there is perhaps no spot more dull to look at, more Lethean in aspect, more corpse-like or more cadaverous than Spanish Town. It is the head-quarters of the government, the seat of the legislature, the residence of the Governor—but nevertheless it is, as it were, a city of the very dead.'*[34] He recommended the removal of the capital to Kingston, though the Jamaica assembly had no intention of paying for the reconstruction of a new judicial, legislative, and administrative set-up when perfectly serviceable facilities already existed in King's Square.

In the 1860s, in the midst of an economic crisis, a major refurbishment of the King's House was licensed as a relief programme, though Governor Eyre had some work done cheaply at the General Penitentiary's workshops in Kingston and used the rest of the assembly's grant to order new furniture from England. All of this largely futile expense occurred as many Spanish Town residents slipped into abject poverty.[35] When Sir John Grant arrived to take over as governor in 1866, bursting with reforms for the island in the wake of the Morant Bay rebellion, he only lived in the King's House for three weeks before moving to his new estate in the Port Royal Mountains, with its 'incredibly delicious' climate.[36] Compared to the King's House, the house on the Craighton estate was like a cottage, but homely and set in lovely gardens enjoying magnificent views over Kingston harbour—which Governor Grant viewed as he contemplated the transfer of the administration from unloved Spanish Town.

The town's loss of political supremacy in 1872, when Jamaica became a Crown colony with Kingston as its capital, sealed its fate. Spanish Town slumped. The property market crashed, townspeople fell out of work, and petitions were studiously ignored. Grant was keen to ensure that the splendid buildings of King's Square did not fall into disuse, and hoped that Spanish Town would find a new role as the island's intellectual capital. As part of this project, King's House became a university with the opening of Queen's College Jamaica in September 1873.[37] But despite the arrival of 200 caps and gowns from England, a dearth of students killed off the enterprise within the year.

---

* *Miss Sarah Jack of Spanish Town, Jamaica,* published in 1861.

After its abandonment as the home of Jamaica's governors and its failure as a university, King's House found several uses. Its servants' quarters, for instance, were used until 1924 as the Cathedral High School for girls. But then came a fire that destroyed the King's House in October 1925. Its shingle roof and timbers burnt fiercely and the conflagration could be seen for miles around. The only building in the compound to survive, the old stables, were full of rum barrels, which the local people tried to persuade the government to move. As it was, only the relatively windless conditions and the attentions of the fire brigade prevented the King's House fire from causing wider damage. Afterwards, the St Catherine Parish Council proposed the erection of a hospital on the site, though this was rejected and the charred walls continued to dominate the square. In 1926 the authorities considered pulling the walls down for safety's sake, although a subsequent earthquake failed to move them. The Society for the Protection of Ancient Buildings adopted a resolution in 1929 expressing astonishment that no steps had been taken to repair the fire damage. In the same year Sir Martin Conway, addressing the House of Commons, said that the King's House was 'regarded by professional opinion as the finest example of Georgian architecture in the Western Hemisphere'.[38]

Hubert Corlette was commissioned in the 1930s to report on the King's House. The Jamaica assembly was considering 'proposals to preserve what remains of what was a very fine National Monument, and to reconstruct, as far as possible, the parts destroyed'.[39] 'Let me make it quite plainly clear', he said:

> That the central, built, visible, monument of all your past, and the foundations on which your future history may be, and should be, constructed, is not in one neglected, half-destroyed, building in Spanish Town. It is to be seen, felt and known in the whole complete group of buildings that surround what is now, and I hope will always remain, The King's Square. It is a great historic monument as a whole. It is a venerable pile of fine buildings suffering from neglect and from decay. It is a valuable record of English architectural traditions. And as such it is a piece of fine art worthy of admiration by all. But it needs repair, and, by some means, it should be preserved for your posterity.[40]

Corlette's exhortations went unheeded. In 1959, a new campaign was launched to restore the King's House. Introducing the scheme, Governor Sir Kenneth Blackburne said that:

> No one who passes through the main square of Spanish Town can fail to be struck with its beauty; it has rightly been described as the most striking

Figure 10. Contemporary view of King's House.

collection of 18th century buildings in the New World. But no one who looks closely at the façade of the old King's House—and still less penetrates to the desolate scene of ruin and decay behind the façade—can fail to be struck by a feeling of fear that this historic site will soon be lost to future generations unless urgent steps are taken for its preservation.[41]

Revival: Goodwin, Rockefeller, and the birth of 'Colonial' Williamsburg

In 1926 Williamsburg was a typical small southern town—generally impoverished and proud of its heritage. Yet its historic buildings were not well cared for, and many had been demolished. Early twentieth-century expansion and the growth of nearby Penniman as part of the First World War munitions industry had led to the intrusion of hastily erected buildings lacking architectural character, which jostled their genteel old neighbours on every side. Ugly galvanized structures replaced colonial-era dwellings;

thirty buildings, ranging from a bank to a pigsty, crowded together on the colonial era Market Square, obscuring the magazine that originally had dominated the once elegant open space.[42] Unsightly power cables appeared in the town's streets. A Williamsburg resident lamented the changes that had taken place, writing that:

> Where once the garden bloomed and the beauty of the Palace Park invited their excellencies to take the air, a knitting mill has been erected and number-less, small houses are going up as homes for the workmen employed therein. The locomotives of the Newport News and Mississippi Valley railroad already go shrieking through the sacred precincts.[43]

But Williamsburg was to be spectacularly revived through the endeavours of two men, the Reverend Dr W. A. R. Goodwin and the philanthropist John D. Rockefeller, Jr. Goodwin had first experienced Williamsburg as rector of Bruton Parish Church (1903–7). When he returned to the town in 1923 as head of the Department of Biblical Literature and Religious Education and director of an endowment campaign at the College of William and Mary, he was shocked by the extent to which twentieth-century buildings had encroached on the memorials of the town's past. Williamsburg's, and with it America's, history was disappearing. He set about trying to persuade Rockefeller to sponsor his vision to revive the town.

In the 1920s a new breed of preservation campaigners began to articulate a growing interest in America's colonial heritage and the protection of its historical sites.[44] In 1897 the Association for the Preservation of Virginian Antiquities (founded in 1889) had acquired the site of the Capitol building and marked out the outline of its colonial-era foundations. Goodwin crusaded to preserve and reconstruct Williamsburg, believing that the public buildings could become memorials to the foundation of the federation that created the United States of America, a unique window onto the national past. His pitch to Rockefeller was that Williamsburg was the one colonial city left that had not been obliterated or swallowed up by urban growth.

This vision appealed to Rockefeller and the two men agreed to meet in Williamsburg so that Goodwin could explain his ideas first hand. After wandering around the town, Rockefeller declared that this was an irresistible opportunity, not to restore the town piecemeal, but to reconstruct it in its entirety, giving Goodwin far more than he had bargained for: a blueprint for the transformation and preservation of the entire town, not just a selection of its historic buildings. As he wrote, it 'offered an opportunity to restore a complete area entirely free from alien or inharmonious surroundings as well as to preserve the beauty and charm of the old buildings and gardens of the city and its historic significance'.[45] The aim was to return every structure in the city to its original eighteenth-century appearance.

In 1926, restoration and reconstruction of the major elements of the historic city commenced using information obtained from old documents, records, plans, drawings, and inventories. In the 1930s 120 of Williamsburg's eighteenth-century buildings were either restored or entirely rebuilt as part of the Rockefeller project. What became known as 'Colonial Williamsburg' offers an intriguing insight into America's vision of its own past, for it reveals as much about the use of history through restoration and re-enactment as it does about the past itself.

As for the Capitol building, it was decided to reconstruct the original 1705 Capitol building rather than the later replacements. This was because the original was more thoroughly documented and considered of greater architectural distinction than its two successors. It was to be built on its

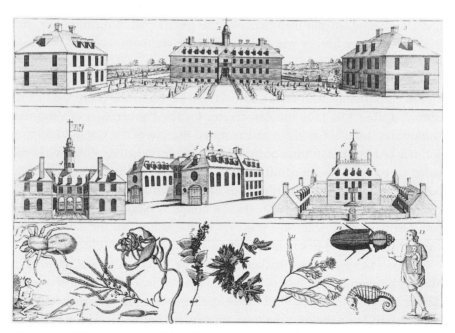

Figure 11. The famous Bodleian Plate, invaluable in the reconstruction of Williamsburg's key buildings, including the Capitol. Modern impression taken from the original 1740s copperplate now in the collection of the Colonial Williamsburg Foundation (Bodleian Plate re-strike).

original foundations and furnished according to surviving architectural information, about which there was a wealth of data available to the architect's research teams. A crucial document in the reconstruction of the Capitol was the Bodleian Copperplate, the only known eighteenth-century architectural drawing of Williamsburg's main buildings. Discovered in 1929 at the University of Oxford's Bodleian Library and dating from about 1740, it was presented to Rockefeller by the Curator of the Bodleian. Rockefeller called it the 'foundation upon which we have based the restoration of the Wren Building and the reconstruction of the Governor's Palace and the Capitol. Without it, we would have been acting in the dark; with it, we have gone forward with absolute certainty and conviction.'[46] In 1934 President Franklin Roosevelt visited Williamsburg to mark the completion of the first phase of restoration. Sixty-one buildings had been restored, and ninety-four rebuilt. In his own words, he had come 'to see how thorough the renaissance of these physical landmarks, the atmosphere of the whole glorious chapter in our history, has been recaptured'.

Heritage today

'You are ready to visit the eighteenth century', the official guidebook to Colonial Williamsburg declares, inviting tourists into a world of 'authentic' dress in which the life stories of 'residents' are played by a small army of re-enactors. Visitors are 'taken back in time' through the use of colonial currency to buy goods in the town's shops and taverns, the sight of militiamen drilling on Market Square, and a fife and drum corps marching down Duke of Gloucester Street. In this colonial era museum-cum-theme park, tourists are actively encouraged to get involved, to 'take part' in the history of America through the activities offered in reconstructed Williamsburg:

> Debate the Stamp Act with Thomas Jefferson, Patrick Henry, or George Washington. See prominent colonial citizens wearing the fashions of the eighteenth century. Encounter the African-American slaves and free blacks who made the Virginia colony's prosperity possible ... Smell the aromas of foods cooked on a hearth in an eighteenth century kitchen ... Experience what it was like to live in the capital of Virginia on the eve of the American Revolution. A visit to Colonial Williamsburg is a journey into America's past.[47]

The 'preservation' of this colonial town-museum, Tindall writes, is almost wholly artificial:

Its present-day appearance is a sign not of a genuine persistence of the past, but of the wealth of present-day America and of the important role of tourism in the economic scheme of things. 'Time has passed by old Williamsburg', in the language of the tourist brochure, but what in fact time had done to it by the early part of the twentieth century was to turn it into a decayed backwater almost indistinguishable from many others...It is money and special interest and a considerable reconstruction that have turned the town back into a simulacrum of itself in 1765, when the Stamp Act was denounced there in the Capitol building at one end of Gloucester Street, thus lighting the fuse that exploded into war.[48]

Goodwin was to be feted as a 'preservation hero as well as prophet', the 'first person in America to conceive of the restoration of an entire city and thus influence the course of American preservation'.[49] In an interesting twist, the Capitol building that was erected by the mass preservation and reconstruction effort of the 1930s turned out to be different from the original in several key respects because the architects simply could not get into the minds of their architectural forebears, to the extent that they ignored compelling evidence. The reconstruction was executed by architects from the Boston firm of Perry, Shaw, and Hepburn. Their assumptions about the placement of the great west door ignored the archaeological evidence, and had profound consequences for the overall plan and reconstruction.[50] Their stubborn rejection of the evidence was based upon their deeply rooted aesthetic preference for compositional balance and axial symmetry. The fact was that the archaeological evidence challenged their preconceived notions of colonial design. The architectural training of the day meant that they misread the intentions and realities of the colonial architecture, and tended to embellish or improve beyond what the historical evidence warranted. They were unable to conceive that a major public building would be erected with an asymmetrical façade, which is just what the architects of the 1701 building had done with the Capitol. As Carl Lounsbury's work has shown, in that earlier period architectural quirks abounded: regularity was illusory, though this was ignored by the restoration architects, who missed the spirit of the colonial building process.[51] The reconstructed Capitol, therefore, stands as a monument to the near past and tells us as much about the influence of Beaux-Arts design principles of the 1920s and 1930s as about the architecture of the colonial period.

All of this matters in that it leads to a very confused historical record and historical 'experience'. The confusion, and the suspension of belief or pure

make-believe inherent in much of the American heritage past, was epitomized by Rockefeller himself, who dedicated the Capitol building upon its
reconstruction. More than any other building, the Capitol symbolized the
patriotic ideals that had motivated him to underwrite the massive reconstruction of Williamsburg. After it had been completed in 1934, it was
tempting, he wrote, to sit in the Capitol in silence, 'and let the past speak to
us of those great patriots', to whose memory he dedicated the reconstruction. Yet the building in which he sat was not one in which any one of those
men would have set foot. Indeed, it was a copy of one that had been
destroyed by fire in 1747—not of the one in which the momentous events
of the 1770s, about which Rockefeller pondered in silence, had taken place.

Today, Spanish Town remains a treasure, though a tarnished one. The
faded grandeur of its neoclassical government buildings is the only reminder
of the town's former status. On the eastern side of the square, the old House
of Assembly now houses the offices of the St Catherine Parish Council,
part of the county of Middlesex. On the south side of the square stands the
burnt remains of the former Law Courts, built in 1819, destroyed in 1986.
Next to it is the St Catherine District Prison. Behind the Rodney Memorial
are the Archives Office and Records Office. The colonnaded portico and
façade are all that remain of the King's House, once a state-of-the-art residence and proconsular entertainment centre surrounded by all the buildings
necessary for the maintenance of a royally appointed governor and his
household. A Folk Museum, part of the 1959 restoration project, exists in
the former stables, but the hoped-for restored national monument and
museum have so far failed to materialize.

3
Fort St Angelo, Malta

The squat medieval ramparts of Fort St Angelo jut out into Malta's Grand Harbour opposite the Renaissance city of Valletta. Its history embodies key aspects of the British imperial experience, chief among them the importance of military and naval force in gaining colonies and sustaining Britain as a global power. Occupied by the British as a naval headquarters until 1979 (fifteen years after Malta gained independence), Fort St Angelo performed a central role during the most dramatic events in Malta's history—the Great Siege of 1565 and the 'second siege' of 1942. It became a potent symbol of Maltese national identity, appearing on stamps and souvenirs and forming the backdrop for events such as the independence ceremonies of 1964 and 1979 and the celebrations marking Malta's accession to the European Union in 2004. The story of Fort St Angelo—Her Majesty's Ship *St Angelo* to the British—illustrates the extent to which the Royal Navy was bound up with the social, cultural, and economic history of numerous overseas ports, and how colonial status could have grave repercussions for colonial subjects, especially during times of war.

Occupying a commanding position at the centre of Grand Harbour, Fort St Angelo stands at the tip of the promontory of Città Vittoriosa ('Victorious City'), the name given to the city of Birgu to mark its heroic role during the Great Siege. Fort St Angelo was part of a system of fortifications defending Grand Harbour, which it did with its four tiers of gun batteries designed to counter broadsides fired from ships of the line. Dating from at least the twelfth century, it was developed by the Knights Hospitallers of the Order of St John of Jerusalem (founded 1085), and later by the British. The Knights of St John, drawn from across Europe, was a Christian military order dedicated to defending the Holy Land and caring for pilgrims. After the Muslim capture of Jerusalem, the Order moved to Rhodes. Ejected from Rhodes by Suleiman the Magnificent in 1522, Charles V of Spain gave Malta and Gozo

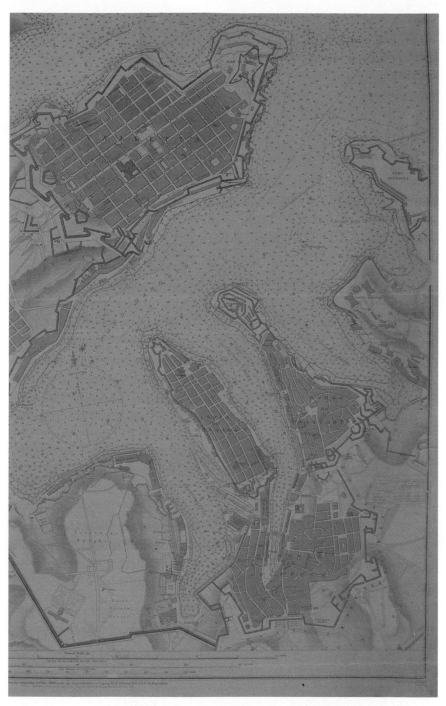

Figure 12. A map of 'Valletta Harbours' dating from *c.*1888 and based upon Royal Navy surveys. It shows to good effect the relative positions of Valletta and the 'three cities' across the main water of Grand Harbour. Valletta is at the top, showing Fort St Elmo at the tip of the peninsula. Fort Ricasoli is visible opposite right, the buildings of the Royal Naval Hospital on the shorter promontory next to it, and then the peninsulas of Vittoriosa, with Fort St Angelo at the tip, and Senglea to its left.

to the knights on the condition that they wage incessant war against pirates and infidels.

To orient oneself in Grand Harbour and understand the role of Fort St Angelo, the numerous strongholds surrounding this large body of water need to be considered. At the tip of the peninsula of Mount Sceberras stands Fort St Elmo, the major fort on the right hand side of Grand Harbour as one approaches from the sea. Behind it lie the elegant streets and squares of Valletta, itself designed as a fortified city boasting massive rampart defences.*
On the left-hand side as one entered Grand Harbour was Fort Ricasoli. Along with St Elmo, Ricasoli guarded the harbour's mouth. But the defensive scheme also depended on extensive fortifications *inside* the harbour: those on the peninsulas of Senglea (Fort St Michael) and Città Vittoriosa (Fort St Angelo) on the left side, and the Lascaris battery opposite St Angelo on the Valletta side. The harbour defences were completed by fortified walls to the south. Whoever held the inner harbour forts, particularly St Angelo, could control Grand Harbour.

In 1930 David Niven, then a subaltern in the Highland Light Infantry, arrived in Malta to join his battalion, then serving as part of the colony's garrison. Like countless other visitors he sought to capture Grand Harbour and its appearance, framed by Valletta on the one side, and the 'Three Cities'—Vittoriosa, Cospicua, and Senglea—on the other:

> The ship was filled mostly with Service families heading for Egypt, India, and the Far East... The *Kaisar-i-Hind* dropped anchor in the deep blue Grand Harbour of Valetta just as the sun was setting and it was an unforgettable sight, tier upon tier of honey-coloured houses rising on one side and Fort Ricasoli, built in 1400 by the Knights of Malta, brooding benevolently on the other. In between lay the leviathans of the greatest navy in the world. 'Retreat' was being sounded by the massed bands of the Royal Marines on the Flight Deck of the giant carrier *Eagle*, while astern of her lay three more—*Furious*, *Argus*, and *Ark Royal*. Ahead there was a line of huge battleships and beyond them again, the tall rather old-fashioned looking County class cruisers... the light cruiser squadrons, the destroyer and submarine flotillas... Pinnaces, Admirals' barges and shore boats slashed the blue water with white... As the final plaintive note of the 'Retreat' floated out from *Eagle*, the sinking sun kissed the topmost houses and churches of Valetta with gold and all over the Grand

---

* The city was named after Jean Parisot de la Valette, Grand Master of the Knights of St John (1557–68). La Vallette died on 22 August 1568 and was buried in the Chapel of St Anne in Fort St Angelo, later reinterred in the Church della Vittoria, which he himself had built, in Valletta.

Harbour as signal lights winked from a hundred mastheads, the White Ensign
and Union Jacks of the Royal Navy were lowered.[1]

Niven's description captures the essence of what at the time was the headquarters of Britain's Mediterranean Fleet, one of the most important naval
bases in the world, crammed with warships and framed spectacularly by the
honey-coloured splendour of the surrounding cities. Across the centuries
travellers have sought to capture Grand Harbour's unique appearance. In
1972 Nigel Dennis wrote that 'Approached from the sea...the sight is one
of the most astonishing in the world...It rises out of the Mediterranean
like some wonder from the sea in Classical legend.'[2] In 1840, George Angas
wrote of 'the vivid novelty of some city seen in dreams'.[3] These reactions to
the four cities chiselled out of the rock surrounding Grand Harbour apply
today just as they have done for the past five centuries.

Malta, described by Napoleon as 'the hinge of Europe', has the highest
concentrations of military works anywhere in the world. This is because it
was coveted for its strategic location and the fact that it possessed two of the
world's finest anchorages (Grand Harbour and Marsamxett). Whoever possessed these harbours could decide who passed from one end of the Mediterranean to the other. Malta's geographical location placed it athwart the
lines of communication of three mighty empires. Mightiest of them all, it
became a vital link in the British Empire's communication and defensive
network.[4] From Phoenician remains to knightly vedettes and British radio
masts and machine-gun posts, successive occupiers contributed to Malta's
military architecture across the centuries.

Early beginnings: Fort St Angelo,
the castle by the sea

It is thought that a temple to the goddess Astarte, known throughout the
Mediterranean world and identified with the evening star, stood on the site
of Fort St Angelo until about AD 878, when it is believed that the first
fortification—an Arab fort—appeared on the promontory. Phoenicians,
Romans, Byzantines, Normans, Arabs, Ottomans, Angevins, Aragonese, Cas-
tillians, Turks, French, and British—all fought for or fought from this strategic redoubt at one time or another. When in 1283 an Aragonese armada
destroyed an Angevin fleet in Grand Harbour, the defenders retreated to the

safety of Fort St Angelo, then known as Castrum Maris, the 'castle by the sea'. The heights where St Angelo now sits, at the end of the promontory of Vittoriosa, were built up by these successive waves of invaders. In 1090 the Norman count of Sicily ejected the Arabs, and in the sixteenth century it came under the control of Emperor Charles I of Spain (who, in turn, offered it to the Knights of St John).

Within Fort St Angelo's sturdy walls stood a range of buildings, for accommodation, defence, surveillance, storage, and worship. On its upper-most level was the Magistral Palace, sometime home to the Castellan leader, later to the Grand Master of the Knights of St John, later still to the British officer commanding the fort. The British Army called it St Angelo House; the Royal Navy referred to it as the Captain's House as it was home to the captain of the 'ship' HMS *St Angelo*. There were two churches, the Church of St Anne, also on the upper level, and the tiny Church of the Nativity of the Virgin Mary a level below. Nearby, an oubliette was rediscovered by the British in 1913, an underground cell used to punish errant knights. Its graf-fiti of names and illustrations indicate that it was in use from at least 1532.

Overlooking the fort's high entrance gate is the massive bulk of the cava-lier tower, topped by the St Angelo Bell, a bronze bell between two pillars dating from 1716, one of the sentry bells which were sounded by the Knights on occasions of rejoicing or as a warning of approaching danger. Nearby is a cemetery where the Grand Masters of the Knights of St John, as well as many of the knights who perished in the city's defence, were buried. Dur-ing the Great Siege more than 10,000 people perished within four months. Those who died in the fort needed to be interred on site because there was no access to the exterior. There was also the need for mass burial when the Plague struck Malta in 1676.

Under the knights, Fort St Angelo and the Vittoriosa peninsula were at the heart of medieval Malta. Its adjacent creeks—Kalkara Creek on one side and what the British named Dockyard Creek on the other—offered shelter even in the roughest weather.[5] Upon their arrival the knights needed to secure their base and improve accommodation and the only protection of any consequence was the half-ruined Castle of St Angelo. Their first task was the reconstruction of the Chapel of St Anne. Most urgently, the knights also needed to improve Fort St Angelo's defences; its greatest drawback was that its battlements were dominated by the high ground of the peninsula opposite, on which, in 1566, the new city of Valletta was built. The piled-up character of Fort St Angelo, almost like a medieval castle, is entirely due to the need to match the height of the peninsula opposite, and it comprises a concentric sequence of three different levels of defence.[6] The palace of the Grand Master, which stands on the loftiest part of the fort, was enlarged and beautified with stuccoes, frescoes, and mosaics, and surrounded by gardens and courtyards, including a grotto, or 'Nymphaeum'.

On his arrival, the Grand Master of the Order of St John set up his residence in the fort and the Florentine engineer, Piccino, was employed to draw up proposals for improvements and repairs. He designed a massive square cavalier with two chamfered corners on the landward end of the fort. This formed a platform from which guns could fire onto the harbour entrance, supporting Fort St Elmo, and out across the land front of Vittoriosa. Below the cavalier a broad ditch was excavated, capable of holding galleys and turning the fort into an island. On the south front Piccino built the Homedes bastion.[7]

By now, the fort that is visible today had largely come into being. Fort St Angelo was soon surrounded with batteries, and Malta was considered the strongest place in Christendom.[8] The fort is entered by a drawbridge and gate, over which is a Latin inscription:

> Under the happy auspices of Grand Master Adrian Wignacourt and by the previous consent of the Grand Master Caraffa, Fort St Angelo, once a renowned temple of Juno but now a strong bulwark of Christendom, was restored by Charles Grunenberg, Knight of Devotion and Commander in the Army of the Catholic King; he contributed his talents and his money to restore to a better condition this fort, decayed by age, in the year of Salvation 1690, the first of the Magistery.[9]

From the main gate a steeply ascending ramp (ramps rather than steps are found throughout the fort to facilitate the passage of horses) leads to the first tier of batteries and continues to the Upper Fort, where there is a large parade ground, at the end of which stands the cavalier, a lofty and massive building, its summit forming a gun emplacement, its interior used as accommodation for soldiers. On this level, hewn from the living rock, is the tiny Chapel of the Nativity of Our Lady, built by Roger of Normandy in 1090 and the oldest Christian church in the island.[10] Another short ramp leads from the parade ground to the next battery level, and thence by a short flight of steps through a tunnel in the ramparts to the summit, where the Grand Master's Palace stands. Nearby is the charming Chapel of St Anne, set amidst spacious gardens and courtyards, the remains of the top tier guns still visible.

The Great Siege

In 1565 Fort St Angelo was at the centre of the island's resistance to Emperor Suleiman the Magnificent, who swore to sweep the knights out of Malta. The island was a thorn in the side of his campaign against a Christian European alliance fighting for mastery of the Mediterranean. His forces appeared in columns on the horizon, sails billowing as they advanced. Fort St Angelo braced itself. In 1534 the ditch of the Castle had been deepened, so that the promontory on which the fort stood became virtually an island, connected to Vittoriosa only by a narrow causeway on the Kalkara side and a small wooden bridge on the Dockyard Creek side. Now, with the Turks in sight, Grand Master de Valette ordered the drawbridge destroyed to discourage any thought of retreat.

As the headquarters of the Grand Master, the fort was manned by 50 knights and 500 soldiers. Nicolas Monsarratt describes events:

> As it was, St Elmo lost was the key to Maltese victory...the delay in taking it was fatal to the Turkish plan. Eight thousand of them had been killed, in exchange for 1,500 soldiers and 109 Knights...When he entered the ruins of St Elmo, Mustapha Pasha found 1,300 corpses of the defenders, and all the dead Knights. But as he mourned the monstrous total of his own dead, he could only say: 'If the daughter cost us so much, what will be the price of the mother?'
>
> The mother was St Angelo.[11]

On the evening of St Elmo's defeat, the Turks sent the headless bodies of four knights across the water to Fort St Angelo, the mark of the Cross gashed into their breasts, each corpse lashed to a crucifix. St Elmo then bristled with pikes, each one bearing the head of a knight, his armour mounted beneath to supply his name and rank. La Valette's answer, reportedly, was to kill all his Turkish prisoners and fire their heads back across the harbour from St Angelo.

The knights and soldiers inside St Angelo had two frontiers to guard, namely the ditch behind the fort, and the harbour defences. The harbour side remained impregnable, even though the Turks brought up some eighty galleys dragged on rollers nearly a mile overland by slaves and oxen. Maltese fishermen helped confound this ploy, though the Turks also tried tunnelling and mining, eventually making a breach in the fort's walls. As the siege unfolded, the fate of Malta was watched by the world. Elizabeth I said that

'If the Turks should prevail against the Isle of Malta, it is uncertain what further perils might follow to the rest of Christendom.' She ordered prayers for Malta to be read in all the churches in England, three times a week for six weeks.[12]

Though eventually defeated, the Great Siege emphasized the strategic position of Mount Sceberras. It was decided that it should be fortified and maintained as the main stronghold of the Order, and thus was born Valletta. From the date of the fortified city's completion in 1571, St Angelo's importance declined. It was used only as the state prison of the Order, though still had a military purpose in the event of another siege. Damaged by bombardment and partially repaired, so it remained for many years until, in the 1680s, Colonel Don Carlos de Grunenberg, in a scheme for the protection of Grand Harbour, proposed to build water-level batteries on the rocky ledge at the outer face of the fort. The shelving rock there was broad enough to take three long batteries, one above the other.[13]

The arrival of the British

During the course of the Revolutionary and Napoleonic Wars, Napoleon descended on Malta with hundreds of ships and thousands of troops, occupying Gozo and most of Malta en route to Egypt. This, in turn, brought British involvement. As Sir Mark Wood wrote to William Pitt in November 1796, 'were Providence to give us the power to place an impregnable fortress and harbour on any spot in the Mediterranean, most suitable to the views of our country, it would hardly be possible to select one preferable to Malta. It would give us complete command of the Levant; . . . the coasts of Spain, France, Italy, and Africa must be subject to our control.'[14]

Britain needed a good naval base in the Mediterranean. Gibraltar was taken, but something further east was necessary too. When Minorca was lost in 1756, the British approached the Knights of St John about the prospect of using Grand Harbour as a base. Bound to be neutral in the Seven Years' War, however, they could not accede, and the knights reinforced their harbour defences lest the British try to take the port by force. On several occasions the shore batteries had to open up on British ships attempting to capture French prizes in Maltese waters.[15] But the Napoleonic Wars presented the British with fresh opportunities, though not before the French had established themselves on the island. Soon after the French had taken

Malta, the garrison Napoleon left behind became so unpopular with the Maltese people that they had to barricade themselves into Valletta. A stalemate ensued, with the Maltese controlling the countryside, the French the harbour. The Maltese sought to enlist the help of the British, who blockaded the French garrison, increasing its discomfort. This situation pertained for two years, the French only forced to surrender when their food ran out.

As soon as the French capitulated the provisional government handed over to the British all the properties previously used by the Order's navy. The Royal Navy soon began transforming the built environment of Vittoriosa and the creeks either side. An ornamental gate was built into the Marina Grande—the Victualling Yard—in 1819 to allow parish processions to pass through. In 1842 the old arched Galley Arsenal, serving as a masthouse, was demolished to make way for the enormous new Naval Bakery next to Fort St Angelo (today the Maritime Museum) catering for the whole navy in harbour and at sea in the Mediterranean. This reflected the expanding demands being made of the Victualling Yard, which by 1817 had a storage capacity of six months' supply for 10,000 men as well as facilities for sail-making and rope-making. The army garrison protecting Malta rose from 2,000 in the 1820s to 10,000 by the 1900s. The number of Maltese workers employed in the naval dockyards rose and fell with the cycle of military activity in the region, booming in times of war, slumping thereafter. Nearly 14,000 were employed during the First World War, for example, a figure that had fallen back to 6,000 by 1921. Up to a third of the local population depended on the British military for their livelihoods. The jobs, for which Maltese people competed fiercely, could be dangerous: a store house for explosives on the waterfront exploded in 1806 killing 150, and during the Second World War the docks were pasted with enemy bombs.

Sir Ralph Abercromby, Commander-in-Chief of British forces in the Mediterranean (1800–1), wrote to the Secretary of State for War and the Colonies, offering the opinion that 'as a military station Malta may be pronounced the most complete in His Majesty's possessions'.[16] The Treaty of Paris (1814) recognized Malta as British, and the island became Britain's watchtower in the Mediterranean, its importance growing stronger when a new route to India opened through the Suez Canal. Now that the island was officially 'theirs', the British undertook a thorough survey of the defences inherited from the knights, noting the need for urgent repairs and renovations. During the course of the nineteenth century the British, like their predecessors, found that they needed the fort to cover the harbour entrance. An enemy ship that succeeded in penetrating Grand Harbour's outer defences would then have to face St Angelo's batteries: eleven guns at sea level, ten 8-inch guns on the second tier, seven along with six mortars on the third, and eight on the topmost tier.[17]

From the 1830s, fear of the reappearance of a French fleet and the impact of new technology, such as naval guns with grooved rifling firing explosive shells, made change essential if Malta was to be defended. A new battery was constructed in Grand Harbour in 1854, sited on the Valletta side and intended to provide support for the guns of Fort St Angelo across the harbour. The onus of protecting the harbour entrance fell on this, the new Lascaris battery, and Fort St Angelo opposite. Grand Harbour developed as a major fleet sustenance and maintenance base and a coaling station, and it was heavily used by British and French warships and transports during the Crimean War.

In addition to the warships of the Royal Navy, a sizeable garrison of British troops and artillerymen, soon supplemented by Maltese units, was required in order to ensure the island's security should an enemy manage to get ashore. As Stephenson writes, though not defenceless, the vast network of baroque bastions and ramparts inherited from the knights were rapidly being rendered obsolete by technological developments. Fortifications constructed out of masonry had become vulnerable to armoured ships firing the tapered explosive shells that had replaced the solid round shot which the maritime fortifications around the harbour area had been designed to withstand.[18]

Given this, the forts were modernized and more powerful guns installed, the British investing heavily in new fortifications across the island up until the First World War. New coastal forts were erected from 1870 to protect Malta in case the Mediterranean Fleet was called away, and later in the century the Victoria Lines were built across the entire island along a geological fault north of Mdina in case the island was invaded from the north. Screw-driven steam ships, heavily armour-plated and mounting more ferocious guns than ever before, were capable of getting closer in to the shore batteries. The older forts needed modernization: the first of Fort St Angelo's heavy guns, fourteen 68 pounders, arrived in 1841. Rapid technological developments and Great Power rivalries meant that Malta was essentially involved in an arms race. The Italian navy's purchase of 100-ton Armstrong guns in 1877, for example, compelled Britain to arm Gibraltar and Malta with equal calibre weapons. Loophole walls were built to seal off the flank of St Angelo's sea-level or the Fleur D'Eau battery. In the 1870s the British built a case-mated battery designed to house three 9-inch rifled muzzle-loading (RML) guns on No. 2 battery (the second tier) overlooking the mouth of the harbour. As late as 1884, Fort St Angelo still mounted fourteen 64- and 32-pounder RMLs and three 9-inch RMLs behind shields; it also mounted forty-three smooth bores, howitzers, mortars, and carronades, and six bronze mortars. Nineteenth-century photographs show these guns, their cannon balls neatly stacked in pyramids.

Structurally the fort was little altered from the days of the knights. The most significant additions were the new No. 2 battery, a number of magazines fitted to the parapets of the batteries, and the defensive wall pierced with musketry loopholes designed to seal off the seaward approaches to the sea-level battery. In 1878 there were six store magazines capable of holding 9,785 barrels. Magazines D, E, and F were situated inside the three casements of the cavalier, and were protected to the rear by a thick screening wall of soft stone ashlar 34 feet high. At this time the Chapel of St Anne, on the fort's uppermost level, was used as an artillery magazine. The walls of this venerable church were hung with hammers, poles, compasses, rammers, sponges, spiking irons, and other items associated with the use of cannon. Later, it returned to more dignified use. In 1880 it started functioning as a school and in 1935 was consecrated according to Church of England rites and began operating as the Chapel of HMS *St Angelo*. There were other minor adjustments to Fort St Angelo: the cavalier barrack room was converted by the British Army into a magazine, and later, when the Navy took over, it was turned into messes and dormitories.

At the end of the nineteenth century a significant shift in Fort St Angelo's role loomed on the horizon, as the usefulness of great fortifications in warfare declined. In 1888 it was recommended that the obsolete guns be removed. In the same year, generals Nicholson and Goodenough reported that 'it is scarcely possible to imagine works so unsuitable for the purpose of coast defence under modern conditions, and offering such advantages to the attack of ships as the castles of St Elmo and St Angelo. These are the most conspicuous examples, but the rest of the ancient fortifications are almost equally hopeless.'[19] Money spent on them would be wasted and so Fort St Angelo was 'stood down' as a fighting fortress and artillery platform. Thus began a new chapter in its history. The British Army departed the fort, and the Royal Navy moved in.

The Royal Navy takes over

Though the age of siege warfare was passing, the need to defend Malta as well as to project power from it meant that the military presence grew. The Mediterranean Fleet was one of the largest and most powerful naval formations in the world, and by the 1890s the garrison defending the naval base stood at 12,000. The island had become a fully fledged front-line naval base capable of sustaining a large fleet of warships of all classes in every way required. The dockyard, equipped with dry docks to enable ships to be taken entirely out of the water for maintenance and repair purposes, meant that even the largest warships could be repaired in Malta; the bakery, housed in the beautiful and elaborate building next to Fort St Angelo on the Vittoriosa peninsula, enabled Malta to feed tens of thousands of men on a daily basis, the naval hospitals, such as the magnificent Royal Navy Hospital at Bighi, across Kalkara Creek from Fort St Angelo, meant that casualties could be treated to the highest standards; Malta's extensive barrack infrastructure meant that thousands of men could be accommodated ashore; and the expensive breakwater (1903–9) meant that the harbour was as well protected from the elements and potential enemy attack as was possible. The breakwater featured 'state of the art precast construction techniques developed on Dover harbour', and its completion 'transformed Malta's chief port into one of the world's finest deep-sea harbours'. The breakwater increased the berths for warships in the creeks either side of Fort St Angelo and the Birgu promontory, meaning that twenty-five large warships could find safe moorings there all year round.[20] The irony of this was that everything came together just as peace broke out between Britain and its two main rivals in the region, France and Russia. But as the twentieth century unfolded, other enemies loomed.

By the beginning of the twentieth century the fort had been completely disarmed with the exception of five saluting guns fitted on the cavalier. Its main use now was as a naval barracks and administration and communications centre. In 1902 the wharf known as the Jetty was built in front of the fort's main gate in Dockyard Creek, to accommodate a battleship alongside. The hulks of HMS *Egmont* and *Cruiser* were berthed alongside and used as depot ships and accommodation for naval ratings, the officers quartered in the fort itself. Various sailing warships had been used, but in 1855 HMS *Hibernia*, a first-rate ship of 110 guns, was specially fitted out at Portsmouth as the 'Receiving and Guard Ship' for Malta. *Hibernia* continued in service in Grand Harbour until 1909, when she was broken up locally. Her successor was *Achilles*, a first-class armoured cruiser built in Chatham in 1863, and she in turn was specially fitted out for service in Malta. At first renamed *Hibernia*, she was rechristened *Egmont* in 1904 and she had three other ships as tenders, *Cruiser, Bulldog,* and *Firefly. Egmont* was towed back to England in 1912, and the fort took on her name as the naval depot and flagship of the admiral in command of Grand Harbour. The figureheads of the old *Hibernia* and *Cruiser* were placed ashore in the fort when the hulks were finally towed away. *Cruiser's* figurehead was installed on the north-west corner of the parade ground, *Hibernia* in the entrance of the fort inside the main gate. Both trophies were returned to Britain during the withdrawal in 1978.

A complex of new administrative buildings soon developed on the Jetty though all have now gone. In 1902 the fort also became the depot ship for the Mediterranean Fleet's submarine crews and its Maltese ratings and in 1912 Fort St Angelo was commissioned as the 'base ship' for the entire Mediterranean Fleet. Inside the fort, the British adapted what they found—extending, for instance, the tunnels in the old Slave Quarters, and building new things such as a Distillation Station of Maltese limestone designed to convert seawater into drinking water. A new defensive complex and single-storey barrack buildings intruded upon the medieval structure and numerous accommodation and office blocks were built around the fort's central parade ground and a wireless station was created. A hooter announced the arrival of seaplanes landing in Grand Harbour and, in true naval fashion, a mast was fitted on top of the fort's highest point, signifying its status as a ship of war, one of the Empire's many 'stone frigates'. Beneath it was the Saluting Base, which comprised an elegant structure housing a small drawing-room with doors opening high above the water's edge onto the stunning vista of Grand Harbour and Valletta. From here the commander took the salute of warships entering the harbour. The old mast that once proclaimed St Angelo a British warship is still there, and the view from the Saluting Base remains breathtaking and unchanged. To conform to the British Naval Discipline Act, the commissioning pendant of the captain of *St Angelo* had to be flown afloat; in the early years of the century his flag was carried by a small brass-funnelled picket boat moored in Kalkara Creek, and after 1945 a motor fishing vessel did the honours.

The world wars

Though major units of the Mediterranean Fleet were controversially with-drawn to home waters on the eve of the First World War, the fleet grew exponentially with the onset of the Dardanelles campaign for which Malta was the main mustering point and rear base. By April 1915 there were fifteen battleships, five heavy cruisers, sixteen light cruisers, sixteen monitors, thirty-six destroyers, and sixteen submarines. Base facilities were heavily reinforced, and soon there were also five depot ships, two repair ships, two salvage ships, a survey ship, and a seaplane carrier.[21] With the increase in German subma-rine attacks on Mediterranean shipping, Malta was the natural base for the coordination of convoy operations and Grand Harbour filled with the growing numbers of escort vessels necessary for this task as well as a small armada of minesweepers, for which Malta provided many of the locally recruited ratings, freeing Royal Navy personnel for service elsewhere. As well as British vessels, Grand Harbour played host to American, Australian, French, Greek, Italian, and Japanese warships. It also reprised its Crimean role as the 'nursemaid of the Mediterranean', and fifteen new hospitals were opened giving the island a bed capacity of 25,000. Fort St Angelo was inte-gral to the island's role, as a supply base, accommodation and administrative facility, and as a communications centre. Its position made it the ideal loca-tion for a powerful wireless installation, and good cable facilities enabled it to handle hundreds of messages every day.

The inter-war years saw Malta continue as the home of the Mediter-ranean Fleet, though naval life became more gay with the return of peace. Writing in 1930, Sir Harry Luke recorded the social life of the establish-ment: 'To say that Malta was a social place would be a notable understate-ment, particularly between the Wars, when it was the base of the greatest single naval force then in existence, the British Mediterranean Fleet. Par-ties (except in the hot summer months, when they took the form of bath-ing picnics) had to be arranged weeks in advance, while minor entertaining was continuous... A highlight of summer parties was to dine in a battle-ship anchored in Grand Harbour, then adjourn to the quarter-deck and from a comfortable armchair enjoy a good film to the accompaniment of a Havana cigar.'[22]

But from 1935 Britain was again forced to invest in the island's fortifica-tion. New aerodromes, coastal batteries and infantry defences were constructed

and the strength of its garrison forces and anti-aircraft defences was increased.
By 1939, it was estimated that to take Malta by force would cost an aggressor
up to 60,000 lives. At the time of the Abyssinian crisis, the Mediterranean
Fleet comprised forty-nine major warships, including six battleships, five
cruisers, and twenty-seven destroyers. Within a month of hostilities opening
in 1939, it had risen in strength to sixty-seven warships. But given the seri-
ousness and proximity of the Axis air threat to Malta, it was soon decided to
withdraw the Fleet's heavy units to Alexandria. The people of Malta, meanwhile, prepared for what became known as the second Great Siege, practis-
ing responses to poison gas attacks and enduring mock air raids. Though the
garrison was built up and anti-aircraft defences improved, the island was a
mere 60 miles from the nearest Italian air bases but nearly 1,000 miles from
the nearest British bases at Gibraltar and Alexandria. At 0655 on 11 June
1940, the day after Mussolini declared war on Britain, the sirens sounded as
the first Italian air raid came in. As the battle for the Mediterranean developed Malta's position became desperate. On 15 February 1942, the day Singapore fell, Malta was under air raid alert for 19 hours and 59 minutes.

Like St Paul's Cathedral in London, Fort St Angelo became a prominent
symbol of Malta's defiance and resilience during the blitz. From 1939 the
fort was armed with four twin Lewis guns on anti-aircraft mounts. In January
1941 they were complemented by three Bofors 40 mm guns manned by the
Royal Marines, taken over by the Royal Malta Artillery in May 1943. The
actor Alec Guinness captured the grim spirit of Malta under siege:

> It was late in the afternoon of a hot sultry day when we arrived in Malta. I
> hadn't seen the Grand Harbour Valletta . . . since the spring of 1939. Then all had
> been sparkling, with great battleships and cruisers, very spick-and-span, at their
> huge moorings, brass-funnelled Admiralty barges speedily chugging their way
> to the Customs House steps hooting shrilly, Liberty Boats full of raucous sail-
> ors, dghaisas—gaily painted red, green and white—plying for trade, bugles calls
> echoing from Fort St Angelo and flags flying everywhere. Now all looked
> dilapidated and sulky. The Navy was there in force but grim and unlit.[23]

Between March and May 1942, at the height of the war in the Mediterranean, 6,700 tons of bombs were dropped on Grand Harbour. Fort St Angelo
received sixty-nine direct hits though the structure's massive walls remained
relatively unscathed. The raids sank twenty-one ships, four fleet destroyers
and four submarines in the harbour and its approaches.

Meanwhile, Fort St Angelo continued to perform its headquarters role,
and female naval staff of the Women's Royal Naval Service (WRNS) arrived

as cypher clerks and telephonists as the staff work increased. The war inevitably led to further alterations to the fort in addition to the arrival of new guns. Every advantage had to be taken of its defensive capabilities given the severity of the bombing. Three long chambers in the mighty cavalier, for instance, were used by the Royal Navy as junior ratings' messes. At the foot of the first ramp leading down from the fort's narrow main gate lie, somewhat perversely, some of the most modern parts of the fort—tunnels built during the war to protect the inhabitants as the living and working quarters of the fort's entire population went underground. These new living and working spaces were extensions of the Slave Quarters that had been tunnelled deep into the rock during the war against the Turks in the sixteenth century. With the threat of aerial bombardment brought by the Abyssinian Crisis of 1935–6, the Slave Gallery had been increased in size by forming two large rooms in the d'Homedes Bastion and tunnelling towards Kalkara Creek in case the work of Fort St Angelo had to go underground.

This earlier work proved to have been prescient when Axis bombs began raining down in 1940. Nearly a mile of new tunnels were dug beneath the fort. The dungeons of the Captain's House were turned into an air-raid shelter, but most of St Angelo's life during the siege went on in the tunnels below decks in the old Slave Quarters. The captain of HMS *St Angelo* and his officers lived there and had their offices there, the Captain's Office and the Commander's Office converted into Boat Gear Stores after the war when the offices were able to move to the 'top deck' once again.

The Operations Room of the Rear Admiral Malta was located in the tunnel by the sea-level gate, and next to the Operations Room were the Pay Offices. There was a Signal Distributing Office, an important communications facility which, after the war, became the Trophy Store and Electrical Workshop. There were also senior officers' cabins, a large dormitory, storerooms, and a cinema, all opening onto Kalkara Creek. The Operations Room, an important nerve centre, was moved across the water to the underground facilities beneath the Lascaris Bastion.* This meant that the Operations

---

* Located 400 feet under the Upper Barracca Gardens and the Saluting Battery in Valletta, across the water from St Angelo (and reminiscent of the Cabinet War Rooms in London), the Lascaris War Rooms have been restored and are now open to the public. These extensive underground rooms took over the defence of the island from Fort St Angelo and were where planning for offensive operations in the Mediterranean took place. It also housed the RAF's Fighter Control Room and an Anti-Aircraft Gun Operations Room. There was also a combined operations room and a facility for the encryption machines used to receive and send secret communications. In July 1943 it was used as the advanced Allied headquarters for the invasion of Sicily. Following the war

Room could be used to accommodate naval officers, who had been moved out of Fort St Angelo for safety reasons, only to have their new accommodation, Admiralty House Vittoriosa, demolished by enemy bombing in April 1942. So, they moved back into the fort and into its new underground chambers.

The former Operations Room now housed the Wardroom (the naval equivalent of the army's 'mess', the dining and social space of commissioned officers) which in 1942 became home to the Black Bat Club. The Captain of the Marines, Captain Clark, designed a replica of a country pub which was built by the Barrackmaster and his staff. The distance to England— 1,294½ miles—was carved on a milestone. The new Wardroom was completed just before Christmas Day 1942. All of the rooms and tunnels in the old Slave Quarters, especially the Wardroom, were renowned for their dampness. Rain percolated through, and clothes went mouldy in twenty-four hours. Dust and masonry fell from the carved-out ceilings and walls, and the first ENSA (Entertainments National Service Activities) Party entertained by the Wardroom performed in raincoats and seaboots.

There was significant damage elsewhere in the fort. A sallyport connected the sea-level battery to the Wardroom garden. It was used as an officers' landing, but a bomb hit the garden in April 1942, filling in the sallyport with rubble and completely blocking it. The quarters of the battery crew were used as a sick bay.[24] The hulk of HMS *Cruiser*, moored alongside the fort, was damaged by the same bomb which hit the Church of St Anne. (A plaque from 1947 records the navy's restoration of the building). On another occasion during the period of intense air raids the Chapel of the Nativity of Our Lady was wrecked. The eastern buildings on the parade ground and the ramp to the Captain's House were destroyed and the ramp from the main gate and various bastion walls were damaged. When King George VI visited Malta to bestow the George Cross upon the island and its people, the guns of St Angelo crashed out the general salute as the bells of Valletta and the Three Cities rang out.

Valletta and the Three Cities had suffered terribly from bombing, their honey-coloured houses, in Manley's words, sliced in half like pieces of cheese, the streets choked with rubble and the inhabitants, many living a

it became headquarters of the Mediterranean Fleet, and from 1967 was taken over by NATO as a strategic Communications Centre for the interception of Soviet submarines in the Mediterranean, in which role it remained until finally closed in 1977.

troglodyte existence in caves, scared and war-weary. Valletta's population fell from 21,000 to 6,000 and 35,000 houses were destroyed or damaged in the crowded cities around the harbour. Over 5,000 Maltese citizens had been killed or wounded. Grand Harbour and its surrounding cities were placed on air-raid alert 3,340 times during the two years that the raids lasted; this amounted to 2,357 hours in shelters, of which 2,031 came in 1942.[25] HMS *St Angelo*, nearly 1,000 years old and standing proudly across the harbour from Valletta with the White Ensign and Admiral's flag flying high each day, symbolized the people's unbroken resistance.

Fort St Angelo and the British draw-down in the Mediterranean

There was a great deal of work for the Mediterranean Fleet to do from its Maltese bases following the Second World War, including fleet operations off the coast of Palestine during the crisis there in the late 1940s and the clearance of 12,600 mines from the Mediterranean. Fort St Angelo retained its role as headquarters of the Mediterranean Fleet. Its function was to provide logistical support for visiting warships and act as a base for the coordination of naval activities in the Mediterranean. The captain of the fort was also Chief Staff Officer to the Flag Officer Malta until mid-1977.[26] In 1947 the five guns of the Saluting Battery, which had been removed in 1941, were returned. Even as the British Empire contracted, RAF Shackletons and Canberras based on Malta shadowed Soviet submarines.

The post-war decades witnessed the draw-down of the base infrastructure and the thinning out of Britain's military presence. The naval dockyards shut in 1958 and were sold for commercial use. Other naval establishments closed too, and Sliema Creek was no longer the haunt of destroyers and frigates. On the occasion of Maltese independence on 31 September 1964, Royal Navy ships in Grand Harbour were floodlit. But a Defence Agreement meant that the Royal Navy remained, and Grand Harbour continued to act as an important 'fleet maintenance unit' for the Royal Navy and its allies, based in Fort St Angelo; NATO and the US Navy's Sixth Fleet used the island's facilities, though this tailed off after the election of Dom Mintoff's government in 1971 and its move towards a non-aligned foreign policy.

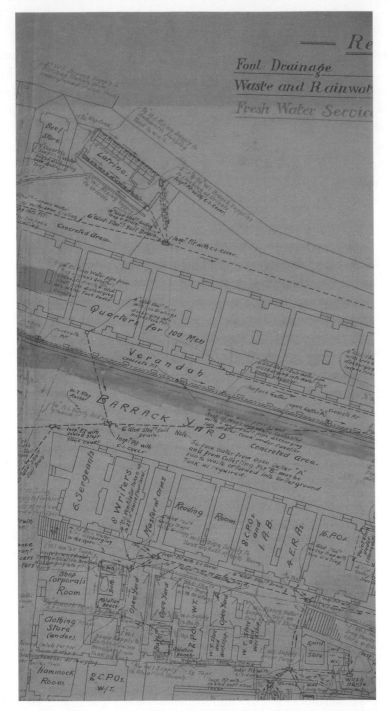

Figure 13. Detail from a plan of Fort St Angelo dating from 1916. The plan was specifically prepared to detail drains and water tanks but offers a fascinating insight into the range of different buildings and rooms crammed into the Fort and the uses to which they were put. The National Archives of Malta has thousands of similar plans of the numerous British military installations on the island.

Despite the post-war draw down, the British remained deep into the 1970s and continued to adjust and develop their Maltese military establishments accordingly. Britain's continued military reach required a complex base infrastructure, and Fort St Angelo was at the centre of its provision and was extensively modernized. The Malta Archives, housed in a charming building in Rabat, contain thousands of plans detailing British bases throughout the island, including many maps and diagrams of Fort St Angelo. The meticulous plans provide an excellent picture of the multifarious uses to which the fort was put, as even the installation of a new water closet for signalmen or a skylight in the Smoking Room required a draughtsman's plan. Electricity was installed throughout the fort, including in the Chapel and in the squash court in 1973. Rectifiers and frequency chargers were installed; in 1968 street lighting was introduced to Oil Wharf and Garden Reach Wharf, and a diving school was opened in the former Distillery Station that the British had built at water level. In 1946 additional accommodation was constructed for Maltese ratings, and in 1969 new offices were opened for moorings, salvage, and boom officers. There was a new Maltese stokers mess, an underground refuge, and detailed plans for the removal of effluent and foul water. In 1967 a new fleet canteen and a WRNS office was opened.

The fort had a purpose-built cinema with its own small bar, erected in the 1920s (and until recently used by a pigeon-racing club), a NAAFI, an engineering workshop, an air-crash disaster store, a surgery, and an underground sick bay (by torchlight in the bowels of the building, one can still find a large illustration of a cheery matelot with his arm in a sling at its entrance). There was a chief petty officers recreation room, a senior ratings mess, an armoury, a dentist, the port signal station, a tennis court (the hazard here was that mishit balls dropped into the sea), a library, galley, junior ratings latrine, a victualling yard, a distillery, a prominent boiler tower, and a WRNS bath.[27] In 1966 deteriorating stonework on the fort exterior was replaced. Meticulous plans of the individual stones requiring attention were prepared, indicative of the preservation work undertaken by the British. Deserted now, until the late 1970s Fort St Angelo was a bustling community of hundreds of men and women of the British armed forces.

When Admiral Sir John Hamilton, the last Commander-in-Chief Mediterranean, departed Malta in 1967, the only force remaining on the Malta station was one escort squadron of frigates. From 1967 the Flag Officer Malta was in charge of the naval base, and also held the office of Commander

South East Mediterranean Area within the NATO command structure. For six more years he flew his flag from the tall flagstaff of *St Angelo*. But things slowly but inexorably began to close down as the British withdrew and their many military establishments were handed over to the government of Malta. Supervising this complicated endgame was Rear Admiral Sir Nigel Oswald Cecil, the Commander-in-Chief British Forces Malta. There was much to be done as the British withdrew. There were, for example, the thousand-plus plans of the fortresses around Grand Harbour, as well as a great deal of other paperwork, to be handed over to the Maltese government. The large defence estate itself had to be transferred to new ownership: Admiralty House in Valletta, for many years the residence of the commanders-in-chief Mediterranean, became the National Museum of Fine Arts. Former Royal Navy hospitals were turned over to the Maltese government, including the magnificent Bighi Naval Hospital designed by Colonel George Whitmore (1830–2), which had closed in 1970 (and now lies derelict). There was a good deal of haggling involved over the transfer of the military estate, even (allegedly) coming down to a bed once slept in by Admiral Nelson and Lady Hamilton that had been evacuated to Malta on the fall of Naples in 1943.

During this phased withdrawal, the British invested money to encourage other industries to replace the imminent loss of the naval and dockyard revenue that had been Malta's mainstay for nearly two centuries. The British withdrawal meant the loss of an annual sum of £35 million paid for the use of the bases, and finding alternative sources of income was difficult. As the British left, however, the yachting industry grew rapidly. Big marinas began to prosper where not long before the sleek hulls of the submarines lay alongside the quays, and buoys once occupied by trots of destroyers and frigates became home to pleasure yachts and sightseeing steamers. Today Fort St Angelo is the mooring point for the enormous yachts of the superrich, which are tied up alongside the British-built jetty. Here, where once there was a forest of military buildings representing an overspill from the fort, there is now just a car park. But alongside it, where once the hulk of HMS *Cruiser* had been moored as an extension of the fort, there are berths for the biggest yachts. Further down, Dockyard Creek is packed with lesser yachts, the warships long departed.

As a military base, no encouragement had been given to visits by private yachts. It was only after independence that there were significant moves to attract such visits. The growth of tourism offered some hope for a Maltese government concerned about its income once the British had departed as, for a while, did the prospect of the privatized dockyards. There were drawn-out negotiations between Valletta and London over the amount of the British subsidy. The renegotiated 'Military Facilities Agreement' of 1972 gave the British facilities in Grand Harbour up until 1979. Now the base was only to be used by ships of the Royal Navy, and not to be used as springboard for a British or NATO attack on any Arab country. Britain pledged to keep Maltese employed in their bases, and the NATO headquarters was transferred to Naples. Though there was no longer a permanent Royal Navy force based on Malta, it was still frequently used, fifty-seven British warships calling in during the course of 1977 alone. As 1978 drew to a close, the Royal Navy's bases and many of its historical treasures were in the process of being trans-ferred to the Maltese government.

The final eighteen months of Britain's 180-year military presence in Malta were supervised from Fort St Angelo, the headquarters British Forces Malta. During this period the Captain's House was occupied by Colonel Peter Seabrook of the Royal Artillery and his family. Seabrook was Chief of Staff to Rear Admiral Cecil, Commander British Forces Malta, Flag Officer Malta and, until the appointment lapsed in 1977, NATO Com-mander South East Mediterranean. Cecil handled the withdrawal with a splendid sense of history.[28] He struck his flag in *St Angelo* on 12 March 1979 prior to the withdrawal of the last British forces on 31 March, and raised his flag aboard the guided-missile destroyer HMS *London*, which had arrived in Malta to act as Cecil's flagship during the final stages of the withdrawal. He left his residence, Admiralty House, and moved to a Flori-ana hostel. The Royal Naval Port Division was disbanded. Cecil attended, with Commander Jack Duffett, the last Commanding Officer of HMS *St Angelo*, a final mass in the ancient chapel of St Anne standing on the fort's upper deck.

Three Royal Fleet Auxiliary vessels, *Olna, Sir Lancelot*, and *Tarbatness*, arrived to lift the departing British forces. Now a series of nostalgic events followed one after the other as the clock ticked down to the final departure date. On 22 March the last Royal Marines, Salerno Company, marched, symbolically unarmed, from RAF Luqa to Vittoriosa, where they embarked in *Sir Lancelot*, moored alongside Fort St Angelo. The following day the Royal Marines Band and that of the Armed Forces of Malta marched down Republic Street in Valletta and beat retreat before the Grand Master's Palace. The two bands then gave a concert in the Manoel Theatre on 25 March,

Figure 14. This photograph of HMS *Ark Royal* was taken as the ship entered Grand harbour on Monday 6 November 1978 during her 'farewell' tour. The photographer was Petty Officer (Phot) Stuart Kent, one of the ship's photographers and as such he probably took it from a helicopter (Westland Wessex) from one of the squadrons embarked. At the foot of the picture is Fort St Angelo, the Chapel of St Anne clearly visible on the left, the buildings of the Captain's House in the centre, and the tower of the desalination plant on the right.

climaxing in a joint rendition of the 1812 Overture. Admiral Cecil and the president of Malta, Dr Anton Buttigieg, then came on stage and a choir joined them and sang the 'Parting Song', the words written by the president, the music by the Admiral. There followed an emotional rendition of 'Auld Lang Syne', and the cars of both men were mobbed as they departed the theatre. Cecil later broadcast a farewell message from aboard HMS *London*.

Dom Mintoff insisted on marking Britain's final withdrawal with a new Independence Day, making Malta the only British colony to celebrate two such occasions. On 30 March Fort St Angelo was turned over by the Royal Navy to the Maltese people; in all its history, Peter Elliot writes, it had seen no more significant day. The Royal Marines mounted their last parade there, then sailed in *Sir Lancelot*, lining the decks as she left harbour. On 31 March an impressive ceremony was held before a large crowd outside the gates of St Angelo. A monument had been erected (designed by Mr Mintoff himself) and one minute before midnight a young sailor from HMS *London* lowered the Union Jack, and a dockyard worker hoisted the Maltese flag in its place. Church bells were rung, and a great display of fireworks was let off.[29] Mintoff and the General Secretary of the General Workers Union climbed the rocks and lit a flame that was to be kept forever burning. This was an important moment in Malta's history, its significance indicated by the fact that even today many Maltese people date their independence from *this* moment, not the arrival of constitutional, or 'flag' independence, in 1964. The actual day on which independence is celebrated has become a bone of political contention between the main political parties. Today, both days are marked, along with the anniversary of the Great Siege, as national holidays.

At the midnight ceremony on March 31 the president, Dr Buttigieg, said in his speech that apart from rejoicing in their 'Freedom Day', the people had gathered to swear never again to have a foreign military base on their soil. Malta, he said, had freed itself from the foreign military base not out of hate or vengeance, but out of a strong act of faith, because it wanted to fulfil a new mission of peace in the Mediterranean in the interests of world peace. Commander Jack Duffett, the last captain of HMS *St Angelo*, gave the White Ensign that had flown from *St Angelo*'s flagstaff to the grateful president of the Vittoriosa Historical and Cultural Society. Then, on 1 April, HMS *London* made her final departure before throngs of people lining the quays and Barracca Gardens, sailors lining the decks. From Luqa airport there appeared a lone RAF Nimrod, piloted by Air Commodore H. D. Hall, the last Air

Commander Malta. He flew low over Grand Harbour and the crowds, dipped his wings in salute, then made a last circuit of the island's shore before setting his course towards Gibraltar.[30]

After nearly 200 years as a British base, Malta had been evacuated. Fort St Angelo faced an uncertain future, though it remained central to Maltese national identity. When Malta joined the European Union in 2004 a dazzling laser-light display featuring the EU flag and the legend 'Welcome Europe' were projected onto the fort's exterior walls. The Captain's House has reverted to its older title, the Magistral Palace, and has been home to the Knight Resident in Malta since an agreement with the Maltese government in 1998 allowed the Order of the Knights of St John to reoccupy the upper level of the Fort. While the top level is well-maintained because of this arrangement, including the Chapel of St Anne, the rest of the Fort is neglected, its upkeep, restoration, and ownership contested.

4

Botanic Gardens,
Christchurch, New Zealand

The city of Christchurch owes its foundations to the Canterbury Association, the energy and ideas of the colonial settlement theorist Edward Gibbon Wakefield, and the Church of England's Oxford Movement. It was named after Christ Church, Oxford, alma mater of John Robert Godley, one of the city's founding fathers. The city centres upon Cathedral Square and its Anglican cathedral, its foundation stone laid in 1864 (though subsequently demolished as a result of the destruction wrought by the February 2011 earthquake). A dominant feature of the city from its inception was a large open space a few blocks from Cathedral Square. This was Hagley Park, extending over 500 acres, and the botanic gardens that it contained were an integral part of the vision of Christchurch's founders. They have been at the centre of the city's cultural and recreational life ever since, and a key aspect of its claim to 'garden city' status. When the Canterbury Association was succeeded by a provincial government in 1855 a law was passed laying Hagley Park aside forever for the enjoyment of the public, an early example of the green belt manifest in the colonies.

When the first settlers arrived in 1850, what was to become Hagley Park was dominated by scrubby grassland and shingle, criss-crossed by creeks feeding the swampy river, soon named the Avon. The dense forests and swamplands that confronted early colonists were both intimidating and attractive. The new city developed on land used by Maori for hunting, a strange environment in which to found an idyllic city of trees and gardens. In the 1860s it was still a frontier town, a group of shacks with the usual drainage and health problems, standing on the bleak, treeless plains over the Port Hills from Lyttelton. Until it was cleared and had its fringes planted with willows, the Avon was choked with flax.[1]

Christchurch was, and remains, perhaps the most notably 'English' part of New Zealand. The Canterbury settlers intended their new city to have green spaces. The park was subdivided by two major avenues into three units, one of which included a botanic garden located in a loop in the Avon River. The park and garden were marked out by elms, beeches, and chestnuts imported from England, heralds of a series of botanical transformations that were to turn this little patch of a distant land into an oasis of Englishness. The planting of introduced species which transformed Hagley Park into an essentially English landscape of open parkland and woodland began in the mid-nineteenth century and continued into the twentieth, before a reaction against the decline of native flora and fauna set in. Christchurch Botanic Garden covers nearly 52 acres of horticultural displays, conservatories, memorials, garden art, and walking tracks.[2] Christ's College was built on Hagley Park as was the museum and the hospital, as the city centre and suburbs such as Beckenham, New Brighton, and Sydenham developed.

Ever since the foundation of Canterbury by settlers sponsored by the British Parliament and the Church of England, the presence of a large area of public space close to the city centre has had a profound effect on the

Figure 15. Christchurch Botanic Gardens: Armstrong Lawn bedding and Curator's House.

character of Christchurch and the life of its people, and the sobriquet 'garden city' remains important to its self-identity to this day. The symbolic moment of foundation for the botanic gardens came on 9 July 1863 when Yorkshireman Enoch Barker, the first Government Gardener, planted an English oak on the occasion of the marriage of Prince Albert Edward, Victoria's son, to Princess Alexandria of Denmark. The site duly became known as First Tree Lawn. The large surrounding acreage of Hagley Park was named after the Worcestershire seat of Lord Lyttelton. Both the park and the gardens were created on an area that had for long been home to the Ngai Tahu tribe of Maori. Once Europeans arrived and claimed the land for themselves, a special area for Maori to rest in when visiting the city— Pilgrim's Corner—was established in Hagley Park, illustrative of the manner in which indigenes were 'moved on' as they became guests in their own country. Repeatedly in the 1860s and 1870s Maori unsuccessfully presented their claims for land in the Hagley Park area. On one occasion the provincial government suggested they surrender the land in exchange for land elsewhere, but it does not seem that they were given any.[3]

Christchurch Botanic Gardens and Hagley Park contained features typical of Victorian and Edwardian town planning, leisure, and civic memorialization. The Peacock Fountain (1911) was imported from Britain by the Christchurch Beautifying Society; the Bandsmen's Memorial Rotunda (1926) honoured the fallen New Zealanders of the First World War; and Victoria Lake, the major water feature, was excavated from the park's naturally occurring swamp to mark the Queen's 1897 jubilee. It was soon stocked with imported perch, and became a favourite spot for sailing model boats. Other memorials in the gardens included a stone gateway commemorating Evelyn Couzins, Mayoress of Christchurch during the Second World War, and the Kate Sheppard Memorial Walk in honour of a noted campaigner for female suffrage (it was here that the world's first white camellias were grown). The Cockayne Memorial Garden, opened in 1938, commemorates Sheffield-born Leonard Cockayne who had a profound impact on New Zealand's botany.

Botanic gardens and the British Empire

The development of botanic gardens went hand in hand with the rapacious exploitation of the New World for plantation development and the production of cash crops. Botanic gardens were significant institutions in the growth of the British Empire, repositories of living plants gathered for the purposes of scientific research and conservation as well as display aimed at entertainment and education. The botanic garden traces its roots back to Renaissance Italy and the gardens established in Pisa and Padua for the study of plants. At the turn of the twentieth century, 102 botanic gardens, 38 per cent of the world's total, were located in the British Empire.[4]

In 1765 the first botanic garden in the Western Hemisphere was established on the island of St Vincent by the governor of the Windward Islands, General Robert Melville, assisted by the Royal Society. Breadfruit trees from those originally introduced by Captain Bligh in 1793 survive to this day. The Royal Botanic Gardens in Calcutta were opened in 1787:

> Not for the purpose of collecting rare plants as things of curiosity or furnishing articles for the gratification of luxury, but for establishing stock for disseminating such articles as may prove beneficial to the inhabitants as well as the natives of Great Britain and which ultimately be tend to the extension of the national commerce and riches.[5]

The development of botanic gardens, domestic gardens, and agriculture led to a global cross-pollination of plant species. Some specimens were collected in the pursuit of scientific knowledge and for medical purposes, others in pursuit of riches or for their aesthetic value.

With ties to Britain and strong links to India, colonial botanic gardens, sponsored and supported by the Royal Botanic Gardens at Kew in Richmond, Surrey, provided a network of scientific enquiry and economic trade. Seeds and entire plants crossed the oceans, often in Wardian cases—tightly sealed, glazed plant cases introduced in the 1830s—and there was a ceaseless flow of information back home in personal diaries, correspondence, ledgers, and sketches. By the nineteenth century botanic gardens, especially Kew, were sending botanists on plant-hunting expeditions and establishing colonial botanic gardens as outposts to hold and propagate plants destined to be sent back to the parent institution.[6] For Sir Joseph Banks, Kew was to act as 'a great exchange house of the Empire', and by 1879 its *Flora and Fauna of the British Empire* ran to twenty-two volumes. Kew's directors were regularly consulted by colonial botanic gardens seeking new members of staff, an example of the types of expert networks that the Empire nurtured and sustained.[7]

The spread of botanic gardens marked a global race to find new riches as what were to become essential commodities spread around the world. Tea from China was cultivated in South Asia. Rubber plants migrated from the Amazon to England, and thence to Ceylon, Singapore, and elsewhere. Twenty-two seedlings taken from Ceylon to Singapore in 1877 became the ancestors of most of South-East Asia's rubber. Cinchona trees from the Andes went to Ceylon and India. Coffee, pineapple, cocoa, and spices also moved around the world. The significance of botany in expeditions of discovery and scientific enquiry rose. Kew's global role was underscored by Joseph Banks' appointment as botanic adviser to the king and the first unofficial director of the Royal Botanic Gardens. Banks dispatched plant collectors all over the world and Kew became an unparalleled centre of botanical exploration and horticultural experimentation. The impact of this activity was often transformational. Along with botanic gardens, the Empire sprouted agricultural and forestry institutions.

The Christchurch Botanic Gardens illustrate the coincidence of the growth of botanic gardens and the advent of the public parks movement. In addition to their economic purposes, botanic gardens became places of recreational resort as well as learning institutions, and their collections began to be arranged and displayed within redesigned grounds of a picturesque park-like nature. At the same time, parks became more like botanic gardens with the planting of exotic trees and the addition of display beds for flowers.[8] This was very much the case in Christchurch, where the botanic gardens grew as part of the large recreational and leisure facility of Hagley Park.

Home gardening also took off in Britain and overseas settler dominions such as New Zealand, and became a notable feature in Christchurch. With 'an almost missionary zeal professional and amateur gardeners set about transplanting and cultivating plants from across the globe', and gardeners in Britain and New Zealand alike formed all manner of societies for the competition cultivation of vegetables, sweet peas, or roses.[9] This 'botanical imperialism' encouraged people to recreate tropical scenery in their own homes, a phenomenon which had an impact on how non-European flora were viewed and classified by Europeans. Regardless of where they were from or what was necessary to make them grow, plants that appeared strange were labelled 'exotic'. The cultivation of 'exotics' in British gardens brought the unknown world into British towns and homes, developing people's understanding—imaginative as much as factual—of distant lands, a subtle aspect of the imperial experience.

It was not just on Britain's great estates that this occurred. Even in the smallest gardens, and interiors with pots and window boxes, an expanse of domestic imperialist culture was opened up. The love of gardening became associated with civilization and diffused throughout society. 'Primitive' countries were often described as having plants in an aboriginal stage of development. As James Ryan writes, 'images of vegetable pandemonium . . . signified not only the rich potential of the land, but also the absence of indigenous industry and labour'.[10] One by one, in Rebecca Preston's words, the planet's plants and animals were to be drawn out of the tangled threads of their life surroundings and rewoven into European based patterns of global unity and order. The Great Exhibition at the Crystal Palace was significant in rendering exotic gardening accessible to the public. Countless foreign plants were incorporated into the Victorian exterior, many of which have since been subsumed into the so-called 'English' garden.[11]

Settling New Zealand

The Dutchman Abel Tasman was the European discoverer of what he christened New Zealand, sighting land in 1642 on an expedition sponsored by the Dutch East Indies Company. Both he and Captain Cook, a later visitor, were greeted by indigenous people, some of whom wanted to kill and eat them (not necessarily in that order, as Piers Brendon remarks). Maori thought Cook's sailors were gods, their gunfire thunderbolts, and *Endeavour* a white-winged whale. Cook became a model for New Zealand nation-building, more suitably British than Tasman as a founding father. Cook literally put New Zealand on the world map when he charted its coastline.

European contact with New Zealand in its initial phases was shaped by explorers, whalers, traders, and sealers. This developing contact, and its reportage back in Europe, wove fantasies around the Maori and their lands. Added to this, tales of Maori and the degrading impact of the roguish Europeans in contact with them—whalers, for instance, who established whaling stations supported by enslaved Maori—attracted missionaries. It was clear to them that here was another fertile glade of God's earth where there were wrongs to be righted and souls to be saved. Maori were considered by missionaries such as Reverend Samuel Marsden to be a 'noble race', though one in need of conversion and upliftment. He gathered Maori complaints against Europeans in order to secure imperial backing for his mission in the Bay of Islands. For their part, the Maori were more interested in buying and selling than adopting a foreign scheme of worship and morality, and were also rather keen to keep their own land, though not averse to working in part-nership with Europeans or employing them and their firepower to pursue their own internal disputes. But as European influences and settlers pressed in, Maori were displaced, often to the detriment of other peoples, such as the Moriori of the Chatham Islands, whose population reduced from 1,600 in 1835 to 101 in 1862.[12] The musket wars of the period had horrendous effects, killing thousands, redistributing tribes, and causing massive popula-tion displacement.

The British imperial state, meanwhile, moved slowly from its position of 'minimum intervention' to a larger role in New Zealand's affairs. Christian imperialism was to the fore in this changing dynamic, tempered by the pro-viso that it must not cost the Treasury any significant sums.[13] Moves from men on the spot—often British officials from New South Wales—made it appear likely that New Zealand would become some form of British pro-tectorate, initiatives that had sufficient Maori support to be credible. Mis-sionary societies cautioned against the evils of unchecked colonialism, and highlighted the need for some imperial regulation so as to mitigate what might otherwise become a fatal impact of Europeans on yet another part of the non-European world. The region was also beginning to loom large in Whitehall's strategic calculations as British interests grew in Asia and the Pacific and opportunities opened up in China, a perfect storm of coalescent imperial impulses.[14] Thus imperialism and humanitarianism marched together towards the annexation of New Zealand.

Christchurch was a particularly notable fruit of the model colonization movement which sought to found societies overseas that represented all that was 'best' about the British social order—in essence replicating the Great Chain of Being, with aristocrats, yeomen, artisans, tradesmen, farmhands, and domestic servants, all in their God-appointed place and happy with their station. Of course, this feudal never-never land had never existed in Britain itself, but that did not prevent people from looking to a Lucky Jim-style 'merrie England', before the factory and the machine had begun to blight the rural landscape. New Zealanders cherished the myth, eagerly fostered by Wakefield, that their colony was a reincarnation of England, a rural Elysium, the Britain of the south. This sat ill with the 'counter myth' which emphasized the colony's progressiveness, in fact, its modernity.

The New Zealand Company had been established for the purposes of colonization, inspired in part by Edward Gibbon Wakefield. Wakefield advo-cated emigration as a release from overpopulation and high unemployment, while extolling its capacity to civilize 'savages' and acquire new fields for British industry to exploit and develop. Wakefield was a curious blend of charlatan and visionary, and the Colonial Office, representing the British government, had no interest in his colonization ideas, a typical measure of how officialdom viewed many of the private initiatives that tended towards the spread of empire. James Stephen of the Colonial Office said that acquiring sovereignty over New Zealand would 'infallibly issue in the conquest and extermination of its present inhabitants'.[15] But the government was in no position to stop enthusiastic private citizens sailing to New Zealand especially when they were, in Melbourne's double entendre, 'quite mad to go there'.[16] In 1838, furthermore, the House of Lords Select Committee on New Zealand endorsed Wakefield's settlement plans.

By 1839 there were at least 2,000 settlers in New Zealand. Warnings of an Aboriginal genocide were not sufficient to deter people. The horror stories about cannibal feasts, the Maori worship of muskets, the spread of venereal and other diseases, and the trade in women and tattooed heads were ignored, and as happened in other parts of Britain's expanding empire, bad things only served to inspire a certain type of Briton to endeavour to get overseas and make a difference.[17] The British public's humanitarian impulse was at its strongest at this point, and in the view of many people, nothing short of annexation could protect natives from whites and vice versa. The Treaty of Waitangi, by which the differences between British settlers and the indigenous inhabitants were thinly mitigated, was taken to mean different things on both sides. The British thought that it secured sovereignty in exchange for protection and civilization, while Maori thought that it denoted vague British overlordship (the 'shadow' to Victoria, the 'substance' to us, as they thought) in exchange for access to goods. In signing the documents involved, the tragedy was that Maori could not foresee the rapid arrival of scores of thousands of land-hungry migrants who were to irrevocably transform their land and their lives.

In 1839 the New Zealand Company—from which the Canterbury Association purchased its land—instructed surveyor William Mein Smith to set aside land for a town belt around what would become Christchurch, and to reserve land for a botanic garden and a park. As the business of colonization got underway, the Ngai Tahu found that the Crown's guarantee of their land and food supplies was ignored by the Canterbury Association. The town site was bordered by a large wetland and separated from the port by hills. Captain Joseph Thomas, the chief surveyor and a former Royal Engineer, was sent out with a team of surveyors to select and prepare a site for settlement. He completed a trigonometrical survey of the Canterbury block by the end of 1849 and laid out the port of Lyttelton and seaside suburb of Sumner as well as Christchurch before the settlers arrived. Thomas originally placed the principal town of the proposed settlement at the head of Lyttelton Harbour, but when he realized there was insufficient flat land there to meet the Association's requirements, he relocated Christchurch to where he had previously placed a town called Stratford at a point on the Avon. Refugees from Wellington's earthquake of 1848, as well as Maori, Australian convicts, and carpenters from Hobart, were recruited to build roads and prepare the new city. The chosen location presented challenges, such as a lack of timber and extensive swampland and the tendency of the Waimakariri River to flood (its waters ran through the streets of the city in 1868). Also, unbeknownst to the city's founders, there was an earthquake risk in this area despite the fact that it was far from major active faults.

Of all the New Zealand settlements founded by Wakefield, Christchurch came closest to his ideal of transplanting a cross-section of English society. The Canterbury Association gained support from the Archbishop of Canterbury and other members of the elite, such as Lord Lyttelton, the Association's chairman. Settlers of different classes were actively sought, posters proclaiming 'Emigration for the Working Classes', the organizers hoping to transplant a 'slice of England cut from top to bottom'.[18] Godley arrived in Lyttelton as the leader of the new settlement in April 1850 and spent two years in New Zealand acting as the de facto governor of Canterbury. The first four ships carrying immigrants arrived in December 1850 and within a year a further fifteen ships had arrived bringing the population of the settlement to over 3,000. Initially, the 'streets' of Christchurch, writes a Canterbury historian, 'were little more than ploughed furrows through tussock and toetoe'.[19] Though extensive pastoralism developed on the Canterbury Plains, most of the Canterbury Association settlers set up homes in or about Lyttelton and Christchurch.

Christchurch began life as a wooden settlement, a scattered village of small wooden buildings awaiting the day when wood would be replaced by masonry. Many colonists built huts along the banks of the Avon in what is now North Hagley Park, weatherboard fronts, hinged doors, and framed glass windows under Maori whare-style 'V' roofs thatched with native flax. But right from the start it was properly laid out in accordance with British ideas about town planning. Edward Jollie's map of 1850 shows Town Reserves, Hagley Park, and the Government Domain (now the botanic gardens), and the grid-based street system, starting at Antigua Street, which ran the length of the eastern boundary adjacent to the Government Domain and Hagley Park encircling it. In the middle of the original grid sat Cathedral Square. Formal geometric lay-out followed the fashion of the day, streets arranged on a grid broken by the course of the Avon River, and diagonal roads, the first leading from the city to Ferrymead, and the second to Papanui Bush.

In 1864 the Canterbury Horticultural and Acclimatisation Society was established and it soon decided to create a botanic garden in Hagley Park. It was agreed that the Government Domain would be used, and that plants and animals that might be useful in the colony would be introduced and first established there in order to see how well they adapted to the climate. The Canterbury Acclimatisation Society developed aviaries and fish-breeding ponds and in the 1860s trout arrived from Tasmania and salmon ova from Britain. Within fifteen years all the streams and lakes of Canterbury were stocked. Hundreds of thrushes, blackbirds, linnets, and skylarks acclimatized here, and pheasants, doves, Canadian geese, partridges, redpolls, rooks, finches, and emus were also imported. There were also animal enclosures, for silk worms, deer, ferrets, kangaroos, monkeys, even a tortoise and a Californian bear. The area became known as 'the zoo' until the Acclimatisation Society was relocated in 1928. (The area is now 'The Woodland', planted with hundreds of deciduous trees such as oak and ash.)

Christchurch was envisioned as an especially civilized settlement, an Oxford of the Southern Hemisphere, its status underpinned by prosperous economic activity and embellished by its cathedral, college, Gothic architecture, gardens, and intellectual infrastructure, which included a noted museum. The new cathedral and public buildings represented the considerable ambitions that men like Wakefield entertained for Christchurch, a model garden city that was to represent the highest Victorian municipal ideals, a centre of education and intellectual endeavour for the whole of New Zealand. The city's status as a seat of learning was important; Wellington was the seat of government, Auckland the commercial capital, and Dunedin the financial centre. Christchurch needed something of its own to shout about, and education and greenery were it. Improving societies, educational institutions, and newspapers were founded almost immediately. These included Christ's College, a colonists' society, a masonic lodge, the Christchurch Club, and a mechanics' institute. There was a musical society, an agricultural and pastoral association, an acclimatization society, and churches of all denominations. The museum was built in Hagley Park at the other end of Worcester Street from Cathedral Square in an area zoned in Edward Jollie's original plan of 1850 for intellectual and cultural institutions.[20] It stands next to Christ's College, both buildings backing onto the park and adjacent to the Botanic Gardens.

The natural environment

The native vegetation of Hagley Park and the botanic gardens was almost entirely eliminated by the nineteenth-century plantings. Native plants such as ferns, tussock, cabbage trees, and flax were replaced by 'English' plants, such as beech, elm, chestnuts, pines, and oaks. The first recorded major plantings in Hagley Park were the avenue of Oriental plane trees in the North Park in 1870. Pines were also planted in 1870 in the north-east corner of the park and near the swamp which later became Victoria Lake. The line of Wellingtonias by the United Tennis Club courts across the river from the gardens was also in place by the 1870s. Between 1870 and 1872 the tree nursery produced 763,034 trees, which were distributed throughout Canterbury, including the thousands of oaks planted by the Railway Department along the south line.[21] Government Gardener Enoch Barker established a nursery and planted an avenue of trees around the park. Plants first arrived from Tasmania and later from China, India, and Nepal. Most early curators had trained on English or Scottish estates and were steeped in Victorian and Edwardian gardening fashions. In the 1870s and 1880s Scotsman John Armstrong as curator was keen on local flora, but introduced and acclimatized 4,000 alien plant species, many of which arrived by sailing ship in Wardian cases.

The 'garden city' sobriquet had been used by numerous American cities as part of the 'City Beautiful' movement. The designation was first conferred upon Christchurch by Sir John Gorst when he revisited the country where he had lived as a young man. He had in mind the sort of city being advocated by the British Garden City Movement. But the term as it was applied to Christchurch soon lost the architectural and town-planning overtones of the British concept and was understood to refer to the presence in Christchurch of extensive public and private gardens. The settler community of Christchurch fostered a strong tradition of home gardening. The Christchurch Beautifying Association and the Horticultural Society ran competitions, and the former was instrumental in the ornamental planting of the city's streets. There were more specialist groups too, such as the Sweet Pea Association. People competed in street competitions, best-kept garden competitions, and competitions for factory gardens and railway station gardens.

Hagley Park was from the beginning associated with sports and leisure activities. A cricket club was established in June 1851, and a match was played at the sports meeting held amidst the tussock and scrub of Hagley Park in December 1851 to mark the first anniversary of the Canterbury Settlement. Foot and horse races also marked the occasion, and the *Lyttelton Times* commented that it was hard to believe that the settlement had only been there for one year, 'so English was the appearance presented by that part of the great grassy plain in which the revellers assembled'.[22] Later a cricket oval and pavilion were built in South Hagley Park. Archery Lawn, adjacent to the Herbaceous Border in the botanic gardens, was one of first parts of the Government Domain to be levelled and sown as a lawn, and between 1873 and the early 1900s it was a meeting place for those engaging in sports such as archery and croquet. The first golf course was established in the park in 1873. If one was of a more aquatic bent, it was possible to punt through the botanic gardens from the Antigua Street boat sheds. Horse racing was first held in the park in 1851, there was a championship bicycle meeting in 1880, and roller-skating also developed as a popular activity. In 1906 over 100 acres of Hagley Park was used for the New Zealand International Exhibition, 14 acres of which was covered with temporary buildings including a Maori pa built alongside Lake Victoria. One of the enormous exhibition entrance towers contained a lift so that people could view the city. Hagley Park found other interesting uses, too, such as the occasion in 1885 when it was the scene of a protest against a new railway line attended by 25,000 people.

The Domain Board responsible for the botanic gardens began attempts to cultivate plants such as olives, tobacco, and arrowroot in an effort to finance its upkeep. The botanic garden also developed standard ornamental and feature beds and borders. There were azalea and magnolia gardens, a New Zealand garden, and an Australian border. The first rose garden was established in 1909, the largest in Australasia containing 132 beds and 2,500 rose bushes. It was redeveloped in the mid-1930s with four paths converging at a mirror pool in the middle of a circular design (the pool later replaced by a sundial). Gravel and stone excavated from the Water Garden was used to build many of the paths of the growing city, and the pits left behind were developed as a cluster of ponds. In 1917 the development of a rock garden began. As the gardens were hewn from the natural environment, the gravel, sand, and timber removed was used in the construction of the city growing up around Hagley Park.

The botanic garden became home to numerous buildings, including a range of conservatories. Advances in the manufacture of iron and glass had introduced prefabricated parts into building technology, enabling the construction of large-scale conservatories with curving sides and glass roofs admitting the maximum amount of sunlight.[23] In 1844 Decimus Burton, working with iron-founder Richard Turner, had built the Palm House at Kew, 363 feet long by 100 feet wide and 66 feet high, influencing the erection of similar, if more modest, structures in colonial botanic gardens such as Christchurch. Here, Cunningham House was a large Victorian glasshouse with a tropical collection and an orchid and a cactus house attached. Another conservatory building was Townend House, an elegant begonia house given by Annie Quayle Townend, a noted early settler (the current Townend

Figure 16. Christchurch Botanic Gardens: Cunningham House and Central Rose Garden. (NB: photograph was taken sometime after 1925 and before 1939 as there was a new rose garden by then replacing the one shown in this image.)

House is a 1950s replacement). Other buildings included a Tudor-style Curator's House erected in the 1920s, now used, according to the garden's official walking guide, for 'fine dining and education'.[24] The gardens were also home to the Magnetic Observatory (1901), where explorers such as Scott and Shackleton calibrated their equipment before heading for the South Pole. The Climatological Station and Magnetic Observatory took daily readings for over a century, measuring cloud cover, visibility, wind direction, and rainfall, information that was sent to the national Meteorological Service.

European settlement had changed the natural landscape and ecosystem in fundamental ways, including the almost total eradication of wetlands and displacement of native vegetation. In the late twentieth century, a new focus on retaining what was left of the city's natural heritage emerged, and a focus on replanting with native rather than exotic species became evident in the city's management of public open spaces. Many New Zealanders came to dislike the work of the Acclimatisation Society and wanted a return to nativism. People came to value the very 'wilderness' that the first settlers had been so determined to eradicate. The area of surviving bush around Deans farm was bought by the city, preserving a small patch of swamp forest in the midst of an urban landscape now heavily dominated by introduced species such as oaks, limes, willows, poplars, Tasmanian blue gum, pines, macrocarpa, and the like. Travis Swamp was also purchased by the city council. From a vision of England in a distant land to a celebration of New Zealand's native flora, fauna, and culture, things had come full circle—though the land had been transformed along the way.

In 2011, the city and its Botanic Gardens were extensively damaged by a 7.1 magnitude earthquake.

5

Gezira Sporting Club, Cairo

The island of Zamalek, also known as Gezira Island, lies in the middle of the Nile as it flows through central Cairo, a hop, skip, and a jump from the British Residency, the Museum of Egyptian Antiquities, and Tahrir Square.* A corniche road lined with flame trees runs along the front of the Gezira Palace (now a sumptuous Marriott hotel), the Nile on one side and elegant turn-of-the-century buildings on the other. The names of these buildings—Dorchester House, Park Lane, Nile View— evoke the days of British prominence in this part of Cairo. Just beyond them lies the main entrance to the Gezira Sporting Club, its trim lawns and playing fields occupying 100 acres of what was once a botanic garden laid out as part of Khedive Ismail's vision of a perfect city.[1] The main entrance lies on the bustling Al Saray al-Gezira Street, though there are four other entrances spaced out at intervals around the club's extensive perimeter wall.

From the 1880s until the 1950s the Gezira Sporting Club was a bastion of the colonial elite, an English enclave in the middle of one of the world's most venerable cities. Along with the Turf Club it was often described as the British 'headquarters' in Cairo. It was a home away from home for privileged Britons, and widely regarded as the finest sporting club in the world. It became central to the nostalgic memories of colonial Cairo following the British ejection from Egypt in the 1950s:

> One could dance all night and as dawn came up ride out to Mena House for an early morning swim followed by a large breakfast before going out into the

---

* Gezira Island is commonly known as Zamalek, 'Gezira' meaning 'island' in Arabic. To confuse things further, the northern end of Zamalek/Gezira Island is often referred to as the Zamalek district, the southern end, including the Gezira Sporting Club, as Gezira. To avoid confusion, Zamalek is adopted here as the name of the entire island.

desert to shoot; and after a siesta, spend the afternoon at the club in preparation for dressing for dinner and starting the whole thing over again.[2]

In this bygone age, the club was a feature of daily life for many Britons.
'I used to lunch off sandwiches and beer by the Lido swimming-pool at
Gezira', recalled Laurence Grafftey-Smith in 1916. Here on Zamalek 'pashas
and senior British officials had their elegant villas and the Royal Flying
Corps their headquarters in the Gezira Palace Hotel'.[3]

The history of the iconic Gezira Sporting Club—which since its foundation in the 1880s has been the most prominent sporting club in the Middle East—allows us to consider colonial constructions in a part of the world
that was not officially British, but in which British power was strongly
manifest. Britain was in Egypt because of the strategic significance of the
Suez Canal, and from the moment its 'temporary occupation' began in 1882
until the nationalization of the Canal by Gamal Abdel Nasser in 1956, Britain's military presence compromised the independence of this proud country, and was widely resented.

Despite the dominant role that the British came to play in the history
of modern Cairo, much of the city's European-influenced architecture was
French or Italian or, in the case of the remarkable garden city suburb of
Heliopolis, the result of the activities of a Belgian industrialist and amateur
Egyptologist, Baron-General Edouard Loius Empain, whose whacky
'palace', inspired by Angkor Wat in Cambodia, can still be seen, forlorn and
deserted beside a busy road. But the Gezira Sporting Club, built on a prime
spot of central Cairo real estate, was very British. Soon after the invasion,
Khedive Tewfiq had been persuaded to lease the British Army a piece of
land carved from his botanical and palace gardens on Zamalek. What developed was a British officers' sports and social club that became an elite
expatriate watering hole and social and recreational venue. It contained
polo, cricket, and hockey grounds as well as shaded pavilions, tennis courts,
and croquet lawns, all centred on a Lido surrounded by the club's administrative buildings. As well as demonstrating the role played by sport in
British imperial society, the 'GSC' reflects the importance of the social
space provided by 'the club', and the distance between alien and indigenous
society that it emphasized. Even though there were a few members drawn
from the upper echelons of Egyptian society, the Gezira was very much a
European club, and 'local' members sometimes suffered the indignity of
being barred from 'European only' events.

Clubs

Throughout the colonial world the club was a place for social interaction and the reaffirmation of cultural identity. In British enclaves overseas everyone tended to belong to a club. It provided a meeting place, a centre for all kinds of sports and games and regulated social activities such as dancing and gaming. It was the place where expatriates could gossip, eat, drink, and play bridge and an array of sports, shielded from the gaze of the indigenous people amongst whom they lived and worked as a racially exclusive ruling elite. Margaret Sheenan strikes a familiar chord when describing her experience of the clubland of the British Empire:

> We lived the life of Riley. We were looked after by our servants. We had a nice garden. It was easy to get into clubs— Tanglin, Singapore Yacht Club ... It was a very leisurely life. We knocked off at five o'clock. No overtime ... Every Saturday night we were dancing at the Tanglin Club or the Swimming Club or somewhere, always in black tie, of course—we even wore black tie to go to the cinema in those days.[4]

The British established social clubs, sporting clubs, yacht clubs, gymkhana clubs and the like wherever they went, essential social institutions alongside masonic lodges, racecourses, theatres, and libraries. They built them in an array of styles, from plain bungalow-style premises to the grandest of confections such as the Royal Bombay Yacht Club, a curious mixture of Hindu and Swiss, or the mock-Tudor of the Selangor Club, known as 'the Spotted Dog', founded in Kuala Lumpur in 1884.

To this day the traveller might happen upon a club still run as if the imperial masters had never departed, long bars, leather armchairs, sporting prints, slow-moving punkhas stirring the heavy afternoon air as immaculately uniformed servants carry drinks on silver trays. The club has even become part of the heritage industry in neo-colonial societies, a tourist attraction offered to those pursuing nostalgia and luxury with delicate hints of deference and a sense of 'what it must have felt like' to be a sahib. In 2010 the Shanghai Club was reopened for the first time since the Japanese invasion of 1941 ended the period of European dominance. After being put to several different uses, including a brief spell as Shanghai's first Kentucky Fried Chicken outlet, Waldorf Astoria restored the club to its original glory with the express intention of recreating the atmosphere of colonial Shanghai. Noël Coward once remarked of the club's famous 110-foot Long Bar that 'one could see the curvature of the earth along it'.[5] The club's elegant lobby featured a barrelled glass ceiling, columns, a marble floor, and the first lifts to be imported into China.

The club was probably the most important social institution of the Empire. As George Orwell put it in *Burmese Days*, 'in any town in India the European Club is the spiritual citadel, the real seat of British power, the Nirvana for which native officials and millionaires pine in vain'.[6] Even for the pukka Briton, a member of the Indian Civil Service or a swish cavalry regiment, say, clubdom at home and overseas represented a carefully graded ladder, progress along which depended upon background, the prestige of your employer, your seniority, and the size of your purse. Socializing with fellow Europeans, playing sport, and attending functions was part of the encouraged culture of settlers, colonial administrators, and military officers. The club provided important functions—such as helping to prevent loneliness or the temptation of getting too familiar with the locals, frowned upon in racially segregated societies. It also provided practical services such as accommodation and a forward mailing address. Clubs also maintained, as they still do, reciprocal arrangements with other clubs, so a person travelling around the world could enjoy club facilities in other cities by virtue of his 'home' club membership.

Different types of expatriates had access to different types of clubs. For the more raffish and distinctly upper crust there were establishments such as Kenya's famous Muthaiga Country Club which opened on New Year's Eve 1913. It began as a home from home for settlers making their way to Nairobi for Race Week because the Nairobi Club was the preserve of colonial officials, whom did not always see eye to eye with the settlers. The Muthaiga became part of the lore of 'white mischief' Kenya, the unofficial headquarters of the colony's hedonistic, drink- and drug-fuelled settlers (the truth, naturally, was somewhat less brazen). It was here that Karen Blixen first met Denys Finch Hatton in 1918.[7] In contrast, the Gezira Sporting Club was an establishment club for the 'high ups' drawn from the official community: not a club of mavericks and rebels like the Muthagai; certainly not a club for box-wallahs or aspiring indigenes and creoles. Nor was it for the middle- or lower-level employees of Barclays, Thomas Cook, or the government. There were very few Egyptian members, and those who were on the books were royals, such as King Farouk, pashas, and beys. There was also a smattering of other Europeans and Armenians and Jews.[8]

Figure 17. Aerial photograph of Cairo showing the location of the Gezira Sporting Club in relation to the Nile. Taken from the Cairo Tower, one gets a sense of the expanse of open space occupied by the Club's grounds in a crowded city. Visible upper centre right, a square building is a wing of the Marriott Hotel. On its other side is the original Khedival Palace, now the showpiece centre of this hotel.

Cairo and Zamalek Island

Despite Cairo's status as one of the world's great cities and centres of civilization, in the nineteenth century the British came as rulers and added their own concepts of urban life, laying out distinct spatial zones and creating their own institutions. Commonly they usurped the cultural and architectural heritage of those among whom they were temporarily resident: in spite of its glories and its former power, Cairo became a playground for the British, epitomized by the 'tarboosh game', in which British servicemen travelling on the back of lorries would entertain themselves by knocking the fezzes off the heads of Egyptian men, and by their appropriation of the Pyramids.

Separation from the indigenous city was an enduring theme of the colonial experience in Cairo, as Europeans created gated communities and cultural enclaves. Penelope Lively recalls her youth in colonial Cairo:

> It was home, the only place I knew, but even then I realized our mystifying otherness, that apparently we really belonged to a distant green land that

I could not imagine. And I also saw that Cairo and Egypt, with which I identified entirely, were a wonderful, vibrant, and bewildering brew of people and
that, here, everything happened at once—time became insignificant. Pharaonic,
Roman, Greek, Mamluke, the boulevards of the nineteenth century—everything co-existed. We went out to the Pyramids or up to the Citadel, we ate
ice-creams at Groppi's and swam in the long blue pool at Gezira Sporting
Club—experiences to be savoured in different ways and which pointed up
the city's dizzying span.[9]

The influx of Europeans and the demands of elite Khedival society—especially the Europeanizing proclivities of an influential Khedive—encouraged
the establishment of the amenities necessary to service them, such as hotels
and clubs, theatres, and opera houses. New guidebooks, such as John Murray's *Guidebook to Egypt* (1858) and Baedeker's publications, offered advice
on what to take and what to see, as Cairo became an extension of the latter-
day Grand Tour and a magnet for literary tourists. Old Cairo hands such as
Ronald Storr mourned the 'multiplication of hotels, and the mass production of peach-fed standardized tourists "doing" the whole country in ten
days'. During the Second World War, amidst the bustle of Cairo as the strug-
gle in the Western Desert ebbed and flowed and the city hosted tens of
thousands of imperial servicemen, the Gezira Sporting Club was an oasis of
calm. The city's wartime atmosphere is ably evoked in books such as Artemis
Cooper, *Cairo at War*; Noel Barber, *A Woman of Cairo*; and Olivia Manning,
The Levant Trilogy.

   During the course of the nineteenth century Cairo changed dramatically
as the manifestations of previous cultures—Pharaonic, Christian, Islamic—
were joined by those of the Europeans, especially the British, and the Khe-
dives. Khedive Ismail presided over the growth of a new, Europeanized
Cairo adding another distinct layer to the city's history. Obsessed with European styles and manners, his extravagant developments were to be his and
his country's downfall, because the indebtedness they created sucked in
foreign financiers and then foreign soldiers and administrators. Ismail aimed
to transform Egypt into a European-style country, reorganizing its institutions and transforming its built environment. He spent vast sums of borrowed money building new palaces and idyllic gardens, railways, roads,
canals, bridges, street lighting, schools, an opera house, and a racecourse.

   Ismail attempted to remodel Cairo in the manner of Haussmann's Paris,
with wide tree-lined boulevards, palaces, department stores, and elegant
parks. Cosmopolitan establishments such as the Continental Hotel overlooking

the Ezbekiya Gardens were opened for rich visitors and residents. After the British occupation, Cairo became home to British soldiers and administrators, unwelcome invaders whose presence was resented. The opening of the Suez Canal had already caused a heavier European presence and now the expatriate community grew. They dwelt in newly built districts that bore a deliberate resemblance to the smarter parts of London, with the Gezira Sporting Club, modelled on the Hurlingham Club, serving as their playground. Like Garden City on the other side of the Nile, Zamalek was a premier location in which colonials made their homes. Here there were dances all the time, and hotels containing well-groomed and eligible young men and women to attend them, along with the recreational activities of the Gezira Sporting Club.

What the British created on Zamalek was an island playground that had more in common with the English Home Counties than with Cairo.[10] There was an expansion in hotels and tours. P&O liners deposited travellers, Nile steamers boomed, and Thomas Cook set up an office in Shepheard's Hotel. As William Fullerton wrote in 1891 'with the polo, the balls, the races, and the riding, Cairo begins to impress itself as an English town'.[11] There was the St James's Grill Room and the Savoy Buffet, and bars such as the New Bar and the Sphinx sold Allsop's and Bass ales.

By the 1920s, a number of prominent Egyptian civil servants and rich landowners had built houses on Zamalek, forming an elite group whose way of life was manifestly more Westernized than that of their forebears. It boasted shaded streets where acacias and poincianas—the famous 'flamboyant' or 'flame' trees—bloomed with vibrant colour in summer. The elegant Qasr al-Nil Bridge, decorated with lampposts and guarded by four bronze lions, was erected by a British company in 1933. The Bulaq Bridge carried a tramway crossing the island from east to west.

Edward Said grew up here in the 1940s. 'Zamalek was not a real community but a sort of colonial outpost whose tone was set by Europeans with whom we had little or no contact... We built our own world within it.'[12] On the other side of the fence, Penelope Lively remembers 'growing up in accordance with the teachings of one culture but surrounded by the symbols of another. Egypt was my home, and all that I knew, but I realized in some perverse way that I was not truly a part of it. [Being English] was of central importance—you were never allowed to forget that—but what it meant I could not possibly have said.'[13] The European elite experience revolved around clubs such as the Gezira and the Turf, Groppi's coffee house, trips on Sunday afternoons to the Mena House Hotel, and picnics in the desert. Humphrey Bowman, a teacher, described the separation between Europeans and Egyptians:

> There was little or no friendly intercourse between them and their pupils; as soon as their work was over, the English masters escaped on their bicycles to the sporting club at Gezira, there to indulge in their own games of golf or tennis or squash racquets, or to sit and gossip at the Turf Club over tea or a whisky and soda with their English friends.[14]

Apart from the mud huts of the fellahin who had occupied the island since it was formed from the deposits of the Nile's inexorable ebb and flow, the sumptuous Gezira Palace had been the first building constructed there. Until the annual floods were partially brought under control by the barrage dams, particularly the first Aswan dam of 1902, little permanent construction was possible on the island. It was Khedive Ismail who transformed it. He commissioned landscaped gardens and nurseries laid out by Delchevalerie, the one-time landscaper of Paris, who also added a U-shaped baroque summer palace. This, the beautiful Gezira Palace, was designed by Julius Franz Pasha and decorated both externally and internally by Karl von Diebitsch. (Once home to the Royal Flying Corps, it is now the Marriott Cairo hotel and boasts beautifully preserved original interiors.)

The Gezira Palace was one of the many Khedival indulgences responsible for bankrupting Egypt. Completed in 1869 and contiguous to the land that would become the Gezira Sporting Club, it was built to impress Ismail's crème-de-la-crème European visitors as they congregated in Cairo for the grand opening of the Suez Canal. In particular, the palace was designed to impress Empress Eugénie, wife of Napoleon III. Its architecture and interior reflected the Khedive's passion for the neo-classical style popularized in Europe. Von Diebitsch, who had studied Islamic architecture and gained fame with entries submitted for the 1851 Great Exhibition in London, designed the interiors. With ornate ceilings and cast iron balconies, the palace's opulent salons included an exact replica of Empress Eugénie's apartment in the Tuileries palace on the banks of the Seine. Oil paintings, furniture, and chandeliers were brought from Europe, many of the items that came to adorn the palace purchased at the 1867 Paris Exhibition. The palace garden, now at the heart of the Marriot Hotel complex, was laid out by Jean-Pierre Barillet-Deschamps, designer of many public parks in Paris.

From this lush Khedival estate on Zamalek, the Gezira Sporting Club was to be formed.

The Gezira Sporting Club

The Gezira Sporting Club was originally named the Khedival Sporting Club, the least the British could do as it was built on land leased by Khedive Tewfik (reigned 1878–92) who gave 146 feddans (a feddan is 1.038 acres) to the British High Command. The name was changed in 1914 to the Gezira Sporting Club because, technically, the British were now at war with the Khedive because Egypt was, again, technically, still part of the Ottoman Empire. Club rules were chartered and the land divided into different recreational playing grounds. At first, the club was for the use of the British Army of Occupation, with a distinctly equestrian focus though also featuring a golf course. It was modelled on the Hurlingham Club which had recently opened on the banks of the Thames at Fulham and which became polo headquarters when the game was introduced to Britain in 1869. Beyond its sporting appeal, polo provided excellent training in horsemanship, allowing the Army to gauge the competence of potential recruits to the cavalry regiments. 'It is on Gezira polo grounds that the officers of the Cavalry Brigade are tested for military efficiency and fitness for command', remarked a British administrator, 'and on Gezira tennis courts that examinations are held to decide as to the desirability or otherwise of retaining in the service the British officials of the Government.'[15]

Beyond its military utility, the club was a place for elite recreation and the reaffirmation of elite status. By virtue of this fact, it was socially and racially divisive. On the issue of barring Egyptians from the Gezira Sporting Club, Percy Martin lamented:

> The want of consideration for the native population particularly the better classes permanently inhabiting the countries in which British men and women but temporarily reside, has frequently provided one of the greatest drawbacks to the gaining of popularity and friendship, even when other of our national virtues are generously recognized...No actual rule as to the exclusion of the Egyptians from the Sporting Club exists; but the natives are not welcomed, and doubtless find themselves ordinarily de trop.[16]

Regarding their separation, William Basil Worsfold, editor of the *Johannesburg Star* in the early twentieth century, wrote that the 'English residents have no

more to do with the picturesque ruins and mud-heaps of Medieval Cairo
than the average West Londoner has to do with the Mile End Road and
Tower Hamlets. Except when they wanted to show a visitor the tombs
of the Khalifs or the Pyramids they only left their villas in the European
quarter to drive to their offices or the Gezira Club.'[17]

Edward Said offers a powerful illustration of this no-man's-land of
belonging but not belonging, and the damage that it caused. Attending the
British-run Gezira Preparatory School during the Second World War, being
taught about the Battle of Hastings and Edward the Confessor, he had what
he termed an 'explicit colonial encounter' in the club's grounds:

> Coming home at dusk across one of the vast outlying fields of the Gezira
> Club, I was accosted by a brown-suited Englishman with a pith helmet on his
> head and a small black briefcase hanging from his bicycle handlebars. This
> was Mr Pilley, known to me in writing as 'Hon. Sec'y' of the club, and also as
> the father of Ralph, a GPS contemporary of mine. 'What are you doing here,
> boy?', he challenged me in a cold, reedy voice. 'Going home', I said trying to
> be calm as he dismounted from his bicycle and walked toward me. 'Don't you
> know you're not supposed to be here?', he asked reprovingly. I started to say
> something about being a member, but he cut me off pitilessly. 'Don't answer
> back, boy. Just get out, and do it quickly. Arabs aren't allowed here, and you're
> an Arab!' If I hadn't thought of myself as an Arab before, I now directly grasped
> the significance of the designation as truly disabling.[18]

Sports and leisure activities, manners, and social ostracism, argues the
social and cultural historian Jean-Marc Oppenheim, were all elements of
socio-cultural imperialism that bequeathed values reflecting the dominance of the colonizer's culture and habits. Functioning as an agency of
social control the Gezira was unique because it was the paramount social
symbol of British hegemony in the country, and it established policies that
confirmed its exclusivity and, in particular, its exclusionary practices. The
club's structure and attitudes were intensely political and bound up with
the alien colonial regime. Until 1914 the General Officer Commanding
the Army of Occupation acted as club president, a role subsequently
assumed by the British High Commissioner. As late as 1951 the British
ambassador was still the president. When Sir Lee Stack, Sirdar of the Egyptian Army and Governor-General of the Anglo-Egyptian Sudan and vice-
patron of the club, was assassinated by nationalists in Cairo in 1924, the
club curtailed all social and sporting activities and cancelled the racing
calendar. The action underlined the spirit prevalent among the club's

decision-makers: that the politically motivated violent death of a member of their fraternity warranted collective action, thus denoting the chasm between the colonizers and colonized.[19]

Aware of the political and social sensitivities that club membership stimulated, when the club committee decided to offer a vice-patronship to the next in line to the Egyptian throne, it sought the views of the British Residency. When it approved, the Resident, as club president, formally presented the offer to the prince. Here the club acted as a reinforcement of the link between British policy and the Egyptian monarchy.

The club could offend its Egyptian members. A celebratory dinner for the Prince of Wales and his brother the Duke of Gloucester in 1928, for example, was declared by the general committee to be 'British subjects' only. Then the club might only fly the Union flag on race days where protocol would dictate also flying the flag of 'independent' Egypt. Another example of insensitivity was provided by the uniforms of the golf caddies—blue galabiehs, white caps, and red sashes—the colours of the Union Jack. Tennis ball boys received the same uniform in 1918, and both remained in use until the 1952 revolution swept the British out of their club and out of Cairo.

Club life

By 1909 the club had thirteen tennis courts, eight croquet pitches, four polo grounds, hockey and football grounds, a cricket pitch, six squash courts, a twelve-hole golf course, two racecourses, a training track, and of course a tea pavilion. A border of tumbling jacaranda surrounded the golf course. A new dining building was completed in time for the 1929 Christmas dance. With a veranda facing the cricket pitch, its oak parquet made an excellent dance floor, and there was an assembly room above looking down into the hall, from where the wallflowers could view proceedings. On normal days, tea was served and family bridge played on this upper floor.

The Lido became the club's focal point, approached along a main drive flanked by administrative and social buildings. Together, the buildings created a space of tranquillity, with their well-maintained walkways and lush foliage. The Lido, erected in 1935, is well maintained to this day. Its facilities retain their original features. The men's changing room for instance, a long and lofty space, is dominated by wooden lockers and mirrors bearing the elegant craftsmanship of their 1930s manufacturers. Behind them lies a

Figure 18. The Lido building, Gezira Sporting Club. Erected in 1935, it is the main building facing the visitor as he or she enters along the Club's main entrance drive. On the other side of this edifice is a swimming pool and terrace, to the left some charming old club buildings and on the right the New Club Building. Note the acronym 'GSC' marked out in flowers in the foreground. The Lido flies the Egyptian flag on the left, and the Club flag on the right.

bustling barber's shop, again an original feature. The deceptively large building also contains a gymnasium, a ladies hairdresser, balconies and terraces and, upstairs, separate men's and women's lounges where children are not permitted. It is a square, stuccoed building, painted cream and dark red, flanked by two wings angled around a large swimming pool with extensive terraces.[20]

The Gezira was a little piece of Victorian England, where proper decorum *à l'anglaise*, discipline, and high standards of sportsmanship were preserved.[21] The dining room served typically British meals, including Welsh rarebit, steak and kidney pie, scones and raisin cake for tea, and trifle for dessert. From their stuffy offices or their houses in Zamalek, people gathered under the awnings of the Lido for lunch. There was also a garden, in one corner of which was a pet cemetery, and a playground where nannies and their infant charges would congregate in the afternoons. This was kept

well away from the serious business of the club, which centred around racing and polo.

From the 1930s the club secretary was Captain Eric Charles Pilley (the
man who had chastised the young Edward Said), who bore the responsibility of protecting and preserving the club. Egyptians privileged enough to
visit regarded him as the epitome of Britishness, touring the grounds daily
on his bicycle and maintaining by his presence the exact orderliness of an
already extremely orderly set-up. Dogs were not allowed in the club grounds
but could be kept in the kennels. Children had to leave the club at sunset,
and Pilley's second in command, Mr Williams, known as 'The Control',
patrolled the premises tirelessly all day long. Pilley lived on site in a charming British-style house, surrounded by perfect lawns with multi-coloured
bougainvillea creeping up the walls.

As a club established for the army, regimental races were a feature, events
including the Lloyd Lindsay, Polo Race, Green Howard Sweepstakes, and
the Horseback Musical Chairs. Race meetings began at the Gezira Sporting
Club in the 1880s, initiated by the Sirdar (commanding officer) of the
Egyptian Army, General Frances Wallace Grenfell. The oldest club tournament, the Egyptian Army Cup, was inaugurated in 1905. There were ten or
twelve polo matches a year, and from 1908 a challenge cup was offered by
Seif Allah Yusry Pasha. Jockeys were imported from Britain and rode
Arabian horses smuggled from Syria via al-Arish and Kantarah, Sinai,
circumventing Turkish restrictions on their export. A regular winner in the
early days was a horse named Adeed, owned by the club's senior trainer. The
Anglo-Egyptians clamoured for the English mare Skittles, which was sent
from Malta and won. Soon the Cairo Derby had been established. The
club's race meetings were on the international social calendar, and the club's
grandstands included the King's Stand, the Grand Stand, and the Public
Stand.

The peculiarly British world of the gymkhana was recreated beside the
Nile. Boaters and straw hats mixed with fly swishes and turbaned Nubian
suffragis brandishing silver platters of game pie, roast beef, ham chops, and
cucumber sandwiches. The Winter Race Meetings were the principal event
of the year, rivalling in all but size those of Epsom and Newmarket. By the
1920s race days had become mini-Ascots with pre-race champagne lunch
parties and elegant women in white cotton dresses and straw summer hats.
Sir Henry 'Chips' Channon, the American-born Tory MP, visited Cairo in
1941, where he attended a race meeting at the Gezira with his hosts, Sir

Miles and Lady Lampson. He was delighted by the ceremonial formalities—
'God Save the King' played as the ambassador entered his box, dressed in a
grey frock-coat and topper, with Lady Lampson in a dress of silk ruffles and
a picture hat.[22] Ambassador Lamspon was himself a regular user of the club.
Once, he surprised a group of competition golfers as he strode across the
fairway with a pair of guns, a loader, and two boys. His targets were scaveng-
ing kites, for which he had a passionate hatred because they stole his golf
balls in the mistaken belief that they were eggs.[23]

By 1914 there were 750 British members, with the Consul-General by
tradition serving as the club's president (the title of the senior British diplomat in Egypt changed from Consul-General to Special Representative to
High Commissioner before finally settling on Ambassador in 1936). During
the First World War a volunteer reserve unit was formed by club members,
which called itself the Pharaoh's Foot. As well as sports and routine social
activities, the Gezira was renowned for its set-piece ceremonial events,
including parades such as the searchlight tattoo on the polo grounds in
honour of Edward, Prince of Wales. It also hosted other peculiarly British
institutions; Edward Said remembers the Cub Scouts meeting behind a shed
on the club grounds. Though initially a military club, it soon opened its
doors to civilians in order to enhance its recreational activities. Grafftey-
Smith wrote of the young debutantes who each year arrived 'to distract the
many eligible subalterns of various cavalry regiments':

> The British in Egypt then assumed that the sun rose and set in their centre,
> and for most British visitors this circle offered world enough: parties, picnics,
> eligible escort and a Gezira Sporting Club where every game could be played.
> The few denizens of a non-British world who were observable there, playing
> bridge or mah-jongg in bad French and good pearls, merely served as a foil
> for Anglo-Saxon attitudes.[24]

During the Second World War the Gezira became a Cairo landmark for tens
of thousands of imperial servicemen, though other ranks were only allowed
in on special occasions, such as in December 1940 when, following an
important victory at the Battle of Sidi Barrani, the club hosted a party for
3,000 soldiers at which Lady Lampson helped serve tea. The club was alive
with British officers, many of whom lived in Zamalek, some occupying
apartments overlooking the club. 'The polo fields and the surrounding flora
was a welcome sight especially the firs from Aberdeen, the azaleas from Sussex Gardens, and the beds of lavender from London', wrote Gerald Frank.

'At his window, listening to the self moans of doves outside, Lord Moyne, the former Leader of the House of Lords, could feast his eyes upon a corner of England itself.'[25] In British military establishments around Cairo the working day started at nine, and broke off at one. 'Then the officers headed for the Gezira Club', writes Artemis Cooper, 'to play tennis and swim, followed by lunch from the buffet piled with chicken, game pie, boiled and roast beef, ham and chops ... The afternoon's work started at four or five.'[26] Penelope Lively relished the 'intoxicating expanse of a real, chlorine-reeking, blue-tiled swimming pool, and green swards of grass with blinding white fences, and a babble of English voices'.[27]

From 1907 the Gezira Sporting Club was the home of Egypt's lawn tennis, with open tournaments and championships held on clay courts for trophies such as the Doherty and Slazenger cups. Noted early players included the Alexandrian Greek Auguste Zerlendi and Sir Cecil Campbell, Marconi's representative in Egypt. A new Centre Court built in 1952 to the design of Henri Fresco hosted a novel 'Holiday on Ice' show, and in 1954 it became a corrida for a bullfight. Centre Court at the northern end of the club's grounds has an air of dilapidation about it now, though still a significant structure. Its entrance hall features large, deteriorating wooden plaques bearing the names of the winners of the Egyptian Lawn Tennis Association's singles and doubles from the competition's inauguration in 1904 up until 1979, names including Pam Shriver, Ilie Nastasie, and Peter Fleming.

The Egyptians take over

Following the reduction of British troops in Cairo after the Anglo-Egyptian Treaty of 1936, the club acquired a strategic importance for the resident British authorities. A special club committee was appointed, comprising the British ambassador, the commander of the nearest British Army brigade, the club chairman, and a few others. Its purpose was to draw up contingency plans for transforming the club into a defended enclave for Cairo's British community in case of serious nationalist disturbances.[28] But despite such planning and mounting tension, to outward appearances at least, it seemed as if things had returned to colonial 'normality' with the end of hostilities in 1945. The Anglo-Egyptian upper crust carried on as they always had. The British still sipped their gin-slings on the terrace of Shepheard's Hotel, there was polo and racing at the Gezira Club, and dancing at the Auberge des Pyramides or Madame Badia's.

But this was a deceptive calm. In 1950, as part of its efforts to oust the British, the Egyptian government had exercised the right of eminent domain to expropriate the northern part of the Gezira Sporting Club to build the Mohamad Ali stadium. Luckily, the 1952 *coup d'état* occurred and the club, along with golf, were saved for a while. In 1952 the minister of interior announced that the club would be taken over for public utility purposes, effectively Egyptianizing this last British bastion. Moreover, all remaining British officials serving in universities, government schools, the ministry of public works, and the Egyptian state railways were dismissed. At this moment the club had 2,453 British members, 594 foreign, and 1,116 Egyptian. Alarmed at these developments, on 24 January 1952 Britain's ambassador, Sir Ralph Stevenson, resigned as club president, and the committee resigned too.

The clock stopped two days later—Saturday 26 January 1952. This was Black Saturday, a day that witnessed one of the most extraordinary upheavals in Cairo's long history. Zamalek was a ghost island and the city centre was in flames as British buildings and symbols were targeted. Barclays, Thomas Cook's offices, the Morris Motors showroom, the British Council, the Turf Club, Shepheard's Hotel—the supports of its spectacular dome melting in the flames and crashing to the Moorish hall below—were all attacked. Ten Britons were killed in the Turf Club fire on Maghrabi Street. The Gezira Club lay abandoned. 'The self-important inglizis and their self-serving toffee-nosed committees', as the club website, rather gleefully, puts it, 'were gone at last. No more Empire Day celebrations and coronation dances. No more parades and searchlight tattoos on the club's polo grounds with poppies raining from the sky.' The city that the British had known and loved virtually vanished overnight, wiped out by the breaking wave of Egyptian nationalism.

Long an offensive symbol in the minds of political and class-conscious Cairenes, the British era was over.[29] The club held an extraordinary general meeting on 29 February 1952. Significantly, for the first time, its subsequent announcement was printed in both English and Arabic, with greater prominence given to the latter. At the meeting a new Gezira Sporting Club board was elected, comprising Egyptian pashas and beys. A distinctly downsized Captain Pilley was asked to stay on as Club Secretary. But it was now very much an Egyptian club.

The Egyptian take-over soon manifested itself in other ways. Nasser was determined to show his power, to stamp his mark on Cairo, and to cut the Gezira Sporting Club down to size. Soon his Cairo Tower, the epitome of Egypt's vibrant new nationalism and independence, rose to dominate the skies above the club's grounds. Rising above the greenery of Zamalek, a slender wickerwork cylinder surmounted by a cluster of viewing galleries and communications masts, it soon became the city's most famous landmark after the Pyramids, as well as its tallest. Nasser also appropriated a huge chunk of the Sporting Club's grounds for the use of the poor. Thus the entire southern part of the club was converted into football fields, today a wasteland of pathways, litter, and dilapidated football pitches. He also split the club's grounds in two with a multi-lane freeway that crossed the Nile, running from downtown Cairo and the Tahrir Square area, across the Nile and Zamalek Island on high stilts, then across the Nile again on the other side of the island to the El Dokki area on the western bank of the Nile. This was the Sixth of October Bridge connecting the city to Cairo International Airport, the name commemorating the day on which Egyptian forces crossed the Bar-Lev Line at the start of the 1973 war with Israel.

After the Egyptian revolution, Zamalek became, in the opinion of Cairo historian Chafika Hamamasy, 'a microcosm of Egypt, a place where ugliness competes successfully with beauty, where attempts to maintain a modicum of aesthetic standards are an uphill battle fought daily by a few valiant souls'.[30] Yet here, as elsewhere in Cairo, British influences made lasting impressions, though Zamalek today stands very much as testament to the lives of Egyptians in their homeland, the aspirations of their first president for a truly independent nation, and his desire to commemorate in concrete a profound turning points in the nation's history. Until the 1950s Cairo was considered one of the most beautiful cities in the world, but its growing population and urban sprawl have transformed it. But the Gezira Sporting Club remains, still in many ways surprisingly the same. Despite its transformation (or perhaps because of it) the Gezira's socio-political symbolism continued. Now its role was to establish the new post-revolutionary social and political elites who emerged after the 1956 Suez Crisis, when Egypt's British and other foreign resident bourgeoisie—the bulk of the Gezira's membership—were either expelled from the country or encouraged to emigrate. In its original anachronistic form, the club would have no place in Nasser's Egypt; but its symbolism and its social and political role remained and continue to this day.[31]

The club today is a vibrant centre of activity, sport, and companionship serving as a verdant sanctuary in the middle of Cairo's urban core, with a bewildering array of things going on and places to explore.[32] There is a bowling green, track and field athletics, basketball, billiards tables above the little mosque, French billiards tables near the office of the notary in the grounds of the Cultural Centre, and croquet lawns (the club has produced several world champions). There is a dressage and show-jumping club and children's horse rides in the tree-lined avenue near the polo stables. Horse racing takes place every weekend during the winter months, and there is a Fencing Centre and a Gezira Soccer Academy. There is a nine-hole golf course, each hole having two greens—meaning eighteen holes are available—a driving range, chipping area, and putting green. There are world-class gymnastics facilities in a building near the Centre Court, handball, hockey, and ping pong. Though polo games now happen at polo fields in other areas of Cairo, the polo horses are still stabled near the western car-park exit from the club, and practices for the Gezira Polo Club are still held in the race track area.[33] Many of the world's top men and women squash players are members of the club, including Karim Darwish and Amr Shabana.

There is water polo and synchronized swimming, forty clay tennis courts, and volleyball. The club supports a range of cultural activities—bridge, cinema, exhibitions of members' work. There is a bank, a seasonal bazaar, a call centre, a doctor's surgery, internet, newsagent, notary, optician, pharmacy, plant store, post office, shoe shiner, and travel agent. Around Centre Court numerous activities take place, including aerobics, yoga, pilates, and massages. The impressive children's area features an arcade; biking; an extensive playground containing slides, swings, and frames; an air-conditioned baby-feeding and changing room; and a children's bookshop. There are numerous food outlets and restaurants—coffee shops, ice cream shacks, hamburger stands, the Rooftop Restaurant and the Elite Restaurant, a bean and falefal stand, and a barbeque garden.

The new club building has a spacious air-conditioned quiet room, a card room, three restaurants, a small library, and an outdoor terrace. The colonial-era villa where the club secretary once lived now acts as a Cultural Centre and library, set in a secluded garden. From here music lessons, painting and drawing classes, and day trips and excursions are organized. The administrative buildings include a membership renewal office in the first of the former colonial-era squash courts. With a new squash complex erected,

Figure 19. The Club Secretary's House, now the Club's Cultural Centre.

these buildings now accommodate ping-pong tables and a cinema showing the 'movie of the week'. There are two mosques, one in the north-east corner of the club, the other near the Tea Garden which lies just north of the New Club Building. There is a pergola near the small track, on the west side of which is an Astroturf pitch for mini-football. Other main buildings include the martial arts building near the Olympic Pool, itself an important addition to the pool on the Lido. People jog around the horseracing track and football pitches. There is a sauna in the men's gym and a masseuse, and one of the colonial-era grandstands lies near to the extensive warren of stables, alive with the activity of stable boys and grooms. On race days, the well-to-do inspect the horses in the paddock.

The flavour today is overwhelmingly Egyptian, and the Gezira has been 'dry' since 1980. The central administration office is occupied by numerous busy men and women, only one (on my visit) speaking any English. All noticeboard signs are in Arabic, as are club chits, invoices, business cards, and stationery. Though thousands use its facilities each day, Zamalek and its famous club are constantly under threat as Cairo expands. Recently the club had to fight off an attempt to develop a shopping centre on one of the football pitches of the Youth Sporting Club land appropriated by Nasser, as well as a car park. Yet despite the challenges, perhaps in part because of them, the club continues to flourish.

6

Kuala Lumpur Railway
Station, Malaya

The 'Two Sisters' are a pair of striking colonial buildings close to Kuala Lumpur's famous Merdeka Square. One is the headquarters of Keretapi Tana Melayu Berhad, the Malaysian Railways Limited, the other, standing opposite across a busy main road, is the city's former central railway station, built in extravagant Indo-Saracenic style. In 1913 J. F. Dijkotra, a visitor from the Dutch East Indies, beheld the Kuala Lumpur Railway Station with something approaching rapture:

> Out of proportion to the place...you cannot imagine yourself in the East. Going from the town of Kuala Lumpur to the Station is like going to the Gare du Nord in Paris. The Station is high like that in Weisbaden, and clean as the Central Station at Amsterdam, and hospitable as a London terminus.[1]

'The Taj Mahal of the Train World' was how others described this arresting snow-white building. 'There isn't a station anywhere to touch it', wrote the well-travelled Scottish railway enthusiast Adam Saylor. It gives the 'sense of an architect pining to create a Sultan's palace. It rose, sixty years ago, like a chandelier in a slum. Kuala Lumpur then was a pretty tawdry township, a community characterized by clusters of attap roofs'.[2] Kuala Lumpur Railway Station remains at the heart of the Malaysian capital, an important commuter hub and now also a hotel trading upon the building's heritage status.

The 'Two Sisters' are located on one of the main routes leading into the city centre, an arterial road during the evolution of this British-created city, and an arterial road still. In the colonial era it was known as Victory Avenue, since renamed Jalan Sultan Hishamuddin. It is a road flanked by a stunning sequence of colonial era 'Indo-Saracenic' buildings as it leads into Merdeka (meaning 'independence') Square, also known as the padang, a space at the

Figure 20. View of the Old Railway Station, Kuala Lumpur, 2011.

heart of the Malaysian nation as well as its capital city. The railway station and the railway administration building lead on to the General Post Office (now the Court of Appeal) and the stunning Sultan Ambdul Samad Building (1897), the major governmental complex of the state of Selangor during colonial times. Across the padang from these two splendid colonial structures stands the Royal Selangor Club (1884) with its mock-Tudor features. Completing the square is St Mary's Cathedral (1894) and, opposite, the National History Museum (1910), formerly headquarters of the Chartered Bank of India, Australia, and China.

The Sultan Abdul Samad Building and its 134-foot clock tower, known informally as 'Big Ben', is an Indo-Saracenic delight. It was named after the Sultan of Selangor and designed by A. C. Norman in the Mogul style that he had observed in Africa and India. With a cream stone appearance achieved by plaster-covered brick, it was the centre of British administration in the Selangor province, housing the Public Works Department, the Mines Department, the Sanitary Board, district offices, and the Treasury. The private members' Royal Selangor Club was built as a social centre for the city's elite, its original timber and attap-roofed structure replaced by the smart Tudor-style clubhouse.

These colonial buildings enclose the green expanse at the centre of Merdeka Square, the padang, formerly the cricket ground of the Royal Selangor Club. New architectural styles joined the colonial era buildings as

Kuala Lumpur developed into a federal capital in the 1950s and the cultural junction box of a new nation.[3] While in so many ways a quintessentially colonial space, Merdeka Square also became symbolically associated with the foundation of independent Malaysia. It was here that independence was officially marked as the Union flag was lowered for the last time, and the square now features a towering, 311-feet-tall flagstaff bearing a huge, slowly undulating Malaysian flag. This was a project of Prime Minister Mahathir Mohamad (in office 1981–2003), who wanted to erect the tallest flagpole in the world.[4] It stands on the spot where the new nation's flag was first unfurled on Independence Day 1957. Cricket is still occasionally played on the padang, and it is the focus for the annual National Day Parade. Towering above the buildings of Merdeka Square are modern skyscrapers of the post-colonial era, including the iconic 'twin towers' and the headquarters building of Petronas, Malaysia's flagship oil and gas company. It is a breathtaking space that fuses the old and the new.

Transport and communications

Many of the British Empire's most significant and long-lasting constructions were associated with the infrastructure of transport and communications. Private and public investment in railways, roads, bridges, and airports was central to the development of the Empire and part of the self-image of progress that its advocates perceived. Such technological developments, including submarine telegraphy and steamships, fostered ever-speedier communications, making the world a smaller place and deepening the inter-connectivity of the global economy. The Royal Mail, aided by subsidized private companies such as the Peninsula and Oriental Steam Navigation Company, contributed to the nineteenth-century communications revolution and enabled people in the 'British world' to keep in ever closer contact.

The British prided themselves on the technological advances that they pioneered and, as technical imperialists, gasworks and water-towers were as characteristic of their rule as courts of justice or government houses.[5] As befitted a maritime empire, the British acquired, improved, and created ports all over the world. Karachi was built by the British from scratch from what had been a humble fishing village when they arrived in 1838: engineers created a deep-water harbour by building a causeway to an offshore island

and dredging its basin. Remarkable feats of engineering accompanied British rule across the globe. The Ganges Canal, for example, opened in 1854, was one of the greatest works of engineering of its day, 810 miles long with 2,000 feeder canals.

In Tasmania, the first postal service was established in 1816, connecting Hobart in the south to Port Dalrymple at the mouth of the Tamar on the north coast. The Government Messenger, Robert Taylor, would leave Hobart on Sunday morning and travel the 120 miles north, and on the following Sunday reverse the process, most of the journey accomplished on foot and with no road to follow.[6] From such small acorns mighty oaks did grow: the post office on Bourke Street in Melbourne—which in 1855 looked like a 'Wild West' film set—grew into the enormous General Post Office building (now a shopping mall). By 1914, Cable and Wireless maintained 253 cable and wireless stations across the globe manned by over 8,000 staff.[7] The company and its network of cables, buildings, and staff controlled 164,000 nautical miles of submarine cable, over half the world total.[8]

In 1926 Lionel Fenzi drove a 12 horse-power Riley the 300 miles from Mombasa to Nairobi, pioneering what would become a major new arterial road. Fenzi, founder of the Royal East African Automobile Association (today's AA Kenya), had asked British car manufacturers to donate vehicles for him to test under trying conditions as he staked out major new road transport routes. Indicating the spread of this mode of transport, and the creation of dusty and precarious 'roads' that would eventually become major highways, by the time of Fenzi's 'capital to coast' journey the East African AA had over 2,000 members. Fenzi also pioneered the Nairobi–Dar-es-Salaam–Nyasaland route, and was the first man to drive from Nairobi to Khartoum.[9]

By the 1850s the British had linked Calcutta and Bombay by a metalled road running across the subcontinent; they had driven the Great Hindustan and Tibet Road through the foothills of the Himalayas to Simla; and they had recreated the Grand Trunk Road, otherwise known as the Grand Military Road, running from the outskirts of Calcutta to Peshawar, the gateway to Afghanistan. It was marked along its path by monumental milestones, transit camps for marching troops, official lodgings, police stations, post offices, and cemeteries for those who died along the way. In its last section alone, the 260 miles between Lahore and Peshawar, it crossed 550 bridges and tunnelled through six mountain ridges.[10]

Railways

Railways were strategic instruments.[11] In Central Asia, for example, they increased the threat to India and decreased the importance of the sea-power upon which Britain's strength was founded.[12] From the turn of the century, therefore, defence of empire in the east became inextricably tied to strategic railways, building them oneself or stopping rivals from building them. The British wanted a Baghdad to Haifa line in order to protect Iraq and link new Middle Eastern territories to the Mediterranean, but opposed German development of a Berlin to Baghdad line. In the north, the Russian Trans-Siberian line threatened India.

By 1930, over 146,000 miles of railway track had been laid in the Empire outside of Britain, and by 1920 some 1.2 billion passengers and 90 million tons of freight were carried annually on the Indian railway system.[13] Using the clever elision 'railpolitik', historians Thomas Otte and Keith Neilson argue that the growth of the railways from the 1840s fostered the development of modern capitalism and facilitated the birth of modern nations.[14] In Britain, the railway facilitated the growth of railway towns such as Crewe and Swindon. The phenomenon was soon translated to the colonial world, bringing with it the opening-up of communities previously lost in rural torpor, the ever-faster circulation of ideas, the deeper penetration of central government power, and the exchange of goods and services and development of extractive industries. Railways, steamships, and telegraph wires shrunk time and space within and between regions, and were a potent symbol of the colonizers' ability to cross continents and create vast new political entities such as Canada and India. (The Canadian Pacific Railway was central to the emergence of a unified Canada.)

A line through the Khyber Pass was completed in 1926, while the Darjeeling Railway (1878) climbed over 6,600 feet in 37 miles with gradients of up to 1:19.[15] The Khojak Tunnel, the longest in India when completed in 1891, carried the Chaman Extension Railway to the Afghan border. Commenced in 1883 it was a secret strategic line designed for the rapid deployment of troops over the frontier to Kandahar. The line also carried refrigerated fruit trains bearing grapes, peaches, and nectarines. Thousands of men were employed to drive the tunnel through the Khwaja Amran Mountains, including Welsh miners who had worked on the Severn Tunnel.[16] Eight hundred died in the winter of 1890 alone from typhus. The work was finished in three years—12,780 feet in length built with 20 million bricks fired on the spot. The tunnel was entered through a spectacular fortified entrance featuring castellated turrets and battlements, and high loops apparently for the pouring of burning oil.[17]

Seeking to expand its position in the world, Berlin viewed railway lines as vehicles for the projection of German influence. For their part, the British viewed railways as a diplomatic tool to block the expansionism of other powers. Both powers were also keenly aware of the commercial advantages to be accrued from involvement in worldwide railway expansion. Railways were one of the main instruments used in the opening-up of the non-European world, including South America, where the British were the main investors and builders of the Argentine railway system. Both the Central Argentine Railway Limited and the Buenos Ayres Great Southern Railway Company had their headquarters in London. Equipment, from locomotives to railway terminals and signal boxes, was shipped out from Britain and the first train to run along the Western Railway Company's track, Argentina's first, was built in Leeds.[18]

Railways often featured in the Empire's military ventures. Thirty years before Kitchener's railway helped him achieve victory at Omdurman in 1898, Lieutenant General Sir Robert Napier took 13,000 soldiers, 26,000 labourers, and over 40,000 animals, including elephants, from Bombay to the East African coast. In order to facilitate the unloading of the 280 ships transporting this mass of soldiers, ammunition, and equipment, a new port, complete with piers and warehouses was constructed, as was a narrow-gauge railway reaching 20 miles into the interior.[19] The Uganda Railway was viewed as an integral part of British efforts to shield the Upper Nile Valley against the designs of other powers in order to protect Britain's position in Egypt.[20] This 'Lunatic Express' was the railway line that drew the British government into the affairs of Uganda. Elsewhere in Africa, Cecil Rhodes dreamed of cementing British suzerainty from 'Cape to Cairo' by way of a transcontinental railway. In Ceylon, meanwhile, the Royal Engineers used dynamite to drive a railway into the central highlands in order to dominate the kingdom of Kandy in the central highlands.

Because of all of this development, the railway station became one of the most significant buildings of the age, the cathedral building of the nineteenth century, a monument to industrial and social progress.[21] Throughout the Empire, as in Britain itself, railway stations came in all different shapes and sizes, from the quaint rural halt to the grandiose urban landmark. Many

Anglo-Indian stations were simple wooden shelters built in local styles, or hill-station halts like resort bungalows. Some were built with defence and fortification in mind, and after the Indian Mutiny it was decreed that stations in the north should be easily defensible. The new station erected at Lahore in 1864 was built in this manner, a great fort with closable arches, turrets, musket slits, and a stone curtain wall.

There were then the striking set-piece stations, such as Victoria Terminal in Bombay, a vast edifice with a tower, like Wren's Tom Tower in Oxford, on top of it, and a multitude of galleries, loggias, and elaborate windows below. Opened in 1887 in time for Queen Victoria's Golden Jubilee, it is adorned with monkey gargoyles, sculpted dripstones, portraits of Victoria and colonial notables, heraldic medallions of elephants and locomotives, and an allegorical figure of Progress. The building featured domes, pinnacles, turrets, and Corinthian columns of polished Aberdeen granite.[22]

Kuala Lumpur and the Malayan railways

Kuala Lumpur was founded in 1857 as a trading post for miners at the confluence of the Klang and Gombak rivers. The early Chinese traders found that they could pole no further up-river than this point and so established a settlement to supply the tin mines at nearby Ampang.[23] Soon, Kuala Lumpur was being cut out of the secondary jungle beside a Chinese tin-mining settlement. Like many colonial settlements, the town developed a 'wild west' frontier edge, with gang wars, violence, and brawls. A major change in the settlement's fortunes came when Frank Swettenham, the British Resident in Selangor, moved his administration to Kuala Lumpur and rebuilt it from scratch, pulling down the wooden huts and replacing them with stone and brick structures. The development of the railways was associated with global economic shifts; as the Cornish tin industry became exhausted, deposits in Bolivia, Malaya, Nigeria, and Sumatra were turned to. As the tin industry expanded and European mining replaced established Chinese operations, new means of transport were needed; roads were very poor, bullock carts unsatisfactory. It was in this context that the railway made its first appearance in the 1880s.

The railway was integral to the development of Kuala Lumpur. In 1886 a line was constructed to connect the settlement to the port of Klang, and a decade later Kuala Lumpur became the capital of the Federated Malay

States. Wealth started to flood in from tin revenues, and the new tin millionaires built themselves impressive mansions along the Jalan Ampang.[24] The population grew rapidly, supplemented by thousands of Indians who arrived as labourers for the rubber plantations and men of the Ceylon Pioneer Corps brought in to build the railways. Earthworks, masonry, and locally sourced sleepers of hardwood were their materials, along with quarried ballast stone. The prospect of the Malayan railways becoming part of a great communications link between India and Australia via Singapore caught the imagination of Frederick Weld, governor of the Straits Settlement during the 1880s.[25] He mused on the possibility of linking a Malayan line to a Burmese line, perhaps requiring the annexation of intervening Thai territory (even if this meant compensating France with the rest of the kingdom). The Burmese railway system would then link to the Indian network. Such a scheme would also have the benefit of blocking Ferdinand de Lesseps ambition to build a canal through the Kra isthmus which, it was feared, would draw trade away from Singapore.[26]

The first section of railway to be laid in Malaya was the 7½ miles of track between Taiping and Port Weld, opened in 1885. The line was built to serve the main mining area of Larut. In the following year a stretch of line was opened between Kuala Lumpur and the Klang River as railways expanded across the peninsula. A station opened in Kuala Lumpur, near Market Street, though it was soon considered too small. This original station was a little north of the present site, known as Residency Station because it terminated at the British Residency. A new building was erected on the current site in 1892, its centrepiece a gable-ended hall surmounted by a vaguely Italianate clock tower, fronted by a porte cochère with a classical balcony.[27]

With the growth of the town and of Malaya's rail traffic, it was not long before this new station was itself too small, and it was decided to construct a building on much more ambitious lines which would be capable of meeting all requirements for many years.[28] Thus was created the station that still arrests the visitors' eye in the centre of Kuala Lumpur. Looking more like a mosque than a railway station, it is a riot of Moorish—sometimes referred to as 'Raj' or 'Neo Moorish'—architecture with scalloped eaves, keyhole arches, minarets, and cupolas.[29] Its towers form its dominant feature and give it an imposing skyline. It features ground-level linear halls, with a continuous deep-fronted loggia providing shelter and shade, with the platforms laid out in parallel behind. The station was part of Kuala Lumpur's development as the hub city of a new federation.

Figure 21. The spires of the Kuala Lumpur Railway Station frame skyscrapers.

The building's stunning façade offers a fine example of colonial era East-meets-West architecture, designed by Arthur Benson Hubback who worked for the government of India before taking up an appointment with the Malayan government in 1901. As architectural assistant to the director of the Public Works Department, he was inspired by Anglo-Asian styles in India and his previous work on the colony's mosques, notably the Jamek Mosque. He spent the year 1907–8 planning for the new station, trying to get the project to come in on budget. When he took his plans to the High Commissioner in Singapore in May 1908, he had nine separate ones.*[30] There followed a debate over which style of architecture should be chosen, won by those who favoured the 'Moorish' style courtesy of chief architect A. C. Norman's casting vote. The *Straits Times* commented that 'the Moorish style of architecture which has become such a feature in the Federal capital' had been chosen, no doubt because it was in keeping with buildings that already existed.[31] The Kuala Lumpur Railway Station building and train-shed were conceived as one architectural whole and the trains entered what seemed like a cross between an extravagant Oriental palace and a mosque.[32]

---

* In November 1912 Hubback took up the commission to design the terminal of the Kowloon-Canton railway in Hong Kong. He was the commanding officer of the Malay State Volunteer Rifles sent to Europe during the First World War, and was wounded in France in July 1917.

Though designed in an Eastern style, building materials were shipped in from Britain. The building and its three platforms covered about 140,000 square feet (3.3 acres), the building measuring 450 feet long by 150 wide. There were two storeys with a mezzanine, or half storey, containing the bathrooms attached to the second-floor bedrooms. Two subways, one for passengers and one for luggage, connected the different platforms, and a red sign on the platform displayed the destination of every train departing from Kuala Lumpur. The construction of the new station was watched keenly by the press, which reported on the planned interior:

> The bottom storey will be taken up with booking halls, waiting rooms, and a large refreshment room, besides porters' rooms and stores and other offices. The second storey will project over the lower sufficiently to allow carriages and motors to put down passengers under cover, also a covered stand for rickshaws...It is to be built entirely of concrete, cement, and iron, and will be fire-proof, and of quite a unique and beautiful style of architecture...The Hotel containing thirty bedrooms, restaurant, bar, etc., is part of the same building.[33]

In 1910 the new Kuala Lumpur Railway Station became the town's main station. Designed with distinctive minarets, horseshoe and ogee arches, and chatris, it remains a striking edifice. Inside, the platforms are covered by a steel-framed roof that was originally glazed and partially open to allow smoke from steam locomotives to escape, and the station to breath. Celebrating its fiftieth anniversary in 1935, the Malayan Railways published its history, proudly and justifiably proclaiming that 'the Station Building, including the Hotel and the Central Railway Offices immediately opposite are two of the finest buildings in Kuala Lumpur'.[34] The second building was erected as the 'Central Railway Offices', completed in 1917. Tenders were called from India and Malaya, wrote the author of *Fifty Years of Railway in Malaya, 1885–1935*, 'as at the time few buildings of such size had been attempted by local labour. The contract was secured, however, by a local Chinese firm.'[35]

Soon the railway extended the length and breadth of the Malay peninsula, embracing Singapore Island. In 1900 the Victoria Bridge was opened over the Perak River in order to benefit the tin industry, and in 1909 the Johore Railway was completed, delivering most of the mail from central and western regions of the peninsula to Singapore. The Federated Malay States Railways (FMSR) was formed in 1901 in order to rationalize the early profusion of companies. It was not until 1909 that the spinal railway of Malaya was completed, connecting the rubber plantations to the capital, Kuala Lumpur, north to Ipoh and Penang, and later (after 1931) up the pan-handle to Thailand. In 1913 FMSR purchased the Singapore Government Railways, and in 1918 the Malayan railway system was connected to the Thai railway system, partially realizing the vision of an interconnected pan-Asian network.

In 1923 Singapore was connected to the state of Johore in Malaya by a causeway and Singapore station, instead of being merely an entrance to a small island system, became a portal to Malaya and ultimately Thailand. In the late nineteenth century a succession of small lines had been built to connect the Malayan tin mines to the coast, and now they were connected to a central mainline from Singapore in the south to Thailand in the north. The local stations on this system ranged from the simple wooden buildings at Batu Gajah and Tampin to the large, airy, open-sided barn style at Teluk Anson. In 1935 the network extended to 1,321 miles of track.[36] There were 213 permanent stations and 76 halts. In 1929 the Malayan Railways employed 25,000 people, but by 1935 this had shrunk to under 12,000 as a result of the cessation of new construction, reorganization, and a reduction in traffic.[37]

Kuala Lumpur Railway Station and the people

The station became a part of people's daily commute; it was a workspace for railway employees, hawkers, and petty criminals, and a stop-off for well-heeled travellers using the hotel; it featured in press stories and advertisements; and it was the scene of civic events. The to-ings and fro-ings of officials and dignitaries often began or ended on the station's platforms, their movements widely reported in the press. It was the departure point for government officials leaving for overseas visits, and the point of arrival for visiting notables, touring sultans, religious leaders, and for British battalions serving tours of duty in the region. In 1921 the station was decorated and beflagged with a guard of honour from the Malay States Volunteer Rifles drawn up on the platform, the occasion being the arrival of the new Chief Secretary.[38] The Green Howards, the Worcestershire Regiment, and the 1st Battalion The Suffolk Regiment, were seen off here amidst crowds numbering in their thousands, having done their stint during the Malayan Emergency in the early 1950s. The 'Federation's Coronation Contingent', sent to London to represent Malaya when Queen Elizabeth II acceded to the throne in 1953,

gathered here for a goodbye ceremony. In October 1960 there were emotional scenes at the station as Malaysian troops embarked for the UN peace-
keeping mission in the Congo following Belgium's precipitate withdrawal
from the troubled Central African territory.

The station was also a space used for public display; in 1938 the Federated Malay States Railway stand for the 'Malaya Court' at the Glasgow
Empire Exhibition was displayed here prior to being packed for shipment
to Britain.[39] The display included a 10-feet model of one of the new day-
and-night carriages then being constructed in Malaya. In 1952 the station
was the scene of the All-Malay Gang Show put on by Boy Scouts from
across the Federated Malay States.[40] In April 1924 a large ceremony outside
the station marked the unveiling of the Federated Malay State's War
Memorial.[41]

Like all great urban buildings, the Kuala Lumpur Railway Station was
part of the furniture of everyday life, a recognized institution and edifice
that could be used to advertise products. Imperial Chemical Industries
(Malaya) Limited ran adverts for its 'Pentalite' emulsion paint in the late 1950s
which showed the building: 'An enchanting example of Kuala Lumpur
architecture enhanced and preserved' by this particular brand of paint.[42] The
station was part of the city's cultural life, the railway company, for example,
laying on special train services to the nearby Batu Caves for the benefit of
Hindu worshippers and devotees. The station's restaurant—'that oasis of
colonial charm and lifesaving victuals', as the *Straits Times* described it—was
a popular venue.[43] It was also known for its bathrooms, the spacious waiting
room, and of course the Station Hotel.

Reports of the crimes that took place within the station precincts regularly featured in the press, and included the discovery of a severed head and
decapitated body. Such stories attracted Sherlock Holmes-style headlines
such as 'The Mystery of the Missing Case' and 'Jailed by Clue of the Cigar
Wrapper'. The latter story recounted how fingerprints found on a cigar
wrapper had led to the conviction of a man who had been stealing from the
station canteen.[44] 'Carried Ganja in His Pillow: Arrest in Kuala Lumpur
Railway Station', meanwhile, reported that 'alighting from the Singapore
mail train at Kuala Lumpur Railway Station this morning, a Tamil, who carried a mat and pillow under his arm, was stopped by a detective while he
was on the point of boarding a rickshaw outside the station'.[45]

In February 1929, a Chinese woman was fined $50 at the Kuala Lumpur
Police Court or six months 'rigorous imprisonment' for stealing a sewing

machine at the station.[46] In August 1934, Chong Lam Kong was apprehended at the station and subsequently charged with conveying 'uncustomed' goods, namely two suitcases and forty-one rolls of cloth.[47] In April 1949, 25-year-old P. Ramanathan was charged with kidnapping a 16-year-old Eurasian girl at the station.[48] In September 1952, Lee Keen Ging, a 30-year-old woman, was arrested carrying 700 packets of chandhu, a name for prepared opium.[49] In January 1967, schoolboy K. Ragu Pathy appealed for the return of his certificates, especially his Cambridge School Certificate, after he had been robbed at the station as he returned from a job interview.[50] Under the headline 'Journey's End for Mr Chang' a sad story was recorded of a 65-year-old man who rushed to the station for a 7.30 p.m. down train to Singapore in May 1952. Finding that he had got the times wrong, and that it in fact departed in the morning, he settled down on the platform with a blanket, only to be found dead when a guard tried to rouse him in the morning.[51]

The railway station, and indeed Malaya's entire rail network, played a part in both the Second World War and the Malayan Emergency. Towards the end of the Japanese occupation, the railway system was bombed by American B-29s. This meant that after the war there were numerous incidents of undiscovered bombs going off, or unexploded bombs being found and then defused by the Royal Engineers. Japanese prisoners of war, reported the Straits Times, were employed on 'railway reconstruction' in the Kuala Lumpur Railway Station's goods yards, 'where B-29s played havoc during the Japanese occupation'.[52] In April 1949 a wartime bomb detonated, creating a 20-yard crater just outside the station.[53] Sometimes other repairs were required too, as when in March 1949 one of the station's minarets was hit by lightning and collapsed onto the roof above Number 5 platform.[54] During the Emergency armoured cars were mounted on rail carriages for protection, and extra-thick glass installed in the carriages to deflect bullets, some of which is on view in the station's museum.

Today, Kuala Lumpur Railway Station is still in use as a transport hub. People crowd outside for buses, and inside people await commuter trains. But it has about it the air of decline. In 2001 it ceased to be the city's main station when Kuala Lumpur Sentral was opened a little over half a mile away. The new station took over all cross-country and intercity traffic, relegating the now 'old' railway station to commuter status. Nevertheless, what is now regularly referred to as the 'old' Kuala Lumpur Railway Station has become part of Malaysia's heritage industry. Until recently, the hotel within its precincts was known as Heritage Station Hotel. The manner in which 'essentially foreign cultural systems or objects are assimilated into a national culture is a complex process', writes architectural historian Peter Stocker. Where the constructing agency was colonial, the 'legitimacy' of heritage inevitably becomes part of a wider discussion of national identity. Such is the ambivalent position of Kuala Lumpur's old railway station. Its image now adorns travel brochures and is emblazoned on T-shirts. Its motifs have been borrowed for a state triumphal arch and its interior modernized to coincide with the latest of many challenges in its life.[55] The government strategy which emerged in the early 1980s was for the renovation of major monuments. Thus between 1983 and 1987 the station's technology was updated and the building restored, a process which involved reinforcing and in some cases replacing the domes and pinnacles. Today, the station stands midway between two points, as a functioning train station and as a national monument.

7
Viceregal Lodge, Simla

The hill station was a peculiar British creation, exemplified by Simla in the Himalayan foothills, a settlement which grew from a small Indian hamlet into the administrative capital of the Raj and a hub of elite social activity. For several months every year between the 1860s and 1940s it was one of the great capitals of the world. Here, in the hills above the Punjab, the viceroy of India ruled with absolute power over several hundred million people. His imposing home, Viceregal Lodge, stood on a 330-acre site atop a prominent hill, visible for miles around and designed as a symbol of imperial power. The house and the town over which it presided were extraordinarily incongruous imperial creations. By rights, they simply should not have existed; their equivalent might have been a chief's kraal surrounded by rondavel huts in deepest Shropshire, or a Chinese walled settlement in the Grampians.

Edward Buck described the town in 1904:

> Simla, the summer capital of the Supreme Government, of the Punjab Government and of the army head-quarters, is situated on several small spurs of the lower Himalayas, at a mean elevation of about 7,100 feet above sea level... To the north and east a network of mountain chains, range rising over range, is crossed in the distance by a magnificent crescent of snowy peaks— the mountains of Kulu and Spiti on the north, and the central range of the eastern Himalayas stretching east and south-east as far as the eye can reach.[1]

The central Himalayas, Buck continued, stood out so sharply 'against the horizon through the clear mountain air, that space seems annihilated, and the beholder might well believe that a short day's journey would carry them to their base.[2] Scattered over seven hills, today the city's dense mosaic of buildings runs up the southern slopes, while the northern slopes are undeveloped and thickly wooded.

By the 1870s, Simla was firmly established as the summer capital of the Raj, home of the rulers of British India, nicknamed the heaven-born.

Figure 22. Archive postcard of the Viceregal Lodge in Simla, India with the Himalayas in the distance, by J. and H. King, *c.*1905–10.

Because of this role, Simla was described as the Capua of India, or Olympus. Given its rise to prominence, what Simla needed was a suitably imposing viceregal centre-piece, an abode from which the most important person in India could command the business of empire. In the 1880s, therefore, an extraordinary home was built for Viceroy the Marquis of Dufferin and Ava by an obscure architect named Henry Irwin. Sitting on top of Observatory Hill, it is a stunning Mock Tudor, 'Scottish baronial' edifice, designed to impress and to symbolize British majesty and rule. On a hill of its own and surrounded by tall pine trees, it remains a most imposing structure, its tower heightened by a subsequent viceroy, Lord Curzon, in order to accentuate the building's impact and balance its proportions.

Viceregal Lodge was specifically designed to emphasize the authority of the Raj and its leading representative, one of the most powerful men in the world. India was renowned for its ceremonial splendour, and here in the hills the viceroy could entertain the serried ranks of India's great and good, primarily the nawabs and maharajahs of the princely states and the leading ranks of India's civil and military community, as well as itinerant worthies from Britain and beyond. The lodge is a magnificent building, surpassing all others in the region. 'The pulchritude of the sprawling terraced gardens, the bonanza of flowers and the assiduously trimmed bushes are all in all a paradise of dreamy skies and any attempts to ameliorate it shall be in vain.'[3]

Modern day Shimla (as Simla is now known) houses one of India's finest collection of British colonial architecture, including its library, post office, municipal offices, Gaiety Theatre, and many impressive houses. Here the visitor discovers bandstands, fountains, and rose-ringed cottage porches, quintessential English creations thousands of miles from 'home'—shades of Margate, in Jan Morris's phrase, in the foothills of the Himalayas. Raja Bhasin, a noted historian of Simla and Himachal Pradesh, captures the bizarre nature of the very existence of such a town in such a place, writing that there was something incongruous about the imperial government stationed at Simla, maintaining its links with the rest of the world through the tenuous umbilical cord of a narrow mountain path. For that matter, there was something incongruous about Simla itself: three merchants from Yarkand who visited the station in 1847, having travelled over the snow-covered ranges, were astonished at the sight of a British settlement where logically there should only have been a small Indian village.[4]

The hill station phenomenon and British 'separateness'

The British established over eighty hill stations in India. But Simla was the queen of them all, renowned for its social life and its role as the administrative and military capital of the Raj—'red-tape tempered with picnics and adultery', as one wag described it.[5] Sir John Kaye considered it to be 'the cradle of more insanity than any place within the limits of Hindustan'.[6] Hill stations came to prominence in the mid-nineteenth century and were known for their mixed architectural styles, including the Gothic pleasure villa, Georgian spas, half-timbered Alpine chalets, and rustic cottages. Hill stations developed in close proximity to the major cities in which the British population of India lived and worked. There was Naini Tal in the Kumaon hills, Mussoorie above Dehra Dun, Murree above Rawalpindi, and Darjeeling 250 miles north of Calcutta. What also marked hill stations out was the speed with which they developed. No slow accretion of foreign styles here; instead, they represented the sudden implantation of an alien architecture and way of life. Unlike other Indian cities and their colonial-era buildings, they shunned 'eastern' influences in their design. Their buildings sought on the one hand to recreate 'home' for the British, and on the other to build monuments of imperial power (with which to further the project of mastering the indigenous inhabitants). For many British people in India the hill stations were associated with periods of leave and relaxation, and the social activities that accompanied the 'Season'. But for members of the Indian civil service and the Army's general staff, Simla was strongly identified with paperwork and decision-making as well. Many hill stations were strategically located in order to serve as military outposts or sanatoria for convalescing soldiers.

As Simla grew, so did the desire to develop its English character, which became its chief feature. Here, at least, was a bit of India that was *theirs*. The architecture of Simla explains a great deal about the British desire to recreate home wherever they went overseas, and to emphasize their superiority. Hill stations were not only about escaping from the heat of the plains, but about escaping *the country* too. They were places of exile, places from which to exclude India to the greatest extent possible and to think of England. Privet hedges, amateur dramatics, teashops, and the ubiquitous 'Mall' promenade kept hill stations British, and kept India at bay. Their buildings reflected this separateness, which was accentuated by contemporary ethno-medical theories that declared that hill stations were healthier locations for Europeans and, later, by the desire to remove Indians from the European areas— out of sight, out of mind, discreetly present in the background to provide the myriad acts of personal service upon which colonial life depended, but not cluttering the Mall or spoiling the view.

Simla's early history

Following their war with the Gurkhas in 1815, the British retained several hill bases as military posts. The Maharaja of Patiala was given lands around Simla for helping the British during the campaign, and was allowed to purchase other tracts, in effect becoming a hill chief. At the time Simla was described as an obscure village surrounded by 'dense jungle infested with wild beasts', and early visitors were struck by its cool temperature.[7] 'Semla' was first mentioned in 1817 in the diary of two Scottish officers as they surveyed and mapped the newly subjugated hill states.

Captain Charles Kennedy founded the future summer capital when posted as garrison officer and thereafter as political agent and commanding officer of the Nasiri Battalion stationed at nearby Sabathu. From Sabathu cantonment the thickly wooded ridge of Simla was clearly visible and the area became a favourite hunting ground for officers posted there. Kennedy built Simla's first permanent house in 1823, a gabled cottage called Kennedy House. By 1827 Captain Kennedy claimed to have achieved the subjugation of the hill territory, and developed a 12-feet-wide road between Pinjore and Bushahr, a distance of 200 miles. From small beginnings the summer capital of the Raj slowly emerged. The magnificent forests became speckled with cottages and bungalows belonging to Europeans lured by the beauty and climate of the hills. In the northern distance, the snow ranges could be descried. Here, away from the plains, Britons could revel amidst oak and rhododendron, cedars, ferns, mist, and moss, and find enough snow to validate the dispatch to England of cards bearing wintry scenes at Christmas.[8]

Simla became known as a sanatorium, and in 1830 the government of India directed negotiations with the chiefs of Patiala and Keonthal in order to buy the land necessary to form a station. Houses began to sprawl, set in generous grounds where potatoes, cabbages, flowers, and shrubs were cultivated, wild flowers mixing with rhododendrons in burgeoning English gardens. The climate soon became famous, and invalids from the plains ventured there, and built houses, instead of risking the journey to the Cape. A broad road was built round Mount Jakko, the highest point on the ridge, 3 miles in length.

But it took more than these efforts to turn this inaccessible backwater into the capital of India. It required, in fact, the patronage of the monarch's own representative, the Governor-General. In 1827 Simla was chosen for a visit by Governor-General Lord Amherst (1823–8), who arrived in state with an entourage supported by 1,700 coolies (a word derived from the Tamil for hireling). He stayed for the summer at Kennedy House, his visit creating a significant precedent. Governor-General Lord Bentinck (1828–35) acquired land—4,000 acres—for the government. (He was also responsible for the purchase of Darjeeling.) Not having their own viceregal home, however, they had to 'camp' out in rented abodes ill-suited for their purposes. Bentinck's visit in 1831 made Simla the 'establishment' hill station. Thereafter, every successive governor-general visited the town at least once. In 1836

Plate 1. Michelangelo Hayes (1820–77), *Military Parade in Dublin Castle*, 1844. The Georgian Bedford Tower was built on the original thirteenth-century entrance. The statues of Fortitude and Justice stand on top of the internal arches.

Plate 2. Aerial view of Fort St Angelo with Kalkara creek on one side, Dockyard creek on the other. Courtesy of Birgu Local Council.

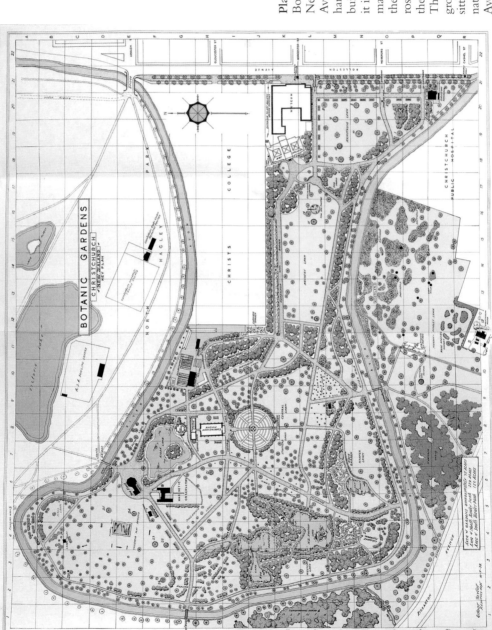

Plate 3. 1958 plan of the Botanic Gardens, Christchurch, New Zealand. Rolleston Avenue runs along the right hand side, with the Museum building marked. Behind it is Archery Lawn. Also marked are Victoria Lake, the glasshouses, the circular rose garden, and the site of the Magnetic Observatory. The map illustrates how the grounds of the Botanic Garden, sitting within Hagley Park, are naturally bordered by the Avon River.

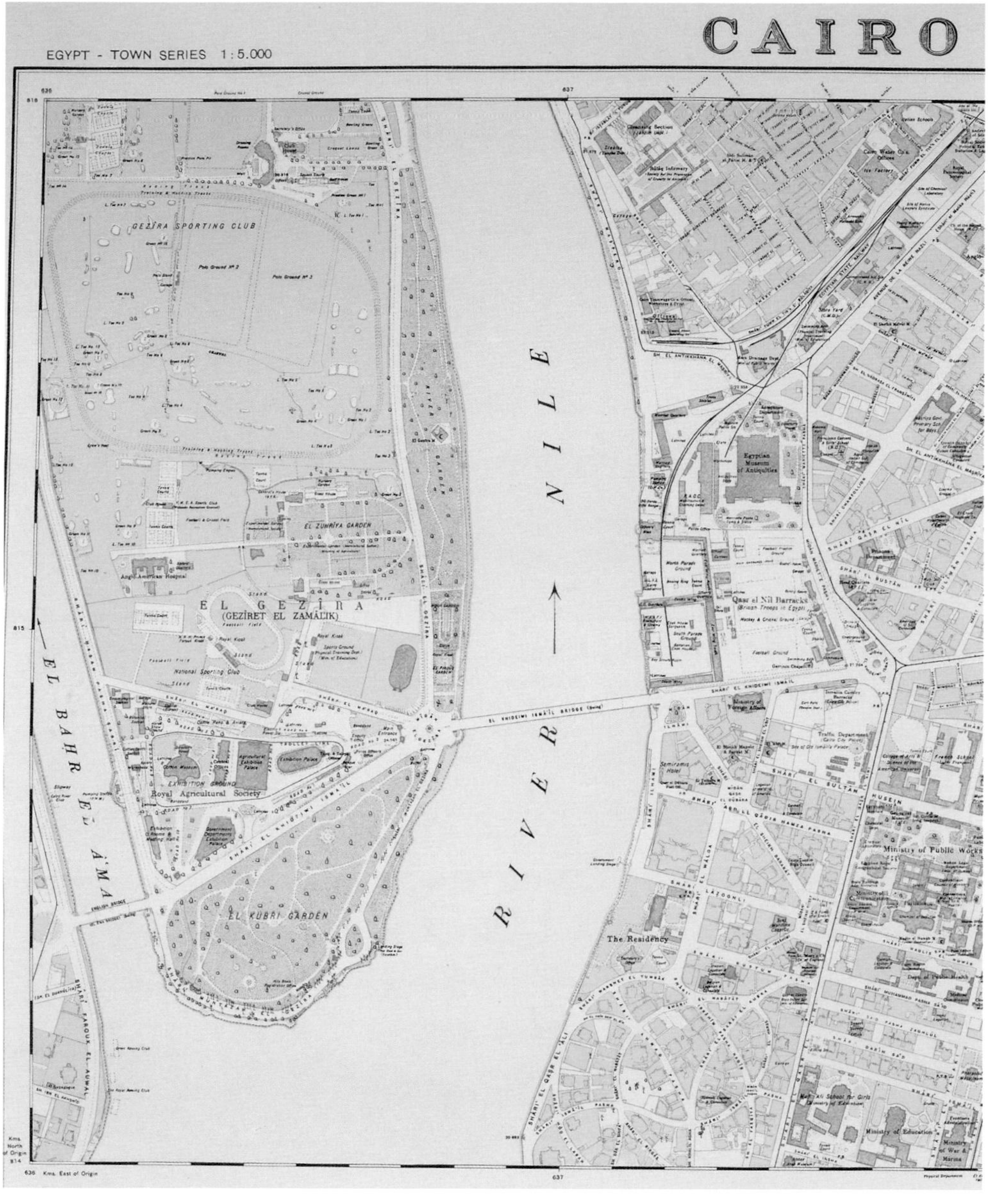

CAIRO

Plate 4. Detail from a map of Cairo produced by The Survey of Egypt in 1936 (this is the November 1944 reprint). The map captures several bastions of British power and influence in Cairo. On the right-hand bank of the Nile, the British Residency (opposite the tip of Gezira Island) and, directly across the bridge, the Qasr el Nîl Barracks (with what is now Tahrir Square to its right). The famous Museum of Egyptian Antiquities lies above the barracks. On Gezira Island, meanwhile, the extensive grounds of the Gezira Sporting Club are marked out. Within the large perforated circle that forms the race track can be seen polo grounds 2 and 3, surrounded by golf course tees and bunkers. Extreme top left are tennis courts and the Secretary's House. Moving along the road from left to right the Lido and its swimming pool are visible.

Plate 5. Contemporary View of the Old Railway Station (left), in Kuala Lumpur with the Railway Headquarters building on the right. Together, they form the 'Two Sisters'.

Plate 6. Painting of Viceregal Lodge by Viceroy Lord Lansdowne's Private Secretary.

Plate 7. Contemporary view of the Viceregal Lodge, now the home of the Indian Institute of Advanced Study.

Plate 8. Opening of the First Parliament of the Commonwealth of Australia by HRH the Duke of Cornwall and York (later King George V), 9th May 1901. 1903 by Tom Roberts (1856–1931).

Plate 9. Historical postcard advertising the Raffles Hotel in Singapore. This period of the hotel's life, *c.*1915, was considered the benchmark when it was extensively redeveloped in the 1980s.

Plate 10. Exterior of HSBC Building, Hong Kong, surrounded by other buildings, both contemporary and colonial, including the Old Supreme Court/Old Legislative Council Building in the foreground, designed by Sir Aston Webb and Ingress Bell and opened in 1912. To the left of the HSBC Building is the Old Bank of China.

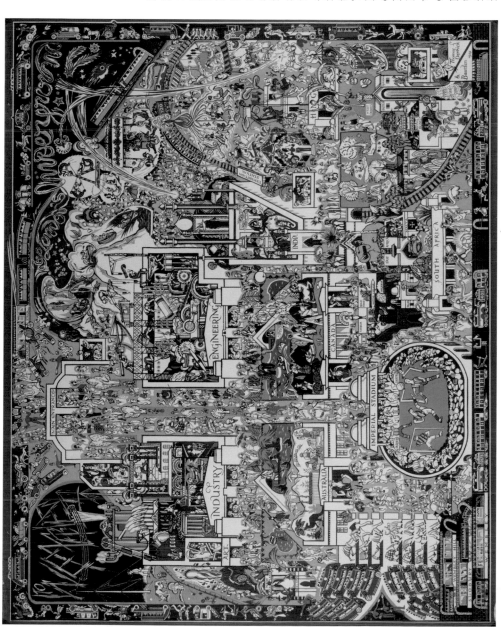

Plate 11. London Underground Museum poster advertising the 1924 Empire Exhibition. This poster was commissioned by the Underground in 1924. The brief was an illustrated map of the British Empire Exhibition at Wembley. Frank Pick approached Edward Bawden for the commission on the recommendation of Bawden's tutor at the Royal College of Art. Pick rejected Bawden's first proposal and brought in the more experienced designer, Thomas Derrick. Derrick handled the cartography and overall design, and Bawden was left to provide the illustrations. From a distance the poster was hard to read, but it was extremely popular with the public for its exquisite attention to detail. The Empire Stadium itself appears at the foot of the illustration, left of centre.

Plate 12. *Metro-Land* guide-book, showing one of Wembley Stadium's famous twin towers. One of a series published by the Metropolitan Railway (Met) over 17 years (1915–32). It describes the places served by the Met and includes photos, a general report of the British Empire Exhibition, and a guide to 'How to get about London'. The term 'Metro-Land' was coined by the Met to refer to the new suburbs that grew in northwest London as a direct result of the developing railway line.

Governor-General Lord Auckland (1836–42) bought a large house for the use of himself and his sisters. Two years later, Auckland House hosted a durbar when an embassy from the Lion of the Punjab, Ranjit Singh, was received in state. It was attended by a company of Gurkhas, mace bearers, and viceregal servants dressed in scarlet livery. In the same year the house also hosted a ball and supper to commemorate Queen Victoria's birthday.

By 1830 a township of thirty British-owned houses was scattered over the Simla tract. Simla soon established a reputation for gaiety, as it was visited by affluent, fashionable military and civil members of the East India Company, its popularity growing with wives and families. British social and sporting activities soon followed, including hack races and rickshaw races. The first funfair took place at Annandale, an open space used for sport and recreation, in September 1833 to raise funds for a girls' school at nearby Sabathu. By the late nineteenth century the Annandale ground had been enlarged for gymkhanas, polo, cricket, and football, and the famous Durand Football Tournament was inaugurated in 1888. Simla boasted a hundred houses by mid-century, occupied by over 300 Britons resident during the summer months. By 1859 the town gave the appearance of a conical hill covered with white bungalows and a white church.

Despite its growing popularity, accessing Simla remained difficult. The 41-mile-long winding and precipitous hill path from Kalka to Simla was only passable on foot or on horse or mule. But political vicissitudes in the Punjab, as well as its growing resort reputation, gave a major impetus to Simla's growth. The deployment of British troops to the region during the Sikh wars necessitated sanatoria and convalescent homes for which Simla was well positioned, and the area formed a valuable strategic base as it was possible to rush troops down to the plains at short notice. It was an important base in the preparation for the conquest of the Punjab, plans for which led successive governors-general to tour the northern provinces so as to be near the area of military activity. With attention focused on Afghanistan in the late 1830s, Lord Auckland spent two years in the region, accompanied by advisers, secretaries, and staff. Governor-General Dalhousie (1848–56) spent three consecutive summers in Simla between 1849 and 1851 as the conquest of the Punjab proceeded. For him, Simla was an 'eyrie from which to watch the newly annexed plains that stretch below'.[9] The construction of the Hindustan–Tibet Road brought more people to Simla including an increasing number of holiday visitors. Hunting and sightseeing trips became popular.

Imperial Simla

Why should the government of India have found it expedient to travel over
1,200 miles from Calcutta, across the length of Indo-Gangetic plain, to gov-
ern from Simla? Its remoteness and mountainous location made it an
unlikely destination, and what became the annual migration of clerks and
files from Calcutta (later New Delhi) amounted to a huge expedition. The
government progressed cumbrously from Calcutta to Amballa by train,
where the government official would hire a gharry for the journey to Kalka,
crossing the Ghaggar river in a bullock cart. Staying overnight in a hotel at
Kalka, he would thence move on to Simla by cart. When Viceroy Lawrence
formally assembled the executive council at Simla in 1864, 484 persons from
Calcutta gathered for a six-month period. The viceregal migration took up
a lot of space in Simla and its environs—even the forests of the hill state of
Dhami were reserved for the viceroy and his entourage as a shooting
ground.

There were health reasons for the government's annual pilgrimage to
Simla. A government press release explained the six-month sojourn as a
'source of vigour and energy to the men who expend and exhaust their
strength in administering the affairs of the Indian Empire'.[10] Viceroy John
Lawrence (1864–9) decided that Simla was the place for the Raj's summer
capital, and deployed every argument to get this accepted by the India
Council in London. 'No doubt there is the danger of being cut off from the
seat of Government', he mused. 'Still, on the other hand, railways will lessen
the danger.'[11] To his mind there was great advantage in having one foot in
the Punjab, the other in the North-West Provinces, and his choice of Simla
had much to do with his preoccupation with the affairs of those regions,
and fear of Russian expansion. Calcutta, it was felt, was not central enough
as capital of the ever expanding Indian Empire. Lawrence also claimed that
he could do more work in one summer's day at Simla, than he could in five
in Calcutta, and his doctors made residence in the hills in the hot weather a
condition of his taking the job.[12]

There was also the fact that Simla's population was considered 'docile'
and the hill rulers 'submissive', important considerations in light of the
Indian Mutiny. Its growing accessibility by road and rail made it attractive
too: the construction of a line from Calcutta to Delhi and then to Amballa
occurred in 1869 and there was a cart road from Kalka. The first passenger

train arrived at Simla in 1903. Designed by chief engineer H. S. Harington, the construction was a 60-mile engineering feat. From Kalka at 2,100 feet above sea level it rose to Simla, 7,000 feet up, climbing the ascent by a series of loops and tight curves. Five miles were covered by 103 tunnels, and a further 2 miles by viaducts.

Beyond this, there were yet more reasons for choosing Simla. Hill stations were becoming more important as the British population in India increased, and in the 1850s district and provincial administrations began to move their summer headquarters to them. The Bengal government, for instance, moved to Darjeeling, and Simla became the summer capital of the government of the Punjab. The military also moved in. General Frederick Roberts's house, Snowdon, in central Simla, was acquired as permanent residence of the commander-in-chief, and scarlet-liveried messengers bustled along the Mall between there and Viceregal Lodge. With both regional and pan-Indian governments and the army high command converging, Simla became, in Kipling's famous words, 'the abode of the little tin gods'. Thereafter the military constituted about a third of the town's official establishment. On the terrace above Army Headquarters was Simla's magisterial law-enforcement bulwark, the Kutcherry, housing the court and offices of the deputy commissioner of Simla, built in 'Norman Baronial' style. Between Army Headquarters and the courts was the Roman Catholic Church, designed by Henry Irwin in French Gothic style, and Ripon Hospital lay to the east of Army Headquarters, also designed by Irwin.

In the eastern part of Simla, Barnes Court, set in 46 acres of land, was purchased as the residence of the Lieutenant-Governor of the Punjab. Demolition of Upper Bazar at the Ridge provided a flat stretch of land in the centre of the town which became the city centre and served as a piazza, its western corner dominated by Christ Church, built in Tudor style and designed by Colonel J. T. Boileau. On the Mall, Irwin designed a Tudor brick-and-timber structure for the Post Office and a telegraph office. The Town Hall included all that British society needed: a theatre, a library, and a large hall for suppers, balls, exhibitions, and durbars. The ground floor comprised the Gaiety Theatre, a masonic hall with a vaulted entrance, the municipal offices, and the police station. The Mall was well maintained, watered daily, and even oiled before ceremonial functions. Seventy-two oil lamps were erected in the 1880s, and its European character was reinforced when a tunnel was dug underneath it giving access to the Lower Bazar, allowing Indians to be largely kept out of sight. By the 1880s improvements had reshaped Simla to meet European needs. There was now a continuous water supply and drainage and sewerage system. The Ridge had been cleared of Indian shops and European-style shops opened on the Mall, the Bazar had been tidied away, and government offices were open. Simla had developed into two distinct and interrelated entities: Bazar Ward, the Indian part of the town—or the Indian 'excrescence' as less enlightened Britons viewed it—and Station Ward, 400 privately occupied cottages, villas, and castles, each built on an acre or more of land. But despite all these developments, still the viceroy had no suitable home of his own, making do with a house called Peterhoff, rented from the Raja of Nahan.

Viceroys Lytton and Dufferin and the construction of Viceregal Lodge

When Lytton made his first viceregal visit to Simla in 1876, the place struck him as a 'mere bivouac'.[13] He was dismayed at the makeshift temporary arrangements, but what particularly irked him was the lack of a viceregal residence. Lytton, as an imperialist and an aristocrat, found Peterhoff unsuitable, uncomfortable, and cramped, describing it as 'a sort of pigstye'.[14] Architect of the great Delhi durbar of 1877 which proclaimed Victoria Empress of India, he was very keen on durbars and the dispensation of the honours that bound the Indian princes to Britain. Durbars at Simla were held in a marquee on the lawns of Peterhoff, an arrangement that really didn't suit Lytton's style at all. What was needed in Simla, in the eyes of grand viceroys like Lytton and Dufferin, was a great deal more splendour. But someone had to pay for it, and some viceroys and some secretaries of state for India in distant Whitehall were more parsimonious than others. The India Office was loath to sanction any significant expenditure on government facilities until the fate of Simla as a summer capital had been decided. All government offices were in rented accommodation—in 1875, for instance, the Home Office was in St Mark's, Finance in The Yarrows, Public Works in Herbert House, the Foreign Office in Valentines, and Revenue and Agriculture in Argyll House. In 1882 the government of India was renting eighteen private houses to accommodate their offices, the establishment including 103 officers and 1,082 clerks. The whole government, never mind the viceroy, was camping out in Simla.

Lytton began the process which led to the creation of the resplendent Viceregal Lodge by selecting the site on Observatory Hill in western Simla. The growing imperial self-awareness of the later nineteenth century generated buildings intended to convey messages about British power and permanence. The Simla Imperial Circle of the Public Works Department was set up in 1877 with the task of translating official ingenuity into drawing-board sketches and earth-bound construction. After half a century of ad hoc growth it was decided that the restructuring of Simla would transform its higgledy-piggledy-ness and reflect Britain's confidence in its imperial destiny. Captain Cole, architect and engineer of the Simla Imperial Circle, outlined the principle that buildings should bear a distinct classical or Gothic impression: since the Moghuls had left exemplars of Muslim architecture, the British as successor imperialists should create structures that bore the stamp of ideal European architectural forms.[15]

Cole was deputed to prepare designs for a new Viceregal Lodge during a stay in England. He drew a fairy-tale palace, exhibited at a fine arts show in Simla in 1878. Lytton had a pretty shrewd idea that nothing would happen in a hurry, certainly not during his tenure as viceroy. Viewing Cole's etchings, he described it as 'a prospect so distant that it is only possible to the eye of faith'. From the 'airy nothing' to which his constructive genius has given 'a local habitation and a name' is that visionary Viceregal residence which 'never is, but always *to be* built' at Simla.[16]

Henry Irwin (1841–1922) of the Public Works Department, a member of the Institute of Civil Engineers, London, was appointed superintendent of works to the Simla Imperial Circle in 1880. He produced a second design for a new house. But the scheme to build a new viceregal lodge was postponed by the India Office and Lytton's successor, Lord Ripon (1880–4). Opposed to pomp and the idea of a new palace, Peterhoff continued in service. But the next viceroy, Lord Dufferin, was much more of the mind of Lytton, and it was he who finally forged ahead.

Dufferin had a choice of three plans—the Cole and Irwin designs as well as Irwin's design for a restructured Peterhoff. Initially he went for the latter, and Irwin began work in February 1885. But when Dufferin arrived at Simla for the first time in April, the decision was revoked. To this cultured and aristocratic diplomat, who enjoyed durbars, receptions, and fancy-dress balls, a new viceregal abode was clearly needed. Both he and Lady Dufferin thought Peterhoff unsuitable for viceregal events. Before leaving Calcutta, the notion of redesigning Peterhoff had been put to them. Upon arrival,

they rapidly decided that this just would not do. Lady Dufferin, in her journal, recorded that the house was a 'cottage', quite adequate for family
domestic life, but not for the official life of someone as important as a viceroy. It was not tiny, though; Lady Dufferin thought it quite all right for dinners of up to two dozen, but anything beyond that (and viceregal dinners
were often far beyond that) would lead to 'horrible crushes'. She also dis-
liked the idea of renovating Peterhoff because of the 'proximity of our prec-
ipices': there was barely a yard to spare out the back, and just enough room
for a tennis court out the front, the abodes of the viceroy's subordinates, as
she put it, sliding off the surrounding mountainside.[17]

So the plan for a house on Observatory Hill was revived. Lord Randolph
Churchill, the new Secretary of State for India, was by happy and necessary
coincidence more amenable than his predecessors on the subject of funding
a new viceregal abode. Dufferin delighted in the prospect of overseeing its
construction personally. He had wanted to build a grand house on his estate,
Clandboyes in County Down, Ireland, and later wanted to build an official
residence in Quebec when he was Governor-General of Canada. Lack of
funds had prevented both projects, so the opportunity to build at Simla was
one that he relished. Dufferin himself suggested the general plan of Viceregal Lodge, and until the designs were completed, continually examined
and modified the drawings in detail. For two Simla seasons his hobby was
to visit the site almost every morning and evening, to the dismay of Public
Works Department officials.[18] Lord Dufferin helped further Irwin's career
at the same time that he was also hosting and promoting the career of one
Rudyard Kipling. The Kipling family was part of Dufferin's informal social
set in India, and *Plain Tales* was published in the same year as Irwin's most
prestigious architectural project was completed.

Viceregal Lodge occupied the most commanding position in Simla.
Lying to the extreme west of the town, the lodge is one of the first things
to catch the eye on the approach from Kalka. The summit of Observatory
Hill was lopped and levelled to provide a plateau on which to build. The
incline of the hill was used as part of the building's design; viewed as a cross-
section from the side, Viceregal Lodge descends the mountainside like three
downward steps, the hill's contours employed to allow for the building's different heights. While the main block consists of three storeys and the east
wing two storeys, this use of the hillside meant that a five storey north wing
could be accommodated into the design. This north wing featured a base-
ment—an abnormality in British India—which contained the laundry,

kitchens, scullery, wine rooms, and linen and china stores. Built on the side of the precipice, this block commenced three storeys below the ground level of the main block and east wing. This meant that when viewed from the north-east the house presented a lofty, somewhat forbidding appearance, looking like a medieval castle.

The building was erected by thousands of Indian workers and cost thousands of lakh rupees. Working in winter was costly as workers demanded high wages, while carpenters were as rare as hens' teeth. The work in progress presented a fascinating sight, as Lady Dufferin recorded:

> D. took Hermie and me, all over the house in the afternoon. We climbed up the most terrible places, and stood on single planks over yawning chasms. The workpeople are very amusing to look at, especially the young ladies in necklaces, bracelets, earrings, tight cotton trousers, turbans with long veils hanging down their backs, and a large earthenware basin of mortar on their heads. They walk about with the carriage of empresses, and seem as much at ease on top of the roof as on the ground-floor; most picturesque masons they are.[19]

All the construction material came from India. The masonry was light-blue limestone, and the wrought stonework sandstone with a beautiful light-grey tint. The sandstone was from Kalka and the limestone was quarried at Kareru on Prospect Hill, transported to the lodge on mules. Concrete for the foundations was manufactured in Simla. The iron girders, beams, and trusses came from Bombay. Burmese teak had been procured several years before the construction, while deodar, walnut, and kail were axed from the forests around Simla. The structure concealed concessions to the tropical environment, as well as incorporating the engineering skills of the Victorian age. The two new materials, iron and glass, were moulded into the structure, the former to strengthen and reinforce, the latter for light and ventilation.[20]

The façade of the Viceregal Lodge is impressive and imposing. Verandas and terraces adorned the buildings on multiple levels and columned arches along the façade were echoed in the arches of the alternating widths supporting the verandas.[21] The column arches supported the verandas on the first and second floors, and the verandas were roofed by glass cubes laid into T-shaped angle frames of iron. They were meant to diffuse the rays of the tropical sun, even as it streamed into the rooms. The roofline was broken up with curbed gables, a domed turret with a weathercock, and prominent chimney stacks.

The lodge was a classic Victorian statement, and a building of power. A small tower surmounted the house from which a flag was flown when the viceroy was in residence, the practice adopted from the palaces and homes of monarch and dukes. The tower contained the water tanks supplied from the municipal mains, prosaic, everyday features and functions cleverly concealed in a building intended to embody higher sentiments. The corrugated-iron roofing, typical of most Simla houses, was concealed by red pantiles manufactured in Simla.[22] Minor iron spiral staircases, designed in English Renaissance style, were made to allow cleaning staff to reach the roof from the outside and then descend to the bathrooms, the lowest of the low carrying 'night soil' and kept out of sight. Rain and bath water was carried in cast-iron pipes and discharged into a concrete drain which surrounded the plinth and brought the water into four reservoirs.[23]

Moving day for the Dufferins was 23 July 1888, with beds and everything else moved from one house to the other. Dufferin and the girls went up in the evening, when everything was brilliantly illuminated by the novel touch-button electric lights. 'After dinner we went down to look at the kitchen', wrote Lady Dufferin, 'which is a splendid apartment, with white tiles six feet high all around the walls, looking so clean and bright.'[24] The lodge could accommodate 800 guests for balls and garden parties, and could seat nearly seventy guests for formal dinners. No sooner had the Dufferins moved in than they began putting the house to its intended use. Lady Dufferin's journal records the first formal state dinner, held on 8 August 1888:

> We had our first entertainment in our new house tonight. It looked perfectly lovely, and one could see that everyone was quite astonished at it and at the softness of the light. First we had a large dinner for sixty-six people at one long table. The electric light is enough, but as candelabras ornament the table we had some on it. At one end of the room there was a side-board covered with gold plate, etc, and at the other end double doors were open, and across the ballroom one saw the band which played during dinner. We had all the Council and 'personages' of Simla, and the Minister, Asman Jah, from Hyderabad, who brought his suite. After dinner people began to arrive for the dance. When not dancing, everyone was amused roaming about the new rooms, and going up to the first floor, whence they could look down upon the party.[25]

The interior and the viceregal estate

A flight of steps and porticoes led to the entrance hall which featured a teak stairway ascending through three storeys. The building was centred upon the teak-panelled gallery. The carved pillars and treads were made of teak and the carved balusters of walnut. The concealed portion of the framing of the stairs was made of deodar. The gallery rose to the full height of the building, 90 feet long, 50 feet high, and 18 feet wide. It was lit by a glass ceiling and by large mullioned windows. The upper gallery was hung with Japanese paper in white and embossed gold. It was further decorated with a collection of Indian arms and, above the mantelpieces, mirrors in frames of Burmese glass mosaics, looted by Lord Dufferin from King Thebaw's Palace at Mandalay. Heavy velvet curtains divided the gallery from the ballroom, which measured 70 feet by 30 feet with a side annexe 70 feet by 10 feet on the west, and a vestibule 17 feet by 30 feet on the east. Another velvet curtain divided the ballroom from the state drawing-room, its wall panels hung in silk tapestry. The state dining-room was panelled in teak, the upper 2 feet in pierced strap work supporting the coats of arms of past governors-general and viceroys of India. The walls were divided pilasters supporting the ceiling beams, their upper portion hung with crimson silk and woollen tapestry.

The furnishings of the house were provided by Messrs Maple and Company of London's Tottenham Court Road, who sent staff out to India to supervise the installation. Other fixtures were made by Punjabi carpenters. All the state rooms were hung with damask, sky-blue and pale green in the two drawing-rooms, yellow in the ballroom, and crimson in the dining-room. The latter was also hung with Spanish leather and the drawing-room with brown and gold silk. Heraldic beasts supported the chimney-piece of the immense hall, which was as tall as the house itself, and everywhere there were elaborate carved details of teak, deodar, and walnut such as a walnut ceiling with a Kashmiri design. A beautiful carved screen of teak in the dining room was made under Curzon's instructions on the model of the screen that stood behind the emperor of China's throne at the Imperial Palace in Peking. The Council Chamber was adorned with engraved portraits of past governors-general and viceroys, a result of Curzon's genealogical and heraldic researches. The house also featured an indoor tennis court.

In order to appreciate the scale of the new Viceregal Lodge, one must consider the wider 330-acre estate over which it presided. There were lawns and gardens on the south and north fronts, which were used for state garden parties, and an avenue of limes and shrubs screened the eastern face of the house. The viceregal estate covered the whole of Observatory Hill, Bentinck's Hill, Prospect Hill, and a portion of the hill on which Peterhoff stood. The estate included twenty-six houses, and at the turn of the century accomodated forty Europeans and 800 Indians. Over 700 staff maintained the house, its formal gardens, and the estate. To the east of Viceregal Lodge stood Observatory House, residence of the viceroy's private secretary. Behind Observatory House was the steam-powered electrical engine house for the lodge, and the little chapel of All Saints. Between here and the stables near the entrance gates stood a gun-shed containing a canon that was fired daily at noon and on special occasions. Its unexpected salutes were found to be so disconcerting to equestrian visitors that it was removed.[26] The northern slopes and the summit of Prospect Hill, the fine spur to the south of Viceregal Lodge, were within the boundary of the estate, and the public had free access to this hill. Among the European houses were Squire's Hall, Curzon House, and Courteen Hall (office of the military secretary to the viceroy). Quarters for the clerk of the works, the electrician, the band, the bodyguard, and police guard were erected on other parts of the estate, and there was a half-timbered guard house at the gate. Viceregal Lodge was Simla's first truly modern house, complete with over 1,000 electric lights. The grounds and approach roads were also lit by electricity.

Opinions of the lodge

Lord Dufferin was understandably delighted by the building that he had been so involved in creating. He boasted that at last 'a decent Viceregal residence has been erected ... where Simla maidens will have better opportunities of displaying both their grace and their pretty frocks'.[27] But from its foundation the lodge had its detractors.[28] 'Doz' in *Ragtime in Simla* wrote of the 'spacious medieval stronghold of greystone on Observatory Hill, which is both a joy and an expense forever'.[29] The structure was spectacular, although its aesthetics and appropriateness were repeatedly questioned. The style of architecture drew inspiration from the English Renaissance, with markedly Elizabethan characteristics.[30] Lord Lansdowne, Dufferin's successor, wrote that the 'whole arrangement of the rooms and anatomy of the building [tells] a tale of amateur architecture with its inevitable faults. Waste of space everywhere, absence of sufficient accommodation for guests in spite of the palatial dimensions, rooms in the wrong place considering the purpose for which they were built.'[31] Lansdowne added, however, that 'It is an English house and not an Indian residence, and we shall feel more at home than we have yet felt.'[32] Robert Fermor-Hesketh wrote that the lodge 'was an uninspiring, grey stone Elizabethan-style house. It looks and feels like a hotel in Peebleshire. Inside, the viceroys entertained in a suite of Jacobean-type rooms, ideally suited to performances of Gilbert and Sullivan.' The viceroy himself sat at his desk in an elevated turret with a glorious view of the snow-capped peaks of the Himalayas.[33]

One of the main criticisms of the interior was that the gallery leading to the ballroom, 50 feet in height and 90 feet long, was 'only eighteen feet broad, which is really much too narrow'.[34] This contraction in width came about in order to save money, as it should have been 12 feet wider. Mounting costs and the race to finish in time for the Dufferins to move in had led to modifications to the original plans. Jan Morris describes it as a great mock-Tudor English country house 'encouched in exotic trees and set against the background of the Tibetan Himalaya, which suited the grand anomaly of its meaning and gave susceptible Britons, as they rode past its guardhouse to the salute of the turbaned sentries, perceptible frissons of satisfaction'.[35]

There were more forgiving views too. Trevor Pinch in the *Civil and Military Gazette* called it 'A stately building set amid a panorama of beauty which almost takes the breath away'.[36] Yvonne Fitzroy, visiting Viceroy Lord Reading in the 1920s, wrote of its 'cathedral-like silhouette... You could have found fault with it to eternity and then not have reached the limit of its crimes; on the other hand it was so large, so perfectly complacent, that in the end you grew near to accepting it at its own valuation.'[37] Alan Campbell-Johnson, press attaché to the last viceroy, Admiral Lord Louis Mountbatten, thought it 'an ideal venue for quiet, calm deliberation'.[38] Audrey Harris captured the building's incongruous qualities:

> The hall had an almost loveable naïve ugliness as, I think, had the whole of Vice-Regal Lodge, apart from the outside which glories in spa-like monstrosity. Those who built it had no doubts about the suitability of an enlarged English country-house, with its panelling and cosy galleries, being set down in India. That certain styles aren't suitable on certain scales and certain types of surroundings, didn't worry them in the least.[39]

Lady Curzon was of a similar opinion: 'The first view of Simla amused me so—the houses slipping off the hills and clinging like barnacles to the hill-tops and then our house! I kept trying not to be disappointed. A Minneapolis millionaire would revel in it, and we shall love it and make up our minds not to be fastidious... A look out of the window makes up for all and I can live on views for five years.'[40] Others compared it to Pentonville Prison; Edwin Montagu, when Secretary of State for India, thought it resembled 'a Scottish hydro—the same sort of appearance, the same sort of architecture, the same sort of equipment of tennis lawns and sticky courts'.[41]

Whatever the differences of opinion on the building's design and architecture, few could fail to marvel at the views it offered. 'The house will really be beautiful', wrote Lady Dufferin as it neared completion, 'and the views all around are magnificent. I saw the plains distinctly from my boudoir window, and I am glad to have that open view, as I shall not then feel so buried in the hills.'[42] The 'view from its summit on a clear day is magnificent. To the north, and north-east particularly, the ranges of perpetual snow are seen to great advantage over the peaks of the nearer ranges, while on the west, especially in the rains, there is a grand view of the plains, with the Sutlej winding away in the distance.'[43]

> I went up to the new house this afternoon, and it did look lovely. It was one of Simla's most beautiful moments, between showers, when clouds and hills, and light and shade, all combine to produce the most glorious effects. One could have spent hours at the window of my unfurnished boudoir, looking out on the plains in the distance, with a great river flowing through them: at the variously shaped hills in the foreground, brilliantly coloured in parts, and softened down in others by fleecy clouds floating over them or nestling in the valleys between them. The approaching sunset, too, made the horizon gorgeous with red and golden and pale-blue tints. The result of the whole was to make me feel that it is a great pity that we shall have so short a time to live in a house surrounded by such magnificent views.[44]

As the symbol of British power and home of the monarch's appointed representative, formality prevailed within the walls of Viceregal Lodge. Simla was the exclusive preserve of the British with a protocol that made even six nuns wait in a shed on the road to Viceregal Lodge when they found that they were too early for their appointment with Lady Dufferin.[45] On the death of His Imperial Majesty Nicholas II of Russia in 1918 'court mourning' dress was de rigeur for four weeks, ladies instructed to wear black until the 13 August and half mourning (white, grey, or mauve) thereafter.

But the lodge also had its more relaxed moments. The vicerine's private secretary recalled a party in 1926:

> It was colossal! Reverend gentlemen, renowned hitherto for their eloquence in the Legislative Assembly or the Council of State—or for their dignity of demeanour during interviews with the Viceroy—raced the

length of the ballroom on cushions—danced in solitary defeat blowing gold bugles—tore round the room in teams of four to the strains of John Peel—bleated like sheep or roared like lions and laughed without ceasing...Since then (the guests) have enlarged, on the telephone, on the road, to each other and all and sundry, that never in their lives have they had such an evening.[46]

The British depart: from Simla to Shimla

Simla was a quiescent city until the 1920s, the British preserving it as a uniquely English enclave, restricting town expansion and restricting the growth of the Indian population. As Indian nationalism grew in strength after the First World War, however, even lofty Simla felt the weight of events in the outside world. In May 1921 Gandhi arrived at Simla's Summer Hill Railway Station, greeted by an immense throng. Two days later, when he met Lord Reading, crowds accompanied him to the gates of Viceregal Lodge, chanting 'victory to the uncrowned king'. Gandhi returned in 1931 and again in 1945, though on that occasion he was greeted with black flags in protest at negotiating away Hindu rights when he attended the Simla Conference convened by Wavell at Viceregal Lodge.

Viceregal Lodge played a prominent role in the transfer of power negotiations between the British and the leaders of the Hindu and Muslim communities. Lord Wavell hosted the Simla Conference, the failure of which has been seen as the last chance for a united India to emerge during the final days of British rule. 'I am here alone', wrote a British official at the time, 'with a hundred minions brushing and dusting and refurbishing in preparation for the Conference. Among endless other things I have to arrange a house for Gandhi, one for Nehru (they won't share) and a garage for Gandhi's goats.'[47] Viceregal Lodge, 'with its gilt chairs, silver throne, pictures of Queen Alexandra and tubs of hydrangeas, is full from dawn to dusk with the white-clad figure of Congress *Le Congres Marches*— but there's been no dancing yet, though the atmosphere is friendly and even gay'.[48] There were some splendid incongruities during these pre-partition conferences; Gandhi drinking goats milk beneath a picture of Curzon, Lady Wavell's printed silk dress and Gandhi's loin-cloth together at tea.

With the coming of independence the bubble burst, and the Summer Capital ceased to be. The 'Season' was finally over. The age had gone when osprey feathers nodded in rickshaws, when Whiteaway, Laidlaw and Company retailed the latest in fashion from London and Paris, when the long reaches of power and officialdom trickled down the winding roads, when from Burma in the east and Afghanistan in the west, millions were affected by decisions made among the blooming rhododendrons and the tall cedars. The hill station, a new and wholly British-Indian urban concept, was impelled towards the next stage of its ambulation. There was no one left to balance time between Lady Dufferin's Fund, balls and gymkhanas, files and amateur theatricals, or mild and serious flirtations.[49]

Shimla became the capital of post-partition Punjab before it moved to Le Corbusier's Chandigarh. It then became capital of the state of Himachal Pradesh from 1966. Under an independent government, Shimla's days as a capital city were finished. As early as 1931, when asked where an independent India's capital would be, Gandhi had said: 'We must go down 5,000 storeys to the plains, for the Government should be among the people and for the people.'[50] Simla's 'urban form was a consecration of values that implied detachment from the local people and a commitment to unequal forms of development'.[51] There was a need to create a space in Shimla for indigenous perceptions and experiences, so long squeezed out or denied by its overbearing Britishness, which had cast its spell on Indians, too:

> That Simla was the facsimile of an original British town (which most had never seen) was never doubted. Thus a strange convoluted nostalgia shadows Indian memories: the abiding impression is of a well-planned town, sparkling window-panes, washed roads, even though the majority lived in crouched subservience in the bazar . . . Now, the buildings that have survived fire, termites, decay, and demolition are being restored and conserved. Well-sited and promoted themed heritage experiences are major tourist attractions. It is also hoped in the conservation of the natural forest and built environment, heritage would play a role in neighbourhood regeneration and be used as a catalyst in urban growth strategies . . . The pedestrian stretch of the Ridge and the Mall still evoke 'a Home Counties English Town' and forms the core of the heritage area. Its fame as 'Little England' lingers.[52]

8

Royal Exhibition Building, Melbourne

Set amidst extensive formal gardens in the heart of Melbourne on a street named for Queen Victoria, the Royal Exhibition Building is a cruciform structure centred upon a vast domed hall, inspired by Florence Cathedral. Positioned on a ridge in the landscape, when erected in the late 1870s it was the biggest building in Australia, its distinctive dome, the largest architectural space in the southern hemisphere, forming the most significant feature of the Melbourne skyline. The journal *Architecture* thought the building possessed a 'grandeur and magnificence' which few subsequent buildings managed to attain.[1] This is partly because of the Exhibition Building's overpowering size, but also because of its excellent use of immense space. It was an intensely Victorian building, a product of the Victorian era conceived during a period of overwhelming confidence for the vibrant new colony of Victoria. But beyond its design and its scale, the Exhibition Building was to become of far greater import to the history of the Australian nation than its architectural significance alone merited. It became woven into the fabric of Australian history, associated with many national and cultural activities. 'Is there a more important Australian historic building', asks David Dunstan, the building's chief historian, 'one that has enjoyed a richer past or a wider range of associations?'[2]

The building's historical significance lies in the fact that it is the only remaining great exhibition hall still in use, a breed of building that flowered briefly in the nineteenth century when the international exhibition movement blossomed. What gives the Melbourne Exhibition Building greater significance than the sum of its architectural parts is the ideas that inspired its creation. Though not an engineering innovation, it strove like the Crystal Palace to be symbolic of a world exhibition, rather than a national symbol of the Australian colonies.[3] It was designed to express the ideas developed at the 1851 Great Exhibition, quintessentially Victorian ideas that were central to the development and self-image of the maturing settler colonies created by British expansion. It expressed confidence, optimism, and aspiration, a complacent monument to ideas of progress and civilization and European triumph over the world and its peoples, flora, and fauna. The Melbourne Exhibition Building was the centre-piece of a vision of the city articulated by its liberal intellectual culture, and attempted to forge a nexus between science, the city, and imperialism.[4]

The Melbourne Exhibition Building's ecclesiastical features, including aisle, nave, transepts, fanlight windows, clerestory lighting, and choir and organ dome, combined with its secular function, marked it as a cathedral of industry. It was also a temple to civic pride and nascent colonial patriotism. Today, as well as continuing to perform a host of cultural roles, it stands as a memorial to a certain type of internationalism. This late nineteenth-century internationalism manifests itself in the form of

Figure 23. Royal Exhibition Building, Melbourne, c.1901, the site where the first Commonwealth Parliament of Australia was opened by the Duke of Cornwall and York (later George V) on 9 May 1901.

extravagant exhibitions held in the world's great capital cities—and in recently formed colonial cities such as Melbourne which sought to be numbered among their ranks. The World Fair movement lasted from the middle of the nineteenth century until the First World War, a conflict which put paid to its idealistic, confident, and naïve assumptions. The movement aimed to chart the material and moral progress of mankind through the industrial products of different nations.

The building itself was a cornucopia of traditional references and modern materials and messages. Its walls were constructed of cement rendered brickwork, its roof timbers framed and covered with corrugated galvanized steel and slate. It is built of brick set on a bluestone base, and has long central naves and stunted transepts. The central nave is 500 feet long and 160 feet wide, with extensive side galleries and large cellars of bluestone below. There are four triumphal entrance porticoes, one on each side, with the principal entrance facing south towards the city, with a massive portico functioning both as a triumphal arch and temple front.[5] The building was designed by the Cornish architect Joseph Reed and built by David Mitchell (Dame Nellie Melba's father). He manufactured the building materials at his works in Burnley Street and his steam-powered brickworks at Richmond. William Sangster, a leading horticulturalist, developed the gardens, which remain a classic example of Victorian landscape design, blending Australian and European species. A wide avenue lined with plane trees links the front (southern) entrance of the building with the city beyond. A viewing platform around the dome was reached by a lift, allowing visitors to survey the progress of the booming city stretching out before them. The building was finished in a light-coloured cement stucco with dark-green trim. Within the grounds, two permanent annexes were also constructed, each 460 feet long by 138 feet wide.

Opulent interiors matched the building's external extravagance. The lunettes under the great dome showed Victoria as Peace welcoming Science and Art accompanied by the greeting 'Victoria Welcomes All Nations'. Given the colony of Victoria's protectionist predilections, this provoked amusement. Opposite was another mural depicting the nations of the world responding to Victoria's welcome, with different peoples represented in such a way as to suggest a hierarchy of race which, when related to the classification of technological achievement, allowed the colonial city to appropriate the land.[6] It was quite straightforward, even if subtly stated: exhibition displays about Aboriginals suggested their almost inevitable extinction. The dome was painted to simulate a starry sky with a circle of clouds, the transept and nave painted in a subdued olive green.

Altogether, the Melbourne Exhibition Building is a striking example of Victorian colonial architecture, illustrating the importance of exhibitions, and of museums, as vehicles of civic and national pride and focal points of national unity. It is also testament to the growth of new nations, for in 1901 the building hosted the first federal parliament following the unification of the six Australian colonies as they amalgamated to create the Commonwealth of Australia. The Exhibition Building, which remains at the centre of Melbourne's civic life today, has had a varied career. It was built as the venue for the World Fair of 1880, and eight years later hosted the Centennial International Exhibition commemorating the hundred years since the arrival of the 'First Fleet', Australia's foundation moment. It has found many subsequent roles to perform on behalf of the city, the state, and the nation.

Melbourne and the international exhibition phenomenon

In 1851 the proclamation of Victoria as a separate colony was received with jubilation. Days later major gold discoveries were announced at Ballarat and Bendigo, and the fledgling colony entered a period of rapid economic and demographic transformation fuelled by a remarkable gold rush. In its first decade Victoria's white population grew from 77,000 to 540,000, the population of the capital, Melbourne, rising from under 20,000 in 1851 to 150,000 by 1870. The colony's ambitious and expanding elite soon craved badges of urban civility such as learned societies, exhibitions, and museums. The 1851 Great Exhibition in London had set a new standard, and since that pioneering event, international exhibitions had become a vehicle by which Western nations and settler states sought to showcase their wares and achievements, in the arts but particularly in the spheres of industry and technology. Exhibitions demonstrated their mastery over the environment, including its indigenous peoples, and their skill in classifying all forms of knowledge. About seventy international exhibitions were held between 1851 and the First World War in locations as diverse as America, Britain, Chile, Jamaica, South Africa, and Vietnam. Exhibitions and fairs played a major role in the civic life of colonial cities; anniversaries allowed settlers to celebrate their progress, and royal jubilees were used to mark links between settler communities, 'the mother country', and the Crown (Christchurch's Hagley Park, as has been seen, was home to the 1906 New Zealand International Exhibition). The exhibition was transformed from 'a simple display of technology into a national, quasi-religious, festival'.[7]

Australian exhibits were sent to the London exhibitions of 1851 and 1862. As early as 1854 Melbourne erected its own exhibition building at the site of the Royal Mint on William Street, the design based on the Crystal Palace. This first building was demolished in 1861, considered too small for future exhibitions: Melbourne exhibitions were becoming regular occurrences, growing in size and ambition, and they needed a venue that matched the colonists' aspirations. As a temporary measure, Sir Redmond Barry, founder and trustee of the public library and museum and chancellor of the University of Melbourne, offered the grounds of the public library and museum to serve as a venue for the exhibitions.[8] Exhibitions were staged here in 1866, 1872, and 1875. Each of these Melbourne exhibitions was timed to coincide with major overseas exhibitions—in Paris, London, and Philadelphia—to which the Australian exhibits were then sent. In 1875, Barry suggested that a new site be found, and two years later a plan for a permanent exhibition building was submitted to the Victoria parliament. Giving extra impetus to this plan was a complementary desire to hold a large international exhibition in what was a booming city and colony. The Victorian Commissioners had sent a message to their opposite numbers in France ahead of the 1878 Paris Exhibition, stating that Melbourne was now 'the site of a populous and well-built city presenting all the evidences of wealth and civilization, taking rank with the foremost cities in the world'. The rapid progress of Australia, they enthusiastically claimed, was 'one of the marvels of modern times'.[9]

In 1880 Sir William Clarke, chairman of the Victorian Commissioners and planner of the 1880 Melbourne International Exhibition, boasted proudly that the site of the new Exhibition Building was 'only a generation ago...part of an unknown forest in an unknown land'.[10] A cantata by Leon Caron echoed the claim of the colony of Victoria, 'Queen of the South', once 'sleeping amidst the primeval solitudes' and now harkening to the voice of 'speedy discovery and development'. People were proud of the sudden creation of a sophisticated, Western state on the other side of the world. The Exhibition Building was a celebration of the West's triumph over the 'primitiveness' that their modernity had displaced. In just a quarter of a century Victoria had developed from a pastoral economy to an industrial one with a capital city of a quarter of a million people. How better to publicize the achievements of the colony and the opportunities it offered than by hosting an international exhibition?[11]

The desire to put Melbourne and Victoria on the world map was translated into an international exhibition intended to showcase Australian produce and achievements to the world and stimulate the idea of Victoria as a place in which to invest. Melbourne, it was proudly boasted, was the newest outpost of Western civilization, and the Exhibition Building was designed as a powerful symbol of that fact. It proclaimed to the world the wealth, capacity, and culture of the city and the British colony, and documented the development of the city from a small frontier settlement into a modern metropolis, strongly linked with a world economy and community of ideas.[12]

The gardens and buildings

The land for the Carlton Gardens where the Exhibition Building was sited was initially reserved as part of Superintendent (later Lieutenant-Governor) Charles La Trobe's network of parks and gardens that enclosed the north and east edge of the centre. In the early days cattle grazed on the site and people foraged for timber and used the space as a recreation ground. Bounded on either side by Victoria, Rathdowne, Carlton, and Nicholson Streets, the space in which the Exhibition Building and its grounds lie was marked out by the parliament of Victoria in 1878. The building's foundation stone was laid on 19 February 1879. Covering 64 acres, the perimeter was marked by bluestone plinth and cast-iron palisade fencing, ornamental gates, and cast-iron pots. Joseph Reed's design for the Exhibition Building provided it with a grand entrance, linking it with the clear vista to the central places of democracy and civil administration—Parliament House and Government House—via a *grande allée* entrance in the form of three straight tree-lined paths, which formed powerful converging avenues from entrances in Victoria Street. The adjacent gardens on the north and south sides of the Yarra River, as well as the Fitzroy, Treasury, and Parliament Gardens, heightened the contrived device of the Carlton Gardens and Exhibition Building as set within an endless boulevard of greenery and civic grandeur, reminiscent of European baroque palace gardens.[13]

Reed contributed more to Melbourne's appearance than any other man, and there is hardly a street in the city centre were his work cannot be found (he had his silk handkerchiefs embroidered with the names of his principal Melbourne buildings). Reed's design combined Gothic and Classical elements to create a building that was at once useful and ceremonial, secular, and sacred. Reed drew on his experience of travelling in Europe when he was a Victorian Commissioner at the London International Exhibition in 1862. His winning design was a Beaux-Arts axial scheme with the building as a palace, primarily in the Italian Renaissance style. Reed and Barnes adopted the little-known German Rundbogenstil mode, and other more familiar stylistic motifs from earlier international exhibition buildings in Britain and Europe, to great effect. Rundbogenstil was essentially a 'round arched' style, made popular in northern Germany in the early nineteenth century. This remarkably eclectic building and its surroundings also combined elements from Byzantine, Romanesque, Lombardic, and early Italian Renaissance buildings. Reed nominated Filippo Brunelleschi's pointed double-shelled dome of Florence Cathedral as his model. Its lay-out was influenced by the buildings of Kensington Gardens in London. The building was 'more a temple to industry, the building...is a dramatic testament to the spirit of enterprise and industry of Victorians in late-nineteenth century Australia'.[14]

The aesthetic significance of the Carlton Gardens lies in their embodiment of the nineteenth-century Gardenesque style. They were intended to be part of the attraction and included parterre (formal or symmetrically placed) garden beds, significant avenues such as the southern carriage drive and *Grand Allée*, the path system, specimens and clusters of trees, and lakes and fountains.[15] A level promenade runs along the front of the building, with a semi-circular space centred on a fountain. The ceremonial approach is along a 78-feet-wide avenue with floral carpet bedding, and two other paths radiate from the Melbourne Exhibition Fountain. At 33 feet in height and the largest fountain in Australia, this feature was designed by the German Josef Hochgurtel. Its design reflected the confidence and progress of the colony, and signalled the purpose of world fairs—to display the produce and industry of nations. At the central level of the fountain, four figures dance below symbols of the arts, science, commerce, and industry, such as musical instruments, a telescope, a sailing ship, and a steam engine. Above this are images of Victoria's indigenous flora and fauna, including ferns and platypi, the economic arts being nourished and developed by the storehouse of natural sciences.[16] Holding all of this aloft are four merpeople rising up from the waters of the lower pool. Built during Victoria's boom

years, the spouting water was intended to demonstrate the power and success of the recently established Yan Yean project which had brought potable
water to the city.[17] During the 1880 exhibition temporary buildings covered
the northern portion of the site, which was designed to become a complementary landscape to the building once the temporary pavilions were
removed. There are diagonal avenues of chestnut-leaved oak and Dutch elm.
Part of the land was used for a while as a recreational oval with a grandstand,
later for buildings, then as a car park. It is now the site of the State of Victoria Museum.

The Melbourne exhibitions of the 1880s

Among other things, exhibitions denoted the power of settlers over indigenous communities. They heralded the introduction of new technologies
such as photography and electric lighting, and innovations in steel production, flight, and wireless telegraphy. They facilitated the global dissemina-
tion of goods, technologies, and values and the development of a global
marketplace, not only for goods but also for ideas. Those who attended the
exhibitions were participants, not just observers, and the exhibitions developed Western consumerism and were shop fronts for the industrial revolution. The international exhibition phenomenon reflected a dynamic and
transitional phase in modern history, which saw the growth and spread of
the benefits of industrialization in the form of technological advancements
and social progress, the transmission of ideas and cultural values around the
world, and the rapid development of an extensive international economy.[18]

The construction of the Exhibition Building allowed Victoria to steal a
march on its neighbouring state, New South Wales, for when a venue was
required for a centennial event in 1888, Sydney was not an option because
the Garden Palace had burned down in 1882. Melbourne thus stepped into
the breach. There was some tension between the two states and their capital
cities, New South Wales politicians resenting Victoria's 'go-ahead, Yankee
style and protectionist stance' and opposing federal union.[19] Melbourne was
able to construct a new vision of itself through exhibitions and the exciting
and commanding building designed to stage them. It heralded advances in
public health and the electricity that would revolutionize the city. The
building was connected to the telephone network, and Melbourne was
hooked up to this new technology two years before London. Among other

things, the Exhibition Building and the vision of Melbourne showed how much Australia owed to emerging American technology and urban forms, though it was also inspired by the Paris Exhibition of 1878 and the nineteenth-century development of the French capital itself.

The Melbourne exhibitions of the 1880s took place during a period of economic growth for the colony based on gold and agricultural exports, stock-market profits, and real-estate speculation.[20] It was also a period of notable public building, as wealth from a booming economy was directed to grand and symbolic projects intended to reflect the status and position of Melbourne, Victoria, and the Australian colonies on the world stage. The Melbourne International Exhibition of 1880 opened with 20,000 people on the streets watching a procession led by two brass bands and 800 sailors from the British warships on station, the Victorian Naval Brigade, and visiting German, French, and Italian vessels. It attracted over 1.3 million visitors in eight months and exhibits were sent from America, Britain, France, and Germany. The British court featured carpets, upholstery, chemicals, hardware, paper-hangings, carriages, leather goods, and weighing machines.

Figure 24. External view of Royal Exhibition Building, Melbourne, from Nicholson Street entrance, December 2008.

The Americans offered agricultural machinery, barbed wire, lawnmowers, cottons, and electric lights. There were exhibits of lace, furniture, tiles, and armaments.[21] The largest display was from the colony of Victoria itself, featuring locomotives from the Phoenix Foundry in Ballarat and the Victorian Railway Workshop, local wine, gold, artwork, and crafts. In the Indian court, tea was served by 'Hindoos', and for those desiring something a little stronger, there was a 'German lager beer' pavilion. Pottery ware and fine porcelain were displayed as well as fine art loaned by prestigious overseas galleries. The description of the items of Victorian produce and industry occupied thirty-seven closely printed pages, nearly 2,000 entries in all. The exhibition became a world unto itself, reported on in the daily newspapers. It spawned a range of medals, prizes, and mementoes, and its closure was marked by a grand ball.

The 1888 Melbourne Centennial Exhibition was the first in the world to have night-time viewings. This was because over 60 miles of cabling allowed the interior and exterior of the building to be lit by electricity. By the late nineteenth century the Australian colonies had reached a level of economic and industrial development commensurate with the emerging 'first world'. An international exhibition was just the kind of calling card that would announce the arrival on the international scene of a vigorous young nation. 'The hosting of a world fair seemed to represent Australia's coming of age', and 1888 marked the high-water mark of Victoria's prosperity.[22] The building, therefore, reflected nationalistic pride as Australia developed a sense of itself beyond the ties of empire and the 'mother country', as well as internationalist ideas. It also reflected, in its purpose and its design, the value of education and scientific, cultural, and technological progress, and a belief in the power of modern industrial society to improve the lot of mankind. A key value was the Utopian concept of civilization through technological advancement. Four developments dictated the shape of international exhibitions and all of them related to the Industrial Revolution—mass production, prefabrication, mass communications, and urbanization.[23]

The 1888 exhibition attracted over 2 million people, but cost the Victorian government £250,000, ten times the scheduled sum, which struck a discordant note as the city's boom was coming to an end. It required the erection of huge temporary annexes in the gardens around the main Exhibition Building. There was a working dairy, a quartz-crushing stamper battery, school-room displays from around the world, paintings and sculptures, musical performances, and armaments pavilions. At the opening a choir of 5,000 people performed. Half a million people attended symphony concerts during the course of the exhibition, and over 3,000 paintings were displayed.

In 1880 the window and door joinery was painted green and the rendered walls were left unpainted. The combined effects of trams, horse-drawn traffic, and industrial pollution gradually discoloured the exterior surface of the building. It was repainted with a new scheme for the 1888 International Exhibition and the dome gilded with gold leaf. The Ancient Order of the Druids, with flowing beards and white robes, were part of the opening procession, flanked by trades union members carrying their union banners. The exhibition included such curiosities as a 'Victorian fernery' and a model of the (as yet incomplete) Eiffel Tower constructed from champagne bottles, and an armament court displaying the martial capacity of 'Greater Briton', 'enthralling and reassuring anxious colonists'.[24] There were many visitors to the exhibition from overseas. It opened a new channel of trade and laid the foundations for new manufacturing industries, investment, and employment of British and foreign capital. This acted as a justification for the exhibition movement and the extravagance involved. But this exhibition marked the end of an era, not the beginning of one. The exhibition's closure was a turning point in the downward economic spiral which led to the collapse of the financial system in Victoria in 1893.

After the exhibitions: parliament, museum, monument

Not long after Melbourne's splendid new Exhibition Building was completed, exhibitions fell out of fashion. There had grown a distrust of their purpose as confidence in 'progress' waned; there was an increasing awareness of the element of drudgery in most people's work, even in technologically advanced societies, and of the bane of poverty in the midst of plenty. But even though the days of the great exhibitions were at an end, an array of other activities found a home in the Exhibition Building and its grounds, transforming its utility in the process and reflecting the changing cultural landscape of the city of Melbourne.

In 1901, the interior was redecorated in time for the opening of the first Commonwealth Parliament of Australia. This took place in the Exhibition Building because it was the only building large enough to accommodate the 14,000 people who attended the ceremony and saw the Duke of Cornwall and York (the future George V) open the federal parliament for the first time. The decorations were under the control of John Ross Anderson, also known for the interior design of the ANZ 'Gothic' Bank in Collins Street. In keeping with the solemnity and importance of the occasion, Anderson chose a sober scheme for the interior of the temporary parliament. The great dome was painted to represent the sky. Underneath were four mottos suitable for a new nation: *Dei gracia*—by the grace of God; *Carpe diem*—seize the day; *Aude sapere*—dare to be wise; and *Benigno numine*—with benign power. A frieze shows the products of agriculture and hinted at the wealth of the new nation.[25]

Continuing the symbolic theme, on the arches are lunettes (half-moon shaped spaces where the arches meet cornices) representing Peace, War, Federation, and Government. The Federation image shows Britannia welcoming the six federated states of Australia as young women, while the Government image shows Knowledge enthroned, surrounded by figures representing the arts, education, and defence. Eight women in draped costumes symbolize the Four Seasons, Night and Morning, and Justice and Truth. Under the dome are plaster heads from the first decorative scheme of 1880. They include an indigenous Australian, a Chinese man, and an Indian.[26] For the celebrations that accompanied the opening of the federal

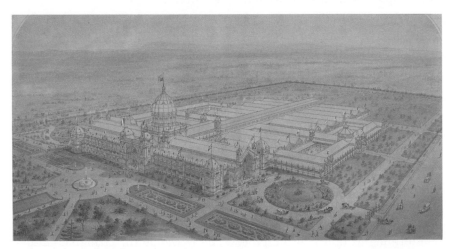

Figure 25. Large framed watercolour of the Exhibition Building, built in Carlton Gardens, Melbourne between 1879 and 1880 for the Melbourne International Exhibition. The watercolour was probably painted by the architect of the Exhibition Building, Joseph Reed, and reflects the changes to the original design that was sanctioned by the Exhibition commissioners in May 1879; these included the addition of a machinery annexe and acres of temporary annexes.

parliament in 1901, the exterior of the building was lit with festoons of small incandescent lights (recently enhanced with fibre optics and digitally created images). Tom Roberts was commissioned to capture the event on canvas, producing a famous grand painting. Royalty, governors, members of the various states of Australia, and the common people—'that's the Empire', said Roberts, 'and this all meets under one roof. And that's what I'm painting.'[27]

After the ceremony, the federal parliament moved to Victoria's State Parliament Building in Melbourne, where it sat until Canberra was ready in 1927. The western annexe, used at the 1880 Centennial International Exhibition as a machinery hall, was converted to accommodate the parliament of Victoria which was thus ejected from its home, and it remained here until 1927. The western annexe was demolished during the 1960s, while the eastern annexe, partially demolished in the 1950s, made way in 1979 for the new convention centre. In 1912 Victoria's first Motor Show was held at the Exhibition Building, where it remained based until 1995 when it moved to the new and larger Melbourne Exhibition Centre. In 1919 the building was used as a makeshift fever hospital during the Spanish Influenza epidemic, accommodating 1,500 people. The building was also the original site of the Australian War Memorial. Part of the eastern annexe became a home for war memorabilia brought home from the First World War by Australian soldiers, and this display enabled the historian C. E. W. Bean to exert pressure on the federal government to create the Australian War Memorial in Canberra. The Exhibition Building remained the main store until the Canberra facility was ready in 1941, some material remaining there until the early 1970s.

The building was used for the Melbourne proms and from the 1890s new museum displays developed, along with a picture gallery, live animal displays, and new garden and sporting attractions. In 1892 there was a cyclorama in the eastern annexe, which showed a view of Melbourne in 1841. In 1907 it hosted the first Australian Exhibition of Women's Work and became the venue for the annual Ancient Order of Druids gala, and before the First World War there were cycle races on the Oval which attracted large crowds. The retailer Sidney Myer threw a giant feast in 1930 for 11,000 poor and unemployed people. There was an exhibition maze, and in 1908 over 30,000 people watched a balloon take off from the Oval. The Exhibition Building hosted annual school and university examinations, as well as home improvement and home ownership exhibitions and car shows, poultry, and dog shows, and rallies of the Australian Natives Association and the Salvation

Army. Adjutant Rattray of the Salvation Army wrote: 'Shall I ever forget that vast concourse of twice three thousand? The sonorous tones of the magnificent Exhibition Organ.'[28] The Exhibition Aquarium was a very popular landmark for many years.

In the 1930s the Exhibition Building served variously as a ballroom, cyclorama, aquarium, and concert hall, and staged bike and motorbike races. During the Second World War it was used for troop accommodation before being taken over by the Royal Australian Air Force as barracks and a training establishment. In 1940, 4,000 men of the 17th Brigade of the 6th Division bivouacked there. From 1949 until 1962 the huts left on the Oval by the air force were employed as the Exhibition Building site was used as a major migrant reception centre. A ballroom complex was developed when the city staged a ball for Princess Elizabeth, and the Great Hall and stadium annexe were used during the 1956 Olympic Games for weightlifting and basketball. The Exhibition Building continued to be used as a venue for major exhibitions, trade fairs, and public events, the anchor events being the biennial Melbourne International Contemporary Art Fair and the Melbourne International Flower and Garden Show.[29]

The colonial museum

Some of the exhibits from the two great exhibitions of the 1880s were acquired by the Industrial and Technological Museum, and now form part of Museum Victoria's collections, including model boats from the Straits Settlement, Minton tiles for home decorating, bars of pig iron and steel, mineral specimens, and samples of rice, rubber, sago, and timber.[30] The Industrial and Technological Museum had been established in 1870, a by-product of Melbourne's 1866–7 Intercolonial Exhibition. From 1870, the museum, along with the Melbourne Library and Art Gallery, were located on Swanston Street behind an imposing classical frontage.

In the late twentieth century the Exhibition Building and its site became a part of the state of Victoria's museum and heritage provision. In 1995 an architectural competition for a new Melbourne museum to be located on part of the Carlton Gardens reserve was announced, and a design was selected. A free-standing building to the north of the 1880 structure was opened in 2000. The Exhibition Building became a museum piece itself, and in 1996 Museum Victoria became responsible for the Royal Exhibition Museum Collection of over 3,000 objects, files, and images. The history of exhibitions and museums had for long been intertwined. The development of exhibitions paralleled the nineteenth-century preoccupation with display, and was demonstrated through the development of institutions such as museums, art galleries, dioramas, and cycloramas. The international exhibition movement was an extension of the principles of classification and comparison developed by eighteenth-century scientists. Contemplation of objects was intended to inspire feelings of human progress and achievement.[31]

A rapidly expanding natural world (not least as a result of expeditions and associated collecting) became ever more subject to forms of taxonomic systematization. Contemporaries were increasingly confident that the natural world could be known and the nineteenth-century museum lay at the heart of this. It constituted the public face of scientific endeavour, the point of contact between scientists and public exhibition, between empirical collecting and theorization, and between such scientific discourse and popular understanding.[32] Creating exhibitions that 'swept the world up into one place seemed to offer an extraordinary insight into the possibilities of scientific globalization. It also stimulated the growth of museums, directly in the form of the South Kensington Museum (later the V&A).'[33] The gathering of material and knowledge was central to the physical expansion of empire and its intellectual underpinning and justification, as well as the developing sense of European superiority over non-Europeans. Railways, telegraph lines, and the surveys associated with them conquered time and distance. Geology, palaeontology, archaeology, and zoology represented the conquest of nature. An important output of this was public display in museums. Colonization involved raiding the natural world, of which indigenous people were viewed as a part. The museum was created by a European vision of the world. Museum buildings and collections carried visions of the past and of the future, and came to evoke civic, colonial, national, and imperial power. It offered a public justification for expansion and the accommodation of nature and peoples to its purpose.[34]

Turning specifically to Australia's museums, MacKenzie writes that they were characteristically founded in each colony by a group of bourgeois dilettante scientists, wealthy businessmen, and influential professionals. Initially, the creation of such museums was designed to forward their own natural historical interests, to establish a club in which they could interact, and to connect them with both imperial and international networks and scientific endeavour.[35] These museums fulfilled a role in transferring flora

and fauna, and human cultural artefacts, to the metropole for the further-
ance of European science and academic knowledge. In 1798, for instance,
Governor Hunter sent a platypus preserved in spirit to the new Literary and
Philosophical Society of Newcastle upon Tyne. Interest in scientific study
was stimulated by land surveys, the need to study water supply, and the
foundation of botanical gardens and observatories. In 1853 Ferdinand von
Mueller was appointed as government botanist and director of the Gardens,
while in the same year Wilhelm Blandowski, a mining engineer from Silesia,
proposed a geological museum and was appointed government zoologist
and first curator of the museum. Melbourne's early prosperity meant that
resources were available for the foundation of new institutions such as the
Royal Society of Victoria. The creation of a colonial museum was at the
heart of all these developments.

In 1899 the museum at the university moved to the city centre's cultural
complex, representing a new philosophy of bringing the museum to the
people.[36] It was housed in a large brick extension named McCoy Hall.
Some of the Industrial and Technological Museum's collections were amalgamated with the National Museum, some sold or stored. This museum
reopened 1915 in the Queen's Hall, formerly part of the library, where it
remained until a new museum was opened in 2000 behind the Royal Exhibition Building.[37]

9

Raffles Hotel, Singapore

Drawing up outside Raffles for the first time, for a split second I failed to recognize it. My brain would not immediately compute, for the building before me as I stepped out of the taxi looked like a miniature of the structure I knew so well from photographs—like one of the two-thirds-sized facsimiles of famous buildings that used to be erected at British Empire exhibitions. The hotel's iconic main building, enormous when first erected, illustrates the difference in scale between grand colonial-era buildings and the modern ones that dwarf them. But its graceful charm was soon apparent; a pristine white structure, its elegance accentuated by lower-level wings in a matching style and further extended after a major redevelopment to occupy an entire block of central Singapore city. Nevertheless, it is in some ways outclassed by the enormous, gleaming, occasionally breathtaking, new buildings that define the city centre, some simply tall, others innovative and almost space age. Like a clash of civilizations, Raffles and central Singapore city's other colonial-era buildings vie with bold post-colonial structures, such as Raffles City across Bras Basah Road from the hotel complex, the stunning erections of the marina, and the forest of skyscrapers that rise directly behind the 1880s Singapore Cricket Club when looking across the padang towards the central business district. The contrast and mixture is utterly exhilarating.

According to Somerset Maugham, the Raffles Hotel 'stood for all the fables of the exotic East'.[1] Maugham fell in love with the hotel—the 'Savoy of Singapore'—upon his first visit in March 1921, and when resident would often sit under the frangipani tree in the left hand corner of the Palm Court. Known for his short stories and plays about colonial life in the East, while staying at the Raffles he corrected the galley proofs of *The Trembling of a Leaf*, a volume of short stories, and worked on the play *East of Suez*. Located at the heart of a city-state dominated by modern buildings, Raffles Hotel stands apart, a colonial-era oasis surrounded by high-rise concrete and steel.

Figure 26. Historical advertisement for the Raffles Hotel in Singapore displaying sharp marketing instinct: Kipling actually said, 'Feed at Raffles' but 'stay at the Hotel d'Europe'.

It presents an arrangement of low-rise, veranda-enclosed buildings painted white, with terracotta-tiled pitched roofs, set amidst courtyards and gardens. The contrast between the lush and generous tropical gardens and turn-of-the-century colonial architecture is its hallmark. As a visitor in the early 1930s put it, 'Besides being a landmark of European civilization in the hub-bub of Asia, the Raffles is a palace among hotels. Compared with the towering piles of New York and Chicago [the visitor condescended], it would look aged and squat and rambling, but here in the eye of the Orient it is germane to its natural setting.'[2]

Raffles's classically inspired architecture features towering windows and doorways framed with 19-feet-tall arches designed to allow as much light into the building as possible. Raffles and its famous Long Bar became synonymous with elegant travel and elite colonial society, though its history is testament to the cosmopolitan nature of empire and the manner in which indigenous elites, and those drawn from amongst non-British alien communities, could prosper under British rule. While the hotel was constructed at the zenith of British power and was associated with the colonial upper crust, there is little that is British about the maze of buildings that house its 103 suites. Built in the French Renaissance style, there has only ever been one British manager, and the Raffles Hotel was created and managed by Armenians—the four Sarkies brothers who were jointly responsible for the world's first great Asian hotel chain. Arshok, Aviet, Martin, and Tigran Sarkies haled from New Julfa, the Armenian quarter of Isfahan.

A chain of opulent hotels sprang up in the ports and cities frequented by travellers in the colonial world. Their growth reflected the volume of itinerant people moving hither and thither about the business of running, working, and touring the empire and the wider world. Colonial administrators, planters, emigrants, missionaries, soldiers, sailors, traders, and their families—young women in search of husbands, children packed off to boarding school in England, peripatetic authors—all followed familiar routes of travel across the oceans, stopping off in port cities and at coaling stations, each with its own clutch of hotels and clubs. In 1917, 50,000 to 60,000 people signed the guest book at the Raffles Hotel, indicating the volume of human traffic transiting through busy ports such as Singapore. Imperial travellers were joined later by wealthy tourists on extended tours or round-the-world cruises, as travel became more affordable and distant places more accessible. Soon these wealthy globetrotters, including royals and titled personages haunting swanky hotels and private drawing-rooms, were joined by Hollywood stars and sports idols. As more people travelled the world for pleasure Singapore became the Clapham Junction of the eastern seas. Everyone, it seemed, stopped there for at least a day, and a visit to Raffles became one of the rites of passage of world travel.[3] To this day, most people passing through Singapore for the first time find it impossible to resist sampling a Singapore Sling in the Raffles Long Bar.

Singapore

Singapore presents the visitor with vivid contrasts, ethnic enclaves and colonial squares jostling the ultramodern, as gleaming skyscrapers loom above Edwardian civic buildings and overcrowded living quarters.[4] Hybridity—cultural, racial, and architectural—are pervasive. The 'Straits Chinese' illustrate the fusion that is such a Singaporean theme. Born locally, and sometimes known as the 'King's (or Queen's) Chinese', members of this community emulated British lifestyle and adopted European clothing. Their homes bore witness to their cultural duality, Ching dynasty tables and chairs side-by-side with massive English-style sideboards and cupboards. Colonial 'planter's chairs', 'with wicker seats and foot-rest extensions, share space with the ancestral altar covered in dragon carvings. Roll-top desks and pedestal-type telephones co-exist with embroidered Chinese wall hangings and mah-jong tables.'[5]

European colonialism in the region originated in the interaction of what the historian Mark Frost dubs the four 'Cs'—curiosity, collaboration, commerce, and conflict. In 1819 Stamford Raffles established an East India Company settlement at Singapore to counter the growing power of the Dutch in the region, part of a high-stakes commercial battle for control of maritime South-east Asia. Raffles selected the island of Singapore because of its perfect location for the China trade, especially the shipments of Bengal opium which had become essential to the East India Company's liquidity.[6] Acting as Lieutenant Governor of Bencoolen in Sumatra, Raffles wrote that in acquiring Singapore 'our object is not territory, but trade, a commercial emporium and a fulcrum, whence we may extend our influence politically'.[7] This Singapore undoubtedly became. Singapore grew as a beacon of capitalism and commerce, and in the twentieth century became the empire's main naval base east of Suez.

Raffles convinced the leaders of Singapore to cede the island in return for an annual payment. On 30 January 1819 he camped on the banks of the Singapore River, with the Union Jack flying within the crumbling ramparts of old Singapura.[8] The island's thousand-strong population comprised a Chinese and Malay minority and the nomadic *orang laut* or 'sea gypsies', the indigenous people of Singapore and Malaya. A treaty of friendship between Raffles and the new sultan and his prime minister, involving an annual salary of 5,000 Spanish dollars, was signed. Soon Raffles's troops began clearing ground, erecting tents, and surveying the harbour for defensive positions, and people started to arrive in large numbers. Immigration began with a handful of Europeans and Indians, some of them merchants from Penang. From as early as 1820 a small trickle of Armenians, already well-established in trade in Brunei and the Philippines, began to arrive, while Chinese people appeared in great numbers. Wealthy Arab merchants also started to arrive, as Raffles, envisioning a thriving free trade port, hoped that they would. By 1821, the population had grown fivefold.

Singapore became a cosmopolitan place, a pioneer town of rootless immigrants, like so many other colonial 'Wild West' settlements around the world, a notoriously lawless one. Trade was Singapore's lifeblood and the British brand of free trade was an exciting novelty. By the 1830s the island had so leapt ahead of the other British settlements at Penang and Malacca that it was made the centre of British government in South-east Asia. The population had grown to 30,000 by 1830 and 200,000 by 1897, an astonishing rate of expansion driven by the success of the port. The volume of trade passing through was enormous, and it had become a major coaling and refitting station for ships across the whole of South-east Asia. The port thrived, based on junk trade with China, Cochin-China, and Siam, and the Bugis trade with Bali, Borneo, and the Celebes. Most ocean-going liners between Europe, the Far East, and Australasia stopped at Singapore, which was excellent for the island's burgeoning hotel business. There was then of course the trade of European shipping lines connecting Europe with the Far East. The conversion of cargo shipping to steam from the mid-1860s, and the opening of the Suez Canal in 1869—which made the Straits of Johore as opposed to the Sunda Straits the main route to the east—saw a dramatic rise in Singapore's trade, which expanded eightfold from 1873 to 1913. Singapore was the hinge between trade in the Indian Ocean, the South China Sea, and the Java Sea, the grand tropical emporium which Raffles had dreamed of.[9] The arrival at the Singapore Botanical Garden in 1877 of the first rubber seeds from Brazil foreshadowed a future economic transformation, as did the growth of the tin industry. By 1903 Singapore was the world's seventh-largest port in tonnage of shipping handled.

The sinews of the global economy grew stronger with each passing decade. In 1867 the record time for a London–Singapore voyage stood at 116 days; three years later, the steamer *Shantung* made it from Glasgow in forty-two days. This led to a rapid expansion of dock facilities, and the cable links that arrived in the 1860s further enhanced the growing interconnectedness of the imperial world. In terms of Singapore's internal transport infrastructure, this developed too. It was connected by railway, and in 1880 the *jinricki-sha* was first imported from Japan via Shanghai. Soon there was a horse-drawn omnibus, and in 1885, the Singapore Tramways Company began operation. In 1889 Rudyard Kipling walked along the beach 'in full view of five miles of shipping—five solid miles of masts and funnels—to a place called Raffles Hotel'. His opinion of Raffles was that 'the food is as excellent as the rooms are bad. Let the traveller take note. Feed at Raffles and sleep at the Hotel de

L'Europe.' He clearly enjoyed his dining experience at the hotel, sampling six different chutneys with his curry.[10]

Singapore's population boom and status as a hub port utterly transformed the built environment. In the 1840s, Munshi Abdullah, a witness to this transformation, wrote: 'I am astonished to see how markedly our world is changing. A new world is being created, the old world destroyed. The very jungle becomes a settled district while elsewhere a settlement reverts to jungle.'[11] When Raffles had first landed in 1819, the only part of the island not covered in swampy mangroves was a small area that became known as the padang ('open space') which eventually became the central focus of the colonial administration. The padang is still the seat of judicial and parliamentary rule, its open space, used initially as a cricket and parade ground, also becoming the traditional setting for state occasions. The Singapore Cricket Club sits at one end of the padang, the Singapore Recreation Club (founded in the 1880s by members of the Eurasian community) at the other.[12] The padang square is completed by the classical City Hall and Supreme Court, opposite the War Memorial.

Raffles chose what buildings went where and what 'zones' the nascent town was divided into—to the north and south of the river, ethnic neighbourhoods and space reserved for government buildings, religious sites, and a botanic garden (reflected in today's 'Little India', 'Arab Quarter', and 'Chinatown').[13] The width of streets, size of houses, and even the materials for their construction were regulated. Between the 1820s and 1860s things started to change, particularly in the European district. The frontier character of the town gave way to a new colonial-style order as the British imposed themselves architecturally on the town. Looming over Singapore's inhabitants by the 1850s were shiny new colonial edifices built of stone and brick.[14]

The Singapore River was the heart of the town, its Boat Quay and Commercial Square backing onto the sea. Europeans started to live on the east bank fronting the Esplanade and along the beach, the 'Mayfair of Singapore', where they erected elegant homes.[15] From the 1830s the Irish superintendent of public works, George Coleman, began using convict labour from India (the convict population numbered 3,000 by the 1850s), building churches, lighthouses, government offices, and public buildings, draining marshes, constructing roads, and building Palladian style houses which set the fashion for Singapore's delicate, graceful colonial architecture.[16]

By the 1870s, the town was beginning to look impressive. The prosperous commercial sector on the west bank of the Singapore River faced the official quarter across the river where the government offices, City Hall, Singapore Institution, and St Andrew's Cathedral stood, all set amid well-kept green lawns. Fort Canning dominated the town, flanked by hills crowned with fine houses. There was a general hospital, a parliament house, a police station, the Raffles Museum and Library, and the Victoria Memorial Hall. There was also the Apostolic Church of St Gregory, commissioned by Armenian refugees from Turkey. The Raffles statue was erected near where he is thought to have landed in 1819, a replica of the original bronze cast in front of the Victoria Theatre in Empress Place.

Raffles Hotel

From Shepheard's on the banks of the Nile to the Peninsula in Hong Kong, the empire's grand hotels were way-stations familiar to generations of well-heeled travellers. They were few, so they became distinctive landmarks. These stepping stones from Europe to the East included the Galle Face Hotel in Colombo, the Taj Mahal in Bombay, the Mandarin and the Peninsular hotels in Hong Kong, and the Raffles in Singapore. Peripatetic people needed places to stay, and taverns, guest houses, chummeries (dormitories for single men), and hotels took root wherever settlements developed, ranging from the opulent to the downright shabby. The Taj Mahal was viewed by many as the quintessence of imperial amplitude, though ironically was not built by Britons but by Parsees, members of a community which had grown rich and powerful through their amicable relationship with the imperialists. The industrialist Jamsetji Nusserwanji Tata, founder of the Tata Group, engaged the English engineer W. A. Chambers to build to a design produced by Indian architects. Opened in 1903, its enormous Indo-Saracenic bulk sits on the waterfront at the Apollo Bunder, the city's main point of embarkation and disembarkation, next to the Gateway of India. In contrast, Watson's Hotel, also in Bombay, was a more modest establishment. The architect Rowland Mason Ordish, known for his work on the single-span roof of St Pancras Station, designed its external cast-iron frame, which was manufactured in Britain and shipped to India.[17]

A variety of accommodation facilities also accompanied the growth of Singapore. In 1827 John Francis was advertising a 'public house' in Singapore to accommodate travellers. Five years later it had become a 'hotel', complete with billiard room and refreshment hall. By the 1840s there was the Ship Hotel, the London Hotel, the British Hotel, the Commercial Hotel, the Hotel de Paris, and the Hamburg Hotel. Raffles's main rival, however, was the Hotel de l'Europe on the Esplanade (now the site of the striking Supreme Court building). An even greater choice of lodgings developed as the overland route to the East became busier. This route ran from Europe via a railway between the Mediterranean and Red Sea, to the sea routes and ports of the Indian Ocean. The opening of the Suez Canal in 1869 greatly increased the traffic between East and West, acting, in the words of Joseph Conrad, 'like the breaking of a dam'.[18] Speedier voyages from Europe and America brought a new wave of European visitors. Tourists in search of a brush with the East expected to have it from the comfort of a quality hotel and itinerant colonial *memsahibs* sought to maintain civilized standards. Europeans visiting Singapore were increasingly less inclined to 'rough it'.[19]

Though a potent symbol of colonial society in the East and an institution in which few Asians would dream of setting foot (unless members of the elite or members of staff), Raffles was founded by non-Europeans on land owned by an Arab trader. Martin and Tigran Sarkies had established a hotel business in Penang, their Malayan portfolio already including the Eastern Hotel, the Oriental Hotel, the Oriental Tiffin and Billiard Rooms (later renamed the Sea View Hotel), and the Crag Hotel, a health resort on Penang Hill. In 1887 the brothers took over a cavernous ten-room Anglo-Indian bungalow in Singapore, and the Raffles Hotel was born.[20] It was the year of Queen Victoria's Golden Jubilee, an event marked in Singapore by the unveiling of a new statue of Stamford Raffles, an event which may well have influenced the choice of name for the new hotel.

The bungalow, which was to morph into the iconic hotel was located on the corner of Beach Road and Bras Basah Road. It had begun life under British rule as 'East India Company Lease 214'. In 1827 the plot was granted to Samuel Milton, a missionary friend of Raffles, who intended to build a church or a school, but two years later it was acquired by Robert Scott, who built an extensive bungalow called Beach House. In 1870 it came into the hands of Sir Syed Mohamed Alsagoff, a wealthy Arab merchant and land-owner. In 1878, he leased Beach House to Dr Charles Emmerson, a veterinarian who also ran a well-known restaurant called the Tiffin Rooms.[21] He renamed Beach House Emmerson's Hotel. Following Emmerson's death, Beach House was leased to the Raffles Institution, a boys' school, which used the building as a boarding house.

It was in this commodious bungalow that the Sarkies began their venture into the Singapore hotel trade, advertising in the *Straits Times* on 19 November 1887:

> Raffles Hotel, 2 Beach Road, Singapore. Messrs Sarkies Brothers have the honour to inform their friends and patrons that they will open the above Hotel on the 1st of December next. The situation is one of the best and healthiest in the town, facing the sea, and within a few minutes' walk of the Public Offices and the Square. Great care and attention for the comfort of Boarders and Visitors has been taken in every detail, and those frequenting it will find every convenience and home comfort.[22]

From these modest beginnings Tigran Sarkies, a man of vision and determination, built up the hotel, calculating that there was a growing market for first-class accommodation and fine dining. In 1889–90 he added a pair of handsome two-storey wings flanking the original bungalow, with twenty-two suites, each benefitting from a private veranda and a sea view. In 1892 he opened the Raffles Tiffin Rooms in the heart of Singapore's commercial district, known as Commercial Square until 1858, and as Raffles Place subsequently. Raffles residents could thereafter 'tiffin in town' beneath punkah fans, at no extra charge, the two establishments being a little over a mile apart.* Back at the main hotel site, in 1894 Sarkies acquired an adjacent piece of land, 3 Beach Road. On this site was developed the famous Palm Court Wing, where guests could look out on an expanse of emerald-green lawn surrounded by stately palms as they lounged. The Palm Court Wing added thirty rooms, each with a private veranda, bathroom, and en suite dressing room. This building and its courtyard established what was to become a Raffles signature—the experience of long verandas, sunny courtyards, and tropical vegetation. In 1896 a billiard room was added, a facility considered essential at the time and which became noted because of the occasion in 1902 when a tiger was discovered underneath its raised floor.[23] The Bar and Billiard Room, still standing, was a single-storey building with a deeply pitched roof, large windows, and an airy veranda encircled by a row of white pilasters.[24]

The next development of the hotel site, from its bungalow beginnings to the famed white edifice that greets the traveller today, came when Tigran

---

* Raffles Place grew from a patch of greenery marked out by Garrison Engineer Lieutenant Philip Jackson RN on the Town Plan of 1822 into the city's commercial hub. With the ocean on its southern side, it is now at the heart of the Downtown Core and home to the city's three tallest buildings.

decided to replace the bungalow with a new structure. Swan and MacLaren, Singapore's pre-eminent architectural firm, was engaged in 1897 to construct the new Main Building. The talented London-trained architect, Regent Alfred John Bidwell, was to do much to improve the city's skyline around the turn of the century, especially with his design for this new Main Building. Bidwell, a graduate of London's Architectural Association, had worked for the Straits Settlement Public Works Department before joining Swan and MacLaren. Thus he was not only well-versed in the classical idioms and technical advances fashionable in Britain, but appreciated the importance of adaptations to suit the tropical climate.[25]

The construction of the Main Building marked a turning point for Raffles Hotel. With its Renaissance influences (Ionic, Doric, Corinthian orders), Palladian windows, endless verandas, and distinctive butterfly wings, it was immediately considered one of Singapore's finest buildings. Surrounded as it is today by skyscrapers, it is all too easy to forget that it was, by the standards of its day, imposing and frightfully modern.[26] The late Victorian Italianate Revival design was extremely fashionable, the iron-frame construction was technologically advanced, and the installation of electricity was considered a marvel.

The Main Building opened with a fanfare on 18 November 1899, when 200 guests sat down to the chef's 'Special Inauguration Dinner' followed by dancing to the music of the band of the King's Own Regiment. Electric lights blazed for the first time, and electric fans cooled the dancers. 'Approaching from the seafront', wrote a contemporary traveller, 'the appearance of the hotel, lit throughout by electricity, is exceedingly fine. It literally blazes into the darkness of the night.'[27] With the opening of the Main Building, Tigran Sarkies's dream of a truly grand hotel was at last realized. A splendid three-storey structure that combined classic features with modern innovations, the Main Building added only twenty-three bedrooms but it had a dining room capable of seating 500. Its 6,500 square feet of floor space, with 36-feet wings, was paced in Carrara marble, and galleries supported by ornate columns and arches looked down on the central portion from both of the two storeys above. This hall was crowned by an elaborately ornamented skylight and ventilator that filtered sun and air to the interior.

This lofty lobby featured an imposing double staircase, broad public verandas, and spacious reading lounges extending across the front of the

Figure 27. Contemporary view of the lobby of the Raffles Hotel in Singapore.

building on the upper levels. Access to the verandas was provided by massive carved doors, while at the far end the main staircase, of wood construction with fine mouldings and flanked by bronze statues set on plinths formed by the stair newels, swept majestically to the upper floors. A wide, richly deco-rated veranda ran round all four sides of the Main Building, sheltering the rooms from the elements. To the world, this now became the 'face' of the hotel.[28] The rather haphazard early development of the hotel's premises remains central to its charm today. It is linked by an intricate network of broad, airy verandas from which archways offer views of the various court-yards, each with a distinctive ambience.[29]

The final major addition was the Bras Basah Wing, which opened in 1904 with twenty suites on the upper floors and one of Singapore's first shopping arcades at ground level. With it, Raffles Hotel became the largest and most successful hotel in the Straits Settlements and fabulous stories began to accumulate around it.[30] 'First Class Travellers only . . . the select Rendezvous of the Elite', proclaimed a 1904 advertisement.[31] Raffles was now the largest hotel in the Malayan peninsula and its reputation was growing. Soon the Bar and Billiard Room had been renovated, the Tiffin Rooms brought from the city centre to the hotel, and a cast iron portico added to the Main Building in 1913, designed by Walter McFarlane of Scotland. The hotel occupied 200,000 square feet and commanded a panoramic view of the harbour and the adjacent islands, conveniently situated within easy reach of the chief business centres.[32] Originally the sea came right up to Beach Road, and at high tide sea water would seep into Raffles Hotel and special steps were built to prevent this.[33] Ever increasing demand meant that there was more expansion to come. In 1921 two upper floors of a three-storey Edwardian edifice along nearby Stamford Road were leased. It was called the Oranje Building, christened 'The Grosvenor' or Raffles Annexe. In 1923 the Sea View Hotel in Tanjong Katong, which belonged to the Jewish businessman Sir Manasseh Meyer, was also leased. This was an establishment which had opened in a coconut grove in 1906 with forty rooms, a beer garden, tennis courts, and a swimming enclosure.[34]

Raffles possessed its own livery stables, laundry, a dark room for patrons to develop their own photographs, and a sample storage room for commercial travellers. Hotel runners were available to board all incoming and outgoing steamers in order to assist passengers with luggage.[35] The hotel had its own bakery, government post office, telegraph office, refreshment room, internal ice and cold-storage plant, slaughter house, and a direct telephone line to every room. Raffles was the first hotel in the Straits Settlements to have electric lights, fans, and call bells powered by its own generators, though the punkah-wallahs were allowed to stay until the 1920s. There was also a 10,000-gallon water tank. The hotel maintained its own transport fleet— rickshaws, bicycles, and a motor stand. There were thirteen cars in its garage in 1917 and three lorries for luggage and goods. The rickshaw pitch outside the hotel was particularly lucrative, and in 1923 400 men fought for position around the Rochore Canal Road near the hotel with knives, sticks, stones, and poles until dispersed by a police baton charge.

With all of these modern conveniences and the attention of an army of servants, hotel residents experienced levels of luxury that even those accustomed to domestic help could find overwhelming. Staying at the Raffles Hotel, a new arrival's reliance on servants could quickly become an addiction:

I am getting into the way of things here. I could not get on without attention, so said to the hotel people I must have boys to wait on me, and to 'put
them on the bill'. Now I appear to have six. They all look the same and I no
longer lack attention or attendance ... If I want anything I pull the nearest
bell-rope—I mean pigtail—and point at something.[36]

Hotel society

The Raffles Hotel was a relaxing refuge for the traveller. 'At the Raffles, the
"hot and inflamed" new arrival', as Colonel R. V. K. Applin put it, 'could
find relief in an "Indian bath" '—which involved a large earthenware jar and
a tin bucket, and which the colonel claimed 'was one of the best he'd ever
had'.[37] The hotel was an increasingly important feature in the social life of
expatriates living and working in Malaya and Singapore, as well as those
passing through. The colony's social life improved as Singapore expanded
and developed all the pleasurable amenities of a bustling colonial metropolis, such as clubs, theatre, dances, 'smoking concerts' (musical performances
during which an all-male audience smoked and conversed), reading rooms,
a public library, museum, and botanical garden. European 'society', Frost
argues, had become institutionalized, and it was now conducted as much
outside the home as within.[38] The European community was dependent
upon dinners and alcohol. Singapore had been firmly established on the
map of world travellers. Postcards and tourist advertisements often portrayed Singapore as a centre of romanticism, exoticism, and easy sex. Colonial police officer Rene Onraet observed in his memoirs that 'all that was
known about Singapore, in most places of the world before the 1914 war,
was contained in the four words: "Raffles Hotel" and "Malay Street"—the
latter being a nearby street known for its Japanese prostitutes'.[39]

By 1915, most of the big architectural developments had been completed,
leaving the hotel poised to benefit from the Roaring '20s, which were a
boom-time for Singapore. The hotel was well known for its generous table.
The breakfast bill of fare in 1899, for example, included porridge, fried fish,
mutton chops, devilled fish, cold beef and salad, boiled eggs, cheese, fruits,
tea and coffee, and Benedictine to 'facilitate the digestion'.[40] Daily routine
around the turn of the century, for men at least, included a ride or walk
early in the morning, tea and biscuits while reading or writing letters, and
then a 9 o'clock breakfast of fish, curry, and eggs, washed down with claret.

After going to the office, at 1 o'clock it was tiffin time, a meal which might consist of curry and rice, fruit or biscuits, with beer or claret. After some more business in the afternoon, and assuming one was still sober, there would be sports before sundown. Then at about 6 o'clock there might be sherry and bitters or some other sundowner. Dinner was at 6.30 or 7 o'clock, and consisted of soup, fish, beef/mutton/turkey or capon, with tongue, fowl cutlets, and vegetable side dishes, curry, rice, and *sambals*, the titbits, such as pickles, finished with dessert, cheese, and fruit.[41]

From an early stage in the hotel's development Tigran Sarkies turned his attention to the hotel's cuisine and, following the great European *belle époque* hoteliers, elevated the experience of public dining in Singapore to an entirely new level—'cuisine of highest character is served at separate tables', ran an 1892 advertisement. (Tigran died in 1912 and is buried in Kensal Green cemetery.)[42] The inspired setting for his feasts was the new main dining room. The 1913 edition of *Seaports of the Far East* claimed that:

> The chief glory of the hotel is its magnificent dining hall, overlooked by balconies on the upper floors. Its handsome pillars, its white Carrara marble floor, and the dainty artistic arrangement of its numerous tables form an ensemble unsurpassed outside Europe and America; and at night, when dinner is in progress, to the accompaniment of the excellent orchestra, the gay and festive scene is one to be remembered.[43]

Despite its origins, from the outset Raffles was a destination for the wealthy and, especially, for the white; Asians were banned until the 1930s. The hotel catered for travellers, but also for long-term residents, mainly bachelors who preferred hotel life to sharing a bungalow in the suburbs. In 1918, 20 per cent of the hotel's 200 rooms were kept by long-term residents. The hotel became synonymous with rich and famous visitors. But in addition to the resident bachelors and the international travellers, Raffles developed a niche market as a social centre as much, if not more, for Singapore residents as for hotel guests.[44] It was treated almost as an exclusive club by the colony's residents. The closure of its main rival the Hotel de L'Europe in the 1930s assured Raffles's position as the colony's social centre for tourists, through-passengers, and for planters down from the Federated Malay States for relaxation and jollification.[45]

The new ballroom, built in front of the main entrance, made Raffles the ideal venue for parties and all sorts of social gatherings for planters, travellers, and residents. The ballroom's grand opening in January 1921 established the hotel as Party Central. Tea dances, special music programmes, balls, cabaret shows, and after-dinner dancing to the sounds of the newly appointed Raffles Dance Orchestra, all kept the stream of expatriates, cruise-ship passengers, dignitaries, and visiting royalty dancing.[46] Raffles became the most popular place in town, thronged nightly with men and women in elegant evening dress.[47] It had succeeded in becoming not only a renowned hotel, but a central meeting place, a tourist attraction in its own right, and the premier social centre for settlers, transient visitors, and the officers of the British armed forces.

The veranda-enclosed ballroom was exposed to public view on the Beach Road side. The spectacle of Europeans enjoying themselves in what non-Europeans considered to be eccentric and morally inappropriate manner (men holding women in their arms for the waltz and so on) became one of the cheapest shows in town for those prepared to loiter and observe the goings on.[48] When taking a break from dancing, people sat at the ballroom's rattan tables and chairs along the edge of the dance floor, drinking gin Pahits, Singapore Slings, and Million Dollar Cocktails. Along with local luminaries such as the Sultan of Johore and Rajah Brookes of Sarawak, members of the wealthy Straits Chinese elite who effectively acted as local intermediaries for the British in the colonial government were high-profile in the ballroom at functions.[49] There were then the globetrotting celebrities of the period, such as Noël Coward, Charlie Chaplin, Douglas Fairbanks, Ava Gardner, Lord Louis Mountbatten, Hayley Mills, and John Wayne (and, much later, the likes of Felipe Massa, David Beckham, Gwen Stefani, Prince Albert II of Monaco, and Jackie Chan).

From the hotel's verandas one could watch the flotsam and jetsam of the port city—deeply tanned rubber planters and tin miners from Malaya, officers from ships in port, pale civil servants, and middle-aged army officers flushed with too much drink—going about their daily business.[50] The chit system, which extended generous credit to large numbers of people throughout the colonial world, added to the financial difficulties which the hotel's proprietors soon found themselves in, and contributed to the low level alcoholism that was prevalent in the colonial world. It has been suggested that cheap drink was 'mainly responsible for that absence of intellectual interests which is a defective feature of British colonial life in tropical countries'.[51]

At Raffles Hotel today extensive gardens take up a fourth of the total land area, with over 50,000 plants representing eighty species, including the paddle-like leaves of the famous Traveller's Palm, frangipani, red ginger, Caribbean 'black magic' heliconia, breadfruit, coconut palm, bird's nest fern, livistona, ginger torch blossom, the giant-leaved colocasia esculenta, banana plants, mango trees, and yellow and orange caesalpinia. These luxuriant borders between the three main sections of the hotel hide secret passages and corridors.[52] In contrast to the modern-day profusion of verdant tropical flora, in the early days the emphasis was on the manicured rather than the 'wild'.[53] Back then, gardens occupied only 8 per cent of the hotel's grounds. Guests in the early twentieth century, Tan argues, would have been horrified if they were to be confronted by a profusion of Kipling-esque jungle fronds. With the evolution of the modern traveller and his taste for exotic experience, however, the shift towards incorporating the natural environment into the scheme of the building gave the gardens of the Raffles Hotel a boost.[54] In the hotel's early years, the backdrop was very different. Sandy beaches, clumps of seaweed, coconut trees, rainforests, jungle, and rivers winding past stilted houses were all around, and the hotel was an oasis *away* from this tropical, Oriental 'disorder'. For these planters and other British residents and travellers, Raffles Hotel was a sanctuary of peace, a kernel of civility in which to seek refuge from the balmy tropical heat and vegetation.[55]

The Second World War and after

The American war correspondent Cecil Brown arrived in Singapore in August 1941. His account of his time in Singapore conveys a sense of the European community's reluctance to face up to the threat that was looming. Arriving on 3 August, he was taken to Raffles:

> I had dinner tonight in the beautiful palm-lined courtyard of Raffles Hotel. Each table, set on the grass, had a pink-shaded lamp and a vase of orchids. The Argyle and Sutherland Highlanders band played for the smartly dressed officials and women in gay print dresses. The members of the band wore plaid hats and white coats and kilts, and the war seemed a million miles away.[56]

Living at Raffles for several months, until the threat of Japanese bombing obliged him to leave, he was stunned to find Singapore's social routine essentially unchanged: 'The bar at Raffles is crowded with people drinking gimlets and *stengahs* during *pahit* time, and everyone is busy being conversational, agreeable, and superior.'[57] Observing Singapore's last days from

room 48, Brown's diary is full of meetings in the hotel's bar or dining room
or palm-court with correspondents, consuls, and British officers. Cocktails,
formal mess jackets, evening gowns and the perennial cry of 'boy', as a
waiter was summoned to refill the glasses, permeate his account. The hotel's
management was reluctant to heed General Percival's pleas about food wast-
age, not wanting to cut its dinners from six courses to three. 'No dancing
except in formal dress' read a notice above the ballroom's entrance, and
though the number of officers dwindled as the war came ever closer, Raffles danced on. But as the Japanese advanced down the Malay peninsula,
hotels, boarding houses, and private homes were crowded with refugees
from up-country, and many restaurants and nightclubs closed down. Though
Raffles Hotel continued to hold its nightly dances, by mid-December it
was filling up with evacuees from up-country. With surrender imminent,
the hotel's vast stocks of liquor were poured down the drain and its silver
roast beef trolley buried in the grounds to spare it the indignity of serving
the Japanese.

The colonial *belle époque* that Raffles came to symbolize was fatally undermined by the Japanese conquest of Singapore in February 1942. During the
ensuing occupation, the hotel was renamed Syonan Ryokan. 'Syonan' meant
'Light of the South', the new Japanese name for Singapore, and 'ryokan' was
a traditional Japanese inn or hotel. Upon the surrender of Japanese forces in
1945 it was employed as a transit camp for British and Allied prisoners on
their way home from Japanese prisoner of war camps. In 1957 Singapore
became independent as part of Malaysia and in 1965 became an independent state in its own right. It set out to be a major financial centre and capital
market, and to become the biggest shipping, ship-repairing, and shipbuilding centre after Japan.[58] In 1969 Singapore outstripped London as the busi-
est port in the Commonwealth, and became the container transhipment
centre for South-east Asia, the third port in the world after Rotterdam and
New York by 1975. Raffles continued to act as a home from home for people visiting Singapore or just passing through, sometimes engaging its
guest so much that they paid only scant attention to the rest of the city
and the island. Susan Kurosawa remembers staying there with her parents
in the 1960s. 'There was a sign behind our guestroom door that announced:
"While at Raffles, why not visit Singapore." Mother didn't take up the
offer, preferring to recline in a rattan chair in the palm-laden garden,
drinking gin slings and blowing smoke rings from under a wide straw hat
purchased especially for "the equator".'[59]

But the post-war decades were less kind to Raffles Hotel, and bankruptcy loomed. The hotel badly needed to regenerate. It was showing its age and the rise of modern, international-style hotels in the Orchard Road area, which was fast becoming the prime shopping district, offered stiff competition.[60] Amid the flurry of reconstruction, with the rise of new towns in hitherto undeveloped areas, the heart of old Singapore city remained the financial and administrative centre. But its appearance changed rapidly, as old shophouses and decaying office blocks were replaced by modern steel and concrete skyscrapers, and Shenton Way (named after Governor Sir Shenton Thomas) became Singapore's equivalent of Wall Street.[61]

The possibility of demolishing Raffles and starting again from scratch was discussed. In 1980 a plan for an entirely new 32-storey building with 774 rooms was put forward by the British architect Frederick Gibbert and Partners and the Singapore firm Architects 61. Part of the problem was that the hotel in the post-war years was living off its reputation and allowing standards to slip. But another problem was that Raffles was increasingly perceived, in a country shedding its colonial heritage and embracing development and nationalism, as an offensive reminder of colonialism and its successes. In 1959 the anti-colonial People's Action Party government came to power and, reflecting changing times, the hotel's Elizabeth Grill, developed to commemorate Elizabeth II's coronation as recently in 1953, was promptly renamed the Epicurean Grill. As the 1960s dawned, Raffles Hotel faced the threat of obsolescence. By the 1970s, visitors to Singapore were opting for the more modern hotels on Orchard Road. A further blow came when flights ceased to stop in Singapore as often, improved aviation technology allowing passenger aircraft to fly non-stop. Despite all of this, *Country Life* reported in 1975, Raffles was 'nevertheless hanging on to its old trappings. The cane-furnished bedrooms are still forty feet long, people still dine by candlelight at the orchid-decked tables in the palm court, sip their Singapore gin slings at the bar where they were invented, and take tea in the Tiffin Room still cooled by old-fashioned propeller fans.'[62]

Fortunately, thanks to those who saw the hotel's history as a singular asset, a bolder, more dramatic plan was approved instead and Raffles Hotel was declared a National Monument in 1987, the centenary of its foundation. The fact that the hotel remains a thriving enterprise to this day when so many of its colonial-era rivals have disappeared is testament to shrewd management, good marketing, the heritage industry, and an enduring appetite for 'colonial'-style experiences. It was clear by the late twentieth century that modern Singapore was squeezing out other aspects of interest to tourists. The government appointed a special task force to investigate, and its proposed solution was an ambitious restoration programme for local architecture and historic buildings.[63] It concluded that Raffles Hotel was possibly more famous than Singapore itself, but what had once been one of the world's great hotels had become a wasting asset, not providing the impact on visitors that its name implied. 'The irony', the task force reported:

> is that the bones of the original building and its gracious spaces are still there, but they have been clogged with gross and unthinking additions and misused spaces in order to provide some semblance of quick fix economic viability. It is still possible to return it to its former splendour and make it the national treasure it should be—the Crown Jewel of the visitor industry in Singapore.[64]

In turning the hotel's fortunes around, it was decided that the best card to play was its history. Richard Helfer, the new chief executive officer, was backed with $160m and charged with reconceptualizing the hotel and its long overdue restoration.[65] This meant a range of changes—for example, converting what had become family suites back to grand suites. The Bar and Billiard Room, defunct since 1917 when it was converted for accommodation, was returned to its original function to become a key space in the newly developed national monument. The hotel was to be returned to its appearance in 1915, which was declared the benchmark year. To achieve this, the hotel had to be completely closed down.

Raffle's said goodbye to its last guests and closed its doors in 1989 in order to embark on a massive restoration project. In order to return to 1915, this meant, among other things, the removal of the 1920s ballroom and its replacement with an earlier cast-iron portico at the entrance, revealing once more the noble façade of the Main Building in all its original splendour. The refurbished hotel now had 103 suites, eighteen of them Raffles State Rooms, dispersed over five wings linked by verandas.[66] A powerful sense of history pervades the rather haphazard arrangement of wings, with their mellow red-tile roofs, polished hardwood verandas, and hidden areas.[67] Recreation and evocation are the order of the day; a billiards table from the old Government House, period lighting fixtures, old photographs, suites themed according to famous guests of yesteryear.

After narrowly avoiding architectural suicide, Singapore now values what remains of both colonial and Chinese architecture and many colonial-era treasures are not only secure but exceedingly well maintained. Colonial-era

Figure 28. The classic Raffles pose. Contemporary view of the Raffles Hotel in Singapore, with Bentley.

treasures in Singapore city include the Empress Building, the original parliament, the Fullerton Hotel (formerly the General Post Office and the premises of the Singapore Club), the Singapore Cricket Club, the fire station, police station, St Andrew's Cathedral, the Convent of the Holy Infant Jesus, the Masonic Lodge, the Anglo-Chinese School (now the Philatelic Museum), Fort Canning barracks and administrative headquarters, and the underground 'Battlebox' command centre, war memorials, the classical City Hall where Lord Louis Mountbatten took the Japanese surrender, and the old central train station, now disused since the relocation of the train terminal to the Woodlands district in the north.

The passage of time has not been particularly kind to Raffles in terms of its location, which is mundane rather than picturesque. Beach Road is no longer a beach road, since land reclamation moved the waterline many hundreds of yards away. While Noël Coward was able to look at the muddy water while sipping a gin sling on the hotel's veranda, there is no longer any sight of the sea. Beach Road is a dull arterial road, and North Bridge Street to the hotel's rear and Bras Basah Street running along its western edge are busy with cars and shops. At the corner of the two, a rather sorry-looking rickshaw and driver sit for the tourists, a lame gesture to the past in a city now bereft of rickshaws. On the other side, Seah Street is a quieter, nondescript thoroughfare with a few original shophouses still intact. In terms of the centre of Singapore city, the *other* side of the padang is where the action is, with the central business district, the picturesque pubs and restaurants of Boat Quay edging the Singapore River and leading on to Chinatown. It is amidst this setting that one finds the marvellous Fullerton Hotel. A grand, columned 1920s structure that is set-off by the skyscrapers that surround it, it is every bit as intriguing as the Raffles, though shares none of its fame.[68]

For sound commercial reasons Raffles, as part of its redevelopment, expanded and became in the process something more than a hotel. It perhaps lost some of its magic in the process, as the hotel site is now more of a 'complex' than just a hotel. Its entire rear is taken up with new buildings— all in matching style—that amount essentially to a very expensive shopping centre. Charming, arcaded, looking in on a courtyard—but a shopping centre nonetheless. These new buildings also contain the relocated Long Bar to which tourists flock, paradoxically, to evoke the colonial heyday and test-drive the Singapore Sling (invented by a Raffles barman early in the twentieth century).

10

Gordon Memorial College,
Khartoum

The Gordon Memorial College is the quintessential building of empire and nation. Built by the British soon after the conquest of the Sudan with the intention of creating a pro-British collaborative elite to help run the country, the college became the main incubator of Sudanese nationalism, stimulating demands for independence from Britain. One of the college's main achievements therefore was the exact inverse of its founding intent. The Gordon Memorial College's history demonstrates the role of education in the British Empire, and some of the common challenges faced by the British in co-opting indigenous people into their ruling structures. It also illustrates the way in which the public-school idea was propagated around the British world as education became part of the 'civilizing' fabric of imperialism and one of the main justifications for imperial rule.

The Gordon Memorial College was part of the dramatic construction of the new city of Khartoum that began after the Mahdi's defeat in 1898. The college occupied one of the most desirable locations on the banks of the Nile, next door to the Governor's Palace itself and set in a wide expanse of fields and gardens. The main building was an impressive structure which was also home to the Sudan government's Department of Education. The main building formed three sides of a square open to the south and facing the Nile. 'A somewhat heavy but impressive building of brick', wrote the architect William Newton, 'with a flat roof and a strongly moulded arcade on both floors, deeply shadowed in daytime'.[1] Its grounds soon sprouted dormitories and sports facilities, and the collector and philanthropist Henry Wellcome endowed the college with important scientific laboratories which aided its development as a higher education institution that eventually became the University of Khartoum.

The Gordon Memorial College was modelled on the English public school, the majority of which were either founded or re-founded in the Victorian era.[2] Public schools flourished throughout Britain and the Empire at this time. Institutions such as the Lawrence Memorial School near Ootacamund in the Nilgiri Hills (motto: 'Never give in') and Islamia College in Peshawar—a beguiling example of Oxbridge-meets-the-East architecture (motto: 'O God, increase my knowledge')—were commonplace. St John's College, Agra was founded by the Church Missionary Society (motto: 'The truth shall make you free'), while Bishop Cotton School in Simla (motto: 'Overcome evil with good') was created, in the words of its founder, 'to provide an education by God's blessing no less useful than Winchester, Rugby, and Marlborough'.[3] Africa also sprouted public schools and university colleges, though in less profusion than Asia. The Prince of Wales School was established in Nairobi in 1931 and designed by one of the British Empire's most famous architects, Herbert Baker. Its bright main building made extensive use of colonnades, partly inspired by Thomas Jefferson's University of Virginia and T. E. Lawrence's belief, communicated to the architect, that all walkways should be shaded from the tropical sun. The school's emblem depicted an impala and the Prince of Wales's fleur-de-lis enclosed with the motto 'To the uttermost'.

Public schools, whether in Britain or the Empire, had an important role to play in supporting British endeavours overseas. Sir Ralph Furse, Head of Recruitment at the Colonial Office (1931–48), said that 'we could not have run the show without them. In England, universities train the mind; the public schools train character and teach leadership.'[4] Schools, historian Trevor May argues, possessed a great advantage when it came to initiating boys into an elite culture; they were closed institutions. Boys were set apart during term time, often in buildings occupying remote rural sites, away from the weakening influence of mothers and other women. Here, they were prepared for a life which, for many of them, would be centred around all-male institutions. Some public schools in Britain had a particular orientation towards the Empire, through scholarships or the facts of their foundation, including Haileybury with its Indian connections and Cheltenham with its Sanskrit and Hindustani expertise.

As well as schools, the colonial period also witnessed the foundation of institutions of higher education around the world. Those in India's presidency towns set out to transfer British ideas and values to the Indian middle class. There was Madras University, built in the Indo-Saracenic style, and

Bombay University, designed in Gothic splendour by Sir Gilbert Scott. At the height of his career, having already built the Albert Memorial, St Pancras Station, and a cathedral in Newfoundland, Scott's Bombay University featured an oblong quadrangle surrounded by two-storey blocks. An open entrance was flanked on one side by a library, on the other by the Convocation Hall. Its design featured ogee windows, elaborately buttressed balconies, open spiral staircases, statue niches, pinnacles, and ornately decorated arcades.[5]

The Battle of Omdurman and after

The Gordon Memorial College's foundation was a consequence of the British conquest of the Sudan. This occurred after a textbook military campaign orchestrated by Major General Sir Herbert Kitchener. 'I think that the enemy have had a good dusting', was his laconic comment after the Battle of Omdurman on 2 September 1898, during the course of which his Anglo-Egyptian army had killed upwards of 11,000 Sudanese warriors and wounded a further 16,000.[6] On the following day, after visiting Omdurman (today a suburb of Khartoum) and ordering the destruction of the Mahdi's tomb, Kitchener sailed up the Nile on a gunboat. He landed at Khartoum on the jetty outside of General Gordon's wrecked palace and examined the stairs on which Gordon had fallen.[7]

The following day a memorial service for Gordon was held in the ruins of the palace, attended by detachments from each battalion of the Anglo-Egyptian army. The troops were drawn up in echelons on the bank of the Blue Nile at the spot where Gordon had alighted fourteen years earlier, with the gunboat *Melik* and other steamers anchored behind them. The Union Jack was run up on the palace roof, followed by the red Egyptian flag. *Melik* fired a salute and the order 'Present Arms!' thundered out. The soldiers stood silently, their officers at the salute, while the band of the Grenadier Guards played 'God Save the Queen', the Khedival anthem and, in honour of Gordon, the 'Dead March' from Handel's *Saul*. The scene is captured by Richard Caton Woodville's painting 'The Memorial Service for General Gordon, 4 September 1898', held in the Royal Collection and commissioned by Queen Victoria.

Many of those in attendance, including Kitchener himself, were moved to tears. The saga of Gordon's death in Khartoum and Kitchener's reconquest of the Sudan had fired the Victorian imagination. This was its culmination, and the celebration of Kitchener's victorious Sudan campaign that September day became an iconic moment in the annals of late Victorian imperialism. This famous event, in which Lee Enfield rifles, Maxim machine-guns, and river gunboats triumphed over technologically backward opponents, was marked in other ways, too, as British rule settled across the vast territory known as the Sudan. One of them was the foundation of the Gordon Memorial College. After winning the war Kitchener became Consul-General responsible for the administration of this new imperial fiefdom. One of his first acts was to found a brand new metropolis—Khartoum—and to call for the creation of a school to be named in memory of General Charles Gordon. Thus the college was born, the consummation of battlefield victory and an imperial hero avenged.

The war correspondent Bennet Burleigh, an eyewitness to these developments in the Sudan following the Battle of Omdurman, wrote of Kitchener's scheme 'for the well-being of the Soudanese'. Kitchener wanted to tend to the benighted country's 'higher needs':

> I knew the Sirdar had long entertained the idea of fitly commemorating General Gordon's glorious self-abnegation in striving to help the native, single-handed, fighting unto death ignorance and fanaticism. A scheme that would provide for the education of the youth of the Soudan, conveying to them the stores of knowledge taught in the colleges of civilized countries, was what he aimed at. The desired institution should be founded in Khartoum, which was to become a centre of light and guidance for the new nation being born to rule Central Africa.[8]

'Dreaming true', as he put it, Kitchener conceived the idea of founding a college in Gordon's memory which, in his own words, would be a 'focus of higher education in Sudan for all time'.[9] Thus was born what was sometimes (perhaps predictably) referred to as 'the Eton of the Soudan' or 'Winchester by the Nile', a fee-paying college that was to train generations of the Sudanese elite.[10] Judging by contemporary British estimations, it would have its work cut out for it; as Burleigh noted, expatiating about Kitchener's 'noble' vision of uplifting the heathen in a land where he'd recently presided over thousands of brutal deaths, there was an abject lack of knowledge. 'The rudimentary knowledge common to British schoolboys transcends all the learning of the wise in the Soudan', he added, articulating a common contemporary view of assumed African backwardness and European superiority.[11]

Figure 29. A British cartoon depicting Kitchener 'Dreaming true' about his planned Gordon Memorial College and the £100,000 he needed to build it.

On 30 November 1898 Kitchener launched an appeal to the British people for funds in order to erect and endow a memorial college 'as a pledge that the memory of Gordon is still alive among us and that his aspirations are at length to be realized'.[12] He told an audience at Mansion House in the City of London that education was vital for the improvement of the 3 million 'emancipated' Sudanese people. Founding such a college would also secure Britain's reputation as a civilizing power. It was quite clear how the British saw their achievements in the Sudan, and the role the college played in this. Within six weeks, the £100,000 that Kitchener had asked for had been raised, the sum eventually topping £135,000.[13] A general council was formed to supervise the foundation, which had its first meeting on 18 January 1899 at the Bank of England.

It has been suggested that Kitchener's foundation of the college was at least in part an attempt to renovate his public reputation in Britain, damaged by his treatment of battlefield wounded and his desecration of the Mahdi's tomb, a holy site, after the victory at Omdurman.[14] Ultimately the college became an incubator of Sudanese nationalism—not the intention of its founding father and his successors. For them, until the final years of British rule, the foundation myth of the college—and indeed of Britain's very presence in the Sudan—remained unchanged: that British rule had delivered the people from the thrall of barbarian rulers and would, in time, uplift them from the state of barbarism itself. It amounted to a justification of imperialism echoed in just about every other colony in the British Empire, particularly in Africa. As expressed by W. H. McLean, municipal engineer of Khartoum and lecturer in engineering at the Gordon Memorial College: 'It will be remembered that immediately after Lord Kitchener had crushed Mahdiism and routed the savage hordes at Omdurman he asked the British people to provide a college for the youth of the country. This institution was the result of that appeal, and it has proved one of the greatest blessings to the Sudan.'[15]

By 1901, the college was supporting an industrial school, two higher primary schools, and a small teacher training centre. Two years later, 150 boys, 58 of them Syrians and Egyptians, were admitted to the college proper. At the outset, the purpose of the college was to train Sudanese boys for service in the lower echelons of government service and the military. It achieved a great deal in a short space of time: by 1914 many of the graduates were employed in the lower ranks of the government and army administration.

Even the sons of the three *khalifas* and of many prominent Mahdist *amirs* were absorbed into government service.[16] Important for its future development, the college always harboured the intention of being a centre of research: this would eventually lead to efforts to upgrade its status to that of a higher education institution and, eventually, a full university.

The new Khartoum

Before considering the construction of the handsome college buildings set on the banks of the Blue Nile, it is worth noting that they were themselves part of a much greater enterprise—the foundation of the new city of Khartoum itself. It was an incredible sign of imperial power, as were new towns and cities built by the British elsewhere in the world. In 1901 a municipality of Khartoum was created, bringing a very British urban organizational structure into the heart of Africa. The ruins of old Khartoum were levelled with the assistance of British troops, and streets were driven through the debris. By 1909 the new city ran for 2 miles along the banks of the Nile, and was a mile deep. Running parallel to the Nile were three main avenues: Khedive, Abbas, and Sultan. At right angles to the river were four avenues: Victoria, Mohammad Ali, Melik, and Kitchener. Of these, Victoria Avenue was the most important, 180 feet wide and centred on the palace, from which, wrote Khartoum's architect, 'there is a most striking vista away to the south, with the luxurious gardens in the foreground'.[17] A statue of Gordon was erected where this street crossed Khedive Avenue, the second most important thoroughfare at 150 feet in width. Abbas Square in the centre of the city measured 800 by 200 yards, and housed the Great Mosque. Away from the central boulevards and stately new buildings was the 'native quarter'.

The city was commutable by steam trams, and public latrines and urinals were constructed throughout the city centre. Other infrastructural essentials, such as water works and an electric-light station, were erected, though there were no sewers; instead a dry-closet system involving the daily collection of 'soil-pails' for transit to a sewerage farm was devised. It was decreed that houses should not be painted white in the tropics because of glare, so greens, dark yellows, and browns were favoured. The foundation stone of the new Anglican Cathedral was laid by His Royal Highness Princess Henry of Battenberg on 7 February 1904. Trees were planted along the city's broad avenues and public gardens were laid out, with the Gordon Statue as the central feature. Naturally, many Britons interpreted this new city as further evidence of the civilization that trailed in the wake of British occupation. This was a British city, with British order and hierarchy, run on British terms, which happened to be on the banks of the Blue Nile. Lord Kitchener declared that the 'old Khartoum was a pesthouse, in which every tropical disease throve and was rampant; now malaria is almost unknown, though mosquito curtains are not in use; and last year there were only eleven cases of malaria in a town of 50,000 inhabitants'.[18] As with all colonial cities, the further one travelled from the European-dominated and architecturally imposing centre and the European suburbs, the more ragged became the buildings and the poorer the people. An aerial shot of Khartoum taken in the 1920s shows the Governor's Palace and the Gordon Memorial College on the Nile in the foreground, behind it the wider city panned out. The photograph clearly shows the transition from the British officials' 'charming houses on the river with their well-irrigated gardens' to the 'dismal rows of houses in the dusty back parts'.[19]

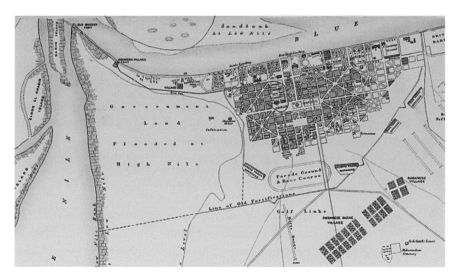

Figure 30. Detail from an early map of the new Khartoum. The GMC is the building top right on the Nile bank. 'British barracks' appear next to it (extreme top right, soon to be replaced by the Governor-General's palace); the Military Hospital is left of the College. Four other barrack blocks appear left and right of the Parade Ground and Race Course. The blocks at bottom right are 'The Sudanese Village'. The 'Union Jack' motif of the plan can be clearly seen.

The college buildings

The Gordon Memorial College, a central and original feature of this new city, was constructed on one of Khartoum's most desirable river-front sites, with the Governor's Palace as its neighbour on one side and the new Blue Nile Bridge on the other. Fronting on to the Nile, at the rear of the college's main building were the college grounds and playing fields. Signifying its lofty foundation, the school was run by trustees and an executive committee based in Britain, created by an Act of Parliament. It met at the Sudan government's London office, located at Wellington House, Buckingham Gate, SW1.

Plans for the college were drawn up by the Khedival architect Dmitri Fabricius Bey (sometimes rendered Fabricius Pasha, 1848–1907). Of the £135,000 raised for the college, it was decided to spend £23,000 on the building and £7,000 on laying out the grounds and providing furniture, fittings, and equipment. The rest of the money was to be invested in an Endowment Fund. The Earl of Cromer laid the foundation stone on 5 January 1899, and the building work was undertaken by the Military Works Department under the direction of Gorringe Bey (later Lieutenant General Sir George Gorringe). The inauguration took place on 8 November 1902, the building ceremonially opened by Kitchener himself—by now ennobled as Lord Kitchener of Khartoum—as he returned from command of British forces in the Anglo-Boer War.

E. N. Corbyn, a former headmaster, offers a description:

> With a central block and two wings, [the college] is a large and impressive structure, the design making use of wide and lofty verandas, suitable to provide shade from the violence of the tropical sun. Inland from the playing-fields are large boarding-houses, and the grounds contain other educational buildings and staff houses.[20]

The main building featured Gothic arches and the construction was of red brick. There were ten football grounds and tennis courts, and the college's technical students extended the pump so that it was possible to water new plants and grass. Education Department officials lavished time on gardening and landscaping, planting lawns, shrubs, and shade trees such as mahogany, and laying out beds of roses and cannas. They even began to cultivate vegetables.

In 1907 a new steam plant was installed to provide power for electrical lighting, cotton ginning, irrigation, and the running of the workshops. The college and its grounds were laid out with room for expansion, which included a primary school for 400 boys and boarding houses for the 100 boarders amongst them, built on an adjoining site a couple of years after the inauguration.[21] Intended as an 'institution of prestige' with an excellent physical environment, the buildings awed the Sudanese students, who were struck by the verdant grounds, technological innovations such as electricity and piped water, and well-appointed rooms.[22] It was an impressive building with grounds to match, and soon became a showcase for the Sudan government, featured in Baedeker's *Egypt and the Sudan: Handbook for Travellers* and Macmillan's *Guide to Egypt and the Sûdân including a Description of the Route through Uganda to Mombasa*. The 1905 version of this guidebook wrote that the 'fine building, which was completed in 1902, can of course at present only be used for the pupils of the primary school, seeing there is no demand as yet for higher instruction . . . Another important adjunct of the college is the very complete instructional workshops, generously fitted by Sir William Mather.'[23] The guidebook's Khartoum section featured a fold-out plan of 'the new city of Khartoum' showing the positions of the college, the Sudan Club, and the Palace ('open to tourists Monday and Friday'). It also showed the positions of the 'British barracks', the hospital, the Government Building ('or Sirdaria'), the post office, and the public gardens— all of these building stretched out along the River Esplanade.

For most of the boys the college was synonymous with the Sudan government, which could present a problem when students failed to find adequate employment in the various branches of the administration and the military. Its association with the government was reinforced by the fact that it was home to the government director of education and his department, and that from the college's foundation it was a common practice for the principal of the college to also be the director of education. Though its trustees and executive committee met in London, the college soon became a departmental institution administered for all practical purposes by the Sudan government.[24] This was formally acknowledged in 1934 when the trustees delegated a major part of their responsibilities to the Governor-General of the Sudan.

Training and education

Gordon Memorial College's educational aims were eclectic, embracing higher education, as per Kitchener's founding 'dream', as well as primary education and practical education. This was because the British, in particular the Sudan government, had specific requirements for Sudanese boys trained at the college. The government needed minor clerks with basic form-filling literacy. They also needed skilled tradesmen—the creation of a competent artisan class—junior administrators, engineers, surveyors, and army officers for the Egyptian Army and, later, the Sudan Defence Force. Wherever they ruled, the British needed indigenous partners to help them in the process. During the vacations boys from the college worked in the Irrigation Department, the Public Works Department, the Railway Department, the Legal Department, the Survey Department, and were commissioned into the Egyptian Army.

In addition to the primary school (with 184 boys in 1907, headed by Hedayat Bey), there were the vernacular and English training colleges (129 boys), an Upper School for the Technical Training of Engineers and Surveyors (twenty-seven boys), and Instructional Workshops (170 boys). On grounds adjacent to the college stood the Khartoum Military School, whose cadets received their general education at the Gordon Memorial College. There were workshop courses for training artisans and a civil engineering course. The college sat at the apex of the rudimentary educational structure that the British threw across the vastness of the Sudan. A 1933 review of education said that primary schools, of which there were ten with 970 students in total, supplied Gordon Memorial College, the sole state secondary school, where 476 boys (60 per cent from Khartoum and Blue Nile Provinces) took vocational and general courses.[25]

Beyond the immediate needs of the Sudan government, there was a longer-term aim as the college was intended to provide the educational and civilizing leaven in the lump of 'uneducated' and 'uncivilized' Sudanese society. Its role, therefore, in the words of a former Governor-General of the Sudan, was the 'diffusion among the masses of people of education to enable them to understand the merest elements of the machinery of government, particularly with reference to the equable and impartial administration of justice', the British desiring that the Sudanese people understood how well they were being ruled.[26] As the sometime principal Robin Udal put it, the immediate aim of government education policy was the 'diffusion of elementary vernacular education among the masses of the people; the creation of a competent artisan class, which was entirely lacking at this time; and the formation of an administrative class, capable of filling Government posts'.[27] The college also trained men in Islamic law in order to provide 'khadis', or

Islamic judges, and the college's work on Mohammedan law was considered to be of university standard.

In terms of recruitment, the college overwhelmingly served the sons of Northern Sudan, reinforcing the north–south chasm that was to inform Sudan's development and eventually lead to the secession of the south in 2011. The college was aimed squarely at the elite: it wanted 'boys of good Arab family' and at the outset, to overcome suspicion, British education officers would visit sheikhs in their homes to attempt to persuade them to send their sons to the new college. The first students were the sons of the amirs and military leaders of the Khalifa's army that Kitchener's forces had so recently vanquished on the battlefield (their military achievements had earned the British significant respect). There were also the sons of tribal and religious dignitaries. In 1937, of the college's 325 boys, most were from Khartoum and the north. There were also a few from Darfur, Kassala, and Kordofan. The boys were mostly sons of officials, the second largest category being sons of farmers, then merchants and officers. Some were the sons of headmen and craftsmen. There were also a few students from British Somaliland, a separate protectorate in the Horn of Africa. This arrangement dated from 1919 when, after a visit from the Commissioner for British Somaliland, the Colonial Office decided to send the sons of prominent Somalis to be educated at the college.

Research and science

One of the most important features of the Gordon Memorial College, that facilitated its subsequent evolution into a higher education institution and then a university, was the emphasis placed upon science and academic research. From the date of its foundation, headmaster James Currie wanted university-quality research to be conducted by the college staff. 'Research sections' supposedly of university standard were built into the college and, while for many years few tutors were in practice able to conduct significant research, it remained a concrete aspiration. Undoubtedly the most important strands of this research culture related to the college's scientific work. When the college was founded the new government, in the words of E. N. Corbyn (headmaster 1926–7), 'needed medical research, chemical research, entomological research, and geological research'. The American pharmaceutical businessmen Henry Wellcome, who became a British citizen in

Figure 31. Sir Rudolf Carl von Slatin inspects a line of African men wearing white robes and turbans in a courtyard outside Gordon College. Khartoum, Sudan, 1926. Von Slatin (1857–1932) was an Anglo-Austrian soldier and sometime administrator in the Sudan.

1910, sponsored the college and established Wellcome laboratories there that deepened knowledge about the Nilotic region and, in particular, its diseases. The new British rulers identified 'pestilence and famine' as the greatest ills afflicting the 'barbaric' Sudan, and the type of ills that their knowledge and technology could help alleviate, thus benefitting the people and allowing the British to fulfil their self-ordained role as agents of civilization and progress.

Henry Wellcome's backing for the college was a boon. He had been one of the earliest visitors to the newly conquered territory, having joined one of the first parties of European civilians to visit the Sudan after the battle of Omdurman. He studied the conditions resulting from the Khalifa's fifteen-year 'reign of terror and devastation'.[28] As he sailed up the Nile from Egypt, Wellcome was horrified by what he saw along its banks. The country was devastated by war; people lived in unclean mud huts and malaria, smallpox, and famine seemed endemic. He believed that scientific research could help to improve both the hygiene and health of the Sudanese people.[29] At Khartoum he met the Governor-General, Sir Reginald Wingate, and was shown the plans of the new Gordon Memorial College. Wellcome's experience in tropical diseases enabled him to quickly grasp the problem and he offered the college the most effectual scientific means of meeting and controlling the situation in the form of fully equipped and up-to-date tropical research laboratories with complete bacteriological and chemical sections.[30]

The state-of-the-art Wellcome Tropical Laboratories opened in 1902, and Wellcome helped pick the first director, Dr Andrew Balfour, and asked him to concentrate on eradicating malaria. Balfour began by draining mosquito breeding grounds and his staff also organized Khartoum's health service, and created a clean water and sanitary system for the whole city. As a result, the death rate from malaria in and around Khartoum was cut by 90 per cent and—true to Wellcome's wishes—the city became the healthiest on the African continent.[31] A setback occurred in May 1907 when fire destroyed the kitchen, dark room, and bacteriological laboratory, though the library, the entomological laboratory, and chemistry department were saved. Despite this early setback, science at Gordon Memorial College grew in strength, and its staff and students conducted important fieldwork throughout the Sudan. In 1907 Headmaster Currie reported that 'Dr Wenyon completed a year's useful and profitable work in the Floating Laboratory on the White Nile, Sobat, and Jur rivers. He has discovered many new blood parasites and has collected a very large amount of material.'[32] The floating laboratory was another fruit of Wellcome's sponsorship, it having occurred to him that from Khartoum it was possible to reach out in various directions and collect materials and specimens for scientific investigation. In 1907, R. G. Archibald was appointed as pathological and assistant bacteriologist. According to the annual report, he had 'recently completed seven months in charge of a Sleeping Sickness Camp in Uganda'. In another branch of the college's research into the Sudan, Dr Beam 'has continued his valuable investigation on Sudan projects, and his analysis of grains, oils, gums, lime deposits, and minerals cannot fail to direct attention to the possibilities which exist for utilizing these various substances'.[33]

This was pioneering scientific work, requiring not only learning but a large measure of intrepidity. It was dangerous work, too. In 1906 Alexander Pirrie was appointed anthropologist to the Wellcome Research Laboratories to work under Dr Balfour. A promising recent graduate of Edinburgh University, he embarked on two expeditions to study the physical characteristics of 'Nilotic negroid tribes', during the course of which he measured the heads, noses, and limbs of people and took impressions of their hands and the soles of their feet. On his second expedition close to the Abyssinian border, he contracted 'tropical fever'. He was invalided to Britain and died in November 1907.

The results of the college's scientific work in areas such as helminthology were sent to the London School of Tropical Medicine, illustrative of the manner in which institutions throughout the Empire fed metropolitan museums, botanical gardens, universities, and other types of research- and collection-based organizations. The college was also known for its anthropological work, and became associated with the documentation and conservation of the Sudan's heritage. Its staff undertook archaeological work and the college itself became the home of the Museum of Antiquities. By 1906, the college comprised five sections—a primary school, a training college for teachers and kadis, an instructional workshop, a secondary division, and a military school. There were also the Wellcome Research Laboratories, the Sudanese Antiquities Service, and the government Geological Survey Unit.[34]

As well as benefitting from the investment of Henry Wellcome, the Gordon Memorial College received a significant boost to its scientific horsepower when the Kitchener School of Medicine was established. As Kitchener had founded the college in memory of Gordon, upon Kitchener's death monies were sought to raise a lasting memorial to his name and his association with the Sudan. When Kitchener drowned off the Orkneys aboard HMS *Hampshire* in 1916, Wingate launched an appeal to build a medical facility in his memory. As the 1916 report recorded, the 'native response' to the appeal had been remarkable—£9,000 already collected 'in a poor country'.[35] The initial appeal raised £13,000, mostly in the Sudan, and a fresh appeal in Britain in 1923 raised a further £54,000. The School of Medicine was initially intended to train medical assistants, rather than fully qualified doctors, and the building was opened by Sir Lee Stack in 1924.

Traditions and ethos

The college was proud of its elitism and the achievements of its old boys, and of its public-school traditions. As Principal Lieutenant Colonel Lewis Whicher wrote in 1952 in an unpublished article commemorating the college's fiftieth anniversary, 'it is a matter of great pride to record that today the Leader of the Sudan Legislative Assembly, the Speaker, and almost all of the Ministers, as well as most of the Sudanese officials in the Sudan Government, were educated in the Gordon College'.[36] The Gordon Memorial College and its educational philosophy were designed to replicate the values of the English public school, and to build a class of well-educated Sudanese men who were loyal to Britain.

Though not intended as such, the college was a crucible for the development of nationalism in Northern Sudan. More than any other colonial-era institution, it shaped a generation of North Sudanese thinkers.[37] The college's alumni association was a precursor to the Graduates' Congress, founded in 1938, which became the major forum for nationalist politics. The college provided direct access to jobs in the government and gave students strong literary education in both Arabic and English, providing access to new communication technologies. It fostered an ethos of self-sufficiency and group spirit among its students, on the playing fields and in the lecture room alike.

The college's education and preparatory work was augmented by a distinct 'socializing intent'—character training and the inculcation of the public school code. For boys at Gordon Memorial College, the headmaster wrote, 'the aim of their instruction...is to encourage pupils to form habits of independent thought as far as possible, and at any rate to check their tendency to unintelligent imagination'.[38] General Sir Reginald Wingate, Governor-General of the Sudan and Sirdar of the Egyptian Army (1899–1916), succinctly captured the aim of both the college's public school foundation, and of the British in the Sudan. 'Our efforts to regenerate the Sudan', he wrote, 'can only succeed if we insist on the vital importance of such character training, this engendering the English public school code of honour amongst the youth of the country.'[39] The college's system of moral instruction, 'whereby the student is brought up to realize that truthfulness, courage, fair play, respect for authority, honesty, self-control, industry, good manners, the duties and privileges of citizenship, and the true patriotism are essential for successful administration, and must therefore be cultivated assiduously'.[40]

Gordon Memorial College adopted the practices of the English public school, including school houses, clubs and societies, prefects, prize giving, scholarships, and special days. Prizes included the Sir Edgar Horne Prize, the Hammill Stewart Scholarship, and the Sir George Arthur Prize Fund. There was an English Recitation Prize, which in 1937 was contested by boys reciting Mark Anthony's Funeral Oration, the Gettysburg address, King

George V's Christmas Broadcast, and the verse of Lewis Carroll.[41] There was the Archer Challenge Cup for 'best all-round boy' (shades of Michael Palin's hilarious *Tomkinson's Schooldays* in his *Ripping Yarns* series), and a silver medal.[42] By the 1950s, there were also Egyptian Government Prizes for final exam performance, and the El Sayed Mohammed el Berberi Prizes awarded for work in Islamic law.

The college venerated traditions and objects that augmented the college's sense of its own evolving history. The trowel with which Lord Cromer had performed a stone-laying ceremony on behalf of the Queen in January 1900 was sent to Victoria. For example, a letter from Buckingham Palace, acknowledging receipt of the college's sympathies on the death of King George VI and signed by Queen Elizabeth, was 'posted under glass cover in the Newbold Library'.[43] As was the British tradition, the college enjoyed the patronage of the great and the good. On the college's foundation, the king was announced as patron and the president was The Right Honourable Lord Kitchener of Khartoum himself. In the 1940s, Lord Cromer chaired the executive committee in London.[44] The Old Boys Day—attended by 300 ex-students in 1919—was a major event in the college's annual calendar. It was held on King's Day, the main celebration of British rule which occurred on 17 January each year, commemorating the occasion on which King George V and Queen Mary had visited the Sudan in 1912 as part of their Empire tour.

The boys were divided into houses (communal dormitories with their own activities, traditions, and loyalties), and words such as 'freshmen' and 'prep' were employed. The houses—Kitchener, Wingate, Stack, Archer, Maffey, and Currie—were named after directors of education and governors-general of the Sudan, 'to assist', as the 1926 report phrased it, in 'the formation of house patriotism and esprit de corps'.[45] Each house had a British tutor, a local housemaster, and a head prefect. The college's administration and governance also ran along British lines. The principal wrote in 1947 that the aim was for a 'system of control' by 'an academic oligarchy' as in the Oxbridge colleges.[46] The clubs and societies typical of the British public school flourished here too. There was the Literary and Debating Society, the Dramatic Society, the Magazine Committee, the Natural History Society, the Art Society, the Photographic Society, the Chess Club, and the Gardeners' Club, which organized the 'rovers' and gardening parties. In 1937 the students put on a Greek Exhibition, and there was a History Room centred upon a wall of pictures and annotated news cuttings that were changed weekly, supplied by the students. In 1917 the Boy Scouts Movement was introduced to the college. By the 1940s there was an annual Study Camp at Erkowit, during which students debated topics such as 'The Arabs and the West'.

The students were kept extremely busy: a standard day's timetable began with first bell at 05.30, baths at 05.45, parade at 06.30, breakfast at 06.45 and morning roll call at 07.45. The day was then occupied with lessons, drill, and games. 'Prep' was between 18.55 and 20.30, and lights out at 21.00.[47] The college's atmosphere was informed by the martial nature of its foundation, coupled with the desire to inculcate discipline and, through Spartan living conditions and games, to build character, the ultimate mission of the public school. 'Ordinary discipline' was left to the prefects, another standard public school practice, based on the notion that boys could best administer their own affairs and ensure justice. Flogging remained until 1937, when it was replaced by caning. The college also employed the familiar public school system of 'fagging', in which, among other things, 'slaves' would make prefects' beds and wash their clothes. It is interesting to note that of the main men in the Sudan at the time of the foundation—Cromer, Kitchener, and Wingate—none had attended a public school: all had attended the Royal Military Academy at Woolwich. The process of moulding the students began on the parade ground, where ex-sergeants of the Egyptian Army gave the newcomers their first introduction to British Army drill.[48]

Sport was a central feature of the public school and its ethos. At Gordon Memorial College, the headmaster wrote, 'each boy plays football twice a week, netball once, swims once a week, spends an afternoon each week watching the 1st XI match, and one afternoon of games'.[49] The fortunes of the football 1st XI were keenly followed. The 1907 report recorded that the team 'was never defeated by any native or Egyptian combinations, while it put up some very credible fights against teams of British soldiers and officials'.[50] The Owen Cup was contested annually between the college's 1st XI and an Old Boys team, and there were regular matches against British military personnel stationed in the Sudan. In 1930, the football 1st XI remained undefeated throughout the season. Five of the twelve matches were played against teams drawn from British battalions stationed in Khartoum—real men against boys' stuff—the college team beating the King's Own Regiment and the Lincolnshire Regiment, and drawing with the Warwickshire Regiment. The 1937 report recorded an 'excellent victory in Khartoum North over the Black Watch 4-0, defeat to Sudan Defence Force 1-3, shortly after they'd won the Governor-General's Challenge Cup'.

Religion, culture, and nationalism

The British were keen not to interfere in matters of religion and custom so as not to affront their Sudanese charges. 'Native custom' in matters such as clothing, food, and bedding was fastidiously observed. The British, as historian Heather Sharkey writes, were careful never to interfere with religion, and the college authorities emphasized the value of Islam. Prayers were encouraged, and the students appointed their own muezzins and imams.[51] As has been seen, throughout its history the Gordon Memorial College served the Muslim north of the Sudan, not the Christian south. It was an instrument for Muslim Sudan, and the government's education policy sowed the seeds of disparity and antagonism between north and south.[52] At the apex of the country's education system, the college was the stronghold of a culture based on the tenets of Islam, as interpreted by the religious leaders of the community.[53] The alliance with this class of elite northerners back-fired on the British rulers. The educated class changed from being loyal minor officials of the government to become dedicated supporters of Sudanese independence.[54]

What was interesting in the case of the Gordon Memorial College was that people doubted the wisdom of its foundation and its intent from the very beginning, questioning in particular Kitchener's vision and anticipating the 'loyalty' problems that were to emerge. Many Sudan government officials were sceptical of Kitchener's plan and considered it dangerous to tamper with Sudanese customs and ways of life. After all, the Mahdi's revolt had started as a reaction to the Turco-Egyptian interference with Sudanese conceptions of a Muslim society.[55] Others objected to the Gordon Memorial College experiment, pointing to the Indian experience, particularly the risk of calling into being an educated class from which political consciousness would inevitably emerge, to the detriment of Britain's position. As Daly writes, considering the Egyptian and Indian examples, spectres of progress or chaos were equally as easily conjured.[56] How much education was wise, how much was dangerous? It was a classic imperial conundrum. Babikr Bedri, the most famous Sudanese educationist, more than once pointed out to British officials that Muslims could never accept infidels as a fully legitimate government.[57]

In line with the powerful trend towards 'indirect rule' which swept through British Africa in the inter-war years, there was a significant change of policy in the Sudan, which affected the education policy of the college.

Sudan's 'tribal societies', it was believed, had been eroded during the rule of the Turco-Egyptians and also during the rule of the Mahdi and the Khalifa. The British should arrest that process and restore the tribal societies. This stimulated a search for Sudan's 'lost' tribes and a new imperative to preserve them, and to identify and work with Sudan's 'natural' aristocracy. Responding to this fad, college authorities began to make a conscious effort to preserve the Sudanese cultural authenticity to avoid creating Bengali babus or African 'Europeanized natives'.[58] Rules were introduced requiring students to wear traditional Sudanese clothes. To preserve 'tribal' identities, the students were divided into teams and houses based on place of origin; proponents of Indirect Rule wanted to emphasize the local, not the colony-wide level, because thinking and communication at this wider level would lead to *nationalism*, colonialism's most potent corrosive.

Political unrest in the early 1920s had provided a pretext for curtailing education and reorienting policy. A reactionary educational policy was therefore explained in paternalistic terms, as best suited to the current stage of the Sudan's development; or, on the level of administrative theory, as inherent in the grand design of Indirect Rule.[59] The chief concern of die-hard exponents of Indirect Rule remained the prevention of modern education in their bailiwicks.[60]

Retrenchment in the education budget during the depression years helped the cause of Indirect Rule. Its exponents shared with colonial administrators elsewhere a conviction that 'literary' education was not only wasted where there was little work requiring it, but also self-defeating since it gave rise to more sophisticated opposition to foreign rule. In the Sudan, modern education had been provided for practical reasons—to train Sudanese for low-paid, subordinate posts in government departments. There had, however, always been a liberal element epitomized by the highly publicized endowment of Gordon Memorial College. In this as in other respects, north and south were treated very differently. Education in the south was first relegated to and later reserved for foreign missionary societies.[61] The policy of Indirect Rule proved a failure, not least because the Sudanese elite objected to its major feature, 'native administrations'. In 1934, Sir James Currie, former director of education, published an article 'provocatively critical of Indirect Rule, its British protagonists in the Sudan, and their deleterious effects on education'.[62] It was not long before the Indirect Rule experiment was abandoned. But it had done little to halt the cause of nationalism.

In the 1930s and 1940s, the students of the Gordon Memorial College were prone to demonstrations aimed at the college's hierarchy and more generally at British rule. As the new principal Lieutenant Colonel Whicher wrote in 1947:

> The position in the college when I arrived in the middle of March was that the students were refusing to take part in any activities outside of the lecture-room. The policy of 'non cooperation', which was intended as a protest against the abolition of the Students' Union and had been in full swing throughout the term, led to the abandonment of a ceremony at which Dr Tothill's departure and my own arrival were to have been publicly acknowledged.[63]

The principal wrote that the college's mission to train the mind and character was not progressing. The Students' Union, he said, was not 'functioning properly' and has been a source of 'continual political unrest'. The students had recently gone on strike. They had threatened demonstrations, and as a result the Union was abolished and a 'Social Club' set up in its place. The principal, rejecting the politicization of the Union, wrote that 'it was always intended' to be no more than a social club. It was clear that while the college authorities were prepared for the students to partake in athletics and amateur dramatics, *politics* was strictly out of bounds. 'Students may not participate in any way whatsoever in public politics.'[64] The college closed its doors for two months as a result of the unrest.

Introduced through their education at the Gordon Memorial College to Western technology, and inculcated with the cultural and political values stressing independence and liberal democracy, the new middle-class Sudanese, like others elsewhere in the Middle East and Africa, turned less and less to the tribe for inspiration and saw in the British administration that dependence and acceptance of authority they had been taught to reject. Scorned by the British officials, who preferred the illiterate but contented fathers to the 'half educated', rebellious sons, and adrift from their own customary tribal and religious affiliations, these Sudanese turned for encouragement and sympathy to Egyptian nationalists in the Sudan, and from that association modern Sudanese nationalism was born.[65]

Young educated Sudanese felt solidarity with Egyptians whom, they felt, were fighting for a just cause—freedom from British rule. They were niggled by local inequalities, resenting for example the fact that British tutors had rooms to themselves, whereas Egyptian and Syrian members of staff shared communal space. The college attempted to replicate the tradition of close, personal interest in the individual student that was common in the British system. Some, however, regarded the English members of staff as distant and conceited. For obvious reasons students tended to communicate better with the Egyptian masters than with the British ones, who were always suspicious of the influence that Egyptian members of staff had over their Sudanese charges. 'The Egyptian teaching element in the college has undoubtedly introduced a good deal of noxious propaganda of the Nation-alistic type among the students.'[66] Subsequently there was a reduction in the Egyptian staff at the college and an increase in men drawn from the Coptic and Lebanese Christians communities, caused by the fear of the influence of Egyptian nationalism.

Expansion and the move towards university status

There was always a tension in the composition of the college. From the start, some saw vocational education and primary education as getting in the way of the college's 'true' mission—to operate at the higher-education level. After the First World War there was an increased demand for well-trained clerical staff and technical personnel. Some wanted vocational courses moved out and more emphasis on academics. As the decades passed, the college devel-oped from an elementary to an intermediate school, rising to become a secondary school and later still a further- and higher-education institution, achieving this by 'shedding its lower branches' as it progressed.[67]

As has already been described, one of the things that marked Gordon Memorial College out was its ambitious plans for expansion and the desire to be a centre of higher-education excellence while embracing all levels of education. It was no more than a low-level primary school when it was established, but was in a permanent state of rapid development during all the fifty-eight years of its existence.[68] The De La Warr Commission's report of 1937 led to the conversion of the college into a true centre of higher educa-tion. The report 'recommended a thoroughgoing separation of technical from secondary education together with the establishment of "higher" schools designed to produce a genuine professional elite'.[69] In 1937 Christopher Cox was appointed principal. A Fellow of New College, Oxford, Cox was consid-ered 'of the right social calibre' and a fitting leader because of his background as a teacher.[70] Cox wrote that the secondary education elements needed to be removed so that 'elements of a future University College, ultimately to develop into a University, may be centred now in the Gordon College'.[71] To facilitate this, in the early 1940s a new GMC secondary school was established at Wadi Seidna (north of Omdurman) to clear the college of its secondary population. The reports into the college's activities of the 1930s, the new Foreign Office attention to the Sudan, and the arrival of Cox resulted in the adoption of a comprehensive scheme for educational advance.[72]

Lord De La Warr's Commission recommended the expansion of primary education and concluded that the improvement and extension of intermediate education was an 'urgent' matter. The commission argued that the standard of Gordon College had to be raised: the British teaching staff were over-worked and under-manned, and new blood was required. Sudanese staff needed improvement and opportunities. For years, notwithstanding the government's denials, British and Sudanese alike had seen the college as a training school for government employment. The Depression and consequent retrenchment turned a shortage of trained Sudanese into a surplus, with no comparable work available elsewhere. This was not because the government alone required men educated to a high standard; rather, Gordon College graduates were *inadequately* trained for private commerce.[73]

In 1937 Ali Bey El Garem of the Egyptian Ministry of Public Instruction visited the college and made recommendations on the teaching of Arabic. Small post-secondary Schools of Engineering, Agriculture, and Veterinary Science were established, along with a School of Law. These 'Higher Schools' awarded diplomas after three-year courses; graduates thus had five years of post-secondary education.[74] The School of Agriculture was based at Shambat College Farm, where it opened in September 1938. It had a 25-year lease of 600 acres for the Faculty of Agriculture and free tenancy of over forty government houses for staff. The college's ambition to acquire university college status came increasingly to the fore from this point onwards.

Unfortunately the war got in the way of these plans; the new school became a hospital and then an American air base, while Gordon Memorial College itself was requisitioned by the Army to become Army Headquarters in the Sudan. The military evacuated the college's buildings in the middle of 1944, the year in which all the existing higher schools in Khartoum were amalgamated into a single higher school to be known as the Gordon Memorial College, administered by a principal and a council.[75] The new college was thus converted from secondary to post-secondary education aiming at university college status. The purpose of the council was to exercise the powers previously exercised by the Governor-General alone.

Things got back on track with the end of the war, boosted in 1945 by a £1 million gift from the British government, placed in trust for the future, and a pledge of £500 per annum over a five-year period from the Rhodes Trust and £500,000 from the Sudan government for new buildings. At the annual meeting of the trustees and executive committee in London in February 1946, the proposed affiliation of the Gordon Memorial College with the University of London was discussed. The arrangement was for degree-granting and was an important step on the way to the college gaining university status, the University of London acting as a 'midwife' for the new university being formed in the Sudan.[76] The link between the two institutions was taken very seriously by Professor (Dame) Lillian Penson, the University of London's first female vice-chancellor, and the college duly became the first non-British institution to enter into a 'special relationship' with the University of London.

The college's ambitions needed to be matched by new buildings and infrastructure. The February 1946 executive committee meeting viewed a model of planned new buildings which were needed if university status were to be achieved, along with new equipment, library accessions, and staff. William Newton, who had recently advised Makerere College in Uganda about expansion as it too sought university status, stopped off in Khartoum on his way back from East Africa in order to help plan new buildings. He made sketch plans of the grounds and buildings that were required. The plans were announced at a luncheon at Brown's Hotel in London on 18 July 1945, hosted by His Excellency Major General Sir Hubert Huddleston, Governor-General of the Sudan.[77] Newton spent March in Khartoum and produced plans to accommodate 500 men and 200 women students. The college needed new halls of residence, lecture rooms, a library capable of holding 200,000 volumes, a mosque, an open-air theatre, and some attractive-looking cloisters that tied together the assembly hall, the existing buildings, and the proposed new library and mosque. New buildings included six student hostels each sleeping sixty students. There were to be cloisters on either side of the original main building and running water channels leading to a Degree Hall. The January 1946 issue of the architectural journal *The Builder* published the architect's model of the completed site, the new buildings extending outwards symmetrically from the original college building, bordered on the south by the Nile and on the north by Kitchener Avenue. By 1951, two hostels had been completed, along with a new laboratory and a science lecture theatre, and work was in progress

Figure 32. Aerial view of Khartoum, showing the Governor-General's Palace and Gordon College in the foreground, 1950. A statue of Gordon stands in front of the college.

on two more and an arts extension. It is interesting to note that in instructing the architect, Principal Wilcher requested hostel buildings 'which would contribute to [the student's] mental make-up through life'.[78]

Other moves were afoot to help the college attain university status. Professor Penson recommended dividing the staff into standard British university grades—lecturers, senior lecturers, readers, and professors. It was announced that the new college was constitutionally independent of the Sudan government, and that it wanted to build up its assets so that it could be financially independent as well. Lord Cromer, chairman of the trustees and the executive committee, launched an appeal for the college's new library in *The Times*. The king and queen led the way, donating books on Windsor Castle and Holbein's drawings at Windsor, and Queen Mary sent twenty-three volumes. The original portion of the library comprised 3,620 volumes, and on his death in 1945 Sir Douglas Newbold bequeathed a further 2,816 volumes.[79] A portrait of Newbold was donated by Mr Licos of Khartoum, and hung in the Council Room.

The Gordon Memorial College achieved university college status in 1946, in special relation with the University of London. The Vice Principal (Student Affairs) was Ibrahim Ahmed Ibrahim MBE. The new University College was divided into schools of administration, agriculture, arts, design, engineering, and science. There was also the Khartoum Veterinary School.[80] The University College of Khartoum was officially opened on 1 September 1951, with eighty full-time teachers, seventeen of them professors. It was officially known as 'The University College of Khartoum incorporating the Gordon Memorial College and the Kitchener School of Medicine', ensuring that illustrious names from the British imperial pantheon continued to be associated with the institution, for the time being at least. October 1953 was the fiftieth anniversary of the college's opening, an occasion marked by a Festival of Sport and a Festival of Art. But the events did not go ahead as planned because the students decided that they did not 'want to participate as it might suggest that they were endorsing the achievements in education of the Sudan Government in the past'. This attitude, the 1953 annual report recorded, made the principal 'melancholy'. It was 'yet another manifestation of the dichotomy which exists in the Students minds between themselves and "the college" and of their tendency to regard the latter as a largely alien entity with no real claim to their loyalties'.[81] But time was running out for the British. Just as the statues of the imperialists were removed when the British departed, so the names eventually changed too. In July 1956, six months after the Sudan attained independence, the University of Khartoum was born, administered largely by Sudanese people. The vice-chancellor was Nasr El Hag Ali, and only six of the twenty-six members of the university council were British.

Many Britons were justly proud of the institutions that the Empire left behind, even if, almost inevitably, they were run differently once they had left. Institutions of state, such as armies and parliaments, retained distinct British traits, as did legal and educational institutions. Former Gordon Memorial College principal Lewis Wilcher believed that the story of the college 'makes a good and timely story, suggesting without stressing the fact that the British haven't done an altogether bad job in the Sudan and that the dreadful Kitchener had a liberal idea or two after all'.[82] Institutions such as the college, and in its modern-day guise as the University of Khartoum, never lost their prominence in society. The old boys' network, with all its informal influence, remains a powerful factor in society, and most of Sudan's elite studied there.

11

Hong Kong and Shanghai Bank, Hong Kong

Hong Kong's waterfront is one of the world's most famous panoramas. Set against the mountainside of Victoria Peak, the central business district features remarkable skyscrapers which are spectacularly illuminated at night. One of the most eye-catching buildings is the headquarters of the Hongkong and Shanghai Banking Corporation Limited, designed by the renowned British architect Sir Norman Foster and situated in prime location—bang in the middle of Des Voeux Road on Statue Square, looking out across Victoria Harbour towards Kowloon on the Chinese mainland. (Occupying an entire block, at the rear the building's address is 1 Queen's Road Central.) Statue Square—Hong Kong's only civic square—is the administrative and financial centre of the city-state and HSBC has been at the heart of its history for over a century and a half. The Hongkong and Shanghai Bank became 'a key British overseas institution', according to its most noted historian. The international financial history of the East cannot be understood 'except with knowledge of the role of The Hongkong and Shanghai Banking Corporation'.[1]

From inside the bank's headquarters building the observer beholds the Hong Kong Club and the colonial-era Legislative Council building (formerly the Supreme Court) on the right, and the Prince's Building and the Mandarin Oriental Hotel on the left. Once known as Royal Square, this space was consciously developed as a royal zone, centred on a canopied statue of Queen Victoria erected to commemorate her 1887 jubilee. She was subsequently joined by statues of her husband Prince Albert and her son Edward VII. There was also a statue of Sir Thomas Jackson, chief manager of the Hongkong and Shanghai Bank in the last quarter of the nineteenth century and, following the First World War, a Cenotaph modelled on the

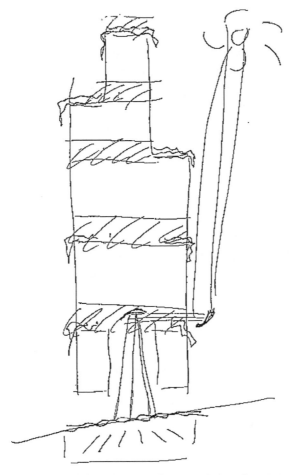

Figure 33. Norman Foster sketch (note from Gayle Mault at Foster + Partners): one of Norman's concept sketches for the HSBC Building, Hong Kong. He made hundreds of sketches in little sketch books during the competition phase for the building and this is the most famous one. It shows what was then a ground-breaking system for letting natural light in to the lower floors.

one in Whitehall. During the Second World War the Japanese took all of these statues to Japan to be melted down, together with the two famous lions that kept guard outside the HSBC building.* Fortunately, the statues evaded this fate, and were repatriated to Hong Kong after the war, Queen

---

* The Japanese used the HSBC building as their headquarters, its massive steel vaults providing an excellent bomb-proof bunker.

Victoria installed in Victoria Park but the lions and Sir Thomas returned to Statue Square, where they remain to this day.

The history of HSBC is the history of capital formation and the growth of the global economy that the British Empire oversaw. The provenance of the bank's current headquarters building, a striking glass, steel, and aluminium skyscraper, highlights the continuation of Britain's colonial experience into the late twentieth century, decades after decolonization had made the term 'British Empire' redundant. The current building replaced a previous headquarters, erected on the same site in 1935, which in turn had replaced the original headquarters building of 1886, which had replaced the 1860s original. It presents a superlative example of modern architecture, conceived in the 1970s as the bank's board looked to the future and sought to cope with rapid growth.

It was the building's design, as much as its size and its cost, which made it unique. For a start, it does not rest on the ground; it is raised on a series of steel columns, its 'ground floor' actually being a large walk-through public space uniting Statue Square with the city behind. It is made almost entirely of steel and glass, full of escalators, and dominated internally by an atrium that spans eleven floors, making it look a bit like a set from *Star Wars*. From inside, the views through full-height panes of glass are stunning: on the one side the lush tropical greenery tumbling down the hillside of the Peak, on the other the brilliant blue of the harbour and the haze of Kowloon spread wide.[2]

The building rises over 586 feet above Des Voeux Road, with a foundation depth of just over 111 feet below ground. There are fifty-two levels, five of them below ground, covering a gross area of 1,067,467 square feet. The building comprised 30,000 tonnes of steel, 3,500 tonnes of aluminium cladding, 1,000 tonnes of raised floors, 1,236,013 cubic feet of concrete, and 344,444 square feet of glass. Nearly 12,000,000 feet of electrical and communication cabling were built into the structure, which upon completion accommodated 5,000 staff, with 116 bank-teller positions.

Many buildings are far bigger. What made the bank different was the building process. Unlike a conventional high-rise building, the steel frame of the bank was not encased in concrete. The frame was like a skeleton; it defined the building's whole appearance and dictated the position of each of its other components. The interior had to be capable of being taken apart and put back together in a different arrangement. It therefore required solid, lightweight, movable parts that could be reassembled in kit-like fashion.

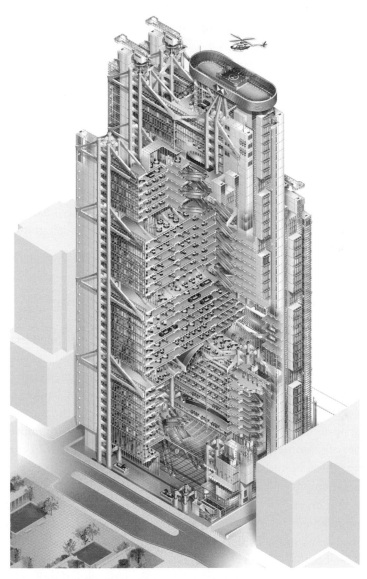

Figure 34. Three dimensional cross-section of the HSBC Building, Hong Kong, produced by Foster + Partners. Ian Lambot Studio.

This meant that the new bank was the modern equivalent of a hand-made building. When all the pieces of the building came together, they had to lock together with the precision of a well-made car door.[3]

Hong Kong had grown into the high-rise financial centre with which we are acquainted today on the ashes of Britain's position in Shanghai. Shanghai had been the eastern capital of British commerce until the Japanese irreversibly undermined Western colonialism throughout the Far East in 1941–2. Despite eventual Allied victory in the Second World War, the British were never to regain their position in Shanghai, which after the war became a de facto part of China as, *de jure*, it had always been. A new centre for Britain's Far Eastern commercial interests, a new capitalist beacon in the East, was required, and Hong Kong stepped in to fill the breach. Like Singapore, it was created virtually from scratch by the forces of British colonialism, a fusion of Western and Eastern culture dynamically charged by the trans-national movement and exchange encouraged by its geographic location and status as a key entrepôt port.

The evolution of colonial banking

The roots of the modern banking system can be traced to medieval times, though it was the modern period that saw the development of state banks, such as the Bank of England, and of 'country' banks. The nineteenth century witnessed the global expansion of banking as the role of banks in public finance expanded, and banks were inextricably linked to the rise of industries and professions. The banking industry made contact with entirely new categories of customer and community, and played a large part in extending the geographical boundaries of the world economy. Warfare and the costs of maintaining empires placed a huge financial burden on the leading nation-states, adding urgency to the need for the management of state debts.[4]

British influence on overseas colonial banks was reinforced in 1846 when all colonial joint stock banks—whether based in London or their home territories—became subject to supervision by the British government. There was a huge investment in Anglo-colonial banks, sixty-eight founded between 1853 and 1913 including the Standard Bank of South Africa (1858) and the Hong Kong and Shanghai Banking Corporation (1864). Reflecting foreign investors' confidence in places such as Hong Kong, the boom in overseas banking was not confined to British territories. HSBC acted throughout

China as well as in Japan, and other regional banks included the London and River Plate Bank in Argentina and the Imperial Bank of Persia.

HSBC became an indispensable institution in bank-rolling China and furthering British interests in the East. Under the leadership of Thomas Jackson, chief manager for most of the period from 1876 to 1902, HSBC took on multiples roles. It acted as agent to Imperial China, as banker to the colonial government of Hong Kong and other eastern states, and as the principal commercial bank in the East.[5] Before its foundation, local banking services for foreign merchants had been provided by the larger European factories. Most of the Western banks in Hong Kong and China were branch offices of Anglo-Indian banks. The Hong Kong and Shanghai Bank was founded by a cosmopolitan group of local merchants (taipans) with an initial paid-up capital of just over £500,000. The founding of the new bank was heralded as a sign of the colony's prosperity, and from the start Chinese capital was a significant part of its assets.[6]

HSBC was not a branch of a European-based bank, but an institution founded in Hong Kong in order to finance trade with China, Japan, and the Philippines. That said, recruitment and training were conducted in London and British values pervaded the bank. Employees came from public schools and the public school ethos was very much to the fore, including an emphasis on team games incorporated into the bank's culture. Executive staff, with a single exception were British, and 'it was thought that their wives most certainly should be British too'.[7] Within fifteen years of its foundation it had spread a network across much of Asia. In 1875 it opened a branch in San Francisco and in 1880 became the first British bank to open in New York. In Hong Kong, it developed into a quasi-central bank, becoming the principal banker to the colonial government of Hong Kong, acting on its behalf in the foreign exchange markets and issuing its local currency notes, which bore the image of the bank's headquarters upon them.[8] The bank financed much of Japan's foreign trade. By 1914 HSBC was leader in Eastern exchange banking and was head of the European China Consortium responsible for major railway and reorganization loans to pre- and post-revolutionary China.

HSBC was an important institution in shaping Britain's policy towards China until the end of the colonial era in that country in the 1940s. As a matter of course it collaborated with the Foreign Office in formulating and delivering British policy. It aimed to uphold China's territorial integrity while advancing Britain's economic interests during a period of intense international rivalry in the Far East.[9] By the close of the nineteenth century it was the leading expatriate bank in the region. The treaty ports, which had resulted from China's forcible 'opening up' to Western trade, acted as bridge-heads. The British government hoped that China could be prised open for European capital and industry by a combination of railways and diplomacy, and HSBC became the essential financial partner in pursuing these goals. The creation of HSBC greatly improved credit facilities just as regular steamship services and the extension of the underwater telegraph cable system, which reached Shanghai in 1871, reduced the time taken for commercial transactions and lowered their cost. Such developments attracted new traders such as Butterfield and Swire to China's treaty ports.

HSBC was intended primarily to finance China's overseas trade, but also to capitalize on new opportunities for business and the raising of loans as China's economy developed. It had privileged access given its position as banker to the colonial government in Hong Kong and also to the Imperial Maritime Customs Administration—China's customs office—which controlled the principal security for public borrowing.[10] Given this position, HSBC was keen to see China remain united, a desire shared by the Foreign Office. HSBC issued China's first foreign loan in 1874 and loaned again in the 1880s. The growth of its foreign loan business strengthened its ties with London. HSBC believed, as did the British government, that China needed to be held together, despite numerous centrifugal forces and the erosion of China's cohesion and sovereignty caused by European and Japanese predations. It wanted to retain the business openings that had come its way, and to avoid a situation in which the government and the Chinese state crumbled, with all the potential for defaults that such a situation threatened. The British government also wanted the ailing regime to survive; if it did not, it was feared that a potentially explosive and costly 'scramble for China' would ensue.

As the Chinese state weakened in the 1890s and 1900s, its reliance on external supporters such as the British government and HSBC deepened. The disastrous war with Japan (1894–5) obliged Peking to borrow from foreign sources on a far larger scale than before, and to look to British protection. Between 1877 and 1895 HSBC raised about £12 million for the Chinese government; between 1896 and 1900, it raised £32 million, indicating what Cain and Hopkins term the growing and increasingly overt convergence of politics and finance.[11] The bank's main business during this period was managing consortia which financed a series of Chinese imperial government loans, including the money to cover Japanese demands for war reparations.[12] There was international competition over shares in China's indemnity loans, as well as for rail and mining concessions. The bank became the main supplier of capital for much of the Chinese railway system.

From 1909 the Foreign Office and HSBC attempted to bind the major powers into a general consortium to finance railway construction. Terms were finally agreed with the Ch'ing government in 1911, at a time when the regime's foreign indebtedness had become a highly sensitive political issue. From Britain's point of view, the 1911 revolution that overturned the dynasty raised the possibility of a default and the implosion of the state. Britain played a leading part in averting this outcome. In 1912, the Foreign Office and the HSBC led the way in forming an International Commission of Bankers to manage custom revenue, and hence to secure loan repayments and help bolster the provisional government.[13] Thus the Foreign Office and HSBC worked together to maintain China's solvency. As late as the 1930s HSBC, along with other British firms and foreign banks, financed over 90 per cent of the foreign trade of Shanghai, the greatest of China's ports.[14]

The building

Given HSBC's central role in managing Britain's relations with China, it is little surprise that its headquarters building was intimately associated with Hong Kong's prosperity in the minds of the local people, both a landmark and an icon. It was sometimes said that the colony was ruled by the Jockey Club, the Hong Kong and Shanghai Bank, and the governor (in that order). HSBC's position in Statue Square denoted the bank's status. Jan Morris remembers this central space, 'a ceremonial plaza of some dignity':

> It opened directly upon the harbour... The steep green island hills rose directly behind the square, and it was surrounded by structures of conse-quence—Government House where the Governor lived, Head Quarter House where the General lived, a nobly classical City Hall, the Anglican cathedral, the Supreme Court, the Hong Kong and Shanghai Bank. The effect was sealed by the spectacle of the ships passing to and fro at the north end of the square, and by the presence of four emblematically imperial prerequisites: a dockyard of the Royal Navy, a cricket field, the Hong Kong Club, and a statue of Queen Victoria.[15]

The first HSBC building built on the present site was erected in the 1860s. It was demolished in the 1880s and rebuilt again. This new building was a remarkable hybrid by the local architects Palmer and Turner, who had opened their office in Hong Kong in 1868. It was in effect two buildings, tropical Mediterranean on one side, monumentally domed on the other, its main south door opening into Queen's Road, its north facing Des Voeux and Statue Square. It was demolished in the 1930s and yet another erected, built in 'Stripped Classical' and Art Deco style and specifically commissioned to be 'the best bank in the world'.[16] It was faced entirely in Hong Kong granite, for the purpose of which the bank had purchased its own quarry. The main banking hall was capped with an enormous mosaic depicting, among other things, the benefits of trade and industry. Commercial banks were enjoying a heyday in terms of the grandeur and style adopted for their main buildings, and expenditure on bank headquarters was especially conspicuous in the inter-war period.[17]

By the 1970s HSBC had outgrown this building as well, and had spilled over into a range of buildings scattered across the colony. The 1935 building had become an uneconomic structure: what was once the tallest building between Cairo and San Francisco represented potential for a new building that could contain three times as much floor space as the current design. But deciding in the late 1970s to demolish an iconic building and start all over again was a decision that the bank's board did not take lightly. It had to be handled with the utmost care, not just in terms of design and construction, but in terms of managing the bank's relations with the people of Hong Kong. The bank's image had become strongly associated with the façade of the 1930s building, which appeared on banknotes and logos, dominating the foreshore and dwarfing its neighbours. Every Christmas, a seasonal lights display adorned the building's façade, which was photographed by thousands of people, and the feet of the lions outside the building had been rubbed to a high polish by countless hands touching them for good luck. The symbolism of the bank was firmly entrenched among the colony's largely illiterate population and it was important, therefore, that the demolition was handled deftly and the replacement building was suitably impressive.

A new building would have to be built on the site of the original, a piece of prime real estate in a colony that by the late 1970s was the world's second largest container port and fourth most important financial centre. Space, therefore, was at a premium. The bank was experiencing a period of quite astonishing growth. In the brief period between 1979 and 1985 it had transformed from a regional bank to a major international financial institution. By the end of 1980 profits were 38 per cent higher than when Norman Foster was commissioned to design the new headquarters in 1979.[18]

Redevelopment of the existing building was seriously considered by the board, fired by the desire to keep a well-loved monument intact and to save a building that, in a city with a high degree of architectural uniformity, was one of its few genuine landmarks. It had become an important element in the colony's feng-shui, and it was feared that its destruction would threaten its stability and prosperity. But change was unavoidable, and the board realized that it had to be fully embraced. What was required was a flagship building fit for the twenty-first century, capable of replacing the 1935 building in the hearts of the people of Hong Kong.

From the outset, the board pursued the world's finest professionals. Deciding on a firm such as the structural engineers Ove Arup and Partners, or Wimpey International as the main constructor, was relatively easy given their established records deciding on an architect was more difficult. An international competition was declared, for which Foster and Partners London office went into overdrive, making regular visits to Hong Kong for presentations and interviews as the selection process unfolded. In the end, the board concluded that 'if we use Foster we shall have to be tough. The benefit of his brilliance and good management could be outweighed by the lack of practicality of his designs.'[19] But the quality of his design won the day, the Foster submission judged to be 'in a league of its own'. The planned building, unprecedented in its complexity and the use of prefabricated components, required over 120,000 architectural drawings for its evolution and was designed to be utterly unique. This was a project that went beyond creating a conventional building of aesthetic merit. It was an attempt to fabricate a building in a way that had never been tried before, using standards of perfection previously confined to the realms of defence or nuclear construction.[20]

The new building was constructed in consultation with feng-shui authorities. Construction began in 1983 and was completed in 1985 at a cost of HK$5.2 billion (US$668 million) making it the world's most expensive building at the time. The building site was extremely constricted—just under an acre, in which 2,500 people (3,500 at peak) worked on a plethora of tasks set by over thirty separate subcontractors. The construction and its management was characterized by enormous complexity, the inevitable problems associated with coordinating massive engineering and design projects across three continents, overspend, and sometimes acrimonious meetings between the board and its chosen architect. Even before the construction could begin, the search for the suppliers of the major components—the steel framework,

the sealed modules that would provide the building's 'floors', and the cladding that would adorn its exterior—led to intense international competition.
At one point there were suggestions that the architects be summarily dismissed, problems having been encountered with regard to the supply of steel
and escalating costs.[21] The tag 'world's most expensive' building was encouraged by headlines such as 'How Not to Build a Masterpiece' (*Asian Wall Street
Journal*) and 'The Sky-high Costs of Building Sky High' (*Sunday Times*). But
Foster kept fighting his corner, arguing that it was not just about the cost of
a building that would be far superior to a 'normal' skyscraper, but also about
what it would cost to run—its 'through life' costs—and here, his innovative
ideas about flexible interior space came into play.

The new HSBC headquarters was the first 'truly original modern building in Hong Kong'. Standing out from the identikit skyscrapers of Central,
'it emerged almost extra-terrestrially'.[22] The design of this incredible late
colonial structure required great ingenuity on the part of Foster. The bank
required a very much larger building than the 1930s structure it was replacing but it had to fit on the original site area; its interior lay-out needed to
be as flexible as possible to accommodate new technology and the changing
needs of a fast-expanding organization until well into the next century; and
it had to be constructed quickly on a very confined site.[23] Foster's solution
was to design a building that utilized a great deal of off-site prefabrication,
with components manufactured all over the world. Having major building
components constructed separately in America, Britain, and Japan required
an extraordinary degree of precision engineering.

The building's design and materials were subjected to rigorous tests—
mock-ups of Hong Kong's Central District and Victoria Harbour were built
for wind tunnel tests, in order to pit the proposed structure against possible
typhoons or tsunamis; the SAS were engaged to simulate terrorist attack.
During construction, six giant red cranes sat on top of the growing structure,
turning it into a 'kind of gigantic kinetic sculpture'.[24] Below ground, a giant
sea-water tunnel, 23 feet in diameter and 350 feet long, was driven from the
building site to the harbour in order to bring cooling water to the building's
main refrigeration system. Once the structural framework was standing, the
gleaming sealed stainless steel modules could be lifted into place. Then, inside,
the demountable partition walls could be installed, along with the liftable
floor panels and the bank's furniture. In developing the interior concept,
Foster and his firm had conducted exhaustive research into the workings of
the bank's departments, their spaces, and furnishing requirements.

Figure 35. Close up of HSBC Building, Hong Kong, at night, showing offices and workers.

The building's core revolves around five steel modules built in Britain by Scott Lithgow Shipbuilders in Scotland; glass, aluminium cladding, and flooring from America; and service modules from Japan. The floors are made from lightweight movable panels—the same material used for aircraft floors—beneath which lie power networks, data and telecommunications cables, and air-conditioning. The floor panels can be lifted enabling the rapid installation and updating of technology. Similarly all internal walls are made of movable partitions so that office lay-outs can be changed and modified as required without the need for structural alterations. There is no internal supporting structure and natural light is the major source of lighting within the building. At the top of the atrium is a bank of giant mirrors. These form part of the innovative, computer-controlled sun-scoop that reflects natural sunlight into the atrium and down to the plaza. Sun shades on the exterior block direct sunlight and reduce heat gain, and, as has been seen, sea water is used for the air-conditioning.

The most conspicuous features of the building are the eight groups of four aluminium-clad steel columns, which rise from the foundations up through the main structure, and the five levels of triangular suspension trusses which are locked into these masts. From these trusses are suspended five groups of floors. They can be seen clearly on the outside of the building—the inverted 'v' sections of the suspension trusses span the structure at double-height levels—giving the building much of its distinctive character. By the use of bridge engineering techniques, and by locating all services in prefabricated modules hung on the east and west sides of the building, Foster eliminated the need for a central core, creating large, unobstructed floor areas that are the key to the building's flexibility and efficiency. The building features express lifts connecting the plaza to the double-height areas, while movement between floors in each zone is by escalator, of which there are sixty-two in the building. A new lobby and an Asian Story Wall were added by Greg Pearce, principal architect of the Hong Kong Airport Express station. The new lobby was designed in a minimalist manner to complement Foster's building.

At ground level, beneath the building, an open public area has been created. Above there is an atrium rising 170 feet through eleven levels. The public banking areas are situated around the atrium and are reached from the plaza by the longest freely supported escalator in the world. Open-plan offices surround the atrium, allowing staff to work under natural light, while noise levels are controlled by means of careful acoustic engineering. On Levels 3 and 5 on either side of the atrium are located black-marble banking

counters manufactured in Italy, with solar powered calculators for customer use set into them. The absence of screens, improving contact between
tellers and customers, provides unobstructed views through the full-height
windows across the harbour to the north, and towards the Peak to the
south. The building, in which over 4,000 people work, was opened with a
party for 2,500 guests and a feng-shui ceremony blessing the entrance
escalators.

Outside the building, the two bronze lion sculptures were reinstalled. Created for the 1935 building by Shanghai-based British sculptor W. W. Wagstaff,
they guard the entrance to the bank on the Statue Square side. Inspired by
lions for the bank's Shanghai building commissioned in the 1920s, they were
cast by J. W. Singer and Sons in Frome to the design of Henry Poole. The
Shanghai lions had become part of the local scene, stroked by passers-by in
the hope that good luck would rub off on them. The Hong Kong lions
became known as Stephen and Stitt, named after bank personalities of the day.
They, too, became venerated by local people. When the Japanese occupied the
colony, the lions were removed to Japan to be melted down, but were saved
when they were recognized by an American sailor in Osaka in 1945 and
returned, Stephen sporting Japanese bullet marks.

Viewing Hong Kong in the 1980s, Jan Morris lamented the changes that
had affected Statue Square. 'It has all been thrown away. Today Statue Square
is blocked altogether out of our sight by office buildings, and anyway only
the spectre of a plaza remains down there, loomed over, fragmented by
commercialism.'[25] The new building served a symbolic purpose beyond its
function as a bank headquarters. For long a symbol of Hong Kong's colonial
status, bank and government officials hoped that the new building would
convey confidence in Hong Kong's future. And although many foreign
firms left Hong Kong in anticipation of the 1997 transition, even more
came to take advantage of the economic opportunities provided by Hong
Kong's reintegration into China. As the largest investor in China, Hong
Kong handled half of China's exports and almost 60 per cent of its total
foreign investment and provided one-third of its foreign exchange reserves.[26]
But over the last twenty years the Chinese presence in Hong Kong has
mushroomed, reflected in Hong Kong's shifting physical landscape. In
March 1990, the Bank of China moved to its new headquarters, a seventy-
storey aluminium-and-glass tower in the Central District designed by
renowned Chinese American architect I. M. Pei.[27] The fifth-tallest building
in the world, it towered over the HSBC building, and cost half as much to

build. Nevertheless, the HSBC building remains enviably located in the centre of the city, part of the stunning harbour backdrop. Fitted with over 700 intelligent lights, it is part of the Symphony of Lights scheme that spectacularly illuminates the harbour at night.

Singapore and Hong Kong are the modern-day success stories of the merchant city-state. Their architecture, Fermor-Hesketh writes, is entirely mercantile in conception and creation, but their very success has destroyed the relics of earlier generations. Continuing progress and vitality have ensured the destruction of many of the great dockland vistas. While this may be a tragedy for the architectural historian, it does have a certain ironic justice. The architecture of a trading empire was its servant rather than its memorial.[28] When HSBC commissioned its new main building in the early 1980s, it was looking for a building that could reassert the bank's importance to Hong Kong as both image and financial powerhouse; the impending hand-over of the colony to China meant that the bank, and Hong Kong itself, needed a public statement of confidence as well as to be firmly bound to the circuit of financial centres and 'world cities'.[29]

12

British Empire Stadium, Wembley

Numerous buildings in Britain betray the country's imperial heritage and its connections with the non-European world, though fewer perhaps than might be expected. Those that do exist include the fanciful façades of early high street cinemas and Oriental confections such as Brighton's Royal Pavilion and Sezincote House in Gloucestershire. There are also the self-consciously imperial erections of the capital city's political and financial districts, and its royal precinct running from Trafalgar Square to Buckingham Palace. There are plenty of institutions with imperial and 'wider world' associations too, such as the schools of tropical medicine in Liverpool and London, academic institutions such as the School of Oriental and African Studies and Imperial College London, the Royal Geographical Society, the Foreign and Commonwealth Office, the Oriental Club, the Royal Over-Seas League, and the currently disused Commonwealth Institute building (1962) on Kensington High Street.

The British Empire Stadium was built by Sir Robert McAlpine and Sons to the design of John Simpson and Maxwell Ayrton. It was completed in time to host the famous 'White Horse' FA Cup Final of 1923. Thereafter the stadium became an icon of world football, 'the cathedral of football', in Pele's words. Wembley Stadium—originally, the British Empire Stadium— was designed and built for the huge 1924 British Empire Exhibition, a lavish exercise in indoctrination as well as entertainment.[1] Heralded at the time as 'the Imperial Stadium, which dominates the landscape for miles around', its creators boasted that it was 'the largest and most complete sports arena in the world', able to accommodate 125,000 spectators, 'one of the greatest concrete wonders of modern times' in the opinion of the journal *The Builder* in 1926. It was the centre-piece of a unique exhibition dedicated to the

British Empire: 'Here during July and August [1924] will be staged a magnificent Pageant of Empire.'[2] But the exhibition was about far more than fun. It was an act of reaffirmation and renewal for post-war Britain as well as a monument to victory and a celebration of the size of the Empire. It was also a bid to stimulate British and imperial trade and economic recovery, and a global media event.[3] Never before had the British public had set before them such a wide-ranging collection of the peoples, cultures, and economies from around the world.[4] At the time, the modest London suburb of Wembley was billed as the gateway to the British Empire.

Surrounded by lakes and pavilions representing all parts of the Empire and approached along King's Way (later, Wembley Way), the Empire Stadium with its famous twin towers was home to marching bands and imperial military pageants before it became the established home of England's national game and the venue for international football matches, domestic cup finals, speedway motor-cycle racing, and 'stadium rock' of the Live Aid variety. The 1924 British Empire Exhibition, repeated in 1925, was intended to showcase the wares of the British Empire and encourage people to 'buy imperial' as well as to entertain and to inform, and was visited by nearly 30 million people. Visitors to the 200-acre exhibition site alighted at Wembley Park Underground Station. An impressive view greeted them. Beyond a large

Figure 36. Aerial view of Wembley Stadium and the Australian Pavilion exhibit at The Empire Exhibition, 1924.

semi-circular formal garden were the parallel paths of King's Way stretching southwards 875 yards to the twin domed towers of the Empire Stadium. For its first 320 yards King's Way was flanked by the huge concrete Palace of Engineering and Palace of Industry, the main exhibition halls for British displays. The Palace of Engineering, the site's largest building, covered 13 acres.

Crossing this axis either side of a serpentine lake were two other paths, the Fairway of the Five Nations and Commonwealth Way, which became Dominion Way to the east. The central position in the exhibition grounds was Unity Bridge. The language of harmony and family was an important aspect of the Empire's self image. From this spot the visitor could look south of the lake to the Canadian and Australian pavilions and the Empire Stadium, westwards to the New Zealand pavilion, and eastwards to the Indian pavilion. A host of other pavilions could be glimpsed: Malaya to the south-west, the Palace of Arts to the north-west, and Burma and South Africa and a number of other colonial pavilions to the south-east. The huge diversity of status in the Empire—dominions, crown colonies, protectorates, mandates, naval bases—were thus brought together, transformed from a ragbag of bits and pieces, to an apparent order, a world bound together under one nation. Here was Wembley's 'great idea'.[5]

Imperial influences in British buildings

It is easy to be aware of British influence when considering the history of the many overseas cities created or influenced by the imperial experience. But it is often harder to detect evidence of empire in the former mother country, and easy for 'metropolitans' to overlook their interaction with the 'periphery'. While it is clear, for example, that cities such as Calcutta, Melbourne, and Shimla have been significantly shaped by the British, it is not as immediately apparent that London and Paris have been similarly marked by contact with, and settlement from, many different regions. The geographer Doreen Massey argues that the identity of places in the modern world is constituted as much by their relation with other places as by anything intrinsic to their location.[6] This is particularly important when viewing the history of Europe's 'metropolitan' cities. To understand the development of London or Manchester, for example, we must look at Africa, India, and Latin America, just as an understanding of the development of Bombay or Kingston requires reference to Britain.[7]

According to the historian John MacKenzie, Orientalism in British architecture was never conscious enough to constitute a movement: buildings in Britain with an Oriental influence seemed to be the product of stylistic fads and fancies.[8] Eastern forms first appeared in the houses, gardens, and parks of the aristocracy, though soon moved into the leisure architecture of the masses. The first Orientalist buildings were exotic additions to gardens—Chinese temples and pavilions were built in the eighteenth century at Stourhead, Stowe, Studley Royal, Alton Towers, Shugborough, Woburn, Wroxton, and Blair.[9] Many such features were inspired by works such as Sir William Chambers's book *Designs of Chinese Buildings, Furniture, Dresses, Machines, and Utensils* (1757). Obelisks, pyramids, sphinxes, and 'Egyptian' mausoleums appeared on English estates and occasionally in town squares and cemeteries. If the great buildings remained classical or, later, Gothic, they did so with their Moorish, Egyptian, or Indian rooms, their Chinese wallpaper, their proudly displayed ceramics and ivories, their 'Chinese' Chippendale furniture, 'japanned' work, screens and chests, musical instruments and cased clocks.[10]

The Egyptian Hall in Piccadilly (1812) was modelled on the Temple of Hathor in Egypt.[11] There were Egyptian houses at Hertford and Penzance, and influences in the Civil and Military Library in Devonport, Temple Mills in Leeds, and the Great Pagoda at Kew. At Blenheim Palace in the 1820s the Arcade Garden led to the New Holland or Botany Bay Garden, and an 8-acre Chinese Garden. In 1824 the 5th Duke of Marlborough used 'Views of India' wallpaper to decorate the Indian Room overlooking the Water Terraces. It is still there, the 'Views of India' images now adorning gift shop souvenirs such as speciality tea caddies and trays. Corals and shells from Mauritius adorned a granite obelisk on Blenheim's Water Terrace; there was a Chinese bridge; and emus and kangaroos wandered in the menagerie. Elsewhere in Britain there were Indian garden temples, pavilions, or 'minarets' at Preston Hall in Scotland, Muntham in Sussex, Melchet Park in Wiltshire, and the Scottish homes of East India Company general Sir Hector Munro at Novar. There were then numerous follies, such as the Mughal dome added by Samuel Pepys Cockerell, architect of Sezincote, to Warren Hasting's Daylesford House in Gloucestershire.

Thousands of British churches contain tablets memorializing servicemen who perished on distant battlefields: street names and street furniture such as drinking fountains reveal roots in Britain's imperial past. In Thornbury, Gloucestershire, for example, there stands an unobtrusive drinking fountain dedicated to the memory of Lieutenant Hector Maclane of the Royal Horse Artillery. Taken prisoner while trying to get water to the wounded, he was subsequently murdered 'in the Camp of Ayoub Khan, near Candahar, on 1 September 1880'. A window in the nearby church also commemorates him, one of nearly a thousand British and Indian troops killed in the defeat at Maiwand in the Second Anglo-Afghan War.

Another piece of public architecture relating to this particular battle is the Maiwand Lion in Forbury Gardens in the Berkshire town of Reading. This large bronze statue commemorates the 300 men of the Berkshire Regiment who died in the battle. The lion remains the town's mascot, and a silhouette of the Maiwand Lion appears on the badge of Reading Football Club (the club's mascot is Kingsley the lion). Another example of these random architectural legacies of empire is the Maharajah's Well in the Chilterns village of Stoke Row. This opulent structure, featuring a golden dome and an elephant astride a well house, was funded by the Maharajah of Benares. A local resident, Edward Reade, had once helped build a well in the Maharajah's state. Later, recalling reports of water shortages in the Ipsden region, he offered the well, which many people travelled to see once it had been erected.

There are many legacies of empire and connections with the non-European world to be found inside buildings throughout the British Isles. The seventeen-panel sequence known as the British Empire Panels adorn Brangwyn Hall in Swansea's Guildhall. Created by Sir Frank Brangwyn (1867–1956) in response to a 1924 commission from the House of Lords to commemorate the dead of the First World War, they were designed to hang in the Royal Gallery at the Palace of Westminster. The resultant profusion of vegetation, animal life and people brought to life in sumptuous (and often bare-breasted) colour, representing the extent of the Empire which the fallen had sought to protect, proved too exuberant a memorial for the Lords, and they were instead installed in Swansea's new civic building.[12]

One of the most notable interiors was Lockwood Kipling's Durbar Room at Osborne and the billiard and smoking rooms at the Duke of Connaught's Bagshot Park, as well as the interior of Maharajah Duleep Singh's Elveden Hall in Suffolk.[13] There were then the more subtle reflections of wider-world architectural influences, such as St Vincent Street Church (1859) with its eclectic classical, Egyptian, and other Orientalist features. Nor should we overlook that most enduring architectural immigrant the bungalow, which proliferated throughout Britain: initially the standard residence in the tropics, it arrived in Britain in the 1860s and became a favoured living space, first as a seaside holiday home and later as a suburban abode.[14]

Imperial London

Joseph Conrad described London as the 'very centre of the Empire on which the sun never sets'.[15] The problem was that the world's 'greatest city' was not a planned city. Unlike recently remodelled Paris, London had not been extensively rezoned, and there was a growing concern that the city did not quite measure up as an urban space to its billing. Critics compared it un-favourably with the spaciousness and stateliness of Rome, Paris, or Vienna. Another criticism was that even the grand buildings that existed in London lacked grand vistas and impressive approaches. In a preface to a book called *Imperial London* (1901), Arthur Henry Beavan wrote that 'the world's capital is a medley of palatial buildings, mean houses, beautiful districts, and squalid regions'.[16] There were plenty of plans afoot to redevelop the city, particularly its centre. In January 1912 *The Builder* published a plan for 'Imperial London' that called for the development of a new Imperial Quarter comprising an imperial parliament, palace, and processional avenue. A new Victoria Memo-rial was to be pivotal to this plan, with avenues radiating out from it, and the Mall forming the principal approach to a new imperial palace.[17]

From the latter half of the nineteenth century until the First World War, London was extensively rebuilt and redeveloped to equip it for its role as the capital city of a world-wide empire.[18] In a large measure, the rebuilding effected the financial and commercial districts while also developing the infrastructure required of a modern city, including sewers, communications, over- and underground railways, and wider streets. London was often described as an imperial metropole and an imperial cross-section—indeed sometimes it was depicted as empire incarnate. It was envisioned as an expression of imperial power, values, and display, with its entertainment and pageant zones mapped out and its darker peripheries—usually centred upon the East End—fantasized. The squalid regions, alive with foreign commodi-ties and foreign people, represented an intrusion of the colonies into the heart of the Empire itself.

Cities such as London, Paris, and Vienna had long contained monuments. It was only in the nineteenth century, Donald Olsen writes, that they attempted to *become* monuments. This process of centralized planning, an effort to configure entire cities as unified and coherent 'works of art', resulted in Haussmann's Paris, 'Ringstrasse Vienna', and, less successfully, in a reworked central London. Increasingly, a goal of London's planners was the transformation of the city into a monument to empire. It was increasingly conceived of as an imperial stage as well as an imperial capital. References to London's imperial pedigree and its imperial locations, monuments, and shrines were to be found in a surprising range of media, including guide-books and advertisements. In 1932, for example, an advertisement for the Underground Electric Railway Company invited people to 'Visit the Empire': all that was required to embark on a tour of the 'wealth, romance, and beauty of the Empire' was a ticket for the London Underground. Australia could be reached via Temple or the Strand, India via Aldwych, and much of the rest of the Empire via South Kensington.[19] A traveller in London could 'span the globe' in the course of a day: one could even see 'The Tropics by Underground'.[20] The London Underground was portrayed as the metropolitan equivalent to the 'All Red' cable route that circled the globe. Politicians contributed to the sense of London as an imperial place, the Conservative Party, for example, celebrating the city's role as an imperial capital.[21] The centrality of London was emphasized in a children's board games, board game publisher John Betts's 'A Tour Through the British Colonies and Overseas Possessions' (1854), which invited players to travel the colonial world with the throw of a dice, the journey beginning from St Paul's Cathedral, described in *Tit-Bits* (1910) as the 'pantheon for our heroes'.

The stage is set: ceremonial London

Government buildings such as the War Office, the Admiralty, and the London County Council headquarters were all designed to reflect a renewed sense of imperial grandeur, and the Colonial Office part of the New Government Buildings (1868–78) was decorated with allegories of the continents and busts of proconsuls and explorers.[22] Spectacles of empire thrived in London's theatres, exhibitions, and jubilees. The success of events such as Victoria's 1887 and 1897 jubilees convinced planners that they were popular and could be used to celebrate the imperial idea.[23] Her death in 1901 was seized upon as an opportunity for the creation of a new imperial space.[24] *The Times* articulated the idea that the Mall 'might be developed in a truly regal and Imperial manner', and it was decided to incorporate a re-designated

Mall within the design for the Victoria Memorial that was to be erected in front of Buckingham Palace.[25] Locating the Victoria Memorial outside of Buckingham Palace elevated the status of what had been a rather unpopular royal residence of little historical importance. The Memorial Committee gave the palace new prominence as a focal point for the metropolis, connecting it symbolically with Trafalgar Square and Whitehall. All of this relied upon the vision of the architect Sir Aston Webb, who designed both the Victoria Memorial and the palace's new façade. Like a great stage set, the long processional route was adorned with allusions to classical Rome and presided over by an enormous statue of the Queen-Empress.[26] Admiralty Arch at the other end of the Mall further added to its utility as a processional route, and the coronation of George V in 1910 launched the Victoria Memorial and the Mall as an imperial space.

There were other spaces in London which were heavily marked by imperial building and usage, including exhibition spaces such as White City, Wembley Park, and even the financial district in the City of London.[27] The symbolic space which framed the idea of the City as the heart of the Empire was Bank Junction.[28] A new Bank of England building was designed by Sir Herbert Baker which contributed to the shaping of late imperial London, as too did India House (1925) and South Africa House (1930). In 1954, plans for a new Colonial Office building in Parliament Square were put on ice because the prime minister, Winston Churchill, wanted to enlarge the square and lay out a 'truly noble setting for the heart of the British Empire'.[29] But this never came to pass; a decade later, the British Empire, amazingly, had all but disappeared.*

Imperial exhibitions

Echoes of the great imperial exhibitions born in 1851 with the 'Great Exhibition' could be found in the 1951 Festival of Britain exhibition on the Southbank and even the Millennium Dome experience at the turn of the

---

* A fascinating aspect of London's association with the Empire relates to the districts in which 'imperial' people resided. In the early years of the nineteenth century, 80 per cent of the directors of the East India Company lived within an area of one by one-half mile in the Marylebone–Baker Street–Harley Street region. St John's Wood was a preferred residential area for retired Indian Army officers, while South Kensington was known to expatriates as 'Asia Minor' on account of the large number of 'colonial-returned' living there.

twenty-first century. On 1 May 1851 over half a million people gathered in Hyde Park as Queen Victoria was driven by carriage to the new Crystal Palace. Inside, 30,000 ticket-holders awaited her arrival to open the Great Exhibition. Disraeli acerbically commented that the spectacle was 'a godsend for the government...diverting public attention from their blunders'.[30] Today, the Albert Memorial, with its gilded statue of the prince, stands close to the original site of the Crystal Palace, Albert holding a copy of the Exhibition catalogue in his hand. The glass wonder that was the Crystal Palace was built by 2,000 men bivouacked in Hyde Park and featured nearly 300,000 panes of glass. When the Exhibition closed on 11 October 1851, there had been 6,063,986 recorded visitors—equivalent to a quarter of the country's population.

Unlike the Great Exhibition, the exhibitions of the late nineteenth and twentieth century were intended primarily to *display* rather than to sell—to transmit ideas and messages rather than to act as a giant mart. Furthermore, while there had been thousands of foreigners at the 1851 Great Exhibition, they had not been intended as exhibits themselves. This had changed by the end of the nineteenth century. Following a trend set at the 1889 Paris exhibition, the display of native people in their 'villages' caught on. At these later exhibitions, objects were increasingly displayed alongside people, as they took on an anthropological element—one might almost say zoological—as 'natives' from various parts of the world were put on display for visitors to gape at. The Franco-British Exhibition of 1908 had a Senegalese village (the 'villagers' having no common background or shared language, but simply being 'black'). There were other changes too following the benchmark exhibition of 1851: whereas the Great Exhibition intended primarily to educate rather than to entertain, by the late nineteenth century the entertainment aspect had come to the fore.

For Londoners, empire and the non-European world was increasingly on show. In April 1836 newspapers carried adverts for a new attraction at the 'African Glen' at the Coliseum in Regent's Park, offering 'views across the New British Settlement of Graham's Town, South Africa's Great Karroo, or desert, Cape Town and Table Bay'. In 1850 Portland Gallery at Langham Place in London displayed an elaborate 'Diorama of the Ganges'; five years later the Egyptian Hall, Piccadilly, was showing 'grand moving panoramic pictures of the Nile', and in 1859 'To China and Back', the illustrated travelogue of Albert Smith.

By the early twentieth century the Crystal Palace, now rebuilt in unfashionable south London after early years on the fringe of smart Hyde Park,

was becoming shabby and the enterprise was running into financial difficulties. In 1911 it hosted the Festival of Empire, organized to celebrate
George V's coronation. Here, as was becoming the exhibition norm, incredibly large, well-built (but temporary) pavilions and other buildings were
constructed, including three-quarter scale replicas of the parliament buildings of the Dominions. There was also an elaborate reconstruction of a
South African diamond field, an Indian tea plantation, and a grandstand
designed by Aston Webb. The Festival of Empire and Imperial Exhibition
included staged entertainments such as the 'Masque Imperial', an allegory
of the advantages of empire.[31] The exhibitions, along with the 'spectacular'
sound, light, music, and dance shows staged by Imre Kiralfy that recreated
far-flung colonial locations, brought the Empire to the British people. Such
pageants were believed to be of educational value, instilling a love of region,
nation, and empire. These exhibitions and pageants—and there were many
of them from the 1880s with specifically imperial or non-European
themes—were seen as an effective way of educating the public in imperial
ideas. Olympia, Earl's Court, and White City hosted many such exhibitions
and events before the First World War. These exhibitions extolled the benefits of empire and served as spectacle, blending both 'science' and entertainment. *Display* was a method of managing Britain's encounter with the
wider world, mastering it through exhibitions and museum displays and
emphasizing Britain's pre-eminence. London could contain the Empire:
'One need not take a tedious journey to the East to realise its glories.
A journey to Olympia in the West will serve as well'; similarly the 'Palestine
in London' guide disclosed that 'the visitor should be able to learn more in
a day than he could otherwise learn by an actual visit in an entire week'.[32]

Wembley and the 1924 British Empire Exhibition

The *Official Exhibition Guide* described the British Empire Exhibition as a
'family party of the British Empire'.[33] By the time the exhibition's pavilions
and the Empire Stadium itself had been erected, Wembley already had quite
a history as a leisure venue with ambitious pretensions. Originally, it was just
a sleepy rural area north of London.[34] But the coming of the railway and the
opening up of London's suburban 'Metro-Land' was to change all that. In
the 1880s, Wembley Park Leisure Grounds contained football and cricket
pitches, a running track, fountains and waterfalls, walkways and flowerbeds.

It was in that decade that the Metropolitan Railway Company opened a line to Wembley as an extension of its Baker Street to Willesden line in order to try to speed up the process of population growth around north-west London.[35] Then in 1889, in a bid to encourage more people to use the railways, Sir Edward Watkin MP, chairman of the Metropolitan Railway Company, decided to build a public attraction at the site in order to entice people onto the trains and out of central London.

The Metropolitan Line had opened in 1863 and was the world's first underground railway. Its extension meant that Wembley began to develop as a suburb. The Metropolitan Railway Company acquired Wembley Park in 1890, and Wembley Park station opened three years later. Watkin, with 280 acres around Wembley now in his possession, had an ambitious vision and soon embarked upon a project to build a huge tower within the Leisure Grounds, inspired by Paris's Eiffel Tower. The only criterion set by the committee established to supervise the project—which received sixty-eight ambitious and bizarre entries—was that the tower be at least 150 feet taller than its Parisian equivalent. Gustav Eiffel himself was asked to design the

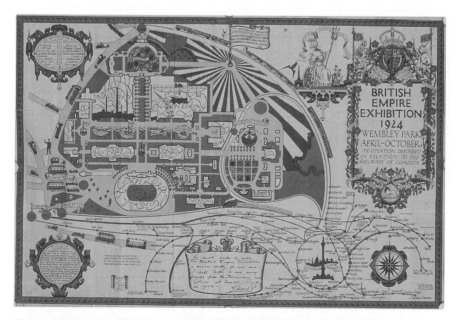

Figure 37. Poster advertising the British Empire Exhibition at Wembley Park, running from April to October 1924. Travel routes are shown, together with a plan of the exhibition space itself.

structure, though declined on the grounds that acceptance would diminish his stock in France. Still, the winning entry bore a marked resemblance to Eiffel's prototype, though carrying lavish Oriental motifs. It was to contain Turkish baths, restaurants, and a dance-hall.[36]

Sir Benjamin Baker, designer of the Forth Bridge in Scotland and the Aswan Dam in Egypt, was appointed consultant engineer and chairman of the competition jury, and the builders of the Blackpool Tower were commissioned to construct the tower. For financial reasons, however, the design was adjusted to four legs, leading to almost inevitable structural defects, and it never rose above 155 feet in height. The concrete foundations started to move, and molten lead was poured in. Subsidence, lack of money, and the death of Watkin stunted its growth and work was gradually abandoned. What inevitably became known as Watkin's Folly stood neglected, pathetically overlooking the Wembley Park Leisure Grounds that it had been designed to dominate. The site was eventually declared unsafe and closed down. The structure was dismantled, and the 2,700 tons of resultant scrap steel sold to Italy. It became a curious tourist attraction in its own right until dynamited out of existence in 1907.

Meanwhile, support for a new British Empire exhibition was growing in important quarters. Lord Strathcona from Canada had been vice-president of the Franco-British Exhibition and in 1913 donated £10,000 towards the fund to acquire the Crystal Palace for the nation. Shortly before his death in 1914 he put forward the idea of an exhibition on the British Empire. A new exhibition site was sought, and the government began planning a British Empire Exhibition featuring a centre-piece stadium which would become a National Sports Ground. The Wembley Park Leisure Grounds, which had by then evolved into an eighteen-hole golf course, was selected as the ideal site. The exhibition area would require 219 acres, and the spot on which Watkin's Folly had stood was chosen as the site for the new stadium.

The lay-out of the exhibition was Beaux-Arts in inspiration, with clear echoes of Lutyens's work in New Delhi, including the domes of the stadium's famous Twin Towers which were influenced by those of Lutyens's Viceroy's House. The principal buildings, the pavilions of engineering and industry and the Australian and Canadian pavilions, were arranged along a processional avenue, King's Way, which led southwards from Wembley Park station to the stadium. All permanent buildings, such as the Palaces of Art, Engineering, and Industry and the Government Building, were made of ferro-concrete as was much else on the site, including refreshment kiosks, drinking fountains, lamp-posts, and seats. Fifty acres were set aside for the Amusement Park, which included a mile-long rollercoaster. John Betjeman considered it to be the largest and most comprehensive pleasure park known to history.[37]

Figure 38. Palace of Engineering at British Empire Exhibition, May 1924, London, from *Supplement to The Times*.

'Never before has an Exhibition on such an elaborate scale been pre-pared', proclaimed the *Official Exhibition Guide*:

> In a single day you will be able to learn more geography than a year of hard study would teach you, and see in each case the conditions of life in the coun-try you are visiting... [The visitor] can travel round the world at a minimum of time, with a minimal of trouble, studying as you go the shop windows of the British Empire... Every aspect of life, civilized and uncivilized, will be shown in an Exhibition which is the last word in comfort and conven-ience... The grounds at Wembley will reproduce in miniature the entire resources of the British Empire. There the visitor will be able to inspect the Empire from end to end.[38]

The British Empire Stadium, as it was originally known, took just 300 days to complete at a cost of £750,000, constructed from thousands of tons of concrete, cement, and steel. The stadium's foundations were built right on top of the remains of Watkin's Folly (which were revealed to view once again in 2000 when the old Wembley Stadium was demolished to make way for the new one).[39] Work on the Empire Stadium began on 10 January 1922 with the Duke of York performing the ceremonial cutting of the turf. The stadium, the first building on the site to be completed, was ready just in time for the FA Cup Final between Bolton Wanderers and West Ham United on 28 April 1923. This was the famous 'White Horse' cup final, attended by anything between 240,000 and 400,000 people eager to see the new stadium. Of that number, Metropolitan Railways conveyed 152,000 to Wembley.

The stadium's construction had been expedited with the Cup Final in mind. Its official capacity was listed as 25,000 seated undercover, a further 10,000 in 'ring seats', and standing room for a further 91,500.[40] Although later on the spectator areas were roofed in, originally only the long sides of the oval-shaped stadium were covered, for a length of 650 feet on each side, these providing the areas of undercover seating. 'There is not in all England', the *Official Exhibition Guide* declared, 'a modern building that can compete with the Empire Stadium in the effect it creates upon the mind of the spec-tator.'[41] The design included a banqueting hall measuring 215 feet by 70 feet to accommodate up to 1,000 people, and a large tea room directly above it, capable of seating 600 people. Both of these large rooms were housed in the 'twin tower' side of the stadium. Incorporated in the design were also a press gallery, royal box, a players' tunnel, and changing rooms which included a concrete plunge bath. There was also a separate 24-feet-wide running tunnel through the structure of the stadium in order to allow a straight running track of a furlong (220 yards).

Intended for both track and field 'sports and games', at its centre was an oblong of grass measuring 492 feet in length and 260 feet in width. The Empire Stadium was a temple to modern architectural techniques and materials, constructed of concrete on a steel skeleton. Giving 'some idea of the immense size of the undertaking', wrote *The Engineer* shortly after the stadium's completion, 'we may say that the overall length of the stadium on its major axis is 900 feet, and that the maximum overall width is 650 feet'. Its construction involved 1,400 tons of structural steel work; half a million rivets; 600 tons of steel rods for reinforcing the 25,000 tons of concrete; 3,500 tons of Portland cement; and 14 miles of concrete beams to form the terracing in the stands. The pitch, too, was quite a feat of engineering. A 10-inch layer of ash and clinker formed the foundation for 5½ inches of subsoil. On top of this were arranged 76,250 turves, each one 18 by 12 inches and 2½ inches thick.

Safety checking this mass of steel, concrete, and cement involved hair-raising techniques that would not find favour with modern health and safety officials. A phalanx of 1,280 labourers, wrote an observer, were 'drawn up outside the building and then marched in, in companies, and led to the banks of seats immediately behind the Royal box'. There, 'under command' of Captain F. B. Ellison, the resident architect, the men were put through a series of movements, such as standing up, sitting down, swaying from side to side and backwards and forwards, and marking time, which they all did in disciplined unison. They were then instructed to jump and shout and wave their arms frantically. The test was then repeated on the other side of the stadium, before gangs of men were ordered to run down several of the flights of the steps. All of this was achieved without visible result, there being no sign of weakness in the stadium's structure. 'It was quite obvious', reported *The Engineer*, 'that the great majority of these men had seen service in the war, for otherwise we do not think that it would have been possible, without preliminary drill—which they had not had—for them to act in unison with such wonderful precision.'[42]

The British Empire Exhibition was officially opened on 23 April 1924, St George's Day, by King George V. His opening ceremony speech was broadcast by radio, the first time that a monarch's voice had been heard over the airwaves, reaching an audience of 7 million people around the world.

It was also released as a record by His Master's Voice. The king also sent a telegram, transmitted from the Stadium Post Office, which circled the globe in a minute and twenty seconds. The purpose of the Exhibition, the *Official Exhibition Guide* said, was 'to stimulate trade, to strengthen the bonds that bind the Mother Country to her Sister States and Daughter Nations... The visitor sees here the ripe product of British achievement in all parts of the earth.'[43] The Empire Stadium was surrounded by hundreds of new buildings including pavilions representing the architecture of the exhibiting colonies. There was also an amusement park, an ornamental lake, parkland, a reservoir, an outfall sewer, and railways and roads. It was an immediate success, and was reopened between May and October the following year, lifting the final attendance figure to 27,102,498 (with 4,500,000 admissions to the Empire Stadium alone).[44]

The Empire Stadium was alive with diverse activities. The Football Association had reached an agreement to use the stadium for cup finals for at least twenty years. While the exhibition was on, the stadium hosted an England versus Scotland football match on 12 April, and 92,000 attended the Aston Villa versus Newcastle United FA Cup Final of 1924. The match, which Newcastle won 2-0, was played on such a rainy day that match programmes were employed as makeshift umbrellas. Consequently few programmes survived in good condition, meaning that among collectors they are the most sought-after programmes of any FA Cup Final. For the exhibition the stadium hosted choral festivals, boxing matches, torchlight and searchlight tattoos, firework displays, and the Pageant of Empire with 12,000 performers. Between 14 June and 5 July 1924 the stadium became a 'Wild West Ranch' when it hosted the popular Great International Rodeo. This featured cowboys from all over the world and displays of steer roping, which attracted the wrath of the Royal Society for the Prevention of Cruelty to Animals.[45] The Boy Scouts Imperial Jamboree involved 12,253 scouts. Bands played daily at nine venues in the grounds, performers including the Edmonton Newsboys' Band from Canada and the British Guiana Military Band. There were evening spectaculars, including 'Eastward Ho!', which told the story of South Africa and India. The *Official Exhibition Guide* promised 'Monster Military Tattoos' and on Empire Day (24 May) the stadium hosted the largest band ever seen in the British Empire. It comprised 1,000 bandsmen drawn from all the line regiments of the British Army and a mounted band from the cavalry regiments.

Around the pavilions

Over seventy dominions and colonies were 'on show' at the British Empire Exhibition, their pavilions and displays spread around 15 miles of road. To navigate the huge site people could hop on and off the 'Never Stop Railway', which had the capacity to carry up to 20,000 passengers an hour. The line connected Wembley Park Station with Exhibition Station and a stop close to the Empire Stadium. There were also hundreds of bath chairs and attendants for those who wished to pay a couple of shillings and be pushed around the site. The idea of separate and distinct national pavilions dated from the 1850s. Whether a particular nation's or colony's pavilion occupied a prime position or was relegated to the periphery proclaimed its relative importance.[46] Pavilions allowed settlers and colonial governments to display their territories. They were designed by settlers and colonial officials, *not* indigenous people; representation aimed at national publics, colonial elites, and other imperial powers.[47]

The pavilions were the elaborate 'homes' in which diverse colonies displayed themselves to the British public. Britain's Government Pavilion, among other things, reinforced the point about this being the Empire on which the sun never set with a working illustration of the sun's vain attempt to do so.[48] But, in a piece of metropolitan modesty, the British building was not placed at the centre of the exhibition grounds. To get to it one went eastwards along Dominion Way, right along Imperial Way, first left down Chittagong Road and continued for 300 yards, past a bandstand and the Palace of Horticulture. There one beheld the British building, flanked by the Newfoundland Pavilion and the combined pavilion of the West Indies and British Guiana.[49] The building's plain portico was supported by columns 32 feet high, 'and the six lions guarding the entrance reduce those around Nelson's Column to mere kittens'.[50] The Admiralty Theatre in the Government Pavilion contained a 72-feet-wide water-stage on which incidents from naval history were recreated, including the Zeebrugge raid, a British attack on the Belgian port mounted in April 1918. The upper floor contained royal state apartments which in 1925 were converted to a 'Court of Heroes' devoted to illustrating, the *Official Exhibition Guide* said, 'those noble qualities of both men and women who have done so much to build up our Empire', centred on a bronze figure of St George.[51] Various government departments explained their work to the public: the Ministry of

Health wowed them with a model of sewage disposal while the General Post Office exhibited a working model of an automatic telephone exchange. A cinema showed films made by government departments, including '3 Million Letters a Day' and 'Clean Milk'.[52]

Entertainment and information were the order of the day. There were things to see, things to do, and things to listen to. Displays of a country's goods and products were central to the event. The pavilions ranged in size from the Australian 'palace' to the smaller West Indies/British Guiana pavilion, which sold cocktails and displayed exhibits about sugar. The West African building was a miniature reproduction of the walled city of Zaria in Nigeria; Ceylon was modelled on the Temple of the Tooth in Kandy; Palestine's pavilion featured a Jerusalem street; and Burma reproduced in Burmese teak one of the gates of a famous pagoda in Mandalay. Hong Kong was represented by a street of Chinese shops, and East Africa by a white-walled Arab building. The Canadian pavilion promoted butter with a life-size refrigerated butter sculpture of the Prince of Wales in the costume of a Native American chief. Life-sized butter sculptures were a peculiarly prominent form of display in the inter-war years, the Australian pavilion sportingly containing one of the legendary English cricketer Jack Hobbs, who toured Australia with England in 1924–5 and scored 865 runs. The Australian pavilion also sold 7 million apples. The Indian pavilion, covering 3 acres, 'reproduces the artistic beauties', the guide claimed, of the famous Taj Mahal and the Jama Masjid mosque in Delhi. It was complemented by an Indian theatre where one could see snake charmers, jugglers, and other performers of a hundred 'mysteries that enchant the East'.[53] But despite the seemingly innocuous verbiage about the exotic East and the wonders of the Raj, Indian nationalists recognized the British Empire Exhibition for the controversial political event that it was, and opposed India's participation.*

Bermuda's history as a naval base was audible in the main hall of the West Indies pavilion where the bell of HMS *Shannon* was rung on the hour. The *Shannon* had captured the American ship *Chesapeake* outside Boston harbour during the Anglo-American war of 1812. The Bermuda pavilion was a replica of Walsingham House, a well-known Bermudan restaurant and pub built in 1651, with a slate roof and green jalousies on the windows. There was a relief map of the island and illustrations of scenes from its his-

---

* In this context see David Stephen, '"Brothers of the Empire?": India and the British Empire Exhibition of 1924–25', *Twentieth Century British History*, 22(2) (2011).

tory. These included the relief of Jamestown, when ships from Bermuda succoured the starving colonists of New England in 1610, and the American naval base on White's Island, showing a staging area used by the American military in the First World War as troops and war matériel were shipped to Europe. The garden surrounding the pavilion was landscaped with native flowers including Easter lillies, hibiscus, pallen, and oleander.

The historian Tom August digs deeper into the intent and layers of meaning conveyed by the West India Committee in its design for the pavilion. He highlights the fact that the Exhibition did not take place in a public-relations vacuum, and that those responsible for 'marketing' the Caribbean today as a holiday destination might take a salutary look at forms of representation and associated narratives of domination and exoticization that were less problematically present during the colonial period. He describes the British Empire Exhibition as the apotheosis of an imperialism quite removed from the music hall jingoism associated with the earlier spectacles in which much less effort was made to familiarize the public with the resources and products of the Empire. Wembley, in contrast, took place in 1924, well after the expansionist phase of modern British imperialism and at a time of severe economic dislocation and indebtedness resulting from the war. Consequently, the Wembley management shifted attention increasingly towards the Empire's commercial value: Wembley was first and foremost a stocktaking of imperial resources and a 'buy British' and 'buy colonial' advertising campaign.[54]

The West Indies and Atlantic pavilion, designed by Messrs Simpson and Ayrton (architects of the Empire Stadium) expressed the cultural values of the European population residing in those territories. There was nothing indigenous about it. It covered 11,000 square feet with another acre for the West Indian garden, showing flora of the Caribbean, the 'Columbus anchor', and a statue of Rodney (the naval hero commemorated in the King's Square in Spanish Town Jamaica). *The Times* said that the pavilion and its garden gave the impression of a museum and a spice market, 'with a bewildering profusion of turtles and flying fish, rim, brilliant seedwork, plaited hats, and live toucans and agoutis and things'.[55] The Chocolate Lounge in the Trinidad and Tobago section was extremely popular, while the Jamaica section boasted a Blue Mountain Coffee Lounge, and the Jamaican Rum Bar, while Horace Myer's stand offered 'real' Planters' Punch. The Planters' Bar and Chocolate Lounge were so popular that the Gordon Hotels chain planned to introduce them into their London and provincial establishments.

British Guiana had one of the biggest sections of the West Indies and Atlantic pavilion. Floor space was expensive, so the organizers of the Guianese exhibit clearly thought the expenditure warranted, a Cinderella colony attempting to raise its profile in the metropole. The exhibition sought to overwhelm and astonish the untravelled Briton with information about the colony's resources.[56] They also had four different types of aboriginal Indians on display as living anthropological exhibits depicting 'typical Indian life', and women weaving cotton and making hammocks, beads, and fans. The British Guiana section also featured a large-scale working model of the Kaieteur Falls (the highest in the world) and examples of the colony's developed and undeveloped natural resources, including timber such as green heart wood, the hardest wood in the world, which had been used in the construction of the Manchester Ship Canal. A working diamond pit was also included, complete with 30 tons of native gravel. Models of dredgers and fine jewellery represented the gold industry. Balata, gums, oils, and resins were on display, and there was also a pyramid made of sugar. The Guiana display was embellished with orchids and the giant Victoria Regina water lily. Films showing scenes from life and work in the colony, produced exclusively for the Exhibition, were displayed for visitors. The blending of the latest commercial intelligence with a postcard exoticism produced a blurred image that was part trade show, part grocery store, and part travel agent fantasy.[57]

Elsewhere on this fascinating imperial site, the path to the Burma pavilion was specially designed, paved with Burmese bricks and featuring a bridge. The pavilion itself was modelled after a royal residence, guarded by seven-sided spires that had been especially shipped to London. Inside the pavilion was a display of scores of different types of Burmese timber, along with wood carvings and crafts including works in ivory, bronze and silver. Films produced especially for the exhibition showcased the teak forests and other natural resources of the country. In the pavilion's theatre, a Burmese troupe performed several times daily as did the juggler Law Paw, who had appeared at the Alhambra and Coliseum theatres.[58]

The Ceylon pavilion included a rubber display and exhibits offered information about its origins and the many consumer uses to which it was put. There was also a display of the Temple of Tooth, and three-quarters of a million pounds worth of gems, including pearls, sapphires, a white ruby, and a flawless blood-red ruby.[59] Completing this display of the colony's natural wealth, the Ceylonese showcased everything from a host of spices, to tobacco, cocoa, and the handiwork of native villagers. Lest there be any doubt about Ceylon's place as a paradise for big-game hunters, one of the largest mounted elephant heads in the world was on display.

The West Africa pavilion took the form of a walled town, a replica of a typical city in the hinterland. 'The exact conditions under which the West African people live will be reproduced', claimed the *Official Exhibition Guide*, 'and special quarters will be arranged for some seventy representatives of the Yoruba, Fanti, Hausa, and Mendi tribes of West Africa—weavers, leather workers, brass workers and others—who will carry on in the Exhibition the chief industries of the West African Colonies.' A special camera party had been dispatched to the 'wilds of West Africa' and returned with 40,000 feet of film, 'which will be on view daily, showing the natural beauties of Nigeria and the Gold Coast'.[60] The exterior of the Gold Coast pavilion was styled on the castles built by European explorers on the African coast. Within, the Ashanti court displayed silk clothing, golden state swords, brass and ivory work, immense wooden idols, and pottery. On loan were Princess Mary's wedding gifts from the people of the Gold Coast, including a silver stool. Other items of note in the pavilion included an executioner's hat made of deerskin and decorated with gold and deer's tails, and a collection of ornate scales for weighing gold.

Exhibits from Britain's South-east Asian colonies were divided into seven categories: forestry, fisheries, mines, commerce, agriculture, arts and crafts, and scenery. The Malay artisans, with their embroidery, beads, silk, gold, silver, and tin work made the arts and crafts section the most popular of the pavilion.[61] The process of tin production was demonstrated, and the main hall featured a reproduction of a Chinese mine, with working models of bucket dredges and hydraulic elevators. The South African pavilion offered people the chance to buy ostrich feathers plucked fresh from any of the thirty live ostriches in the paddock at a cost of six shillings. Other live animals on display included an entire flock of merino sheep and angora goats. The Fiji pavilion contained a collection of forks ostensibly used by cannibals.

All sorts of souvenirs and specially labelled products found their way into the homes of the people who visited the Empire Exhibition. There was souvenir china, music and records, picture postcards, and other postal paraphernalia. An Adams vase of dark-blue jasperware featured the Exhibition's lion logo, as did a Lipton's tea caddy made from brass and a toffee tin with a view of the Exhibition. There was the 'Wembley Willie' mascot doll, an exhibition tea kettle, penknife, and brooch, and a 'Drink More Cocoa' medallion. There were commemorative medals showing the image of the Prince of Wales, Jacob's biscuit tins and Kenyan coffee tins marked with Empire Exhibition designs, and commemorative stamps produced by the Royal Mail.

What people made of the British Empire Exhibition, especially its didactic signals, is open to question. As soon as P. G. Wodehouse's comic character Bertie Wooster arrived at Wembley—itself viewed as a distant outpost compared to the smarter parts of central London that he habitually frequented—he fell for the Planters' Bar and its array of cocktails. Though Sir Roderick Glossop had described the exhibition as 'the most supremely absorbing and educational collection of objects, both animate and inanimate, gathered from the four corners of the Empire, that has ever been assembled in England's history', it did not ring young Bertram Wooster's bell. Not only did the 'citizenry in the mass' put him off and make him feel like he had been walking on hot bricks after quarter of an hour shuffling along, but there was a lack of 'human interest'. 'I mean to say, millions of people, no doubt, are so constituted that they scream with joy and excitement at the spectacle of a stuffed porcupine-fish or a glass jar of seeds from Western Australia—but not Bertram.' The amusement park attracted him, particularly the helterskelter and the Jiggle-Joggle, Switchback, and Wheel of Joy. But Green Swizzles at the Planters' Bar won the day, the British Empire coming off a very poor third. Noël Coward encountered the same problem, and chastised a friend who he'd taken to the Exhibition with the words, 'I've brought you to see the wonders of the Empire and all you want to do is go on the dodgems.'[62] The poet John Betjeman, eighteen years old at the time he visited, was more taken with the exhibition's exotica. He preferred the pavilions of India, Sierra Leone, and Fiji 'with their sun-tanned sentinels of Empire outside' to the Palaces of Industry and Engineering 'which were too much like my father's factory'.*

Though the British Empire Exhibition put Wembley firmly on the map, it was a financial failure and the organizers incurred losses amounting to £2 million. When the exhibition shut in 1925, there was no plan in place for the future of the site or the Empire Stadium, and it was put up for sale. Eventually the land was sold to a speculator for £300,000, and most of the

---

* Revisiting the site in 1972 when filming the television documentary *Metro-Land*, he wrote: 'Oh bygone Wembley, where's the pleasure now?/The temples stare, the Empire passes by...'

structures were quickly dismantled, apart from the massive Palaces of Industry, Engineering, and Arts, which were made over to industrial use. In 1927 the owner, Jimmy White, came close to having the stadium demolished. But new life was found. The running track around the pitch was replaced by a dirt track, and greyhound racing began. This was a vital element in the stadium's post-exhibition survival and became a mass spectator sport.[63]

The owners then managed to attract another sport that could make use of the cinder track used by the greyhounds—speedway motorbike racing, which had arrived in Britain from New South Wales in the 1920s.[64] The first ever Speedway World Championship Final in 1936 was watched by 93,000 people. Regular speedway matches attracted crowds averaging 6,000, the home team, known as the Wembley Lions, going on to race there for twenty-two years. From 1929 the Rugby League Cup also became an annual fixture—the first Wembley rugby final being contested between Dewsbury and Wigan in front of 41,500 spectators. At the request of the American ambassador the stadium hosted two baseball games involving American servicemen in 1934. In the same year a new Empire Pool was opened on the site, today's Wembley Arena.

For the 1932 FA Cup Final, the BBC devised a commentary system involving a pitch divided into eight sections, in which the commentators would describe the action. The cover of the *Radio Times* showed an aerial photograph of the stadium with the grid system superimposed upon the pitch.[65] Wembley was also the major venue for the 1948 Olympic Games, most competitors housed not in a luxury 'Olympic village' but at RAF camps in Richmond, Uxbridge, and West Drayton, as well as some prisoner-of-war camps—the POWs moved out into tented accommodation for the duration. America topped the medal table with thirty-eight gold, twenty-seven silver, and nineteen bronze, followed by Sweden and France. The Great Britain team finished in twelfth place, last place shared by Brazil, Iran, Poland, and Puerto Rico. Holding this prestigious event was good for Wembley's profile, and the seventeen days of track and field and other events were probably the most intensive use of the stadium in its whole lifespan.[66]

Other events cemented the Empire Stadium's role as a national sporting venue. In 1963 40,000 people watched Henry Cooper take on Cassius Clay in one of the epic boxing contests of the era, and the stadium was at the heart of the 1966 World Cup tournament that England won on 30 July, beating West Germany in a classic encounter. In 1968 the stadium hosted the Royal International Horse Show, and in the 1970s it became a major music venue. Even as late as the 1970s, when the British Empire had vanished, football programmes still bore the name 'Empire Stadium' (replaced by 'Wembley Stadium' in 1977). Evel Knieval brought his stunt bike tricks to the stadium in 1975, and there were stock car races and international football matches. The 1985 Live Aid Concert was a fund-raising innovation; the stadium hosted Pope John Paul II; in 1986 American football made its debut at Wembley; and Nelson Mandela appeared there shortly after his release from Robben Island.

Despite its association with a wide range of sports, Wembley became best known for football. Right from the outset the Football Association had taken a keen interest in the exhibition because the plans included a multipurpose stadium. Having decided that their annual showcase, the FA Cup Final, should always be held in London, they found themselves urgently needing a suitably prestigious venue.[67] They had previously used the Kennington Oval cricket pitch, the Crystal Palace stadium, and Chelsea's ground, Stamford Bridge, which was considered very unglamorous and unsuitable. So the chance for the FA to use the biggest and grandest of new stadiums was one considered too good to be missed. Over the years, the stadium was regularly updated and improved. Floodlights were added in 1955 and the electric scoreboard and the all encircling roof, made from aluminium and translucent glass, were added in 1963. Those changes aside, the structure of the stadium remained essentially the same as it was in 1924 and the old stadium was struggling to meet the developing needs of sports fans when it was finally closed in 2000 and earmarked for demolition.

Conclusion

From Empire to Nation

The governments of new nations quickly transformed elements of the colonial cityscape, pulling down monuments and creating their own shrines, triumphal arches, and heroes' acres. This, and the replacement of colonial-era nomenclature—such as the 60 per cent of Delhi's streets that had non-indigenous names—was relatively straightforward. But new national governments were seldom able to change the built environment to any significant extent. Nasser was able to stamp his architectural and infrastructural authority upon Cairo, and Nehru was able to build the unique Le Corbusier city of Chandigarh as a new capital for the Punjab. But such radical changes were rare, and colonial layouts and buildings remained remarkably intact. As Dyos wrote, inertia is part of the dynamic of urban change. Structures outlast the people who put them there and impose constraints on those who have to adapt them to their own use.[1]

The buildings and spaces of the former British Empire can be folded into a narrative of imperial decline, and of the diminishing relevance of the colonial period in the affairs of vigorous new nations. Independence was sometimes marked by the destruction or removal of monuments; discarded statues in a compound at Barrackpore, or those grouped behind Bulawayo's natural history museum. There they stood, when this author happened upon them in 1994, the great and the good of a defunct Rhodesia now dismounted from their main street plinths and standing forlorn in a half circle, in silent conclave, perhaps asking each other, 'Whatever went wrong?'

Sometimes, the statues and monuments remained. Cecil Rhodes still points north outside Mafeking's railway station, anticipating a Cape-to-Cairo line. The Gateway of India, beside the Taj Mahal Hotel in Bombay, was one of the Empire's few grand monuments. It too still stands, though its purpose, and its testimony to Britain's imperial majesty, is long forgotten. The liners no longer come from London, writes Jan Morris, and the only boats around the pier are pleasure craft touting trips around the harbour. 'It is a merry place, an ice-cream place, and not one visitor in a million reads

the text upon its parapet: ERECTED TO COMMEMORATE THE LANDING IN INDIA
THEIR IMPERIAL MAJESTIES KING GEORGE V AND QUEEN MARRY ON 2 DECEMBER
MCMXI.'[2]

The meaning has gone, because the people and the Empire have gone. In
many cities, colonial buildings that have escaped demolition now squat
beside their enormous 'international style' successors, which dwarf them.
Morris and Winchester imagine parents in a former colonial city showing
their children old colonial buildings tucked between skyscrapers. 'See this is
the best they could do', the parents say of the colonialists, 'and then they
went away.'[3] It is not just in the former Empire that 'imperial' aspects of the
built environment have become largely irrelevant; it has happened in Britain too. Wembley Stadium's explicit imperial past is seldom remembered,
and much of London's imperial architectural has become part of a historical
experience for tourists, or subsumed within the variegated flowering of the
country's monarchy, its function, and its marketing. Heavy with tradition
and pageantry, the 'imperial' has been annexed by the 'national', imperial
spaces, empire-building armed forces, imperial monuments and icons
blended into national and cultural events, suffused with the understated
patriotism that the British like to think they do so well. Royal events, anniversaries of military milestones, the trooping of the colour, the Last Night
of the Proms are all redolent of empire, or derived from the days of empire,
yet are not consciously performed or participated in with imperial thoughts
in mind. This is all a sign of how societies 'move on', how the past is discarded or incorporated into the present, how attitudes and mind-sets, as
well as buildings, can adapt or be replaced.

There is more to the study of the buildings and spaces of the former
Empire, however, than that which has passed into history. As well as the
past, they often speak of the present and the future, and of the hardiness of
the institutions established by colonial rule. Also, of the fact that the colonial period *created* the built environment that continues to inform people's
daily lives, whatever people might think of it. In some former colonies,
interlocked heritage and tourist industries have come to value an ideal-
ized version of the colonial period. In other former colonies, meanwhile,
people of all different backgrounds wonder what the future holds for
neglected colonial-era buildings of often sublime appeal, such as the majes-
tic sweep of Rangoon's Secretariat building with its red-brick and yellow-
trimmed exterior and elegant Venetian domes. Preserved by Myanmar's
isolation under military rule, many streets in Rangoon are like vast film sets,

undisturbed by modern construction. But economic growth brings with it
the temptation to raze old buildings to the ground in order to make way for
shopping malls.[4]

Some colonial buildings now appear redundant and anachronistic in the
independent successor states. Others, such as schools and churches, do not.
They are still needed, still used, and still maintained. The same applies to
other types of colonial-era construction, such as railway stations, government houses, and administrative buildings, and those appropriated by the
British, such as Dublin Castle and Fort St Angelo. It is unlikely that the
botanical gardens founded in the colonial period will ever close down or
move site, and many of the world's airports will continue for years to come
to be located on former Royal Air Force aerodromes. As Robert Fermor-
Hesketh suggested, even the most cursory glance at the major colonial cities
reveals a remarkable degree of continuity. Even if the British Empire has
ceased to exist, an understanding of the nature of power has not; and while
a few of the countries that were once part of it have completely abandoned
the old buildings of British government and power, most have retained
them without apparent change of purpose. The sheer volume of what
remains, and its continued use, merits a different, and deeper, assessment of
its historical and artistic worth.[5]

Though a creation of the maligned 'Happy Valley' settlers, Nairobi's Muthaiga Club still exists and serves its original function—providing the Kenyan
elite with both tangible and intangible social goods. If it had not already been
created by the colonial buccaneers of the early twentieth century, the African
successor regime would probably have had to invent it. Likewise the Gezira
Sporting Club: though now alcohol free and entirely Arabic-speaking, it still
performs the functions its colonial creators intended—providing relaxation
and networking opportunities for society's elite. They are Egyptians now, of
course, with a smattering of expatriates, rather than British cavalry officers
and high-ranking civil servants—but a networked elite nonetheless. The
Dodo Club of Mauritius, meanwhile, continues to serve as the exclusive
preserve of the island's powerful Franco-Mauritian minority.

Around the world colonial-era government houses perform the functions of state at the heart of a nation's political life, rechristened 'State House'
or 'The President's Palace' as soon as the British had gone. The ticket halls
of British India's great railway network still bustle with activity. As Morris
and Winchester write of Bombay's Victoria Terminus, it now simply exists—
not any longer the symbol of something either good or bad, not something

invested with either promise or menace. It is simply there, part of the Mumbai scenery, accepted, acknowledged, ignored.[6] The cathedrals and chapels that settlers and missionaries founded still stand for the glory of God even if, as in Baker's Harare Cathedral, the Seshona service overflows with boisterous worshippers while the English-language service languishes amid empty pews and the dirge-like tones of English hymning. The museums, schools, and universities continue to function, the botanic gardens and original town plans still shape the built environment.

The buildings of empire have been indigenized, or returned to their rightful owners, though in the settler states of the Americas and Australasia such buildings continue to proclaim the creation of entirely new societies and the eradication or displacement of indigenous cultures and landscapes. The fact is that half the cities in the world will probably always remain informed by dated colonial theories about town planning, whatever happens to their buildings, and that walking around places such Bellerive Village in Hobart, with its Boer War memorial, colonial homes and Victorian lamp-posts, will always evoke a strong sense of the original settlers' British roots.

In most colonial cities, the new has come to blend with—as opposed to entirely replace—the old. In some cities, the major shrines of national independence are rooted in the power centres of the colonial regimes that they succeeded. Malaysia's Merdeka Square, for instance, contains a fine range of colonial state buildings now dwarfed by the ultra-modern high-rise of independent Malaysia and the enormous Independence flagstaff. The Old Railway Station, with its striking minarets, is often shown in guide-books set against gleaming silver skyscrapers. This is not the case in all former colonies: some city centres have lost their functions as entire new administrative capitals have been built. These include Sri Jayawardenapura Kotte in Sri Lanka, Naypyidaw in Burma, Putrajaya in Malaysia, and Abuja in Nigeria.

It is probably fair to say that many notable buildings look better caught on camera or on canvas than they do in reality. Old colonial buildings often look quaint, rundown, or small, whereas they were built to look impressive, modern, and imposing. But things change. Certainly the scale of architecture has altered significantly in the last century, and buildings constructed on an enormous scale—skyscrapers, for instance—have left their original Western setting and now grow in profusion all over the world. Today, colonial buildings are often noted for their 'faded grandeur', as places where one can catch a whiff of the past—an elegant waiting room, a garrison church, or perhaps the smoking room of a club. But the tourist expecting a nostalgic encounter should beware; sometimes 'faded grandeur', when shorn of pre-arrival anticipation and a frisson of 'connection' with the past on first con-tact, can translate into 'run down' and 'unsatisfactory'.

Ahead of a visit to Kuala Lumpur in 2010, this author was disappointed that online attempts to book a room at the 'Heritage Station Hotel', part of the Old Railway Station, failed. Visiting the city to view the railway station, staying in a hotel located within its walls would have been ideal. Assuming it was fully booked, with genuine reluctance I settled for the five-star Shangri-La Hotel which was offering an attractive deal at the time. On walking to the Old Railway Station, hoping at least to be able to have a drink in the hotel bar and soak up the atmosphere, it became abundantly clear that, swanky website notwithstanding, the hotel was shut. It was, in fact, very shut, and clearly had not been particularly well maintained when open. This prompted an internet search, and it became clear through com-ments on sites such as 'tripadvisor' that when open it had developed a repu-tation for noise, poor service, and dirty linen. It brought to mind a stay at the Queen's Hotel in Kandy, Sri Lanka in 2007, another landmark colonial hotel but a disappointment in terms of basic accommodation given the price being paid. Sadly not a patch, in terms of value for money, on its more anonymous modern rivals. Even some well maintained landmark hotels of the colonial era, such as the Galle Face in Colombo, are simply too small to offer the array of services and standards of service that the big international chain hotels can provide: while it is wonderful to walk around the Galle Face's evocative corridors and verandas, or attend a High Commission cocktail party in its charming palm-fringed, checker-board court looking out over the Indian Ocean, it is nicer to stay across the Galle Road at the Cinnamon Grand. Thus, increasingly, such hotels trade on a name and an era—a diminishing asset unless a country has begun to accept the colonial period as part of its acknowledged heritage—or slip into the ranks of the 'budget hotel'. Few are capable of the kind of transformation that Raffles managed to achieve.

Raffles Hotel succeeded in overcoming the challenge that has destroyed so many other colonial-era establishments. With a more corporate-style management and dedication to unrivalled service, it was able to position itself as more than a hotel, becoming a 'must see' tourist attraction complete with its own private museum, souvenirs, and literature propagating its his-tory and its myths. Today it wins international best hotel awards as a matter of course; it develops clever corporate partnerships, commissioning, for example, a special wine to mark an event or teaming up with a prestigious watchmaker. It has managed to insinuate itself into Singapore's very identity and become part of its interface with the world. Meanwhile, internal innovation is the order of the day, with a touch of historical romanticization thrown in. Thus the recently opened Long Bar Steakhouse boasts a menu inspired by 'honest flavours of early plantation fare'—though its in a part of the Raffles complex that long post-dates the colonial period. Raffles has successfully and fortuitously managed to become part of the 'heritage' package, part of Singapore's identity, the colonial past manifest in the present and the national story going into the future. In the early years of the twentieth century, it was Raffles's astonishing modernity that attracted gilded globetrotters—now, a century later, it is its associations with the past, as well as the very latest in quality service and modern conveniences, that keeps them coming back.[7]

In America the colonial built environment—and the restoration and even re-creation of colonial buildings—remains a powerful force in the nation's self-image, attended by a profusion of re-enactment societies. On a smaller scale, similar things are happening in other former colonies, such as India and Singapore. Singapore has attempted to play a clever game with its historic buildings, not shy to demolish them if they stand in the way of redevelopment, but willing to preserve a few landmarks and even 'create' some new ones if it helps the tourist industry. As Ann Hills wrote in the 1980s, the houses where generations of traders had lived alongside packed quays are being variously renovated as showpieces or destroyed to make way for developments in a tiny country short of land and with mixed views on preservation. The riverside statue to Raffles is safe; so too is the nearest building—Empress Place, dating from the 1860s. The government created a Heritage Link connecting sites of historic, notably colonial, value. 'Second hand, nostalgic experiences may have to suffice for the visitor in future; such is the price of progress. Destruction is rampant—a fact the Singapore Tourist Promotion Board would prefer to turn a blind eye towards as they present packages for future conservation.'[8]

An interesting aspect of the history of colonial-era buildings and sites is what happened during and after the hand-over from British authorities to new independent governments. As with the institutions of state themselves, buildings, establishments, and vast acreages of Crown land had to be transferred also. In Singapore, for instance, the withdrawal of the sizeable military establishment that Britain had maintained meant that large tracts of prime land, together with valuable buildings, schools, hospitals, sports complexes, and other amenities were handed over to the Singapore government.* The government inherited valuable technical installations, particularly the magnificently equipped naval dockyard which became the foundation for a new shipbuilding industry.[9]

In many former colonies, the whole heritage and tourism sphere is unexploited, or does not, or not yet, encompass colonial chic. In some countries, the desire to forget, or stigmatize, the colonial period, has for long trumped any inclination to incorporate it into national history and, in effect, 'move on'. This is understandable, though as time passes—and given that there's money to be made from nostalgia and heritage—things may change. As Raja Bhasin argues in the case of Shimla, if 'under the protective shade of free India's tricolour, we are willing to grant that the post-colonial hangover is done with, and the two centuries of colonial rule are so much water under the bridge, then British-India must be accepted as at least a sub-stream of *Indian* culture'.[10] There are understandably fewer barriers to this kind of incorporation in settler societies, as the example of 'Colonial' Williamsburg demonstrates. But it is an important point, and one that should be interrogated thoroughly—when do colonial buildings become part of a *nation's* history, rather than just part of a *colonial* history that it might want to forget? For 'colonial history' is simply part of general history. As Robert Fermor-Hesketh reminds us, much of the architecture of the British Empire was designed by British architects, and should be judged in that light. After all:

> Roman and Greek colonial architecture is not divided by an artificial barrier of origin; nor is it judged on the merits of what has survived. A Roman court house in England, would, if such a thing existed, be an object of veneration owing to the principles it enshrined and its great antiquity. Its architectural merits would run a poor third, and its relevance as a symbol of Roman colonialism would hardly be considered.[11]

Until relatively recently, the historian Thomas Metcalf argues, buildings in the colonial world were not considered worthy of study, deemed inferior and derivative. Buildings that sought to incorporate indigenous forms, whether in the domestic bungalow or 'Saracenic' architecture, were disparaged as exotics.[12] But for those living in the colonies these buildings performed important functions and marked out power and authority:

---

* Former Middle East Land Forces accommodation blocks now form desirable flats, each sporting the name of a famous British battle above their main entranceways.

As time passes, structures begin to be seen as historically significant and there-fore worthy of study. In settler colonies the imperial past has been assimilated into the national past. In non-settler colonies, however, coming to terms with the buildings left behind by the former rulers has been more of a challenge. The preservation of the colonial architectural heritage has come a poor sec-ond to a host of more pressing tasks. Nevertheless, younger architects and architectural historians in places such as India and Malaysia have recently begun to reappraise the colonial past, to argue for the conservation of build-ings and their acceptance as part of the national past.[13]

Even as the European colonial empires dissolved, Western influence in the built environment was being renewed. As the great American architectural historian Henry Russell-Hotchcock wrote, 'While the West was more and more losing political control of Africa and Asia, its cultural influence on those continents did not necessarily decline, indeed as regards architecture it prob-ably increased.'[14] Where modernism was not a disavowal of imperialism, it was actively deployed as a way of improving the functions of the colonial city, treating the colonies as a laboratory of modernity, elaborating the new rhetorics of hygiene and health and the dualistic narratives of the traditional and the modern, even epitomizing the benevolence of the West.[15]

In some former colonies, governments have sought to use both national and international mechanisms to conserve and protect notable colonial-era buildings. In Jamaica, for example, there is continuing interest in achieving UNESCO (United Nations Educational, Scientific, and Cultural Organiza-tion) World Heritage status for the King's House and Emancipation Square in Spanish Town, though it remains dilapidated and partially ruined. It did manage to achieve UNESCO 'candidate' status, however, which has had the beneficial effect of encouraging an interest in preservation. International grants have paid for a recent stabilization of the Iron Bridge, and a project funded by a European Union grant successfully refurbished the complex of late eighteenth century buildings on the north side of the square.[16] It was proposed to open a museum within the King's House ruins, displaying fur-niture and other artefacts from the Institute of Jamaica's collection. This failed, but a scheme to open a Folk Museum (now the People's Museum of Craft and Technology) succeeded, and today it is housed in the King's House stables. Moves are afoot to regenerate this fallen building and its unique Georgian surroundings but, whatever the outcome of restoration attempts, natural enemies remain: Emancipation Square and its tall palms were rav-aged by Hurricane Gilbert in 1988, and Hurricane Ivan damaged the town in 2004. A modicum of bustle is returning to the town, however, as it becomes a desirable suburb of Kingston.

In Australia, meanwhile, the Royal Exhibition Building flourishes under the protection of the coveted UNESCO World Heritage status. The Royal Exhibition Building and Carlton Gardens were inscribed on the World Heritage list in July 2004, becoming the first building in Australia to achieve this cherished status. During her visit to Australia in 1984 the Queen conferred the 'Royal' title on the building. With its meticulously restored interior, expansive galleries, and soaring dome, the Great Hall continues to offer a magnificent setting for trade shows, fairs, and cultural and community events. Today, the Royal Exhibition Building is a campus of Museum Victoria and the gardens are managed by the City of Melbourne. The UNESCO bid was made on the basis that it is the only surviving example of a Great Hall from a major international exhibition, purpose-designed as the Great Hall of the Palace of Industry. The eastern annexe was partly demolished in the 1950s, and ultimately replaced in 1979 by a mirror-fronted Convention Centre—itself demolished in the 1990s to make way for Melbourne Museum.

To this day, Malta's fortifications dominate the skyline and atmosphere of Valletta and the wider Grand Harbour conurbation. Cannon walls and picturesque vedettes (sentry posts) look out across the harbour, and outerworks such as ravelins, lunettes, counterguards, and bonnets appear across the island, dominating entirely the appearance of Valletta and the Three Cities. Then, as now, Fort St Angelo looks out across Grand Harbour, a round, flat-topped castle of enormous strength squatting like a heavyweight boxer on the end of the Vittoriosa peninsula.[17] Grand Harbour is no longer dominated by British warships and the to-ing and fro-ing of ship-to-shore barges; in May 2011, the only warship in sight was a French destroyer, taking part in operations against Colonel Gadaffi's regime in Libya.[18]

The naval life of cocktail parties, formal guest lists, drills, regattas, shore leave, and Mediterranean cruises is long gone, part of a vanished colonial world. Strait Street, the famous narrow street in Valletta known to generations of sailors as 'the Gut', no longer seethes with bars, brothels, and tattoo parlours vying for the trade of British matelots. It is now a quiet backwater in the middle of the Renaissance city, though one can still make out the odd faded bar name above shut doors. The place was once alive with these bars: Dirty Dick's, the Sunset Bar, the British Bar, Aunty's, the Britannia, Harry's, the Manchester Bar; the bars on the front by Customs House with huge pictures of British warships painted on their walls; the café at the St Elmo end of The Gut where sailors who had been on a spree could get a plate of 'train smash' (tinned tomatoes on toast) before returning groggily to their ships. All have long gone. The Gut was summarily closed by Dom Mintoff as soon as the British had left.* The Knights of St John requested, though were denied, sovereign status for Fort St Angelo. In 1998 they were granted permission, however, to occupy the top level of the fort and today it is home to the Knight Resident, His Excellency Fra John Cretien in 2011. He occupies the Magistral Palace, the only part of the fort currently in occupation and in good repair. The adjacent Chapel of St Anne was included in the arrangement, and is today pristine and well loved, standing in pruned and meticulously planted gardens. Nearby, the little drawing-room that backs on to the saluting base overlooking the glory of Grand Harbour is fit to host a visiting dignitary, and the Magistral Palace is restored, polished, and resplendent, its book-lined study enjoying spectacular views of Valletta and the Mediterranean looking towards forts St Elmo and Ricasoli. The story is not so encouraging, however, for the rest of the fort, the 'lower decks' in the language of the departed Royal Navy. It has had various uses, all failed, most damaging. Parts have been used as a nightclub, a Chinese restaurant, and a pigeon racing club—and damage has been caused by fire and the collapse of a crane. The remains of its brief conversion into a hotel can still be seen, a dry and dilapidated swimming pool and rooms converted from old British mess and office accommodation into en suite bedrooms, now all in ruins.

The fort is a source of continuing political controversy. When the British left, handing over a large defence estate that they had maintained, the Maltese government suddenly found itself with a large collection of historic buildings on its hands, an estate that required either viable occupation or expensive upkeep. Yet the government lacked the expertise, funds, or priority allocation to deal with them adequately. The fort's plight highlights the problem encountered by successor governments suddenly handed control of significant and historical buildings but without the funds or expertise to properly conserve them. Plans are afoot to convert some parts of the fort into a high-class health club and spa resort. The area is regarded as 'hallowed ground' symbolizing Malta's chequered history, a perennial enclave of European sophistication and the focal point of Malta's celebrations marking its

---

* Birgu too had its British bars, such as England's Glory, King George V, Rose, Shamrock, and Thistle, Dockyard Arms, Coronation Bar, The Malaya Bar, British Empire Bar, and Empire Hall.

accession to the European Union in 2004.[19] 'No other place in Malta can be said to have had such a long and important influence in the annals of the island.'[20] It has played a leading part in the island's religious life, as well as in its military history.

In Ireland, Dublin Castle was embraced as the heart of the Irish nation rather than a symbol of colonialism. From 1938 it has been used for the inauguration of state presidents, symbolic of the state's acceptance of the historical importance of the castle. Eamon de Valera himself is credited with the pragmatic decision to use the State Apartments for such functions. He also recognized the importance of accepting its history as part of the story of modern Ireland.[21] Increasingly, Irish people associate Dublin Castle with events in modern political life rather than with the legacy of the British administration.[22] It has been at the centre of state affairs, performing an important role, for example, hosting the talks that preceded the historic Anglo-Irish Agreement (1985) and used to accommodate Margaret Thatcher. The Castle is not a museum or a stately home, but a busy complex of offices and meeting places, and it has always been liable to modernization and change.[23] From 1997 until 2010 George's Hall was home to the Moriarty Tribunal which investigated the financial affairs of former Taoiseach Charles Haughey. In addition to its ceremonial and European Union roles today, the Castle site is home to the Comptroller and Auditor-General, the Revenue Commissioners, and the National Drug Unit. In 2011 Dublin Castle was the central back-drop to a state visit from Elizabeth II, a visit pregnant with symbolism as a British monarch entered Ireland not as a ruling sovereign but as the guest of an independent neighbour.

In other places, more vigorous change came after the departure of the British. The 'chimera' that was Ismail's Cairo did not fare well under Nasser. Things were torn down and freeways driven through the city. The palaces and buildings of Ismail's city were being constantly demolished until lobbying helped slow down the trend.[24] Despite the traffic, Trevor Mostyn writes, Zamalek's streets can be very pretty during the periods of the blossoming of Cairo's myriad flowering trees, and they still retain some of the peace which reflects the island's original ethos as a bucolic retreat. Most of Cairo is now built over, but Zamalek, particularly the southern part of the island, remains moderately preserved. There is still lots of open space—first and foremost the Gezira Sporting Club—but also unkempt public gardens, social clubs, the space around the Opera House, the old Anglo-American hospital, and riverside parks and promenades. Since the building of the fly-over, however, some of the pressure has been taken off Gezira, and some of its former tranquillity has been restored.[25] Importantly, at least there is now a debate in the media about what to develop and what to preserve, and there is a movement to protect the colonial-era built environment. Public space—space truly open and accessible to all—is sorrowfully lacking, making Cairo somewhat unique. Zamalek resident and Gezira Sporting Club member John Harris argues that such spaces are sorely needed to relieve the tensions caused by cramped living quarters. Available public space is mainly in Gezira, but fees and private membership clubs make it inaccessible to many; the number of gated communities and private beaches is also increasing.[26]

In Sudan, the higher education that the Gordon Memorial College did so much to establish has never flourished, stymied by the bitter history of civil war that has blighted Sudan's independence. At the inaugural conference of the Association of Sudanese Academics and Researchers, held at the Africa Centre in London in 1992, it was noted that education had declined and UN statistics showed Sudan lagging behind its neighbours in educational provision. Specifically, the conference, titled 'Ninety Years of Higher Education in the Sudan' and commemorating the foundation of Gordon Memorial College, complained about the policy of Arabicization and Islamization pursued by the country's military junta. 'It is appropriate on the ninetieth anniversary of the Gordon Memorial College', the conference report stated, 'to promote and uphold the principles of liberal democratic education' so at odds with the 'fundamentalist military government and its war in the south'.[27] There remains a discreet legacy of the college in Britain itself, including the statue of a camel-mounted General Gordon removed from Khartoum and erected outside a public school. The Gordon Memorial College's trustees and executive committee still exist, based in Arundel. Its mission is to promote educational development in Sudan, and to support Sudanese nationals studying for postgraduate courses in Britain who intend to return to Sudan at the end of their studies.

Buildings today

Colonial-era buildings are enjoying something of a come-back in certain parts of the world, and there still remain a scattered handful of colonies—now relabelled 'dependent territories'—where building work takes place. Travel agencies offer 'colonial grandeur' in Shimla, 'once the summer capital of the Raj', its 'main street, the Mall, is lined with "fine examples of British whimsy"—

a mock-Tudor post office, for example, and Gorton Castle, its "dour Scottish baronial" style offset with Saracenic arches. The ice rink built by the British survives, as does the racecourse, the Gaiety Theatre, and the "toy train" from Kalka to Shimla. Here, "British grandees once had their retreats" for escaping the heat, so it is "an excellent base for trekkers".'[28] An excellent point, in fact, from which perhaps to 'find oneself', or get a dose of nostalgia and 'the East'—perhaps, even, from which to ponder the outrageous excrescences and penetrations of empire. In the Sri Lankan highlands around Haddon, old estate managers' bungalows have been converted into well-appointed lodges. 'A night in one of these is a return to a nostalgic world of scones, croquet and hot-water bottles slipped between the sheets.'[29]

In the Maldive Islands the British developed substantial military facilities for the navy and the air force, and it remained an important link in Britain's global military chain until the middle of the 1970s.[30] Forty years on, a new use has been found for much of this military infrastructure. As a newspaper's travel section put it, 'the southernmost island, Gan, was the site of a "formidable" RAF base for twenty years from 1956. Much of it remains in good order, including its splendid gardens and officers' mess, which now houses the Equator Village resort', part of the Republic of Maldives luxury tourist infrastructure.[31] This reminds us, among other things, of the extent of Britain's overseas presence into the 1970s, 1980s, and even the 1990s long after, supposedly, 'the British Empire' had ended. Even today, in the second decade of the twenty-first century, the British have a range of overseas territories, some of them containing significant buildings and security infrastructure, such as those in the Sovereign Base Areas of Cyprus, and on the atoll of Diego Garcia in British Indian Ocean Territory.

New building projects provide an interesting and still living postscript to the buildings of the colonial period. Some of Britain's remaining colonies have specific construction needs. RAF Mount Pleasant is a military complex built after the Falklands conflict of 1982. The British government decided that the old airfield at Stanley was not suitable for the purpose, especially as there was a significantly enhanced military presence following the war. The new base, 30 miles south-east of the capital and opened by Prince Andrew in 1986, is the island's international airport and houses up to 2,000 military personnel (and boasts the world's longest corridor). The British undertook some massive infrastructural projects in Hong Kong before handing the colony over to China in 1997. At the heart of a major new road and rail network emerged Hong Kong International

Airport in Kowloon, opened in 1998. Designed by Foster and Partners, it was the most expensive airport complex ever built, voted one of the top ten construction achievements of the twentieth century at the ConExpo conference of 1999.

Emergencies and natural disasters, today as in the past, impact upon the buildings and buildings sites associated with the former British Empire and Britain's remaining overseas possessions. In July 1995 the capital of Montserrat in the Leeward Islands, a British territory since 1632, was hit by a volcanic eruption and evacuated, though soon many of the 12,000 inhabitants returned. This was to prove a tragic mistake. A huge eruption in June 1997 caused the town's permanent evacuation, and a further eruption two months later destroyed or buried the rest of the settlement. Now, the British government is supporting large-scale reconstruction in the safer northern portion of the island. Other places featured in this book have also suffered natural disasters in recent years, notably Christchurch, New Zealand. Here, in February 2011, Christchurch and its Botanic Gardens sustained significant earthquake damage. Buildings were structurally weakened, cracks appeared, and trees felled by liquefaction that turned the earth to jelly. A year later, Townend House, the Fern House, Cunningham House, the Bandsmen's Memorial Rotunda, and the Curator's House Restaurant all remained closed to the public as repairs and earthquake strengthening work was undertaken. But the garden will recover, and will remain an integral part of Christchurch's status as a 'garden city', a key element in its reputation and a national and international draw-card in an era of growing cultural tourism. In a city that is relying increasingly on international tourism to underpin its economy, its reputation as a garden city is an important asset.

The colonial buildings of Shimla, in historian Pamela Kanwar's opinion, must be seen as a moment in architectural history and appreciated for their variety, experimentation, and exuberant vitality.[32] The other noted historian of Shimla, Raaja Bhasin, puts Shimla's built heritage in fascinating context:

> Having been, as an Indian, at the receiving end of the imperial stick, it is hard to be sympathetic to something that was virtually the quintessence of Empire and Britain's imperial dream—Simla. Yet, this quirk seems to strike a chord in everyone, and it is not merely a bunch of 'brown sahibs' come into their own. Enough polemics of Empire and the Raj have emerged in every work connected with the period...and it has somehow become obligatory to rise in defence, or bow to a more recent trend, adopt a wistful expression, and let nostalgia strike the keynote.[33]

My generation has grown up with a dislike of the Raj and all it stood for. But, today, with much of the aura of an English mutant gone, Simla needs to put the arrogance of the British Empire behind it. This town is not sacrosanct and I ask for no diadems, but have always felt that viewed as a whole, the greatest cultural trait of the Indian people is their ability to accept, absorb and adapt to practically every influence to which they are exposed. In this resilience lies the future of Simla. [34]

And what of Viceregal Lodge? Upon independence, it was renamed Rashtrapati Nivas, the 'Presidential Residence'. But it remained underused by the president of the new republic, and in 1964 President Radhakrishnan and Prime Minister Jawaral Nehru made it the home of the Indian Institute of Advanced Studies. Many changes, mainly of room usage and occasionally of decorative detail, have inevitably taken place. 'Built as a residential palace for viceroys, the lodge symbolized imperial domination. Its importance is now highlighted in terms of the Indian nationalist movement and is remembered with images of nationalist leaders', such as Gandhi, Nehru, and Jinnah, all of whom visited. The ballroom is now the Institute's library; the unicorn originally carved over the impressive main fireplace has since been replaced by the Indian wheel of progress. The engraved portraits of British viceroys have departed the Council Chamber, which now houses portraits of Nehru and Tagore. An original Maple and Company chandelier can still be seen, along with a large picture of Lady Elgin above the fireplace in the visitors' lounge. In the grounds still stands a tulip tree planted by the Marquis of Lansdowne, Dufferin's successor as viceroy. And of course, the very fact of the building, redolent with imperial marking such as the royal coat of arms and Lord Dufferin's name, remains intact, along with external furniture such as the crown-topped post box outside the nearby Civil Secretariat building. 'While the lodge retains a large measure of its imperial grandeur, yet small and not so small things proclaim that it is no longer a centre of attention—the locked chapel, the unused tennis courts, painted signs on door panes, [and] unreplaced shingles.'[35]

In 1994 the journal of the Indian Institute of Architecture asserted that the hill stations left by the British were part of a 'precious national heritage'.[36] They had, however, been victims of the country's rapid and chaotic post-independence urbanization. Shimla was degenerating into a decadent urban centre, pseudo-modern architecture—boxes of concrete and glass with pernicious designs—and other concrete monsters gradually swallowing up every available patch of land and blighting the age-old beauty of the wooded world of the hills.

Notes

INTRODUCTION

1. Henry Gunston, 'From Corrugated Iron to Colonnades: Images of British Colonial Architecture', typescript of presentation to Oxford University Department for Continuing Education 'Dominion' Course (2003).

2. Robert Fermor-Hesketh (ed.), *Architecture of the British Empire* (New York: The Vendome Press, 1986), p. 25.

3. H. Y. Sarada Prasad, *The Book I Won't Be Writing and Other Essays* (Bangalore: Chronicle Books, 2003), p. 325.

4. See John MacKenzie, 'Empires of Travel: British Guide Books and Cultural Imperialism in the Nineteenth and Twentieth Centuries', in John Walton (ed.), *Histories of Tourism: Representation, Identity, and Conflict* (Clevedon: Channel View Publications, 2005).

5. This paragraph draws on Jan Morris and Simon Winchester, *Stones of Empire: The Buildings of the Raj* (Oxford: Oxford University Press, 2005).

6. Daniel Headrick, 'Cities, Sanitation, and Segregation', in Headrick, *The Tentacles of Progress: Technology Transfer in the Age of Imperialism, 1850–1940* (Oxford: Oxford University Press, 1988), p 146.

7. See Anthony King, *Colonial Urban Development: Culture, Social Power, and Environment* (Abingdon, Oxfordshire: Routledge, 2007).

8. Jane Jacobs quoted in Ben Looker, 'Exhibiting Imperial London: Empire and the City in Late Victorian and Edwardian Guidebooks' (London: Goldsmith's College, 2002).

9. Gillian Tindall chapter in Fermor-Hesketh (ed.), *Architecture of the British Empire*, p. 90.

10. Khoo Su Nin, *Streets of George Town Penang: An Illustrated Guide to Penang's City Streets and Historic Attractions* (Penang: Janus Print, 1993), p. 5.

11. For the impact of postcolonial architecture, looking down from Penang Hill over George Town, see Mark Crinson, 'The View from Penang Hill: Modernism and Nationalism in Malaysia', in Crinson, *Modern Architeture and the End of Empire* (Aldershot: Ashgate, 2003).

12. Joan Woodberry, *Historic Richmond (Tasmania) Sketchbook* (Adelaide: Rigby Limited, 1977), p. 6.

CHAPTER 1

1. Joseph Robins, *Champagne and Silver Buckles: The Viceregal Court at Dublin Castle, 1700–1922* (Dublin: The Lilliput Press, 2001), p. 4.
2. Richard Killeen, *A Short History of Dublin* (Dublin: Gill and Macmillan, 2010), p. 1.
3. Dennis McCarthy, *Dublin Castle: At the Heart of Irish History* (Dublin: The Stationery Office, 2004), p. 16.
4. McCarthy, *Dublin Castle*, p. 19.
5. McCarthy, *Dublin Castle*, p. 24.
6. McCarthy, *Dublin Castle*, p. 27.
7. Saree Makdisi, *Romantic Imperialism: Universal Empire and the Culture of Modernity* (Cambridge: Cambridge University Press, 1998), p. 98.
8. D. McCarthy, *Dublin Castle*, p. 58.
9. McCarthy, *Dublin Castle*, p. 101.
10. Penny Fitzgerald (A. Native), *Recollections of Dublin Castle and of Dublin Society* (London: Chatto and Windus, 1902), p. 2–3.
11. Fitzgerald (A. Native), *Recollections of Dublin Castle*, pp. 8–9, 10–11.
12. Robins, *Champagne and Silver Buckles*, p. 9.
13. Robins, *Champagne and Silver Buckles*, p. 153.
14. Robins, *Champagne and Silver Buckles*, p. 66.
15. Robins, *Champagne and Silver Buckles*, p. 15.
16. Robins, *Champagne and Silver Buckles*, p. 22.
17. Robins, *Champagne and Silver Buckles*, p. 60.
18. Robins, *Champagne and Silver Buckles*, p. 72.
19. Robins, *Champagne and Silver Buckles*, p. 27.
20. Robins, *Champagne and Silver Buckles*, p. 71.
21. Robins, *Champagne and Silver Buckles*, p. 76.
22. McCarthy, *Dublin Castle*, p. 123.

CHAPTER 2

1. Robert Fermor-Hesketh (ed.), *Architecture of the British Empire* (New York: The Vendome Press, 1986), p. 105.
2. Christopher Baker, *Jamaica* (Peterborough: Thomas Cook, 2007), p. 4.
3. Clinton Black, *History of Jamaica* (Harlow: Pearson, 1983), p. 30.
4. Sybil Williams quoted in Walter Adolphe Roberts (ed.), *The Capitals of Jamaica* (Kingston: Pioneer Press, 1955), p. 3.
5. See Kris Lane, *Pillaging the Empire: Piracy in the Americas, 1500–1750* (New York: M. E. Sharpe, 1998) and David Cordingly, *Life among the Pirates: The Romance and the Reality* (London: Little, Brown, 1995).
6. Ronald Heinemann *et al.*, *Old Dominion, New Commonwealth: A History of Virginia, 1607–2007* (Charlottesville: University of Virginia Press, 2007), p. 31.
7. Black, *History of Jamaica*, p. 55.

8. Carl Lounsbury, 'Beaux-Arts Ideals and Colonial Reality: The Reconstruction of Williamsburg's Capitol, 1928–1934', *Journal of the Society of Architectural Historians* (December 1990).

9. Fermor-Hesketh (ed.), *Architecture of the British Empire*, p. 110.

10. Heinemann, *Old Dominion*, p. 76.

11. James Thompson, *The Birth of Virginia's Aristocracy* (Alexandria, VA: Commonwealth Books, 2010).

12. James Robertson, *Gone is the Ancient Glory: Spanish Town Jamaica, 1543–2000* (Kingston: Ian Randle, 2005), p. 144.

13. Fermor-Hesketh (ed.), *Architecture of the British Empire*, p. 105.

14. Walter Roberts, *Old King's House Spanish Town* (Kingston: United Printers, 1959), p. 11.

15. Hubert Corlette, *The King's House in the King's Square Spanish Town Jamaica: A Report and Historical Review* (London, 1932), p. 10.

16. Fermor-Hesketh (ed.), *Architecture of the British Empire*, p. 206.

17. Sybil Williams quoted in Roberts (ed.), *The Capitals of Jamaica*, p. 10.

18. Robertson, *Gone is the Ancient Glory*, p. 101.

19. Long in Roberts, *The Capitals of Jamaica*, p. 11.

20. George Yetter, *Williamsburg Before and After: The Rebirth of Virginia's Colonial Capital* (Williamsburg, Virginia: The Colonial Williamsburg Foundation, 1988), p. 25.

21. Yetter, *Williamsburg Before and After*, p. 26.

22. Black, *History of Jamaica*, p. 85.

23. Roberts, *Old King's House*, p. 7.

24. Rebecca Tortello, 'The Story of Spanish Town', *Jamaica Gleaner*, 19 May 2003, <http://jamaica-gleaner.com/pages/history/story0049.htm>.

25. Emma Hart review of James Robertson, *Gone is the Ancient Glory: Spanish Town Jamaica, 1534–2000*, H-Atlantic, H-Net reviews, December, 2005, <http://www.h-net.org/reviews/showrev.php?id=11042>.

26. Roberston, *Gone is the Ancient Glory*, p. 163–5.

27. Yetter, *Williamsburg Before and After*, p. 34.

28. Yetter, *Williamsburg Before and After*, p. 36–7.

29. Yetter, *Williamsburg Before and After*, p. 38.

30. Black, *History of Jamaica*, p. 63.

31. Emma Hart review.

32. Sybil Williams quoted in Roberts, *The Capitals of Jamaica*, p. 14.

33. Sybil Williams quoted in Roberts, *The Capitals of Jamaica*, p. 14.

34. Robertson, *Gone is the Ancient Glory*, p. 197.

35. Robertson, *Gone is the Ancient Glory*, p. 201.

36. Jackie Ranston, *Behind the Scenes at King's House, 1873–2010* (Kingston, Jamaica: Jamaica National Building Society, 2011), p. 1.

37. Ranston, *Behind the Scenes at King's House*, p. 13.

38. Corlette, *The King's House*, p. 32.

39. Corlette, *The King's House*, p. v.

40. Corlette, *The King's House*, p. 3.
41. Foreword to Roberts, *The Old King's House*.
42. Yetter, *Williamsburg Before and After*, p. 7.
43. Yetter, *Williamsburg Before and After*, p. 10.
44. Yetter, *Williamsburg Before and After*, p. 49.
45. Yetter, *Williamsburg Before and After*, p. 54.
46. Yetter, *Williamsburg Before and After*, p. 66.
47. Suzanne Coffman and Michael Olmert, *Official Guide to Colonial Williamsburg* (Williamsburg, VA: The Colonial Williamsburg Foundation, 1998), p. 7.
48. G. Tindall in R. Fermor-Hesketh (ed.), *Architecture of the British Empire*, p. 82–3.
49. Yetter, *Williamsburg Before and After*, p. vii.
50. Lounsbury, 'Beaux-Arts Ideals and Colonial Reality', p. 373.
51. Lounsbury, 'Beaux-Arts Ideals and Colonial Reality', p. 373.

CHAPTER 3

1. David Niven, *The Moon's a Balloon* (London: Penguin, 1994), p. 71.
2. Deborah Manley (ed.), *Malta: A Traveller's Anthology* (Oxford: Signal Books, 2010), p. 11.
3. Manley, *Malta*, p. 12.
4. Foreword, Stephen Spiteri, *British Military Architecture in Malta* (Valletta: The Author, 1996), p. iii.
5. Lino Bugaja, Mano Buhagiar, and Stanley Fiorini (eds.), *Birgu: A Maltese Maritime City*, 2 vols. (Msida: Malta University Services, 1993).
6. Denis De Lucca, 'The Fortifications of Birgu', in Bgaja, Buhagiar, and Fiorini, *Birgu*, vol. 2.
7. Quentin Hughes, *Malta: A Guide to the Fortifications* (Valletta: Said International, 1993), p. 185.
8. 'Malta: Its History and the Part Played by Fort St Angelo: A Paper Read at the Accountant Officers' Technical Course', *Naval Review*, 1 (1931), p. 31.
9. 'Malta: Its History and the Part Played by Fort St Angelo', p. 39.
10. 'Malta: Its History and the Part Played by Fort St Angelo', p. 39.
11. Nicholas Montsarrat, *The Kappillan of Malta* (London: Cassell, 2001), p. 282.
12. Peter Elliott, *The Cross and the Ensign: A Naval History of Malta, 1798–1979* (London: Granada, 1980), p. 21.
13. Hughes, *Malta*, p. 187.
14. Manley, *Malta*, p. 93.
15. Spiteri, *British Military Architecture*, p. 2.
16. Spiteri, *British Military Architecture*, p. 6.
17. Spiteri, *British Military Architecture*, p. 221.
18. Charles Stephenson, *The Fortifications of Malta, 1530–1945* (Oxford: Osprey, 2004), p. 32.
19. Hughes, *Malta*, p. 187.

20. William Soler, 'Grand Harbour Breakwater in Malta, 1903–09', *Civil Engineering*, 114 (1996). Thanks to Henry Gunston for a copy of this article.

21. Elliott, *The Cross and the Ensign*, p. 90.

22. Manley, *Malta*, p. 144.

23. Alec Guinness, *Blessings in Disguise* (London: H. Hamilton, 1985).

24. H. G. Bowerman, *History of Fort St Angelo* (September 1947), p. 15.

25. Elliott, *The Cross*, pp. 155–6.

26. Peter Seabrook, 'Fort St Angelo and its Artillery Connections', *The Journal of the Royal Artillery*, CVI(1) (1979), p. 13.

27. Malta National Archives, Rabat, Malta, Map I.5.

28. Elliott's *The Cross and the Ensign* and the opening chapter of Joseph Attard, *Britain and Malta: The Story of an Era* (Malta: Publishers Enterprises Group, 1995) cover the withdrawal. See also Dennis Austin, *Malta and the End of Empire* (London: Frank Cass, 1971).

29. Elliott, *The Cross and the Ensign*, p. 238.

30. Elliott, *The Cross and the Ensign*, pp. 240–1.

CHAPTER 4

1. John MacKenzie, 'Australia: Museums in Sydney and Melbourne', in MacKenzie, *Museums and Empire: Natural History, Human Cultures, and Colonial Identities* (Manchester: Manchester University Press, 2009), p. 210.

2. Official website, <http://www.ccc.govt.nz/cityleisure/parkswalkways/christchurchbotanicgardens/index.aspx>

3. See Te Maire Tau, 'Ngāi Tahu from "Better be Dead and Out of the Way" to "To be Seen to Belong"', in John Cookson and Graeme Dunstall (eds.), *Southern Capital: Christchurch, Towards a City Biography* (Christchurch: Canterbury University Press, 2000).

4. Johnson in Nadine Monem (ed.), *Botanical Gardens: A Living History* (London: Black Dog Publishing, 2007), p. 73.

5. A. J. Christopher, *The British Empire at its Zenith* (London: Croom Helm, 1988), p. 81.

6. Barlow in Monem, *Botanical Gardens*, p. 15.

7. See Daniel Headrick, 'Economic Botany and Tropical Plantations' in Headrick, *The Tentacles of Progress: Technology Transfer in the Age of Imperialism, 1850–1940* (Oxford: Oxford University Press, 1988).

8. Barlow, in Monem, *Botanical Gardens*, p. 15.

9. Rebecca Preston, ' "The Scenery of the Torrid Zone": Imagined Travels and the Cultural Exotics in Nineteenth Century British Gardens', in Felix Driver and David Gilbert (eds.), *Imperial Cities: Landscape, Display, and Identity* (Manchester: Manchester University Press, 2003), p. 194.

10. Preston, ' "The Scenery of the Torrid Zone" ', p. 197.

11. Preston, ' "The Scenery of the Torrid Zone" ', p. 206.

12. Philippa Mein Smith, *A Concise History of New Zealand* (Cambridge: Cambridge University Press, 2005), p. 37.

13. Mein Smith, *A Concise History of New Zealand*, p. 39.

14. Mein Smith, *A Concise History of New Zealand*, p. 43.

15. Brendon, *The Decline and Fall*, p. 85.

16. Brendon, *The Decline and Fall*, p. 85.

17. Brendon, *The Decline and Fall*, p. 85.

18. *The Times*, 5 July 1851, in Charles Carrington, *John Robert Godley of Canterbury* (Sydney: Whitcombe and Tombs, 1950), p. 117.

19. Report, Chapter 1, The Site of Christchurch, p. 11.

20. MacKenzie, 'Australia: Museums', p. 214.

21. <http://christchurchcitylibraries.com/heritage/earlychristchurch/hagleypark.asp>.

22. *Lyttelton Times*, 20 December 1851. See <http://paperspast.natlib.govt.nz/cgi-bin/paperspast?a=d&d=LT18511220.2.11&cl=CL1.LT&e=-------10--1-byDA---0spare+halfZz-hours+edith+searle+grossmann-->

23. Barlow, in Monem, *Botanical Gardens*, p. 16.

24. Christchurch Botanic Gardens walking guide. See <http://resources.ccc.govt.nz/filcs/BotanicGardensWalkingGuide.pdf>.

CHAPTER 5

1. Trevor Mostyn, *Egypt's Belle Epoque: Cairo and the Age of the Hedonists* (London: Tauris, 2007), p. 176.

2. Raymond Flower, *Napoleon to Nasser: The Story of Modern Egypt* (London: AuthorHouse, 2002), p. 102.

3. Laurence Grafftey-Smith, *Bright Levant* (London: John Murray, 1970), pp. 228 and 18.

4. Margaret Sheenan, *Out in the Midday Sun: The British in Malaya* (London: John Murray, 2000).

5. 'First Pictures of Reopened Long Bar', *Weekly Telegraph*, 24 September 2010.

6. George Orwell, *Burmese Days* (Penguin, 2002).

7. See Stephen Mills, *The History of Muthaiga Country Club, 1913–1963* (Mills Publishing, 1996).

8. Jean-Marc Ran Oppenheim, 'The Gezira Sporting Club of Cairo', *Peace Review: A Transnational Quarterly*, 11(4) (1999), p. 553.

9. Penelope Lively, foreword in Andrew Beattie, *Cairo: A Cultural History* (Oxford: Oxford University Press, 2005), p. v.

10. Beattie, *Cairo*, p. 176–7.

11. Mostyn, *Egypt's Belle Epoque*, p. 132.

12. Edward Said, *Out of Place: A Memoir* (London: Granta, 1999), p. 177.

13. Beattie, *Cairo*, p. 179.

14. Bimbashi McPherson, *The Man Who Loved Egypt* (London: BBC, 1985), p. 26.

15. Gezira Sporting Club website.

16. Percy Martin, *Egypt Old and New: A Popular Account of the Land of the Pharoahs from the Traveller's and Economists' Point of View* (London: Routledge, 2013), first published in 1923, p. 206.

17. Worsfold visited Egypt in 1898–9 and wrote *The Redemption of Egypt*. Quote from Terje Tvedt, *The River Nile in the Age of the British: Political Ecology and the Quest for Economic Power* (London: I. B. Tauris, 2004), p. 351.

18. Said, *Out of Place*, p. 44.

19. Oppenheim, 'The Gezira Sporting Club', p. 554.

20. Artemis Cooper, *Cairo in the War, 1939–1945* (London: Penguin, 1989), p. 38.

21. Chafika Hamamasy, *Zamalek: The Changing Life of a Cairo Elite, 1850–1945* (Cairo: American University in Cairo Press, 2005), p. 4.

22. Cooper, *Cairo in the War*, p. 60.

23. Cooper, *Cairo in the War*, p. 239.

24. L. Grafftey-Smith, *Bright Levant*, p. 112.

25. Club website quoting Gerold Frank, *The Deed* (1979).

26. A. Cooper, *Cairo in the War*, p. 122.

27. Beattie, *Cairo*, p. 182.

28. Oppenheim, 'The Gezira Sporting Club', p. 555.

29. Oppenheim, 'The Gezira Sporting Club', p. 556.

30. Hamasamy, *Zamalek*, p. 10.

31. Oppenheim, 'The Gezira Sporting Club', p. 556.

32. John Harris, 'A Rough Guide to the Gezira Club' (2005), p. 1.

33. Harris, 'A Rough Guide to the Gezira Club', p. 4.

CHAPTER 6

1. *Straits Times*, 12 March 1913.

2. *Straits Times*, 25 July 1970.

3. Mark Crinson, *Modern Architecture and the End of Empire* (Ashgate, 2003), p. 165.

4. Crinson, *Modern Architecture and the End of Empire*, p. 159.

5. J. Morris and S. Winchester, *Stones of Empire: The Buildings of the Raj* (Oxford: Oxford University Press, 2005), p. 13.

6. Joan Woodberry, *Historic Richmond (Tasmania) Sketchbook* (Adelaide: Rigby Limited, 1977), p. 12.

7. A. J. Christopher, *The British Empire at its Zenith* (London: Croom Helm, 1988), p. 66.

8. Christopher, *The British Empire at its Zenith*, p. 64.

9. John Johnson Collection, Bodleain Library, Oxford, Empire and Colonies Box 4. *The New Capital to Coast Road: Nairobi to Mombasa, Photographic Record of the First Car, a 12 HP Riley, to Accomplish the Journey* (December 1926).

10. Morris and Winchester, *Stones of Empire*, p. 123.

11. Keith Neilson, 'The Baghdad to Haifa Railway: The Culminating of Railway Planning for Imperial Defence East of Suez', in Neilson and Thomas Otte

(eds.), *Railways and International Politics: Paths of Empire, 1848–1945* (London: Routledge, 2006).

12. Neilson, 'The Baghdad to Haifa Railway', p. 168.
13. Christopher, *The British Empire at its Zenith*, pp. 53 and 60.
14. Neilson and Otte, *Railways and International Politics*, p. 1.
15. Christopher, *The British Empire at its Zenith*, p. 55.
16. Morris and Winchester, *Stones of Empire*, p. 127.
17. Morris and Winchester, *Stones of Empire*, p. 128.
18. Andrew Graham-Yooll, *The Forgotten Colony: A History of the English-Speaking Communities in Argentina* (London: Hutchinson, 1981).
19. Amanuel Ghebreselassie and Jennie Street, *Red Sea Railway: The History of the Railways in Eritrea* (Sheffield: Silver Service Consultancy, 2009).
20. Neilson and Otte, *Railways and International Politics*, p. 8.
21. Neilson and Otte, *Railways and International Politics*, p. 2.
22. Morris and Winchester, *Stones of Empire*, p. 133.
23. Nick Hanna, *Singapore and Malaysia* (Peterborough: Thomas Cook, 2006), p. 56.
24. Hanna, *Singapore and Malaysia*, p. 57.
25. Nigel Brailey, 'The Railway-Oceanic Era, the Indo-China and India-Singapore Railway Schemes, and Siam', in Keith Neilson and Thomas Otte (eds.), *Railways and International Politics: Paths of Empire, 1848–1945* (London: Routledge, 2006), p. 95.
26. Brailey, 'The Railway-Oceanic Era', p. 95.
27. Peter Stocker, 'Kuala Lumpur Railway Station', *Majallah Akitek*, 3–4 (1986), p. 22.
28. *Fifty Years of Railways in Malaya, 1885–1935* (Federated Malay States Railways, 1935), p. 65.
29. Hanna, *Singapore and Malaysia*, p. 61.
30. Stocker, 'Kuala Lumpur Railway Station', p. 22.
31. *Straits Times*, 5 October 1909.
32. John MacKenzie and Jeffrey Richards, *The Railway Station: A Social History* (Oxford: Oxford University Press, 1986), pp. 76–7.
33. *Straits Times*, 25 October 1907.
34. *Fifty Years of Railways in Malaya*, p. 65.
35. *Fifty Years of Railways in Malaya*, p. 67.
36. *Fifty Years of Railways in Malaya*, p. 3.
37. *Fifty Years of Railways in Malaya*, p. 8.
38. *Straits Times*, 10 March 1921.
39. *Singapore Free Press and Mercantile Advertiser*, 14 January 1938.
40. *Singapore Free Press and Mercantile Advertiser*, 14 January 1938.
41. *Malayan Saturday Post*, 12 April 1924.
42. *Straits Times*, 8 December 1957.
43. *Straits Times*, 13 October 1991.

44. *Straits Times*, 20 December 1956.
45. *Straits Times*, 10 September 1936.
46. *Straits Times*, 15 February 1929.
47. *Singapore Free Press and Mercantile Observer*, 15 August 1934.
48. *Straits Times*, 21 April 1949.
49. *Straits Times*, 24 September 1952.
50. *Straits Times*, 1 February 1967.
51. *Straits Times*, 6 May 1952.
52. *Straits Times*, 10 April 1946.
53. *Straits Times*, 24 April 1949.
54. *Straits Times*, 17 March 1949.
55. Stocker, 'Kuala Lumpur Railway Stattion', p. 22.

CHAPTER 7

1. Edward Buck, *Simla Past and Present* (Calcutta: Government of India Central Press/Thacker, Spink, and Company, 1904), p. 1.
2. Buck, *Simla Past and Present*.
3. Ar. Sabeena Khanna, 'Observatory Hill at Shimla', *Journal of the Indian Institute of Architecture* (October–November, 1994), p. 18.
4. Raja Bhasin, *Simla: The Summer Capital of British India* (London: Penguin, 1992), p. 95.
5. Pamela Kanwar, *Imperial Simla: The Political Culture of the Raj* (Oxford: Oxford University Press, 2003), p. 9.
6. Bhasin, *Simla*, p. 97.
7. Buck, *Simla*, p. 4.
8. Bhasin, *Simla*, p. 7.
9. Buck, *Simla*, p. 35.
10. Kanwar, *Imperial Simla*, p. 45.
11. Kanwar, *Imperial Simla*, p. 35.
12. Bhasin, *Simla*, p. 45.
13. Kanwar, *Imperial Simla*, p. 46.
14. Kanwar, *Imperial Simla*, p. 46.
15. Kanwar, *Imperial Simla*, p. 49.
16. Buck, *Simla*, p. 39.
17. Marchioness of Dufferin, *Our Viceregal Life in India, 1884–1888: Sketches from My Journal*, 2 vols. (London: Jonathan Murray, 1889), vol. 1, p. 134.
18. Kanwar, *Imperial Simla*, p. 53.
19. Dufferin, *Our Viceregal Life*, vol. 2, p. 43.
20. Kanwar, *Imperial Simla*, p. 304.
21. The Victorian Web <http://www.victorianweb.org/history/empire/india/10.html>.
22. Bhasin, *Simla*, p. 303.

23. Kanwar, *Imperial Simla*, p. 304.
24. Dufferin, *Our Viceregal Life*, vol. 2, p. 294.
25. Dufferin, *Our Viceregal Life*, vol. 2, p. 294.
26. Buck, *Simla*, p. 50.
27. Kanwar, *Imperial Simla*, p. 69.
28. Bhasin, *Simla*, p. 57.
29. Bhasin, *Simla*, p. 56.
30. Bhasin, *Simla*, p. 56.
31. Bhasin, *Simla*, p. 57.
32. Bhasin, *Simla*, p. 57.
33. R. Fermor-Hesketh (ed.), *Architecture of the British Empire* (New York: The Vendome Press, 1986), pp. 125 and 127.
34. Buck, *Simla*, p. 47.
35. J. Morris and S. Winchester, *Stones of Empire: The Buildings of the Raj* (Oxford: Oxford University Press, 2005), p. 75–6.
36. Bhasin, *Simla*, p. 57.
37. Bhasin, *Simla*, p. 37–8.
38. Bhasin, *Simla*, p. 58.
39. Bhasin, *Simla*, p. 58.
40. Bhasin, *Simla*, p. 75.
41. Bhasin, *Simla*, p. 57.
42. Bhasin, *Simla*, p. 55.
43. Buck, *Simla*, p. 47.
44. Buck, *Simla*, p. 45.
45. Bhasin, *Simla*, p. 127.
46. Alice, Countess of Reading and Iris Butler, *Viceroy's Wife: Letters from India, 1921–25* (London: Hodder and Stoughton, 1969), p. 49.
47. Bhasin, *Simla*, p. 201.
48. Bhasin, *Simla*, p. 203.
49. Bhasin, *Simla*, p. 211–12.
50. Kanwar, *Imperial Simla*, p. 237.
51. Kanwar, *Imperial Simla*, p. 249.
52. Kanwar, *Imperial Simla*, pp. 2, 295, and 297.

CHAPTER 8

1. Robin Boyd, 'Joseph Reed of Melbourne', *Architecture* (October–December 1952).
2. David Dunstan, *Victorian Icon: The Royal Exhibition Building Melbourne* (Museum of Victoria, 1996), p. 7.
3. *Nomination of the Royal Exhibition Building and Carlton Gardens, Melbourne by the Government of Australia for Inscription on the World Heritage List* (Environment Australia, 2002).
4. Boyd, 'Joseph Reed'.

5. *Nomination.*

6. Paul Fox, 'Exhibition City: Melbourne and the 1880 International Exhibition', *Transition* (Summer 1990).

7. Dunstan, *Victorian Icon*, p. 13.

8. *Nomination.*

9. *Nomination.*

10. *Nomination.*

11. Official website: <http://museumvictoria.com.au/reb/>.

12. *Nomination.*

13. *Nomination.*

14. Dunstan, *Victorian Icon*, p. 52.

15. Official website.

16. Fox, 'Exhibition City'.

17. eMelbourne, 'The City Past and Present', <http://www.emelbourne.net.au/biogs/EM02078b.htm>.

18. *Nomination.*

19. Dunstan, *Victorian Icon*, p. 189.

20. *Nomination.*

21. Official website.

22. Dunstan, *Victorian Icon*, p. 3.

23. *Nomination.*

24. Dunstan, *Victorian Icon*, p. 203.

25. Official website.

26. Official website.

27. Dunstan, *Victorian Icon*, p. 272.

28. Dunstan, *Victorian Icon*, p. 5.

29. *Nomination.*

30. Official website.

31. *Nomination.*

32. John MacKenzie, 'Australia: Museums in Sydney and Melbourne', in MacKenzie, *Museums and Empire: Natural History, Human Cultures, and Colonial Identities* (Manchester: Manchester University Press, 2009), p. 1.

33. MacKenzie, 'Australia: Museums', p. 2.

34. MacKenzie, 'Australia: Museums', p. 7.

35. MacKenzie, 'Australia: Museums', p. 120.

36. MacKenzie, 'Australia: Museums', p. 143.

37. MacKenzie, 'Australia: Museums', p. 275.

CHAPTER 9

1. Ilsa Sharp, *There is Only One Raffles: The Story of a Grand Hotel* (London: Souvenir Press, 1981), p. 200.

2. Gretchin Liu, *Raffles Hotel Style* (Singapore: Editions Didier Millet, 2007), p. 7.

3. Liu, *Raffles Hotel Style*, p. 10.

4. For the history of Singapore, see Mark Frost and Yu-Mei Balasingamchow, *Singapore: A Biography* (Singapore: Editions Didier Millet and National Museum of Singapore, 2009), Joseph Yogerst, *Singapore: State of the Art* (New York: Weatherhill, 2000), and Gretchen Liu, *Singapore: A Pictorial History, 1819–2000* (Singapore: Editions Didier Millett, 2001).

5. Nick Hanna, *Singapore and Malaysia* (Peterborough: Thomas Cook, 2006), pp. 24–5.

6. Frost and Balasingamchow, *Singapore*, p. 47.

7. Sharp, *There is Only One Raffles*, p. 5.

8. Mary Turnbull, *A History of Singapore, 1819–1975* (Kuala Lumpur: Oxford University Press, 1977), p. 5.

9. Frost and Balasingamchow, *Singapore*, p. 89.

10. Gretchin Liu, *Raffles Hotel* (Singapore: Editions Didier Millet, 2006), p. 21.

11. Frost and Balasingamchow, *Singapore*, p. 75.

12. Hanna, *Singapore and Malaysia*, p. 36.

13. Frost and Balasingamchow, *Singapore*, p. 66.

14. Frost and Balasingamchow, *Singapore*, p. 119.

15. Turnbull, *A History of Singapore*, p. 46.

16. Frost and Balasingamchow, *Singapore*, p. 46.

17. Barney Henderson, 'Watson's Hotel to Shut 140 Years after Being Shipped from England', *Telegraph*, 3 June 2009.

18. Liu, *Raffles Hotel*, p. 13.

19. Frost and Balasingamchow, *Singapore*, p. 137.

20. Gretchen Liu, *Raffles Hotel Style* (Singapore: Editions Didier Millet, 2007), p. 7.

21. Leslie Danker, *Memoirs of a Raffles Original* (Singapore: Angsana Books, 2010), p. 20.

22. Danker, *Memoirs of a Raffles Original*, p. 19.

23. For a postmodern interpretation of this event, and its subsequent mythicization as a part of Raffles Hotel 'lore', see Lilian Chee, 'Under the Billiard Table: Animality, Anecdote, and the Tiger's Subversive Significance at the Raffles Hotel', *Singapore Journal of Tropical Geography*, 32 (2011).

24. Chee, 'Under the Billiard Table', p. 350.

25. Liu, *Raffles Hotel*, p. 44.

26. Liu, *Raffles Hotel Style*, p. 8.

27. Liu, *Raffles Hotel*, p. 44.

28. William Warren, *Raffles Remembered* (Singapore: Editions Didier Millet, 2010), p. 4.

29. Warren, *Raffles Remembered*, p. 20.

30. Warren, *Raffles Remembered*, p. 4.

31. Liu, *Raffles Hotel*, p. 45.

32. Sharp, *There is Only One Raffles*, p. 49.

33. Dawn Tan, *The Raffles People: Personalities Behind the Great Dame* (Singapore: Angsana Books, 2008), p. 87.

34. Liu, *Raffles Hotel*, p. 85.

35. Sharp, *There is Only One Raffles*, p. 39.
36. Frost, and Balasingamchow, *Singapore*, p. 143.
37. Frost, and Balasingamchow, *Singapore*, p. 141.
38. Frost, and Balasingamchow, *Singapore*, p. 142.
39. Frost, and Balasingamchow, *Singapore*, p. 161.
40. Sharp, *There is Only One Raffles*, p. 219.
41. Sharp, *There is Only One Raffles*, p. 218.
42. Liu, *Raffles Hotel*, p. 20.
43. Liu, *Raffles Hotel*, p. 10.
44. Sharp, *Raffles Hotel*, p. 61.
45. Sharp, *Raffles Hotel*, p. 67.
46. Danker, *Memories of a Raffles Original*, p. 28.
47. Warren, *Raffles Remembered*, p. 4.
48. Sharp, *There is Only One Raffles*, p. 61.
49. Sharp, *There is Only One Raffles*, p. 187.
50. Liu, *Raffles Hotel Style*, p. 11.
51. Sharp, *There is Only One Raffles*, p. 65.
52. Tan, *The Raffles People*, p. 91.
53. Tan, *The Raffles People*, p. 92.
54. Tan, *The Raffles People*.
55. Tan, *The Raffles People*, p. 93.
56. Cecil Brown, *Suez to Singapore* (New York: Random House, 1942), p. 127.
57. Liu, *Raffles Hotel*, p. 93.
58. Turnbull, *A History of Singapore*, p. 307.
59. Susan Kurosawa, 'The Old and the Beautiful', *The Australian*, 22 September 2012.
60. Warren, *Raffles Remembered*, p. 9.
61. Turnbull, *A History of Singapore*, p. 316.
62. *Country Life*, 10 July 1975, p. 75.
63. Hanna, *Singapore*, p. 30.
64. Liu, *Raffles Hotel*, p. 136.
65. Danker, *Memories of a Raffles Original*, p. 119.
66. Warren, *Raffles Remembered*, p. 11.
67. Warren, *Raffles Remembered*, p. 112.
68. Ilsa Sharp, *The Fullerton Heritage: Where the Past Meets the Present* (Singapore: Oro Editions, 2011).

CHAPTER 10

1. 'William G. Newton Gordon Memorial College, Khartoum: Scheme for Redevelopment', *The Builder* (January 1946).
2. Trevor May, *The Victorian Public School* (Oxford: Shire Publications, 2009), p. 5.
3. Jan Morris and Simon Winchester, *Stones of Empire: The Buildings of the Raj* (Oxford: Oxford University Press, 2005), p. 104.

4. May, *The Victorian Public School*, p. 53.

5. Morris and Winchester, *Stones of Empire*, p. 105.

6. Michael Asher, *Khartoum: The Ultimate Imperial Adventure* (London: Penguin, 2006), p. 401.

7. Asher, *Khartoum*, p. 403.

8. Bennet Burleigh, *Khartoum Campaign, 1898 or the Reconquest of the Soudan* (London: Chapman and Hall, 1899).

9. Sudan Archives, Durham University, Whicher draft article 1952, 558/4/22–24 and SudA PK1528.4 GOR, *The Gordon Memorial College Report and Accounts for the Year to December 1937*, Lord Cromer's introduction.

10. Heather Sharkey, 'Colonialism and the Culture of Nationalism in the Northern Sudan, 1898–1956', PhD Thesis (Princeton University, 1998), p. 85.

11. Burleigh, *Khartoum Campaign*.

12. Sudan Archives, Durham University, Wingate, *The Story of the Gordon College and its Work*, reprinted from the story of the Cape to Cairo Railway and River Route, 1887–1925, vol. IV (n. d., probably 1921), p. 7.

13. Sudan Archives, Durham University, 558/4/68. Public Relations Branch, Bulletin 1049, 'Fiftieth Anniversary of the Opening of the Gordon Memorial College'.

14. Gabriel Warburg, *The Sudan under Wingate: Administration in the Anglo-Egyptian Sudan, 1899–1916* (London: Frank Cass, 1971), p. 6.

15. W. H. McLean, 'The Planning of Khartoum and Omdurman', reprinted from the *Transactions of the Town Planning Conference*, October 1910, London, Royal Institute of British Architects (1911), p. 591.

16. Warburg, *The Sudan under Wingate*, p. 91.

17. McLean, 'The Planning of Khartoum', p. 587.

18. McLean, 'The Planning of Khartoum', p. 587.

19. Robert Home, *Of Planting and Planning: The Making of British Colonial Cities* (London: E and F. N. Spon, 1997), p. 110.

20. E. N. Corbyn, 'Gordon College at Khartoum: University College Status', *Nature*, 155(3929) (1945), p. 193.

21. Sudan Archives, Durham University, SudA PK1528.4 GOR, Report 1907.

22. H. Sharkey, 'Colonialism', p. 67.

23. *Guide to Egypt and the Sûdân including a Description of the Route through Uganda to Mombasa* (London: Macmillan, 1905), p. 160.

24. Sudan Archives, Durham University, 558/4/22–24, Whicher draft article for *The Times*, October 1952.

25. M. W. Daly, *Imperial Sudan: The Anglo-Egyptian Condominium, 1934–1956* (Cambridge: Cambridge University Press, 1991), p. 106.

26. Wingate, *The Story of the Gordon College*, p. 11.

27. Sudan Archives, Durham University, Robin Udal, 'The Gordon Memorial College'.

28. Wingate, *The Story of the Gordon College*, p. 15.

29. Penny Bailey, 'Henry Wellcome's Tropical Medicine Laboratories', <http://wellcome.ac.uk/About-us/History/WTX052449.htm>.
30. Wingate, *The Story of the Gordon College*, p. 15.
31. Bailey, 'Henry Wellcome's Tropical Medicine Laboratories'.
32. Sudan Archives, Durham University, 1907 report, p. 18.
33. Sudan Archives, Durham University, 1907 report, p. 19.
34. Sudan Archives, Durham University, Whicher draft article 1952.
35. Sudan Archives, Durham University, 1916 report.
36. Sudan Archives, Durham University, Whicher draft article 1952.
37. Starkey, 'Colonialism', ch. 3, 'The Culture of School: The Gordon Memorial College', p. 81.
38. Sudan Archives, Durham University, 1907 report p. 10.
39. Wingate, *The Story of the Gordon College*, p. 22.
40. Wingate, *The Story of the Gordon College*, p. 22.
41. Sudan Archives, Durham University, SudA PK1528.4 GOR, *The Gordon Memorial College Report and Accounts for the Year to December 1937.*
42. Sudan Archives, Durham University, 1930 report, p. 27.
43. Sudan Archives, Durham University, SA, 558/4, folio 7.
44. Sudan Archives, Durham University, SudA PK 1528.4 GOR, *The Gordon Memorial College at Khartoum, Report and Accounts to December 1907.*
45. Sudan Archives, Durham University, 1926 report, p. 22.
46. Sudan Archives, Durham University, 561/6/63, Whicher note, 26/5/47.
47. Sudan Archives, Durham University, PK 1528.4 HOL, Bjarne Holmedal, 'The Gordon Memorial College at Khartoum: Agent of British Imperialism or Cradle of Independence?', Cand. Philol. Thesis (University of Bergen, 1988).
48. Holmedal, 'The Gordon Memorial College at Khartoum', p. 62.
49. Sudan Archives, Durham University, SudA PK1528.4 GOR, *The Gordon Memorial College Report and Accounts for the Year to December 1937.*
50. *The Gordon Memorial College Report and Accounts for the Year to December 1937*, p. 10.
51. Sharkey, 'Colonialism', p. 69.
52. Holmedal, 'The Gordon Memorial College', p. 142.
53. Holmedal, 'The Gordon Memorial College', p. 143.
54. Holmedal, 'The Gordon Memorial College', p. 16.
55. Holmedal, 'The Gordon Memorial College', 58.
56. Daly, *Imperial Sudan*, p. 114.
57. Holmedal, 'The Gordon Memorial College', p. 62.
58. Sharkey, 'Colonialism', p. 85.
59. Daly, *Imperial Sudan*, p. 104.
60. Daly, *Imperial Sudan*, p. 107.
61. Daly, *Imperial Sudan*, p. 104.
62. Daly, *Imperial Sudan*, p. 109.
63. Sudan Archives, Durham University, 561/6/63 LC Wilcher note, 26/5/47.

64. Sudan Archives, Durham University, Tothill 9/12/46. Agenda Item 4, address by Principal on events of the year.
65. Robert Collins and Francis Deng (eds.), *The British in the Sudan, 1898–1956* (London: Macmillan, 1984), pp. 16–17.
66. Wingate, *The Story of the Gordon College*, p. 86.
67. Sudan Archives, Durham University, Agenda note 6, Department of Education, 2/44.
68. Holmedal, 'The Gordon Memorial College', p. 141.
69. Whicher draft article 1952, 558/4/22–24 and SudA PK1528.4 GOR.
70. Daly, *Imperial Sudan*, p. 110.
71. Sudan Archives, Durham University, report 1937, p. 13.
72. Daly, *Imperial Sudan*, p. 112.
73. Daly, *Imperial Sudan*, p. 111.
74. Daly, *Imperial Sudan*, p. 109.
75. Middle East Centre Archives Oxford, Director of Education to Dr Ina Beasley, Controller, Girls' Education, Omdurman, 18/6/44.
76. Middle East Centre Archives Oxford, 561/6/16, agenda of meeting 1/2/46.
77. Middle East Centre Archives Oxford, 561/5/94–97.
78. 'Gordon Memorial College, Khartoum: A Pair of Hostels Designed by the late William G. Newton', *The Builder* (July 1951), p. 4.
79. Middle East Centre Archives Oxford, 5/5/45 second Council meeting.
80. Sudan Archives, Durham University, SudA PK 1528.4 GOR, Report 1947.
81. Sudan Archives, Durham University, 1953 report, p. 6.
82. Sudan Archives, Durham University, Wilcher letter, 26/10/52, 558/4/21.

CHAPTER 11

1. Frank King (ed.), *The History of The Hongkong and Shanghai Banking Corporation*, 4 vols. (Cambridge: Cambridge University Press, 1986–7), vol. 3, p. xxviii.
2. Stephanie Williams, *Hongkong Bank: The Building of Norman Foster's Masterpiece* (London: Jonathan Cape, 1989), p. 14.
3. Williams, *Hongkong Bank*, pp. 257–8.
4. Edwin Green, *Banking: An Illustrated History* (New York: Rizzoli, 1989), p. 55.
5. Green, *Banking*, p 77.
6. John Carroll, *A Concise History of Hong Kong* (Hong Kong: Hong Kong University Press, 2007), pp. 30–1.
7. King, *The History of the Hongkong and Shanghai Banking Corporation*, vol. 3, p xxviii.
8. Williams, *Hongkong Bank*, p. 15.
9. Peter Cain and Anthony Hopkins, *British Imperialism, 1688–2000* (Harlow: Longman, 2001), p. 361.
10. Cain and Hopkins, *British Imperialism*, p. 366.
11. Cain and Hopkins, *British Imperialism*, p. 370.

12. Williams, *Hongkong Bank*, p. 15.
13. Cain and Hopkins, *British Imperialism*, p. 376.
14. Cain and Hopkins, *British Imperialism*, p. 596.
15. Jan Morris, *Hong Kong: Epilogue to Empire* (London: Penguin, 1990), p. 41.
16. Morris, *Hong Kong*, p. 165.
17. Green, *Banking*, p. 108.
18. Williams, *Hongkong Bank*, p. 267.
19. Williams, *Hongkong Bank*, p. 43.
20. Williams, *Hongkong Bank*, p. 9.
21. Williams, *Hongkong Bank*, p. 193.
22. Morris, *Hong Kong*, p. 175.
23. Unique Headquarters.
24. Williams, *Hongkong Bank*, p. 228.
25. Morris, *Hong Kong*, p. 41.
26. Carroll, *A Concise History*, p. 211.
27. Carroll, *A Concise History*, p. 211.
28. Robert Fermor-Hesketh (ed.), *Architecture of the British Empire* (New York: The Vendome Press, 1986), p. 211.
29. Mark Crinson, *Modern Architecture and the End of Empire* (Aldershot: Ashgate, 2003), p. 20.

CHAPTER 12

1. Jan Morris, *Farewell the Trumpets: An Imperial Retreat* (Orlando FA: Harvest, 1978), p. 132.
2. Oliver Green, *Metro-Land: British Empire Exhibition 1924 Edition* (London: Southbank Publishing, 2004), facsimile of 1924 edition.
3. Mark Crinson, *Modern Architeture and the End of Empire* (Aldershot: Ashgate, 2003), p. 73.
4. Tom August, 'The West Indies Play Wembley', in *New West Indian Guide* (Leiden, 1992), p. 193.
5. Crinson, *Modern Architecture*, pp. 74–5.
6. Felix Driver and David Gilbert (eds.), *Imperial Cities: Landscape, Display, and Identity* (Manchester: Manchester University Press, 2003), p. 4.
7. Driver and Gilbert (eds.), *Imperial Cities*, p. 6.
8. John MacKenzie, *Orientalism: History, Theory, and the Arts* (Manchester: Manchester University Press, 1995), p. 71.
9. MacKenzie, *Orientalism*, p. 74.
10. MacKenzie, *Orientalism*, p. 77.
11. MacKenzie, *Orientalism*, p. 78.
12. Guildhall website, <http://www.swansea.gov.uk/index.cfm?articleid=21964>.
13. MacKenzie, *Orientalism*, p. 82.
14. MacKenzie, *Orientalism*, p. 72.

15. Ben Looker, 'Exhibiting Imperial London: Empire and the City in Late Victorian and Edwardian Guidebooks' (London: Goldsmith's College, 2002), p. 2 n. 4.

16. Arthur Beaven, *Imperial London* (London: J. M. Dent, 1901), preface.

17. Tori Smith, '"A Grand Work of Noble Conception": The Victoria Memorial and Imperial London', in Driver and Gilbert (eds.), *Imperial Cities*, p. 35.

18. Thomas Markus, *Buildings and Power: Freedom and Control in the Origins of Modern Building Types* (London: Routledge, 1993), p. 1.

19. F. Driver and D. Gilbert 'Imperial Cities: Overlapping Territories, Intertwined Histories', in Driver and Gilbert (eds.), *Imperial Cities*, p. 1.

20. Driver and Gilbert, 'Imperial Cities', p. 1.

21. Paul Ward review of Alex Windscheffel, *Popular Conservatism in Imperial London 1868–1906* (Woodbridge, Suffolk: Boydell and Brewer, 2007) in *Reviews in History* 667 (2008), p. 168.

22. Markus, *Buildings of Power*, p. 42.

23. Smith, '"A Grand Work"', p. 23.

24. Smith, '"A Grand Work"', p. 21.

25. Smith, '"A Grand Work"', p. 23.

26. Smith, '"A Grand Work"', p. 30.

27. Iain Black, 'Imperial Visions: Rebuilding the Bank of England, 1919–1939', in F. Driver and D. Gilbert (eds.), *Imperial Cities*, p. 96.

28. Black, 'Imperial Visions', p. 96.

29. Ronald Hyam, *Understanding the British Empire* (Cambridge: Cambridge University Press, 2010), p. 212.

30. Trevor May, *Great Exhibitions* (Oxford: Shire Publications, 2010), p. 9.

31. Deborah Ryan, 'Staging the Imperial City: The Pageant of London, 1911', in F. Driver and D. Gilbert (eds.), *Imperial Cities*, p. 117.

32. 'Palestine in London' guide.

33. Deborah Ryan, 'Staging the Imperial City: The Pageant of London, 1911', in F. Driver and D. Gilbert (eds.), *Imperial Cities*.

34. Patrick Barclay and Kenneth Powell, *Wembley Stadium: Venue of Legends* (London: Prestel, 2007), p. 29.

35. Pete Tomsett and Christ Brand, *Wembley: Stadium of Legends* (Stockport: Dewi Lewis Media, 2007), p. 9.

36. Barclay and Powell, *Wembley Stadium*, p. 29.

37. Barclay and Powell, *Wembley Stadium*, p. 30.

38. *Metro-Land British Empire Exhibition*, number 12.

39. <http://www.brent.gov.uk/regeneration.nsf/Wembley/LBB-149>.

40. 'The Stadium in Wembley Park', *The Engineer* (6 April 1923), p. 358.

41. Tomsett and Brand, *Wembley*, p. 17.

42. 'The Stadium in Wembley Park', p. 361.

43. Tomsett and Brand, *Wembley*, p. 18.

44. <http://www.wembleystadium.com/StadiumHistory/historyIntroduction/>.

45. Barclay and Powell, *Wembley Stadium*, p. 35.

46. Crinson, *Modern Architecture*, p. 72.

47. Crinson, *Modern Architecture*, p. 73.
48. May, *Great Exhibitions*, p. 37.
49. Crinson, *Modern Architecture*, p. 75.
50. *Official Exhibition Guide* quoted in May, *Great Exhibitions*, p. 38.
51. Crinson, *Modern Architecture*, p. 78.
52. From <http://www.20thcenturylondon.org.uk/british-empire-exhibitions-1924-1925>, 'British Empire Exhibitions, 1924–25'.
53. May, *Great Exhibitions*, p. 40.
54. August, 'The West Indies Play Wembley', p. 195.
55. August, 'The West Indies Play Wembley', p. 197.
56. August, 'The West Indies Play Wembley', p. 201.
57. August, 'The West Indies Play Wembley', p. 202.
58. <www.bee1924.com>.
59. <www.bee1924.com>.
60. <www.bee1924.com>.
61 <www.bee1924.com>.
62 John MacKenzie, *Imperialism and Popular Culture* (Manchester: Manchester University Press, 1987), p. 7.
63. Barclay and Powell, *Wembley Stadium*, p. 36.
64. Tomsett and Brand, *Wembley*, p. 20.
65. Tomsett and Brand, *Wembley*, p. 37.
66. Tomsett and Brand, *Wembley*, p. 13.
67. <http://www.wembleystadium.com/StadiumHistory/historyIntroduction/>.

CONCLUSION

1. Pamela Kanwar, *Imperial Simla: The Political Culture of the Raj* (Oxford: Oxford University Press, 2003), p. 251.
2. Jan Morris and Simon Winchester, *Stones of Empire: The Buildings of the Raj* (Oxford: Oxford University Press, 2005).
3. Morris and Winchester, *Stones of Empire*, p. viii.
4. 'Rangoon's Colonial Treasures', Travel section, *The Week*, 21 January 2012; see also 'Letting the Colonial Relics Rot' at <http://viss.wordpress.com/2007/08/01/letting-the-colonial-relics-rot/>. For the creation of colonial Rangoon see Michael Charney, 'The Colonial Centre', chapter 2 of Charney, *A History of Modern Burma* (Cambridge: Cambridge University Press, 2009).
5. Robert Fermor-Hesketh (ed.), *Architecture of the British Empire* (New York: The Vendome Press, 1986), p. 186.
6. Morris and Winchester, *Stones of Empire*, p. vii.
7. Gretchin Liu, *Raffles Hotel* (Singapore: Editions Didier Millet, 2006), p. 12.
8. Ann Hills, 'Singapore's Token Conservation', *History Today*, 37(3) (1987).
9. Mary Turnbull, *A History of Singapore, 1819–1975* (Kuala Lumpur: Oxford University Press, 1977), p. 312.

10. Raja Bhasin, *Simla: The Summer Capital of British India* (London: Penguin, 1992), p. 214.

11. Fermor-Hesketh, *Architecture of the British Empire*, p. 215.

12. Thomas Metcalf, 'Architecture in the British Empire', in Robin Winks (ed.), *The Oxford History of the British Empire, 5: Historiography* (Oxford: Oxford University Press, 2001), p. 589–90.

13. Metcalf, 'Architecture in the British Empire', p. 595.

14. Quoted in Mark Crinson, *Modern Architeture and the End of Empire* (Aldershot: Ashgate, 2003), p. 2.

15. Crinson, *Modern Architeture*, p. 2.

16. James Robertson, *Gone is the Ancient Glory: Spanish Town Jamaica, 1543–2000* (Kingston: Jamaica: J. Ian Randle, 2005), p. 314.

17. Deborah Manley (ed.), *Malta: A Traveller's Anthology* (Oxford: Signal Books, 2010), p. 67.

18. Malta's neutrality remains a sensitive issue: see <http://www.timesofmalta.com/articles/view/20110614/local/french-warships-in-grand-harbour.370562>.

19. *Times of Malta*, 12 August 2009.

20. Peter Seabrook Papers, Private Collection, 'History of Fort St Angelo', typescript, undated, no author.

21. Róisín Kennedy, *Dublin Castle Art: The Historical and Contemporary Collection* (Dublin: Office of Public Works/The Stationery Office, 1999), p. 14.

22. Kennedy, *Dublin Castle Art*, p. 110.

23. Kennedy, *Dublin Castle Art*, p. 16.

24. Trevor Mostyn, *Egypt's Belle Epoque: Cairo and the Age of the Hedonists* (London: Tauris, 2007), p. 172.

25. Mostyn, *Egypt's Belle Epoque*, p. 172.

26. See Fathi Saleh, 'Gezira Sporting Club: A Cairo Landmark', *Egyptian Gazette*, 7 February 2010; Sherine El Madany, 'Attempts to Restore "Cairo's Belle Epoque"', *Daily News Egypt*, 3 June 2007; and John Harris, 'Missing Public Space', *Al-Ahram*, 932, 29 January–4 February 2009.

27. Conference report, 7 November 1992.

28. *The Week*, 5 November 2011, 'Travel'.

29. *The Week*, 29 October 2011, 'Travel'.

30. Peter Doling, *From Port T to RAF Gan: An Illustrated History of the British Military Bases at Add Atoll in the Maldive Islands, 1941–1976* (Bognor Regis: Woodfield Publishing, 2003).

31. *The Week*, 16 April 2011, 'Travel'.

32. Kanwar, *Imperial Simla*, p. 313.

33. Bhasin, *Simla*, p. xi.

34. Bhasin, *Simla*, p. xii.

35. Bhasin, *Simla*, p. 62.

36. Ar. Sabeena Khanna, 'Observatory Hill at Shimla', *Journal of the Indian Institute of Architecture* (October–November, 1994), p. 13.

Bibliography

PRIMARY SOURCES AND SITE VISITS

Bodleian Library Map Collection

Khartoum

E4. 20 *Khartoum (2)*

Cairo

E13. 30 Cairo (4)

E13. 30 Cairo (6)

E13. 30 Cairo (7)

Melbourne

I3. 50 Melbourne (1)

Kuala Lumpur

D25. 30 Kuala Lumpur (1)

Dublin Castle, Ireland

Two visits to the Castle and private tour.

Assistance from staff.

Durham University Special Collections

Sudan Archive. Papers, pamphlets, and photographs relating to Gordon Memorial College, Khartoum.

Wingate, *The Story of the Gordon College and its Work*, reprinted from the story of the Cape to Cairo Railway and River Route, 1887–1925, vol. 4 (n.d., probably 1921).

Robin Udal, 'The Gordon Memorial College'.

558/4/22–24. Whicher draft article for *Times*, October 1952.

558/4/68. Public Relations Branch, Bulletin 1049, 'Fiftieth Anniversary of the Opening of the Gordon Memorial College'.

562/9/36. Michael Grant, Vice Chancellor, 'The First Year of Khartoum University'.

Gezira Sporting Club, Cairo

Three visits to the Gezira Sporting Club.

Specially arranged tour.

John Harris, 'A Rough Guide to the Gezira Club' (2005).

Hong Kong
Visit to HSBC Headquarters.

Kuala Lumpur, Malaysia
Visit to Old Railway Station Kuala Lumpur.
Meeting with Hambali Parjan, Curator, KTMB Museum, Old Railway Station Kuala Lumpur.
Plans of the station.

Malta Archives, Rabat, Malta
Army and Royal Navy plans and maps of Valletta and Fort St Angelo.
Books on Malta's fortifications.
Three visits to Fort St Angelo for specially arranged tours.

Middle East Centre Archives, St Antony's College, Oxford
Ina Beasley Collection, GB165-0022.
File 1 Gordon Memorial College Council meetings, 1944–1947.
File 2 Gordon Memorial College Council meetings, 1946–1950.
File 3 Proposals for the Expansion and Improvement of the Education System in the Sudan.

National Library of Singapore
Newspaper SG Digital Archive.
Straits Times.
Singapore Free Press and Mercantile Advertiser.

Peter Seabrook Papers, private collection
Newspaper cuttings and photographs.
Copy of Lieutenant Commander H. G. Bowerman, *History of Fort St Angelo* (September 1947).
Plan of Vittoriosa and Fort St Angelo, *c.* 1930s.
'St Angelo House', typescript, undated, no author, 6 pages.
'History of Fort St Angelo', typescript, undated, no author, 39 pages.

Raffles Hotel Singapore
Archive images.
Museum visit.
Resident Historian tour.

Rhodes House Library, Oxford
Hubert Corlette, *The King's House in the King's Square Spanish Town Jamaica: A Report and Historical Review* (London, 1932).

Royal Institute of British Architects Library, London
Architecture Malaysia 50 Years Merdeka Supplement, 19(4) (2007).
Robin Boyd, 'Joseph Reed of Melbourne', *Architecture* (October–December 1952).

Paul Fox, 'Exhibition City: Melbourne and the 1880 International Exhibition', *Transition* (Summer 1990).

'Gordon Memorial College, Khartoum: A Pair of Hostels Designed by the late William G. Newton', *The Builder* (July 1951).

Ar. Sabeena Khanna, 'Observatory Hill at Shimla', *Journal of the Indian Institute of Architecture* (October–November, 1994).

Carl Lounsbury, 'Beaux-Arts Ideals and Colonial Reality: The Reconstruction of Williamsburg's Capitol, 1928–1934', *Journal of the Society of Architectural Historians* (December 1990).

'Raffles at Risk?', *Country Life*, 10 July 1975.

'William G. Newton Gordon Memorial College, Khartoum: Scheme for Redevelopment', *The Builder* (January 1946).

Peter Stocker, 'Kuala Lumpur Railway Station', *Majallah Akitek*, 3–4 (1986).

SECONDARY SOURCES

Abu-Lughod, Janet, *Cairo: 1001 Years of the City Victorian* (Woodestock: Princeton University Press, 1971).

Akensimoyin, Kunle, *Building Lagos*

Allwood, John, *The Great Exhibitions* (London: Littlehampton, 1977).

Amery, C., *Lutyens* (London: Arts Council, 1982).

Andrews, W., *Architecture in New England* (Vermont: Stephen Greene Press, 1973).

Angus, M., *The Old Stones of Kingston: Its Buildings before 1867* (Toronto: University of Toronto, 1966).

Archer, Mildred, *Indian Architecture and the British, 1780–1830* (London: Country Life, 1968).

Asher, Michael, *Khartoum: The Ultimate Imperial Adventure* (London: Penguin, 2006).

Attard, Joseph, *Britain and Malta: The Story of an Era* (Malta: Publishers Enterprises Group, 1995).

August, Tom, 'The West Indies Play Wembley', *New West Indian Guide*, 66(3/4) (1992).

August, Tom, 'Art and Empire—Wembley, 1924', *History Today*, 43(10) (1993).

Austin, Dennis, *Malta and the End of Empire* (London: Frank Cass, 1971).

Baker, Christopher, *Jamaica* (Peterborough: Thomas Cook, 2007).

Baker, Herbert, *Cecil Rhodes by His Architect* (Oxford: Oxford University Press, 1934).

Baker, Herbert, *Architecture and Personalities* (Country Life, 1944).

Barclay, Patrick and Kenneth Powell, *Wembley Stadium: Venue of Legends* (London: Prestel, 2007).

Barnett, M. J. et al. (eds.), *A Garden Century: The Chruistchurch Botanic Gardens 1863–1963* (Christchurch City Council, 1964).

Barr, Pat and Ray Desmond, *Simla, A British Hill Station* (London, 1978).

Barringer, Tim and Tom Flynn (eds.), *Colonialism and the Object: Empire, Material Culture, and the Museum* (London: Taylor and Francis, 1998).

Beattie, Andrew, *Cairo: A Cultural History* (Oxford: Oxford University Press, 2005).

Belich, James, *Making Peoples: A History of the New Zealanders, from Polynesian Settlement to the End of the Nineteenth Century* (Hawai'i: University of Hawai'I Press, 1996).

Bence-Jones, M., *Palaces of the Raj: Magnificence and Misery of the Lord Sahibs* (London: Allen and Unwin, 1973).

Bence-Jones, M., *Twilight of the Ascendancy* (London: Constable, 1993).

Beney, Peter, *The Majesty of Colonial Williamsburg* (Gretna, Louisiana: Pelican, 1997).

John Benyon, 'Overlords of Empire? British "Proconsular Imperialism" in Comparative Perspective', *Journal of Imperial and Commonwealth History*, 19(2) (1991).

Berg, Warren, *Historical Dictionary of Malta* (London: Scarecrow Press, 1995).

Berger, John, *Ways of Seeing* (London: BBC/Penguin, 1972).

Berridge, P. S. A., *Couplings to the Khyber: The Story of the North Western Railways* (Newton Abbot: David and Charles, 1969).

Beshir, M. O., *Educational Development in the Sudan, 1898–1956* (Oxford: Clarendon Press, 1969).

Bhasin, Raja, *Simla: The Summer Capital of British India* (London: Penguin, 1992).

Black, C., *Spanish Town: The Old Capital* (Spanish Town: Parish Council of St Catherine, 1960).

Black, C. E. D., *The Marquess of Dufferin and Ava* (1903).

Black, Clinton, *History of Jamaica* (Harlow: Pearson, 1983).

Bonnici, Joseph and Michael Cassar, *The Royal Navy in Malta: A Photographic Record* (Valletta: The Authors, 1989).

Bowerman, H. G., *History of Fort St Angelo* (Malta: Progress Press, 1947).

Bremner, G. Alex, 'Nation and Empire in the Government Architecture of mid-Victorian London: The Foreign Office and India Office Reconsidered', *Historical Journal*, 48 (2005).

Brendon, Piers, *The Decline and Fall of the British Empire, 1781–1997* (London: Vintage Books, 2008).

Brockman, Eric, *Last Bastion: Sketches of the Maltese Islands* (Valletta: Progress Press, 2002).

Brown, Cecil, *Suez to Singapore* (New York: Random House, 1942).

Buck, Edward, *Simla Past and Present* (Calcutta: Government of India Central Press/ Thacker, Spink, and Company, 1904).

Bugaja, Lino, Mano Buhagiar, and Stanley Fiorini (eds.), *Birgu: A Maltese Maritime City*, 2 vols. (Msida: Malta University Services, 1993).

Buisseret, D., *Historic Jamaica from the Air* (Kingston: Ian Randle, 1996).

Burleigh, Bennet, *Khartoum Campaign, 1898 or the Reconquest of the Soudan* (London: Chapman and Hall, 1899).

Cain, P. J. and A. G. Hopkins, *British Imperialism, 1688–2000* (Harlow: Longman, 2001).

Carroll, John, *A Concise History of Hong Kong* (Hong Kong: Hong Kong University Press, 2007).

Carrot, Richard, *The Egyptian Revival: Its Sources, Monuments, and Meaning, 1808–1858* (Berkeley: University of California, 1978).

Caruana, Joseph, *The Battle of Grand Harbour* (St Julians, Malta: Wise Owl Publications, 2006).

Casey, M. *et al.*, *Early Melbourne Architecture, 1840–1888* (Melbourne: Oxford University Press, 1953).

Chang, Jiat-Hwee and Anthony King, 'Towards a Genealogy of Tropical Architecture: Historical Fragments of Power-Knowledge, Built Environment, and Climate in the British Colonial Territories', *Singapore Journal of Tropical Geography*, 32 (2011).

Chee, Lilian, 'Under the Billiard Table: Animality, Anecdote, and the Tiger's Subversive Significance at the Raffles Hotel', *Singapore Journal of Tropical Geography*, 32 (2011).

Chee, Lilian, Jiat-Hwee Chang, and Bobby Wong, 'Introduction—"Tropicality-in-Motion": Situating Tropical Architecture', *Singapore Journal of Tropical Geography*, 32 (2011).

Christchurch Contextual History Overview for Christchurch City (Christchurch: Christchurch City Council, 2005).

Christopher, A. J., *The British Empire at its Zenith* (London: Croom Helm, 1988).

Coffman, Suzanne and Michael Olmert, *Official Guide to Colonial Williamsburg* (Williamsburg, VA: The Colonial Williamsburg Foundation, 1998).

Collier-Wright, Christopher, 'Sir Herbert Baker and the Prince of Wales School', Old Cambrian Society website <http://www.oldcambrians.com/Obituary-Collier-Wright,Christopher.html>.

Collins, Robert and Francis Deng (eds.), *The British in the Sudan, 1898–1956* (London: Macmillan, 1984).

Completion Report of the New Viceregal Lodge at Simla (Calcutta, 1890).

Conner, Patrick, *Oriental Architecture in the West* (London: Thames and Hudson, 1979).

Conner, Patrick (ed.), *The Inspiration of Egypt: Its Influence on British Artists, Travellers, and Designers, 1700–1900* (Brighton: Brighton Borough Council, 1983).

The Contextual Historical Overview for Christchurch City (2005).

Cookson, John and Graeme Dunstall (eds.), *Southern Capital: Christchurch, Towards a City Biography* (Christchurch: Canterbury University Press, 2000).

Cooper, Artemis, *Cairo in the War, 1939–1945* (London: Penguin, 1989).

Corbyn, E. N., 'Gordon College at Khartoum: University College Status', *Nature*, 155(3929) (1945).

Crain, Edward, *Historic Architecture in the Caribbean Islands* (Gainesville FL: University of Florida Press, 1994).

Crinson, Mark, *Modern Architecture and the End of Empire* (Farnham: Ashgate, 2003).

Cundall, Frank, *A Brief Account of King's House, Spanish Town Jamaica* (Kingston: Institute of Jamaica, 1929).

Daly, M. W., *Imperial Sudan: The Anglo-Egyptian Condominium, 1934–1956* (Cambridge: Cambridge University Press, 1991).

Daly, M. W., *Empire on the Nile: The Anglo-Egyptian Sudan 1989–1934* (Cambridge: Cambridge University Press, 2004).

Daly, M. W. and Jane Hogan, *Images of Empire: Photographic Sources for the British in the Sudan* (Leiden: Brill 2005).

Danker, Leslie, *Memoirs of a Raffles Original* (Singapore: Angsana Books, 2010).

Darmanin, J. F., *The Phoenico-Graeco-Roman Temple and the Origins and Development of Fort St Angelo* (Valetta: Progress Press, 1949).

Davies, Helen, *For the Record: James Bennell's Buildings in Early Launceston* (Lauceston, Tasmania: Terrace Press, 2006).

Davies, Philip, *Splendours of the Raj: British Architecture in India, 1660–1947* (London: Jonathan Murray, 1985).

Devonshire, R. L., *Cairo* (Cairo: Sphinx Print Press, 1917).

Dinkell, John, *The Royal Pavilion, Brighton* (1983).

Driver, Felix and David Gilbert (eds.), *Imperial Cities: Landscape, Display, and Identity* (Manchester: Manchester University Press, 1999).

Driver, Felix and David Gilbert, 'Capital and Empire: Geographies of Imperial London', *Geography Journal*, 51 (2001).

Dufferin, Marchioness of, *Our Viceregal Life in India, 1884–1888: Sketches from My Journal*, 2 vols. (London: Jonathan Murray, 1889).

Dunstan, David, *Victorian Icon: The Royal Exhibition Building Melbourne* (Melbourne: Museum of Victoria, 1996).

Dupain, M., *Georgian Architecture of Australia* (Sydney, 1963).

Duperly, A. and Son, *Picturesque Jamaica* (Kingston, 1891).

Dupré, Judith, *Skyscrapers: A History of the World's Most Famous and Important Skyscrapers* (London: Black Dog, 2008).

Eade, John, *Placing London: From Imperial Capital to Global City* (Oxford: Berghahn, 2001).

Eberlain, H. D. and C. V. D. Hubbard, *American Georgian Architecture* (Indiana: Indiana University Press, 1952).

Elliott, Peter, *The Cross and the Ensign: A Naval History of Malta, 1798–1979* (London: Granada, 1980).

Elshahed, Mohamed, 'Facades of Modernity: Image, Performance, and Transformation in the Egyptian Metropolis', MSc. Thesis (Massachusetts Institute of Technology, 2007).

Eylon, Lili, 'Jerusalem: Architecture in the British Mandate Period', Jewish Virtual Library, <http://www.jewishvirtuallibrary.org/jsource/Archaeology/jermandate.html>.

Eyre and Hobhouse Ltd, *Bengal: Palladian and the Picturesque—Colonial Architecture in the Indian Landscape, 1780–1980* (London, Eyre and Hobhouse, 1982).

Farrell, J. G., *The Hill Station* (London: Weidenfeld and Nicolson, 1981).

Fergusson, James, *On the Study of Indian Architecture* (1866).

Fermor-Hesketh, Robert (ed.), *Architecture of the British Empire* (New York: The Vendome Press, 1986).

Fifty Years of Railways in Malaya, 1885–1935 (Federated Malay States Railways, 1935).

Fitzgerald, Penny (A. Native), *Recollections of Dublin Castle and of Dublin Society* (London: Chatto and Windus, 1902).

Foster, Norman, *Foster Catalogue* (London: Prestel Publishing, 2001).

Fransen, Hans, *The Old Buildings of the Cape: A Survey and Description of Old Buildings in the Western Cape* (Cape Town: A. A. Balkema, 1981).

Freeland, J. M., *Architecture in Australia: A History* (London: Penguin, 1972).

Frost, Mark and Yu-Mei Balasingamchow, *Singapore: A Biography* (Singapore: Editions Didier Millet and National Museum of Singapore, 2009).

Gardner, W. J. (ed.), *A History of Canterbury*, 2 vols. (Christchurch: Whitcome and Tombs, 1971).

Goldblatt, David, *The Ball is Round: A Global History of Football* (London: Penguin, 2007).

Goldschmidt, Arthur, *Historical Dictionary of Egypt* (London: Scarecrow Press, 1994).

Gower, S. W., *Christchurch the Garden City of New Zealand* (Christchurch: Christchurch Beautifying Association, 1968).

Gowman, A., *Building Canada: An Architectural History of Canadian Life* (Toronto: Oxford University Press, 1966).

Grafftey-Smith, Laurence, *Bright Levant* (London: John Murray, 1970).

Graham-Yooll, Andrew, *The Forgotten Colony: A History of the English-Speaking Communities in Argentina* (London: Hutchinson, 1981).

Green, Edwin, *Banking: An Illustrated History* (New York: Rizzoli, 1989).

Green, Oliver, *Metro-Land. British Empire Exhibition Number.*

Greenhalgh, Paul, *Ephemeral Vistas: The Expositions, Universalles, Great Exhibitions, and World Fairs, 1851–1939* (Manchester, 1988).

Grieg, Doreen E., *Herbert Baker in South Africa* (Cape Town: Purnell, 1970).

Guide to Egypt and the Sûdân including a Description of the Route through Uganda to Mombasa (London: Macmillan, 1905).

Gunston, Henry, 'From Corrugated Iron to Colonnades: Images of British Colonial Architecture', typescript of presentation to Oxford University Department for Continuing Education 'Dominion' Course (2003).

Hamamasy, Chafika, *Zamalek: The Changing Life of a Cairo Elite, 1850–1945* (Cairo: American University in Cairo Press, 2005).

Hanna, Nick, *Singapore and Malaysia* (Peterborough: Thomas Cook, 2006).

Hart, Emma, review of James Robertson, *Gone is the Ancient Glory: Spanish Town, Jamaica, 1534–2000*, H-Atlantic, H-Net Reviews, December, 2005, <http://www.h-net.org/reviews/showrev.php?id=11042>.

Headrick, Daniel, *The Tentacles of Progress: Technology Transfer in the Age of Imperialism, 1850–1940* (Oxford: Oxford University Press, 1988).

Heinemann, Ronald *et al.*, *Old Dominion, New Commonwealth: A History of Virginia, 1607–2007* (Charlottesville: University of Virginia Press, 2007).

Henare, Amiria, *Museums, Anthropology, and Imperial Exchange* (Cambridge: Cambridge University Press, 2005).

Hewlett, Graham, *The History of Fort St Angelo* (Valetta: Progress Press, 1947).

Hill, Jeff and Francesco Varrasi, 'Creating Wembley: The Construction of a National Monument', *The Sports Historian*, 17(2) (1977).

Hill, Tim, *Daily Mail Complete History of English Football* (London: Transatlantic Press, 2009).

Hills, Ann, 'Singapore's Token Conservation', *History Today*, 37(3) (1987).

Holland, Robert, *Blue-Water Empire: The British in the Mediterranean since 1800* (London: Allen Lane, 2012).

Holmedal, Bjarne, 'The Gordon Memorial College at Khartoum: Agent of British Imperialism or Cradle of Independence?', Cand. Philol. Thesis (University of Bergen, 1988).

Home, Robert, *Of Planting and Planning: The Making of British Colonial Cities* (London: E and F. N. Spon, 1997).

Hughes, Quentin, *Malta: A Guide to the Fortifications* (Valletta: Said International, 1993).

Inside Malta and Gozo (Sliema, Malta: Miranda Publishers, 2005).

Irving, Robert, *Indian Summer: Lutyens, Baker, and Imperial New Delhi* (New Haven: Yale University Press, 1981).

Jackson, Ashley, 'Colonial-Gothic and Narrow-Gauge Tracks: Architecture and Engineering', in Jackson, *Mad Dogs and Englishmen: A Grand Tour of the British Empire at its Height* (London: Quercus, 2009).

Jacobs, Jane, *Edge of Empire: Postcolonialism and the City* (London: Routledge 1996).

James, Harold Hindle, 'Personal Report on Riots in Cairo, 26 January 1952' (transcribed and annotated by John Barnard, May 2009).

Johnson, D. L., *Australian Architecture (1905–51): Sources of Modernism* (Sydney: Sydney University Press, 1980).

Johnson, David, *Christchurch: A Pictorial History* (Christchurch: Canterbury University Press, 1994).

Jones, Geoffrey, *British Multinational Banking 1830–1990* (Oxford: Clarendon Press, 1993).

Jones, Robin, *Interiors of Empire: Objects, Space, and Identity within the Indian Subcontinent, c.1800–1947* (Manchester: Manchester University Press, 2007).

Kanwar, Pamela, 'The Changing Profile of the Summer Capital of British India: Simla, 1864–1947', *Modern Asian Studies*, 18(2) (1984).

Kanwar, Pamela, *Imperial Simla: The Political Culture of the Raj* (Oxford: Oxford University Press, 2003).

Kaplan, F. S. (ed.), *Museums and the Making of 'Ourselves': The Role of Objects in National Identity* (Leicester: Leicester University Press, 1994).

Kearney, B., *Architecture of Natal from 1820–93* (Cape Town: A. A. Balkema, 1973).

Keath, Michael, *Herbert Baker: Architecture and Idealism, 1892–1913: The South African Years* (Gibralter: Ashanti Publishing, 1992).

Kennedy, Dane, *The Magic Mountains: Hill Stations and the British* (Berkeley: University of California Press, 1996).

Kennedy, Greg, 'Maritime Strength and the British Economy, 1840–1850', *The Northern Mariner*, 8(2) (1997).

Kennedy, Róisín, *Dublin Castle Art: The Historical and Contemporary Collection* (Dublin: Office of Public Works/The Stationery Office, 1999).

Kerr, I. J., *Building the Railways of the Raj, 1850–1900* (Delhi: Oxford University Press, 1995).

Killeen, Richard, *A Short History of Dublin* (Dublin: Gill and Macmillan, 2010).

King, Anthony, *Spaces of Global Culture: Architecture, Urbanism, and Identity* (Abingdon: Routledge, 2004).

King, Anthony, *Colonial Urban Development: Culture, Social Power, and Environment* (Abingdon, Oxfordshire: Routledge, 2007).

King, Anthony, *Urbanisim, Colonialism, and the World Economy: Cultural and Spatial Foundations of the World Urban System* (Abingdon: Routledge, 1990).

King, Anthony, *The Bungalow: The Production of a Global Culture* (Abingdon: Routledge, 1984).

King, Anthony, *Global Cities: Post-Imperialism and the Internationalization of London* (Abingdon: Routledge, 1990).

King, Frank (ed.), *Eastern Banking. Essays in the History of The Hongkong and Shanghai Banking Corporation* (London: Athlone Press, 1983).

King, Frank, *The History of The Hongkong and Shanghai Banking Corporation*, 4 volumes (Cambridge: Cambridge University Press, 1986–7).

Kipling, Rudyard, *Plain Tales from the Hills* (London: Penguin, 1994).

Knight, Donald and Alan Sabey, *The Lion Roars at Wembley: The British Empire Exhibition Sixtieth Anniversary, 1924–1925* (New Barnett, Hertfordshire: D. R. Knight, 1984).

Kostof, Spiros, *A History of Architecture: Settings and Rituals* (Oxford: Oxford University Press, 1985).

Lang, Jon, Madhavi Desai, and Mike Desai, *Architecture and Independence: The Search for Identity- India 1880 to 1980* (Delhi: Oxford University Press, 1999).

Leary, F. and J., *Colonial Heritage: Historic Buildings of New South Wales* (Sydney: Angus and Robertson, 1972).

Lee, Hilda, *Malta 1813–1914: A Study in Constitutional and Strategic Development* (Valetta: Progress Press, 1973).

Levy, Pat and Sean Sheehan, *Essential Malta and Gozo* (Windsor, Berkshire: Automobile Association, 2001).

Lewcock, R., *Early Nineteenth Century Architecture in South Africa* (Cape Town: A. A. Balkema, 1963).

Lewis, Colin M., *British Railways in Argentina 1857–1914: A Case Study of Foreign Investment* (Athlone Press, for the Institute of Latin American Studies, University of London, 1983).

Liu, Gretchin, *Raffles Hotel* (Singapore: Editions Didier Millet, 2006).

Liu, Gretchin, *Raffles Hotel Style* (Singapore: Editions Didier Millet, 2007).

Liu, Gretchin, *Singapore: A Pictorial History, 1819–2000* (Singapore: Editions Didier Millet, 1999).

London and the British Empire Exhibition 1925 (London: Ward Lock, 1925).

Looker, Ben, 'Exhibiting Imperial London: Empire and the City in Late Victorian and Edwardian Guidebooks' (London: Goldsmith's College, 2002).

Losty, J. P., *Calcutta: City of Palaces* (London: British Library, 1990).

Lucas, Clive and Philip Cox, *Colonial Architecture* (Melbourne: Lansdowne Editions, 1978).

McCarthy, Dennis, *Dublin Castle: At the Heart of Irish History* (Dublin: The Stationery Office, 2004).

Mace, Rodney, *Trafalgar Square: Emblem of Empire* (London: Lawrence and Wishart, 2005).

MacKenzie, John, *Imperialism and Popular Culture* (Manchester: Manchester University Press, 1987),

MacKenzie, John, *The Empire of Nature: Hunting, Conservation, and British Imperialism* (Manchester: Manchester University Press, 1988).

MacKenzie, John, 'Orientalism in Architecture' in MacKenzie, *Orientalism: History, Theory, and the Arts* (Manchester: Manchester University Press, 1995).

MacKenzie, John, 'Orientalism in Design' in MacKenzie, *Orientalism: History, Theory, and the Arts* (Manchester: Manchester University Press, 1995).

MacKenzie, John, 'Empires of Travel: British Guide Books and Cultural Imperialism in the Nineteenth and Twentieth Centuries', in John Walton (ed.), *Histories of Tourism: Representation, Identity, and Conflict* (Clevedon: Channel View Publications, 2005).

MacKenzie, John, 'Australia: Museums in Sydney and Melbourne', in MacKenzie, *Museums and Empire: Natural History, Human Cultures, and Colonial Identities* (Manchester: Manchester University Press, 2009).

MacKenzie, John, 'New Zealand/Aotearoa: The Canterbury Museum, Christchurch', in MacKenzie, *Museums and Empire: Natural History, Human Cultures, and Colonial Identities* (Manchester: Manchester University Press, 2009).

MacKenzie, John, *The Victorian Vision: Inventing New Britain* (London: V&A Publications, 2003).

MacKenzie, John, and Jeffrey Richards, *The Railway Station: A Social History* (Oxford: Oxford University Press, 1986).

McLean, W. H., 'The Planning of Khartoum and Omdurman', reprinted from the *Transactions of the Town Planning Conference*, October 1910, London, Royal Institute of British Architects (1911).

McPherson, Bimbashi, *The Man Who Loved Egypt* (London: BBC, 1985).

MacPherson, Joseph, *The Man Who Loved Egypt* (London: BBC 1983).

MacRae, M., *The Ancestral Roof: Domestic Architecture of Upper Canada* (Toronto: Clarke, Irwin, 1963).

Mahoney, Leonard, *5,000 Years of Architecture in Malta* (Valletta: Valletta Publications, 1996).

'Malta: Its History and the Part Played by Fort St Angelo: A Paper Read at the Accountant Officers' Technical Course', *Naval Review*, 1 (1931).

Mangan, J.A., *The Games Ethic: Aspects of the Diffusion of an Idea* (London: Routledge, 1998).

Manley, Deborah (ed.), *Malta: A Traveller's Anthology* (Oxford: Signal Books, 2010).

Manning, Olivia, *The Levant Trilogy*, 2: *Fortunes of War* (Harmondsworth: Penguin, 1982).

Mansfield, Peter, *The British in Egypt* (London: Weidenfeld and Nicolson, 1971).

Markus, Thomas, *Buildings and Power: Freedom and Control in the Origins of Modern Building Types* (London: Routledge, 1993).

Martin, Percy, *Egypt Old and New* (London: Allen and Unwin, 1923).

May, Trevor, *The Victorian Public School* (Oxford: Shire Publications, 2009).

May, Trevor, *Great Exhibitions* (Oxford: Shire Publications, 2010).

Metcalf, Thomas, 'Architecture and Empire', *History Today*, 30(12) (1980).

Metcalf, Thomas, 'A Tradition Created: Indo-Saracenic Architecture Under the Raj', *History Today*, 32(9) (1982).

Metcalf, Thomas, *An Imperial Vision: Indian Architecture and Britain's Raj* (Berkeley: University of California Press, 1989).

Metcalf, Thomas, 'Architecture in the British Empire', in Robin Winks (ed.), *The Oxford History of the British Empire*, 5: *Historiography* (Oxford: Oxford University Press, 2001).

Mills, Stephen, *The History of the Muthaiga Country Club*, 1: *1913–1963* (Kenya: Mills Publishing, 1996).

Mitchell, Timothy, *Colonizing Egypt* (Cairo: American University in Cairo Press, 1989).

Monem, Nadine (ed.), *Botanical Gardens: A Living History* (London: Black Dog Publishing, 2007).

Montsarrat, Nicholas, *The Kappillan of Malta* (London: Cassell, 2001).

Devonshire, R. L., *Cairo* (Cairo: Sphinx Print Press, 1917).

Moorhouse, G., *Calcutta: The City Revealed* (London: Penguin, 1983).

Morgan, E. J. R. and S. H. Gilbert, *Early Adelaide Architecture (1830–86)* (London: Oxford University Press, 1969).

Morris, Jan, *Hong Kong: Epilogue to Empire* (London: Penguin, 1990).

Morris, Jan and Simon Winchester, *Stones of Empire: The Buildings of the Raj* (Oxford: Oxford University Press, 2005).

Morrison, Hugh, *Early American Architecture from the First Colonial Settlements to the National Period* (New York: Oxford University Press, 1952).

Morrison, Joan, *The Evolution of a City: The Story of the Growth of the City and Suburbs of Christchurch, the Capital of Canterbury, 1850–1903* (Christchurch: Christchurch City Council, 1948).

Mostyn, Trevor, *Egypt's Belle Epoque: Cairo and the Age of the Hedonists* (London: Tauris, 2007).

Nelson, Nina, *Shepheard's Hotel* (London: Barrie, 1960).

Nicholls, C. S., *Red Strangers: The White Tribe of Kenya* (2005).

Nilsson, Sten, *European Architecture in India, 1750–1850* (London: Faber and Faber, 1968).

Nin, Khoo Su, *Streets of George Town Penang: An Illustrated Guide to Penang's City Streets and Historic Attractions* (Penang: Janus Print, 1993).

Nomination of the Royal Exhibition Building and Carlton Gardens, Melbourne by the Government of Australia for Inscription on the World Heritage List (Canberra: Environment Australia, 2002).

Oppenheim, Jean-Marc Ran, 'Twilight of a Colonial Ethos: The Alexandria Sporting Club 1890–1956', Columbia University, 1991 (PhD thesis; UMI Dissertation Services).

Oppenheim, Jean-Marc Ran, 'The Gezira Sporting Club of Cairo', *Peace Review: A Transnational Quarterly*, 11(4) (1999).

Otte, Thomas and Keith Neilson (eds.), *Railways and International Politics: Paths of Empire, 1848–1945* (London: Routledge, 2006).

Panter-Downes, Mollie, *Ooty Preserved: Victorian Hill Station in India* (London: Hamish Hamilton, 1967).

Perkins M. and W. Tonkin, *Postcards of the British Empire Exhibition, Wembley* (London: Exhibition Study Group, 1994).

Picton-Seymour, D., *Victorian Buildings in South Africa, Including Edwardian and Transvaal Republic Styles* (Cape Town, 1977).

Port, M. H., *Imperial London: Civil Government Building in London, 1850–1915* (Yale University Press, 1995).

Porter, Bernard, 'Architecture and Empire: The Case of the "Battle of the Styles", 1855–61', *British Scholar*, 2(2) (2010).

Pott, J., *Old Bungalows in Bangalore* (London: Janet Pott, 1977).

Raafat, Samir, *Maadi, 1904–1962: Society and History in a Cairo Suburb* (Cairo: The Palm Press, 1994).

Raafat, Samir, 'Gezira Sporting Club Milestones', *Egyptian Mail*, 10–17 February 1996.

Ranston, Jackie, *Behind the Scenes at King's House, 1873–2010* (Kingston, Jamaica: Jamaica National Building Society, 2011).

Rasmussen, Carolyn, *A Museum for the People: A History of Museum Victoria and its Predecessors, 1854–2000* (Melbourne: Scribe, 2001).

Raymond, André, *Cairo* (Cambridge MT: Harvard University Press, 2000).

Rice, Geoffrey, *Christchurch Changing: An Illustrated History* (Christchurch: Canterbury University Press, 2000).

Richards, Jeffrey and John MacKenzie, *The Railway Station: A Social History* (Oxford: Oxford University Press, 1986).

Richards, Thomas, *The Imperial Archive: Knowledge and the Fanstasy of Empire* (London: Verso, 1993).

Ridley, Jane, 'Edward Lutyens, New Delhi, and the Architecture of Imperialism', *Journal of Imperial and Commonwealth History*, 26(2) (1998).

Roberts, Walter (ed.), *The Capitals of Jamaica* (Kingston: Pioneer Press, 1955).

Roberts, Walter, *Old King's House Spanish Town* (Kingston: United Printers, 1959).

Robertson, E. G., *Early Buildings of Southern Tasmania*, 2 vols. (Melbourne: Georgian House, 1970).

Robertson, James, *Gone is the Ancient Glory: Spanish Town Jamaica, 1543–2000* (Kingston: Ian Randle, 2005).

Robertson, James, 'Late Seventeenth Century Spanish Town, Jamaica: Building an English City on Spanish Foundations', *Early American Studies*, 6(2) (2008).

Robins, Joseph, *Champagne and Silver Buckles: The Viceregal Court at Dublin Castle, 1700–1922* (Dublin: The Lilliput Press, 2001).

Sabey, Alan, 'Remains of the British Empire Exhibition', <www.postcard.co.uk/esg/remains.htm>.

Said, Edward, *Out of Place: A Memoir* (London: Granta, 1999).

Samuel, Raphael, *Theatres of Memory: Past and Present in Contemporary Culture* (London: Verso 1996).

Satow, Michael and Ray Desmond, *Railways of the Raj, 1850–1900* (London: Scolar Press, 1980).

Scharabi, Mohamed, *Kairo: Stadt und Architektur im Zeitalter des europäischen Kolonialismus* (Berlin: E. Wasmuth, 1989).

Schneer, Jonathan, 'London's Docks in 1900: Nexus of Empire', *Labour History Review*, 59(3) (1994).

Schneer, Jonathan, *London, 1900: The Imperial Metropolis* (New Haven CT: Yale University Press, 1999).

Scriver, Peter, *Colonial Modernities: Buildings, Dwelling, and Architecture in British India and Ceylon* (Abingdon Routledge, 2007).

Seabrook, Peter, 'Fort St Angelo and its Artillery Connections', *The Journal of the Royal Artillery*, CVI(1) (1979).

Sharkey, Heather, 'Colonialism and the Culture of Nationalism in the Northern Sudan, 1898–1956', PhD Thesis (Princeton University, 1998).

Sharp, Ilsa, *There is Only One Raffles: The Story of a Grand Hotel* (London: Souvenir Press, 1981).

Sharp, Ilsa, *The Fullerton Heritage: Where the Past Meets the Present* (Singapore: Oro Editions, 2011).

Sheenan, Margaret, *Out in the Midday Sun: The British in Malaya* (London: John Murray, 2000).

Sherif, Lobna, 'Architecture as a System of Appropriation: Colonization in Egypt', <http://sea1917.org/heritage/UIA-WPAHR-V/Papers-PDF/Dr.%20Lobna%20Sherif.pdf>.

Sherlock, Philip (ed.), *Jamaica To-Day: A Handbook for Visitors and Intending Residents* (Jamaica: Tourist Trade Development Board, 1940).

Sladen, Douglas, *Egypt and the English* (London: Hurst and Blackett, 1908).

Smith, Philippa Mein, *A Concise History of New Zealand* (Cambridge: Cambridge University Press, 2005).

Spiteri, Stephen, *British Military Architecture in Malta* (Valletta: The Author, 1996).

Stacpoole, J., Colonial Architecture in New Zealand (Wellington: A. H. & A. W. Reed, 1977).

Stacpoole, J. and P. Beaver, *New Zealand Art and Architecture, 1820–1970* (Wellington: A. H. and A. W. Reed, 1972).

'The Stadium in Wembley Park', *The Engineer* (6 April 1923).

Staley, E., *Monkeytops: Old Buildings in Bangalore Cantonment* (Bangalore: Tara Books, 1981).

Stephen, Donald, 'Brothers of the Empire?', *Twentieth Century British History*, 9 (2010).

Stephenson, Charles, *The Fortifications of Malta, 1530–1945* (Oxford: Osprey, 2004).

Stones, H. R., *British Railways in Argentina 1860–1948*, (Bromley, Kent: P. E. Waters, 1993).

Storr, Ronald, *Orientations* (London: Nicholson and Watson, 1943).

Street, Jennie and Amanuel Ghebreselassie, *Red Sea Railway: The History of the Railway in Eritrea* (Sheffield: Silver Service Consultancy, 2010).

Strongman, Thelma, *City Beautiful: First 100 Years of the Christchurch Beautifying Association* (Pelham AL: Clerestory Press, 1999).

Sweetman, John, *The Oriental Obsession: Islamic Inspiration in British and American Art and Architecture, 1500–1900* (Cambridge University Press, 1991).

Tan, Dawn, *The Raffles People: Personalities Behind the Great Dame* (Singapore: Angsana Books, 2008).

Temple, Philip, *Christchurch: A City and its People* (Portland OR: International Specialized Book Service, 1987).

Thompson, James, *The Birth of Virginia's Aristocracy* (Alexandria, VA: Commonwealth Books, 2010).

Tindall, Gillian, *City of Gold: The Biography of Bombay* (London: Maurice Temple Smith, 1982).

Tomsett, Pete and Christ Brand, *Wembley: Stadium of Legends* (Stockport: Dewi Lewis Media, 2007).

Tortello, Rebecca, 'The Story of Spanish Town', *Jamaica Gleaner*, 19 May 2003.

Traditional Art from the Colonies: Catologue of an Exhibition at the Imperial Institute, 25 May to 30 September 1951 (London: HMSO, 1951).

Treasures of the Museum, Victoria, Australia (Melbourne, 2004).

Treiber, Daniel, *Norman Foster* (1994).

Turnbull, Mary, *A History of Singapore, 1819–1975* (Kuala Lumpur: Oxford University Press, 1977).

Twentieth Century Impressions of Egypt (London: Lloyds Publishing, 1909).

'Unique Headquarters', HSBC website, available at <http://www.hsbc.com.hk/1/2/about/home/unique-headquarters>.

Vincent, L. A., *Walk Along the Tracks* (Selangor: The Author, 2010).

Walthew, Kenneth, 'The British Empire Exhibition 1924', *History Today*, 31(8) (1981).

Warburg, Gabriel, *The Sudan under Wingate: Administration in the Anglo-Egyptian Sudan, 1899–1916* (London: Frank Cass, 1971).

Warlow, Ben, *The Royal Navy at Malta, 1900–2000* (Liskeard: Maritime Books, 2002).

Warren, William, *Raffles Remembered* (Singapore: Editions Didier Millet, 2010).

Watt, Tom and Kevin Palmer, *Wembley: The Greatest Stage* (London: Simon and Schuster, 1998).

Whiffen, Marcus, *The Public Buildings of Williamsburg* (Williamsburg: Colonial Williamsburg Foundation, 1958).

Whiffen, Marcus, 'Ornaments of Civic Aspiration: The Public Buildings of Williamsburg', in Robert Maccubbin (ed.), *Williamsburg Virginia: A City Before the State*, (Williamsburg: City of Williamsburg, 2000).

Whitehead, Clive, 'Sir Christopher Cox: An Imperial Patrician of a Different Kind', *Journal of Educational Administration and History*, 21(1) (1989).

Wigram, Henry, *The Story of Christchurch New Zealand* (Christchurch: The Lyttelton Times, 1916).

Williams, Stephanie, *Hongkong Bank: The Building of Norman Foster's Masterpiece* (London: Jonathan Cape, 1989).

Wilson, Granville, *Building a City: 100 Years of Melbourne Architecture* (Oxford University Press, 1981).

Wolmar, C., *Engines of War: How Wars Were Run and Lost on the Railways* (London: Atlantic, 2012).

Wolmar, C., *Blood, Iron, and Gold: How the Railways Transformed the World* (London: Atlantic, 2009).

Woodberry, Joan, *Historic Richmond (Tasmania) Sketchbook* (Adelaide: Rigby Limited, 1977).

Woodruff, Philip, *The Men Who Ruled India*, vol. 1 (London, 1954).

Worsfold, W. Basil, *The Redemption of Egypt* (London: G. Allen, 1899).

Yetter, George, *Williamsburg Before and After: The Rebirth of Virginia's Colonial Capital* (Williamsburg: The Colonial Williamsburg Foundation, 1988).

Yogerst, Joseph, *Singapore: State of the Art* (Singapore: Ian Lloyd Productions, 2005).

Picture Acknowledgements

Index